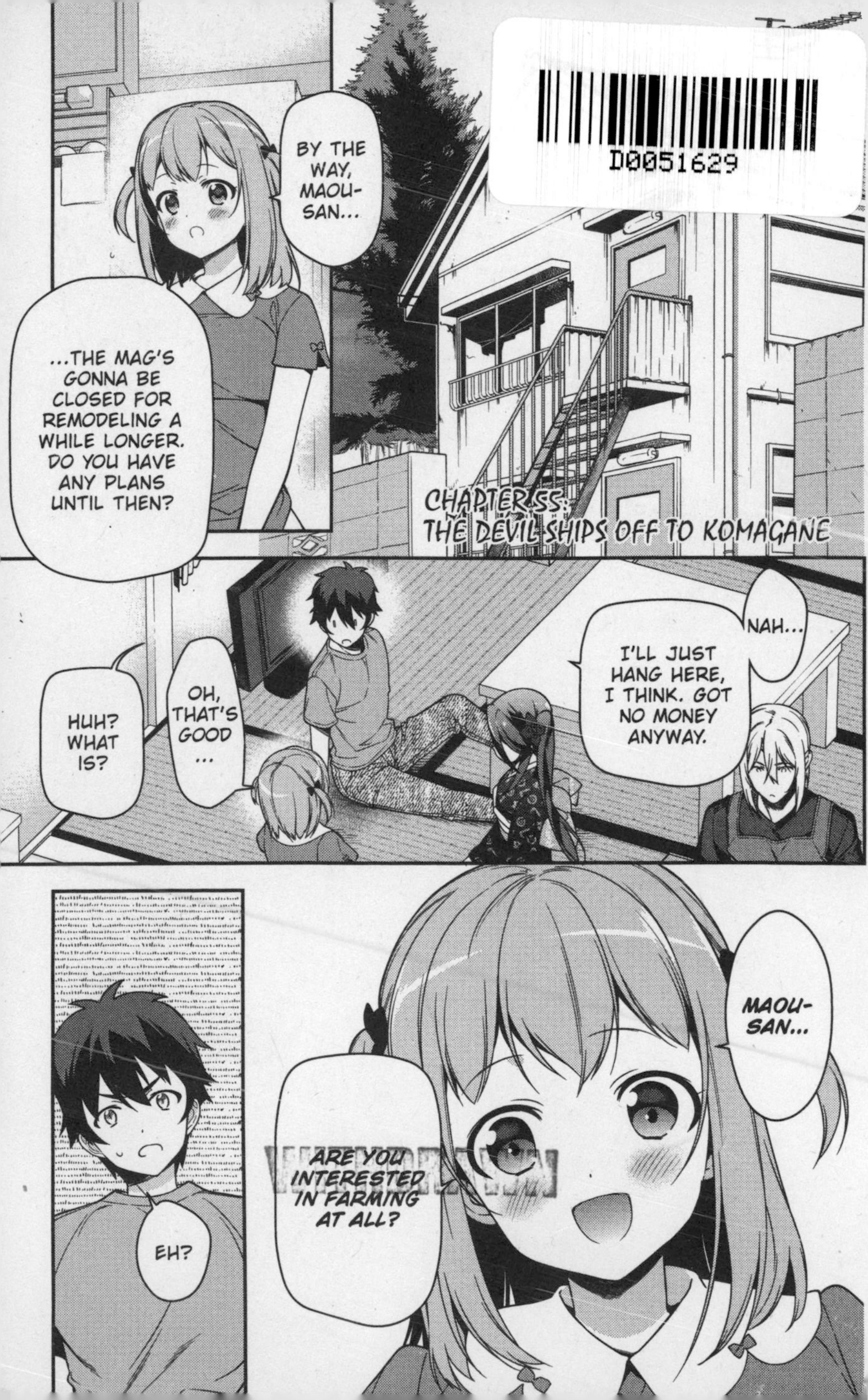
CHAPTER 55: THE DEVIL SHIPS OFF TO KOMAGANE
BY THE WAY, MAOU-SAN...
...THE MAG'S GONNA BE CLOSED FOR REMODELING A WHILE LONGER. DO YOU HAVE ANY PLANS UNTIL THEN?
NAH...
I'LL JUST HANG HERE, I THINK. GOT NO MONEY ANYWAY.
OH, THAT'S GOOD...
HUH? WHAT IS?
MAOU-SAN...
ARE YOU INTERESTED IN FARMING AT ALL?
EH?

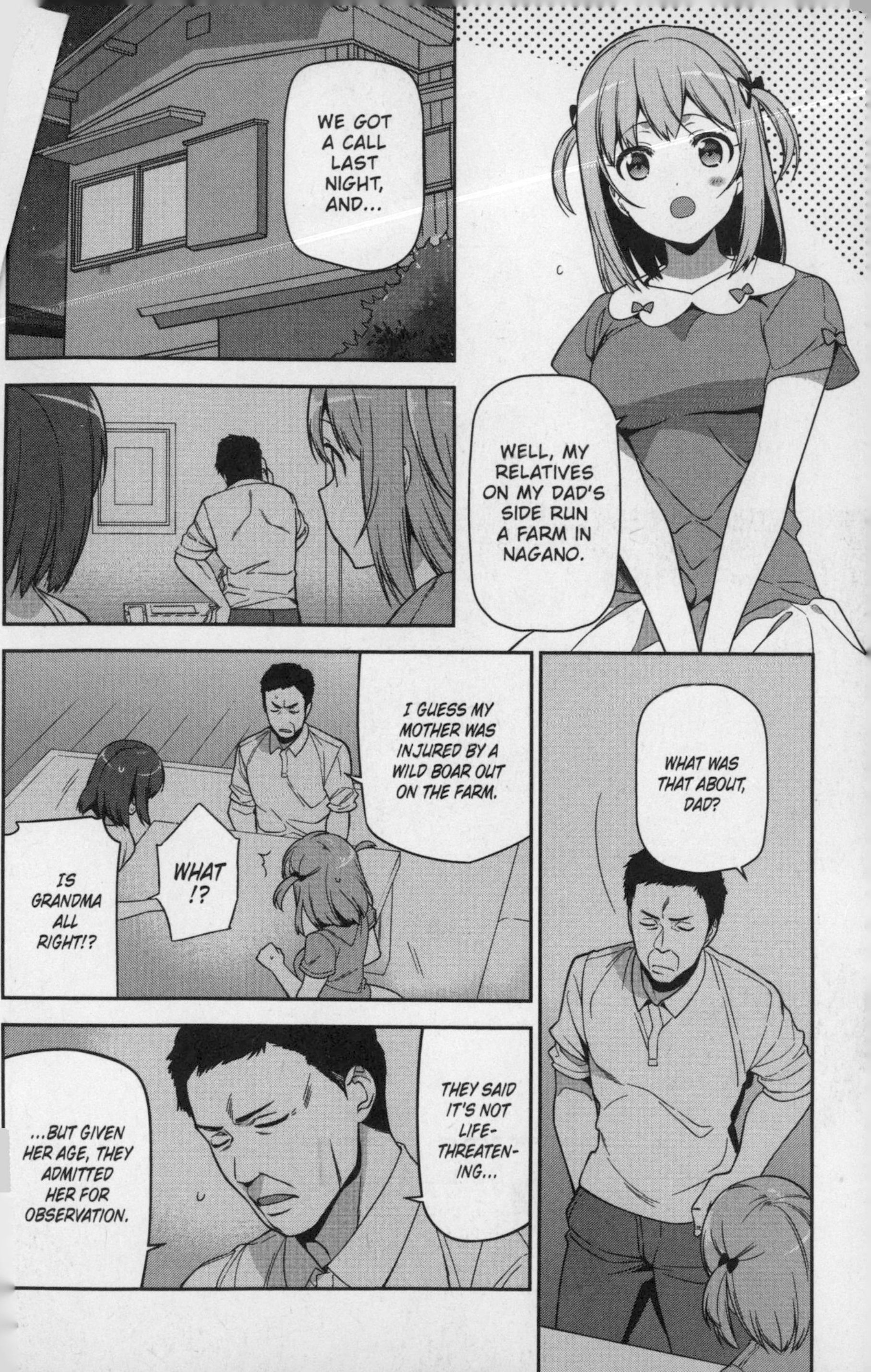
WELL, MY RELATIVES ON MY DAD'S SIDE RUN A FARM IN NAGANO.
WE GOT A CALL LAST NIGHT, AND...
WHAT WAS THAT ABOUT, DAD?
I GUESS MY MOTHER WAS INJURED BY A WILD BOAR OUT ON THE FARM.
WHAT !?
IS GRANDMA ALL RIGHT!?
THEY SAID IT'S NOT LIFE-THREATEN-ING...
...BUT GIVEN HER AGE, THEY ADMITTED HER FOR OBSERVATION.

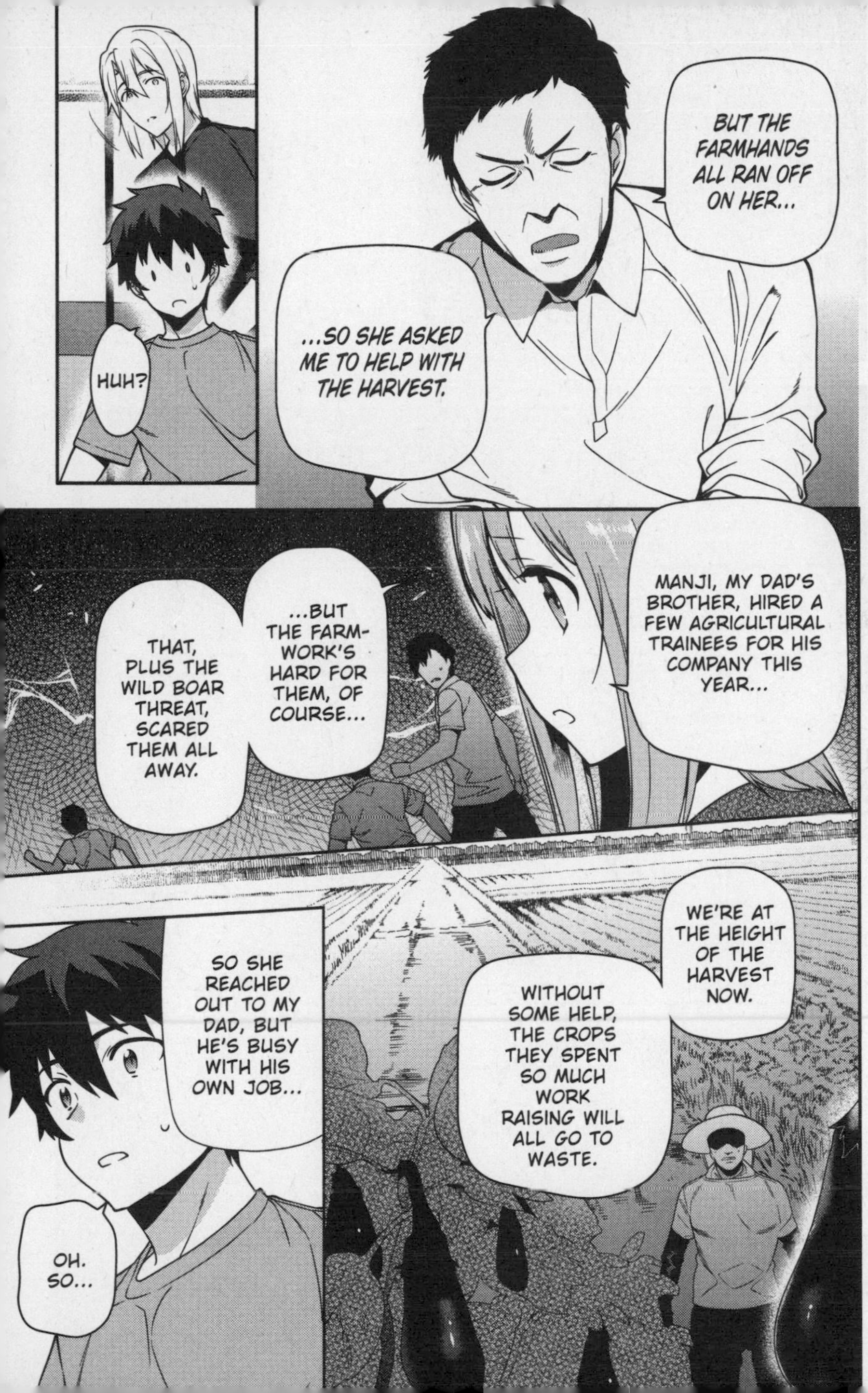
BUT THE FARMHANDS ALL RAN OFF ON HER...
...SO SHE ASKED ME TO HELP WITH THE HARVEST.
HUH?
MANJI, MY DAD'S BROTHER, HIRED A FEW AGRICULTURAL TRAINEES FOR HIS COMPANY THIS YEAR...
...BUT THE FARM-WORK'S HARD FOR THEM, OF COURSE...
THAT, PLUS THE WILD BOAR THREAT, SCARED THEM ALL AWAY.
WE'RE AT THE HEIGHT OF THE HARVEST NOW.
WITHOUT SOME HELP, THE CROPS THEY SPENT SO MUCH WORK RAISING WILL ALL GO TO WASTE.
SO SHE REACHED OUT TO MY DAD, BUT HE'S BUSY WITH HIS OWN JOB...
OH. SO...

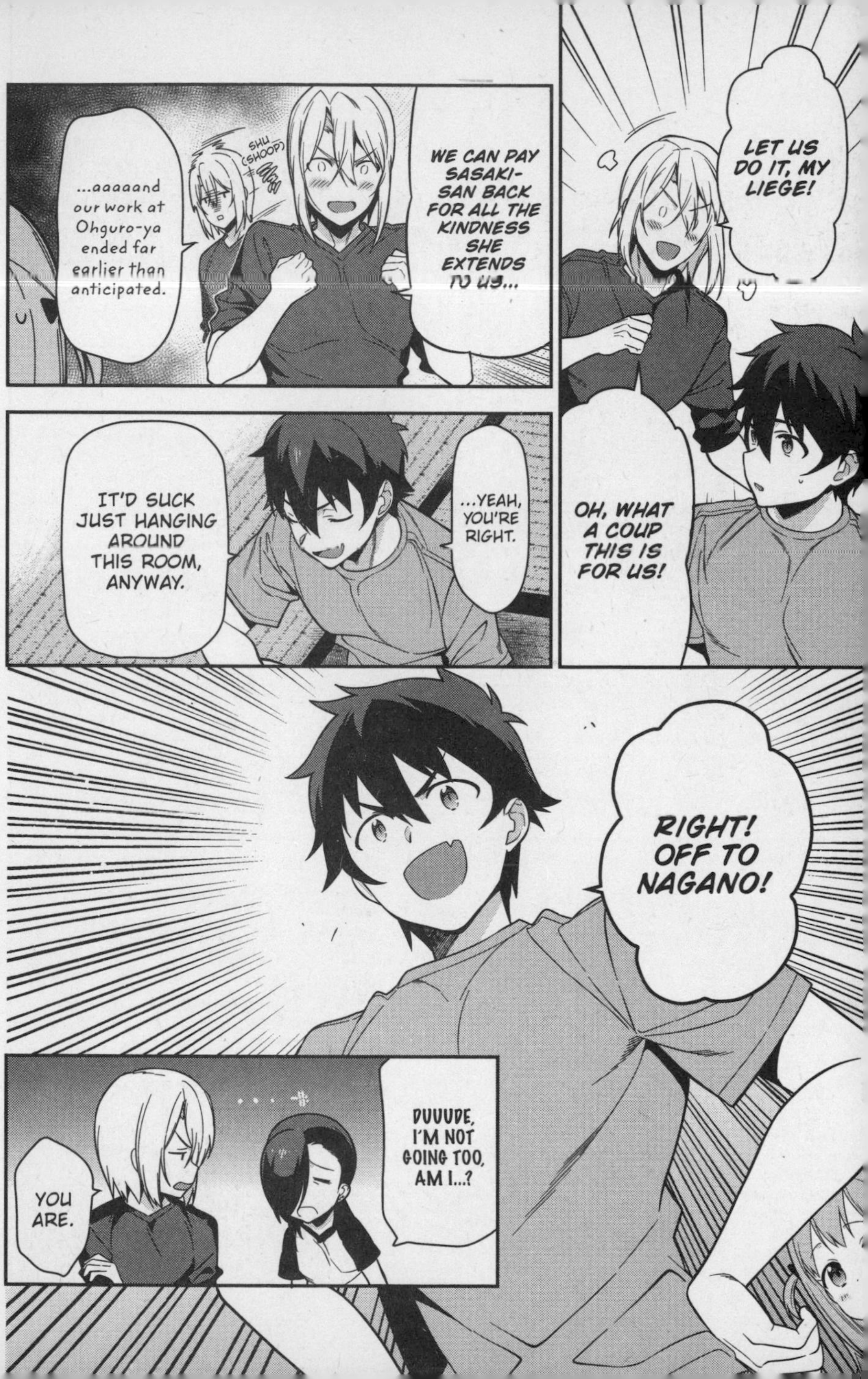
LET US DO IT, MY LIEGE!
OH, WHAT A COUP THIS IS FOR US!
WE CAN PAY SASAKI-SAN BACK FOR ALL THE KINDNESS SHE EXTENDS TO US...
SHU (SHOOP)
...aaaaand our work at Ohguro-ya ended far earlier than anticipated.
...YEAH, YOU'RE RIGHT.
IT'D SUCK JUST HANGING AROUND THIS ROOM, ANYWAY.
RIGHT! OFF TO NAGANO!
DUUUDE, I'M NOT GOING TOO, AM I...?
YOU ARE.

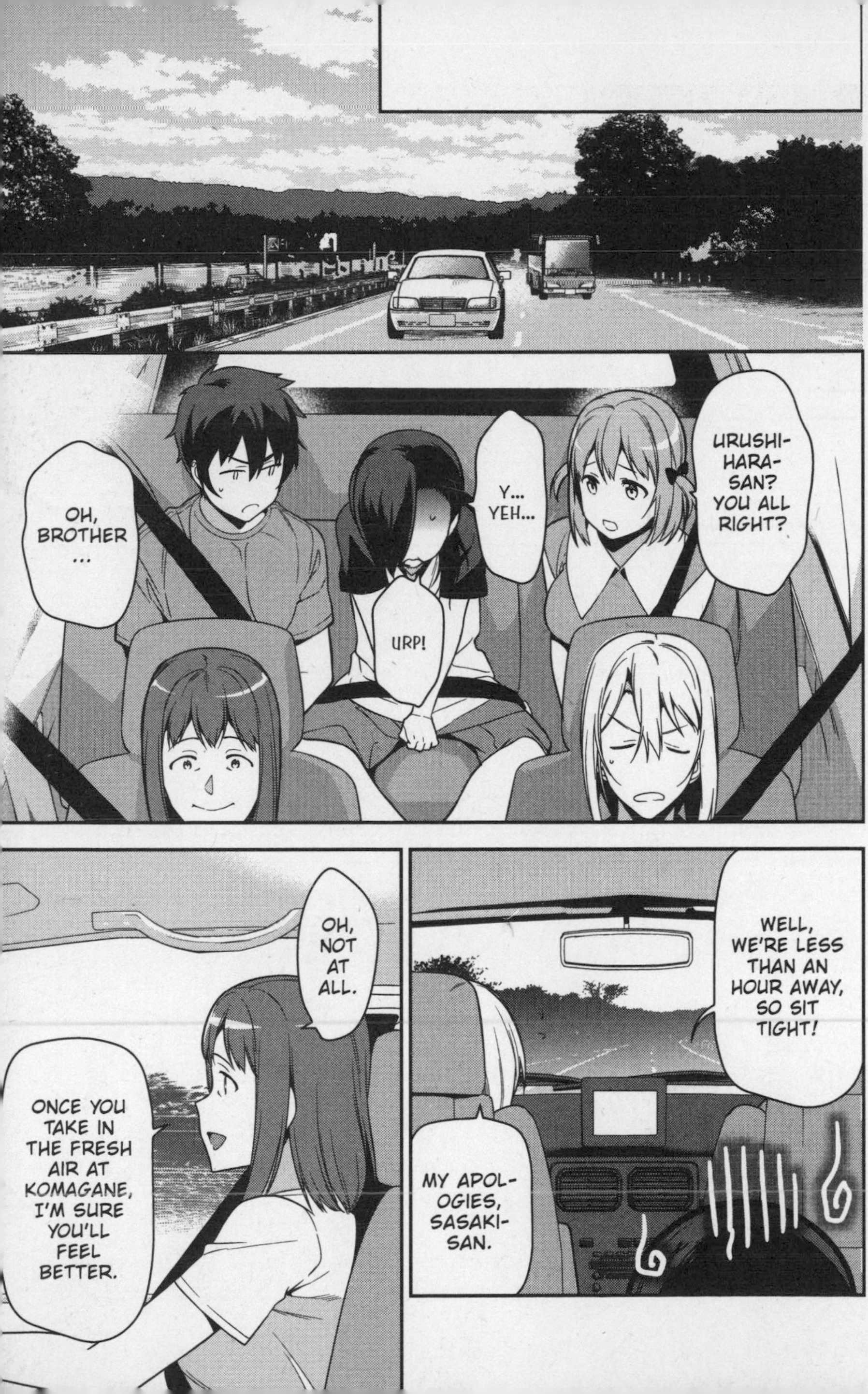
URUSHI-HARA-SAN? YOU ALL RIGHT?
Y... YEH...
OH, BROTHER ...
URP!
WELL, WE'RE LESS THAN AN HOUR AWAY, SO SIT TIGHT!
MY APOLOGIES, SASAKI-SAN.
OH, NOT AT ALL.
ONCE YOU TAKE IN THE FRESH AIR AT KOMAGANE, I'M SURE YOU'LL FEEL BETTER.

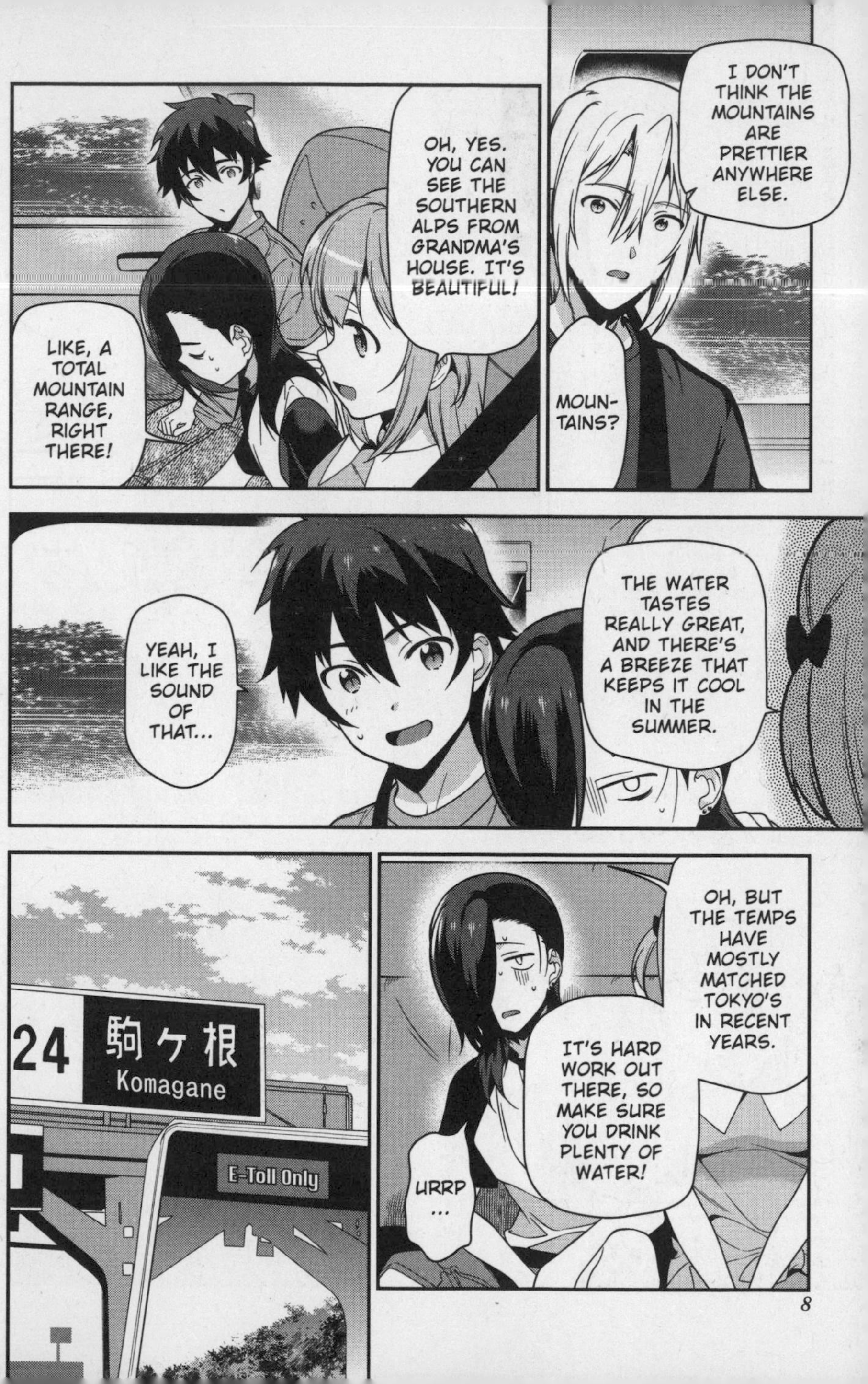
I DON'T THINK THE MOUNTAINS ARE PRETTIER ANYWHERE ELSE.
MOUN-TAINS?
OH, YES. YOU CAN SEE THE SOUTHERN ALPS FROM GRANDMA'S HOUSE. IT'S BEAUTIFUL!
LIKE, A TOTAL MOUNTAIN RANGE, RIGHT THERE!
THE WATER TASTES REALLY GREAT, AND THERE'S A BREEZE THAT KEEPS IT COOL IN THE SUMMER.
YEAH, I LIKE THE SOUND OF THAT...
OH, BUT THE TEMPS HAVE MOSTLY MATCHED TOKYO'S IN RECENT YEARS.
IT'S HARD WORK OUT THERE, SO MAKE SURE YOU DRINK PLENTY OF WATER!
URRP ...
24
駒ヶ根
Komagane
E-Toll Only

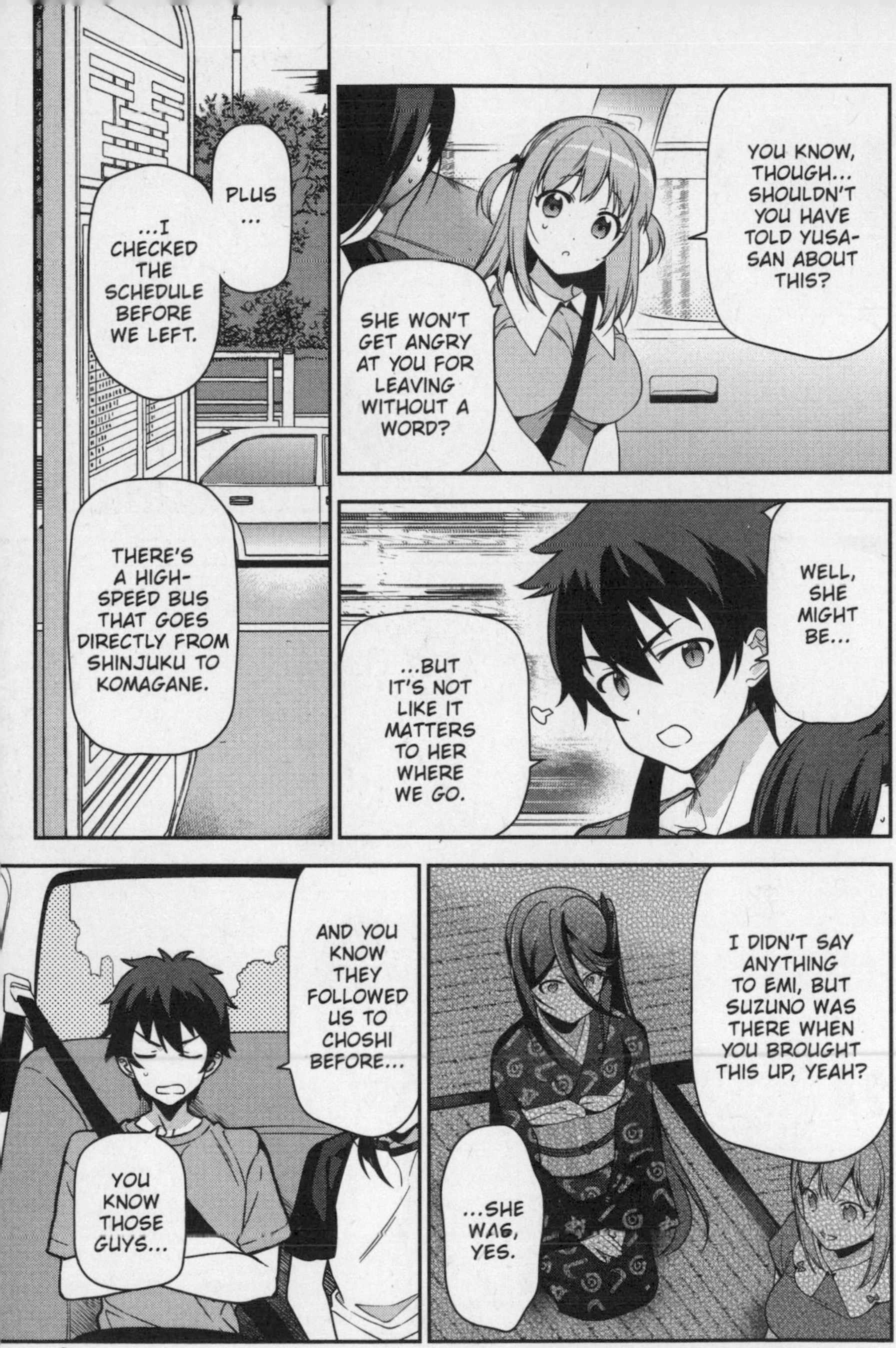
YOU KNOW, THOUGH... SHOULDN'T YOU HAVE TOLD YUSA-SAN ABOUT THIS?
SHE WON'T GET ANGRY AT YOU FOR LEAVING WITHOUT A WORD?
WELL, SHE MIGHT BE...
...BUT IT'S NOT LIKE IT MATTERS TO HER WHERE WE GO.
PLUS ...
...I CHECKED THE SCHEDULE BEFORE WE LEFT.
THERE'S A HIGH-SPEED BUS THAT GOES DIRECTLY FROM SHINJUKU TO KOMAGANE.
I DIDN'T SAY ANYTHING TO EMI, BUT SUZUNO WAS THERE WHEN YOU BROUGHT THIS UP, YEAH?
...SHE WAS, YES.
AND YOU KNOW THEY FOLLOWED US TO CHOSHI BEFORE...
YOU KNOW THOSE GUYS...

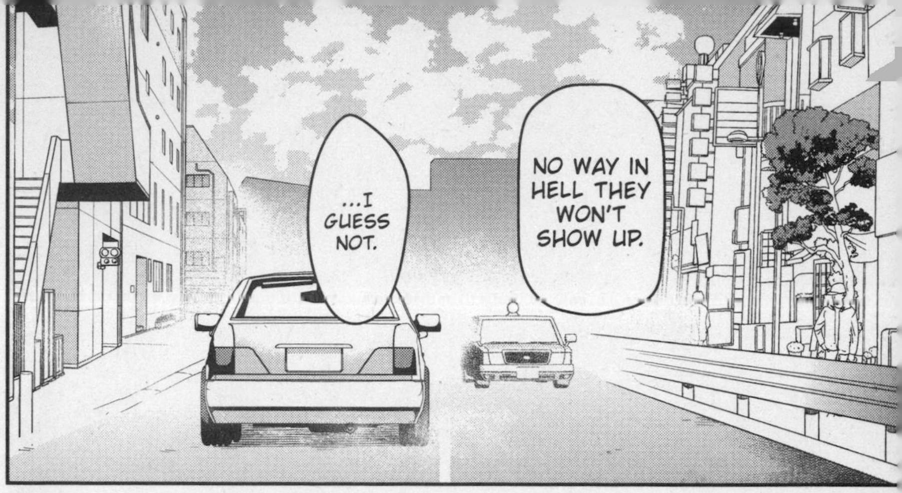
NO WAY IN HELL THEY WON'T SHOW UP.
...I GUESS NOT.

SIGNS: CENTRAL EXPRESS BUS; OVERNIGHT EXPRESS BUS; BOARDING AREA; EXPRESS BUS TERMINAL

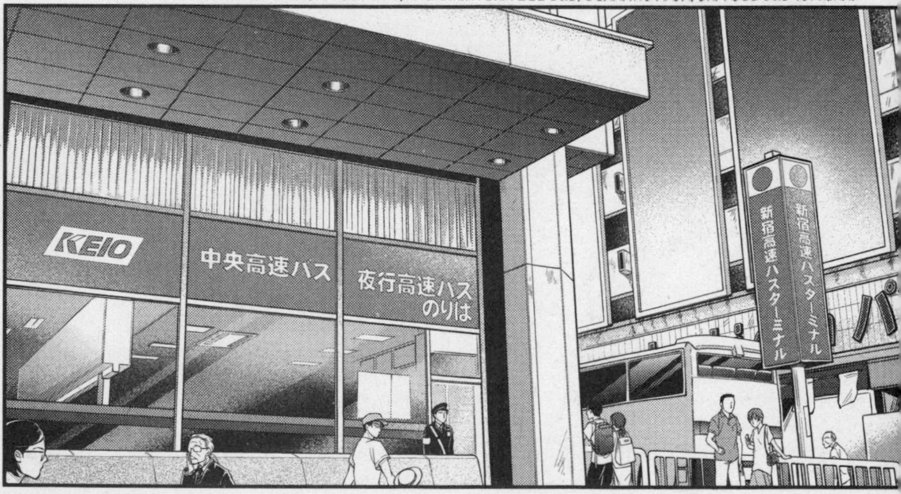
新宿高速バスターミナル
新宿高速バスターミナル
夜行高速バス
のりは
中央高速バス
KEIO

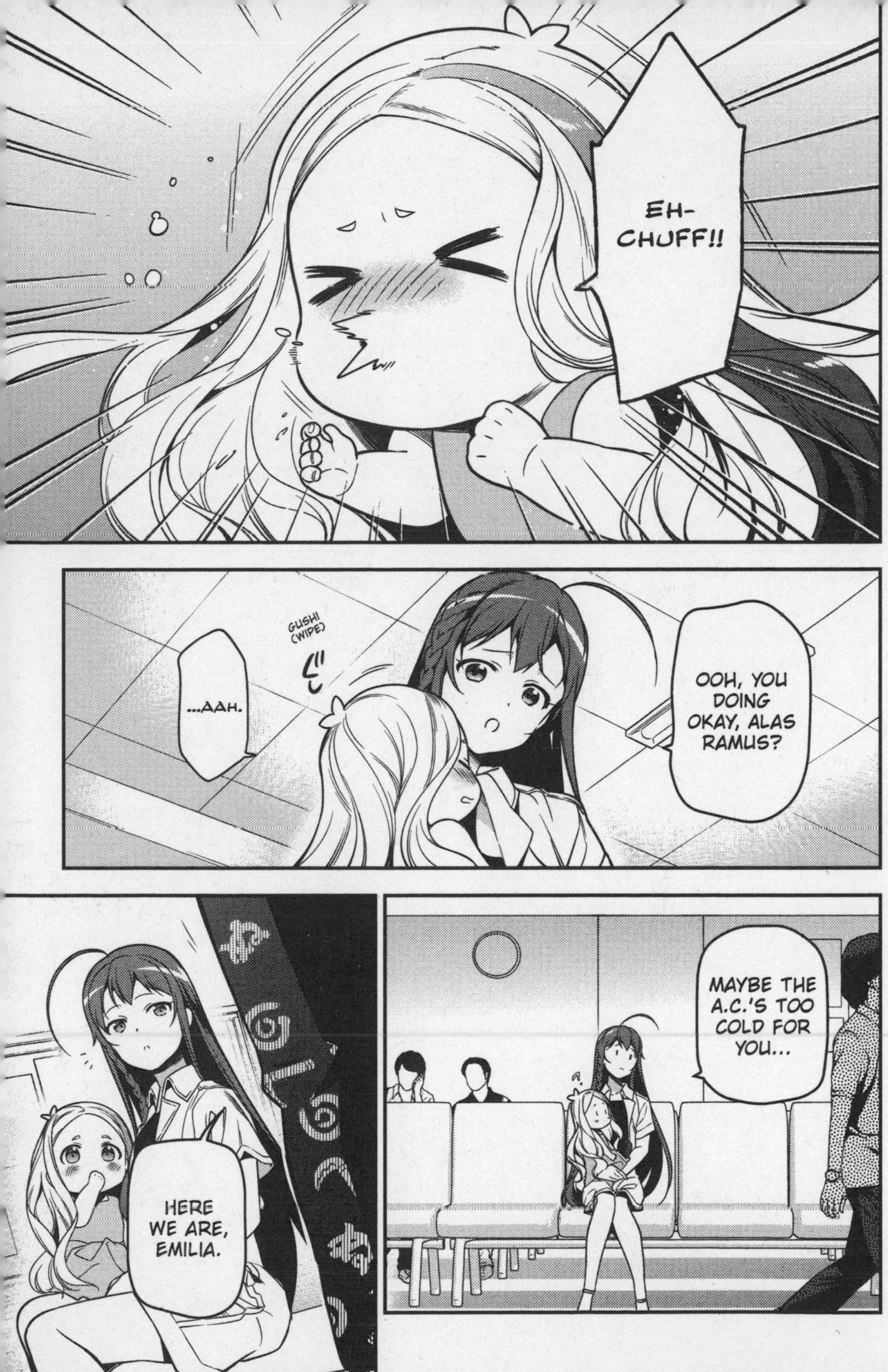
EH-CHUFF!!
OOH, YOU DOING OKAY, ALAS RAMUS?
GUSHI (WIPE)
...AAH.
MAYBE THE A.C.'S TOO COLD FOR YOU...
HERE WE ARE, EMILIA.

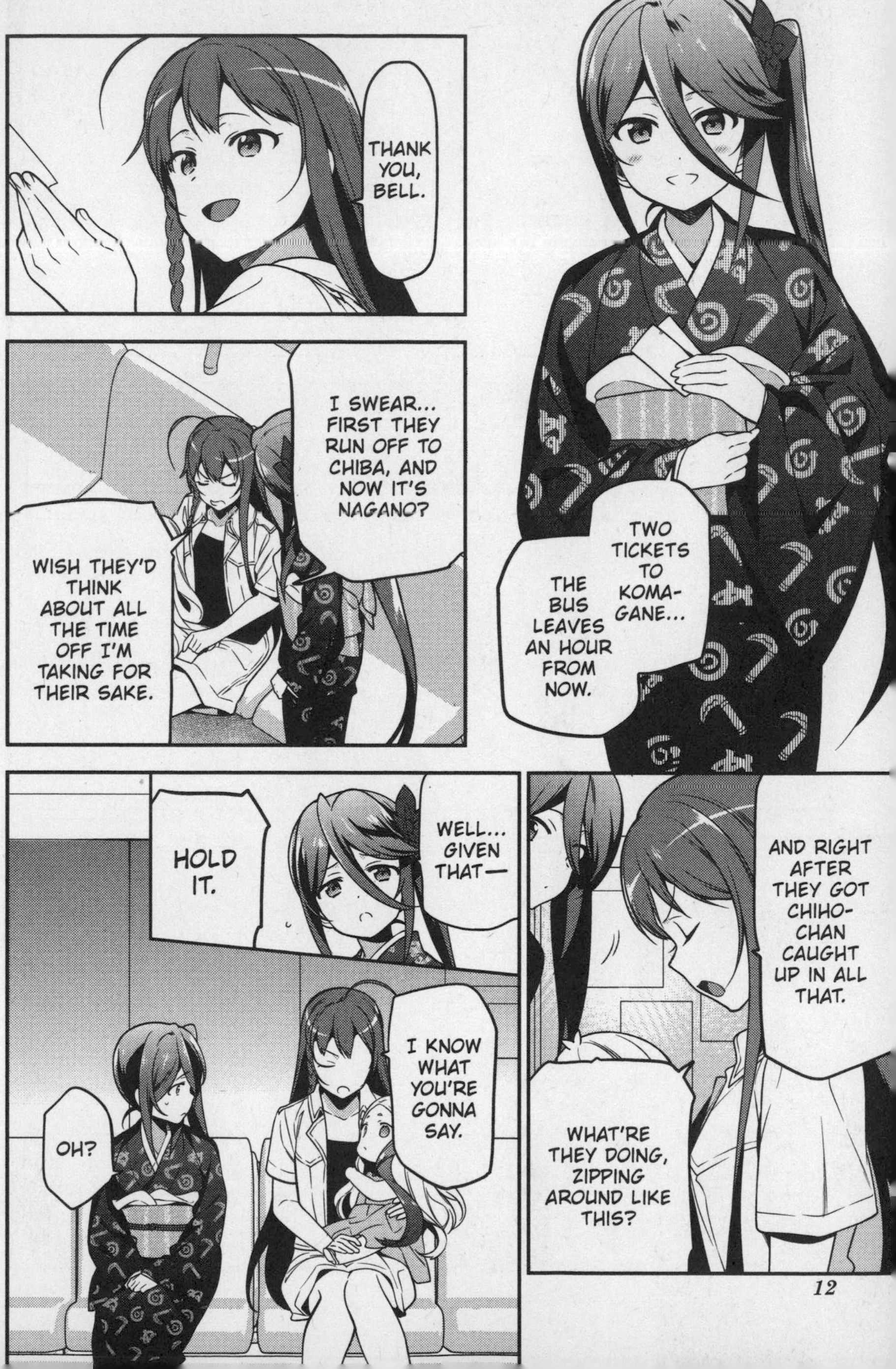
TWO TICKETS TO KOMAGANE...
THE BUS LEAVES AN HOUR FROM NOW.
THANK YOU, BELL.
I SWEAR... FIRST THEY RUN OFF TO CHIBA, AND NOW IT'S NAGANO?
WISH THEY'D THINK ABOUT ALL THE TIME OFF I'M TAKING FOR THEIR SAKE.
AND RIGHT AFTER THEY GOT CHIHO-CHAN CAUGHT UP IN ALL THAT.
WHAT'RE THEY DOING, ZIPPING AROUND LIKE THIS?
WELL... GIVEN THAT—
HOLD IT.
I KNOW WHAT YOU'RE GONNA SAY.
OH?

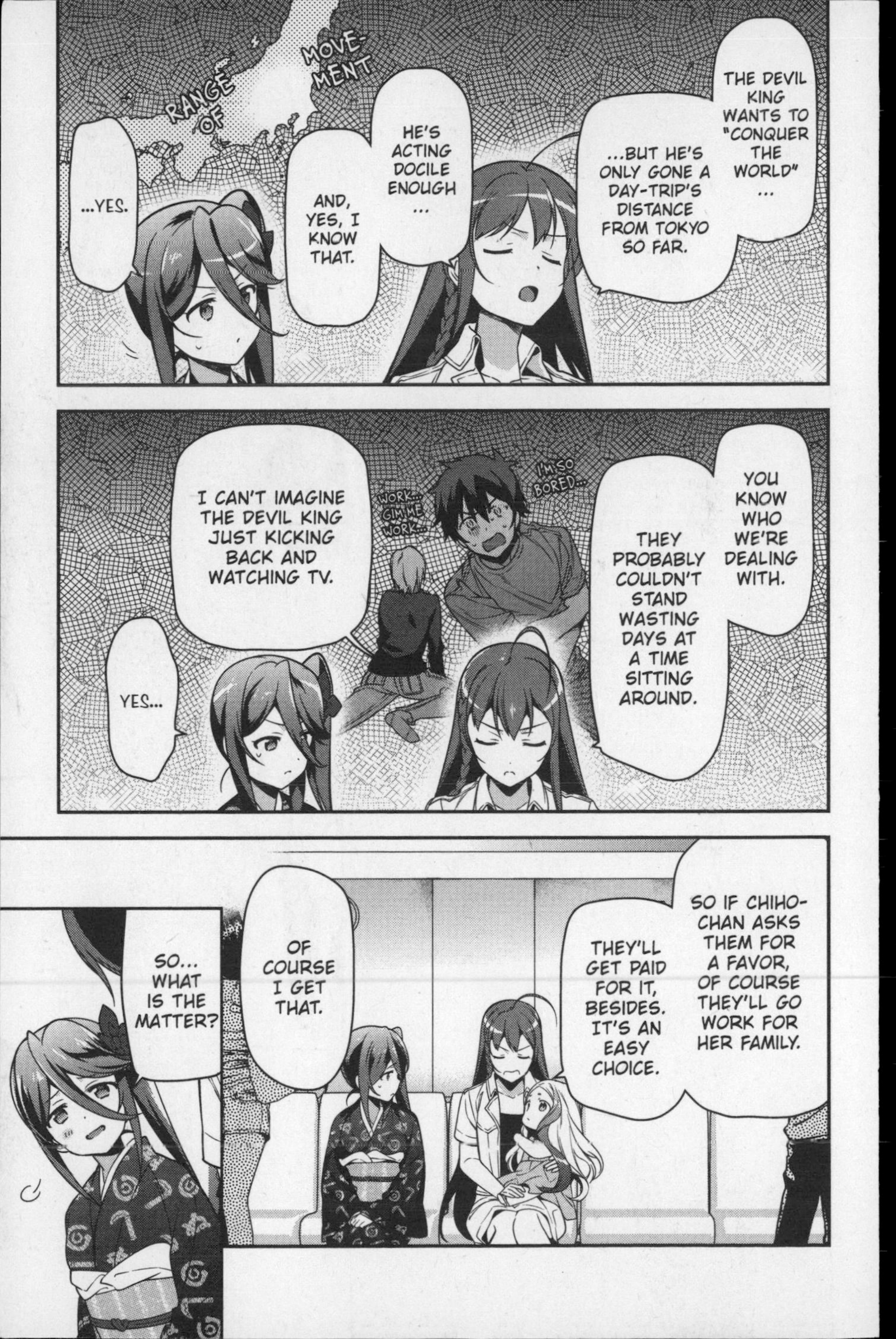
THE DEVIL KING WANTS TO "CONQUER THE WORLD"...
...BUT HE'S ONLY GONE A DAY-TRIP'S DISTANCE FROM TOKYO SO FAR.
RANGE OF MOVEMENT
HE'S ACTING DOCILE ENOUGH...
AND, YES, I KNOW THAT.
...YES.
YOU KNOW WHO WE'RE DEALING WITH.
THEY PROBABLY COULDN'T STAND WASTING DAYS AT A TIME SITTING AROUND.
I'M SO BORED...
WORK... GIMME WORK...
I CAN'T IMAGINE THE DEVIL KING JUST KICKING BACK AND WATCHING TV.
YES...
SO IF CHIHO-CHAN ASKS THEM FOR A FAVOR, OF COURSE THEY'LL GO WORK FOR HER FAMILY.
THEY'LL GET PAID FOR IT, BESIDES. IT'S AN EASY CHOICE.
OF COURSE I GET THAT.
SO... WHAT IS THE MATTER?

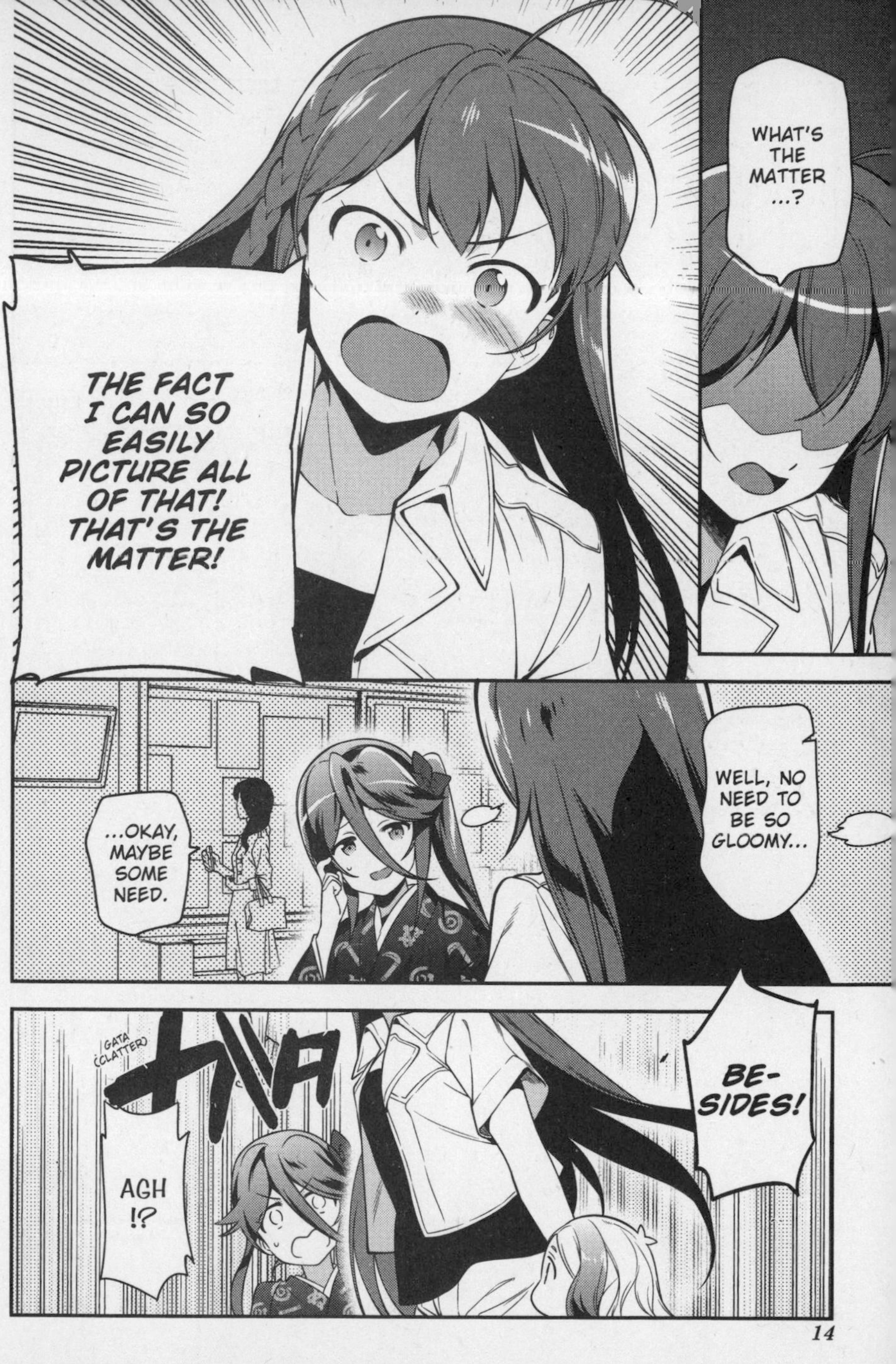
WHAT'S THE MATTER ...?
THE FACT I CAN SO EASILY PICTURE ALL OF THAT! THAT'S THE MATTER!
WELL, NO NEED TO BE SO GLOOMY...
...OKAY, MAYBE SOME NEED.
BE-SIDES!
GATA (CLATTER)
AGH !?

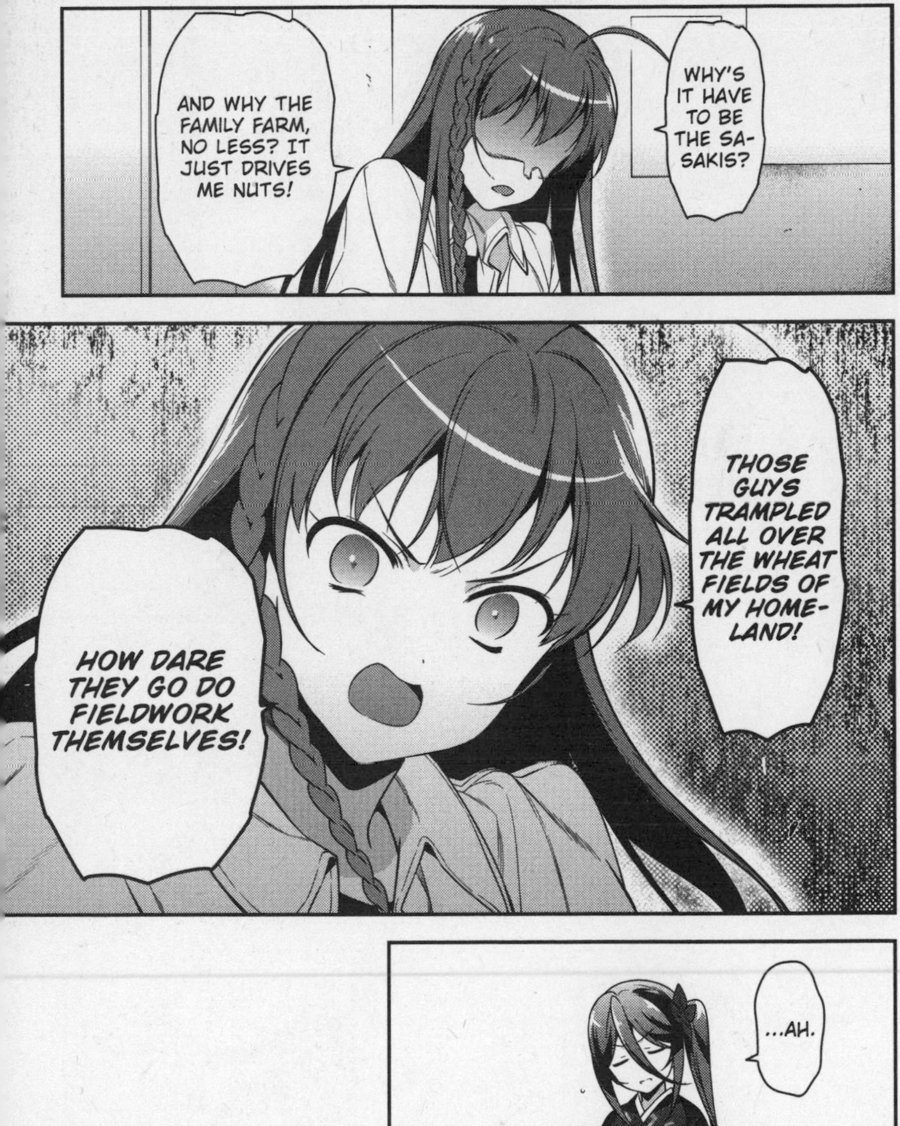
WHY'S IT HAVE TO BE THE SA-SAKIS?
AND WHY THE FAMILY FARM, NO LESS? IT JUST DRIVES ME NUTS!
THOSE GUYS TRAMPLED ALL OVER THE WHEAT FIELDS OF MY HOME-LAND!
HOW DARE THEY GO DO FIELDWORK THEMSELVES!
...AH.

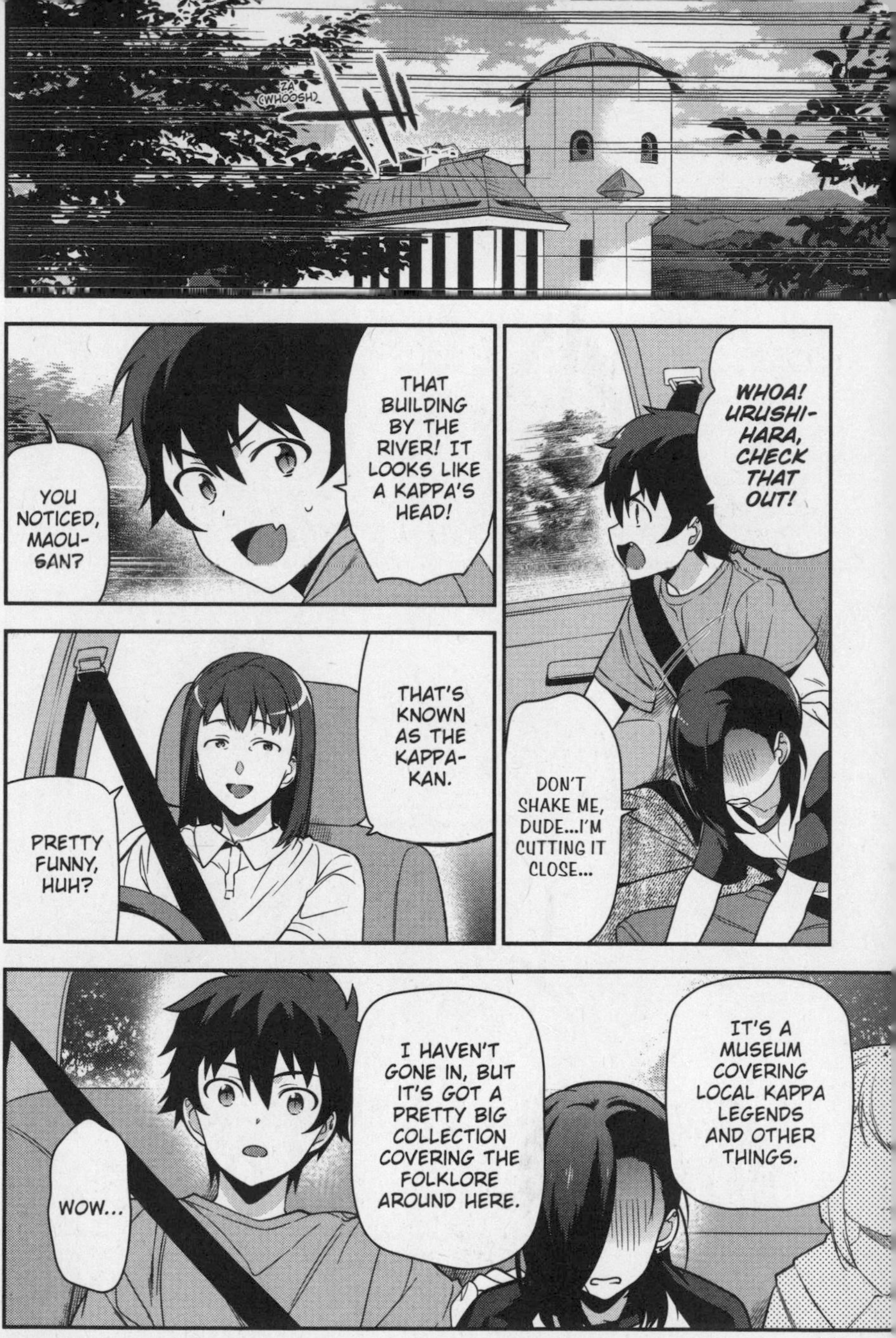
ZA (WHOOSH)
WHOA! URUSHIHARA, CHECK THAT OUT!
DON'T SHAKE ME, DUDE...I'M CUTTING IT CLOSE...
THAT BUILDING BY THE RIVER! IT LOOKS LIKE A KAPPA'S HEAD!
YOU NOTICED, MAOU-SAN?
THAT'S KNOWN AS THE KAPPA-KAN.
PRETTY FUNNY, HUH?
IT'S A MUSEUM COVERING LOCAL KAPPA LEGENDS AND OTHER THINGS.
I HAVEN'T GONE IN, BUT IT'S GOT A PRETTY BIG COLLECTION COVERING THE FOLKLORE AROUND HERE.
WOW...

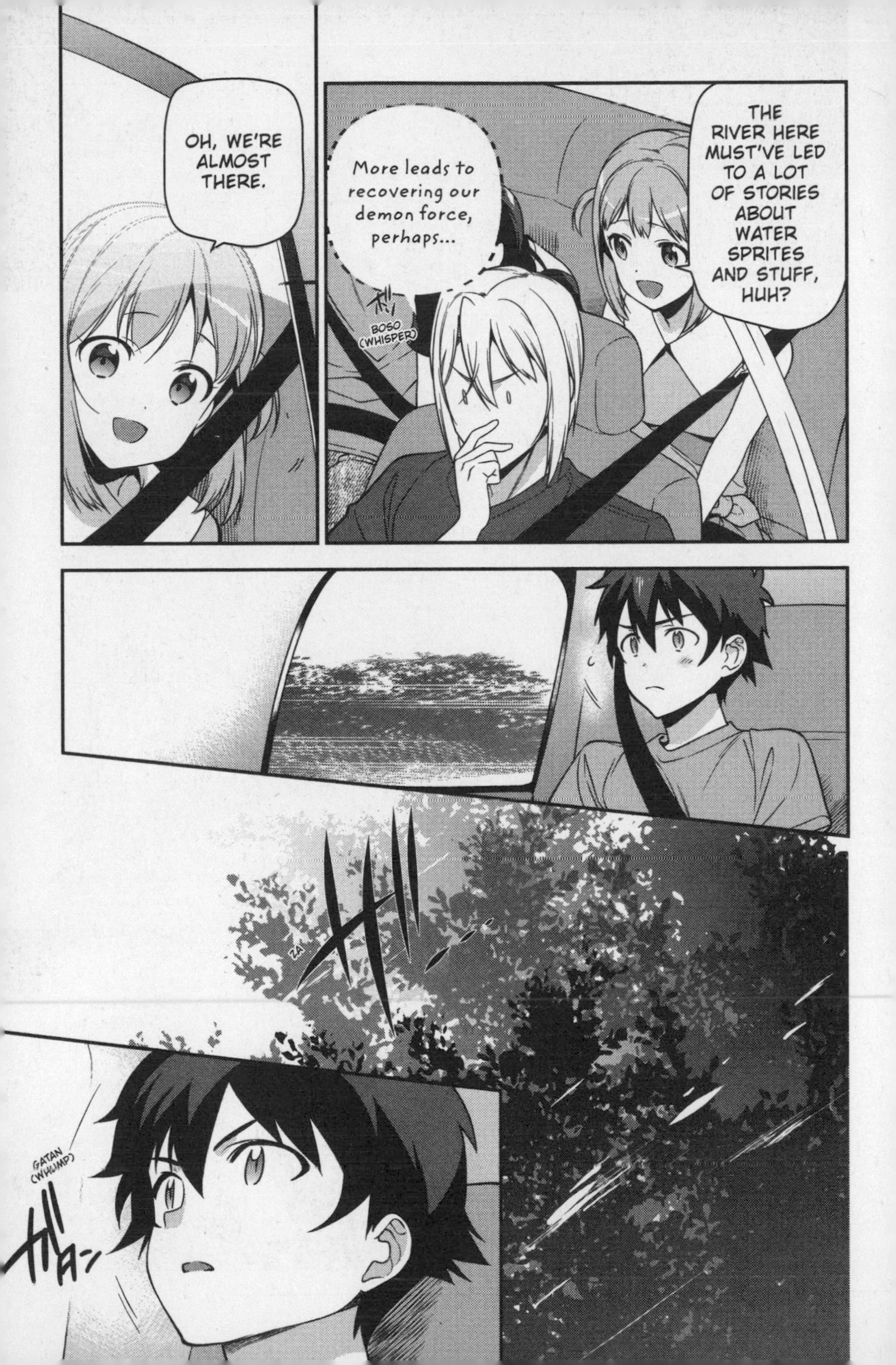
THE RIVER HERE MUST'VE LED TO A LOT OF STORIES ABOUT WATER SPRITES AND STUFF, HUH?
More leads to recovering our demon force, perhaps...
BOSO (WHISPER)
OH, WE'RE ALMOST THERE.
ZA
GATAN (WHUMP)

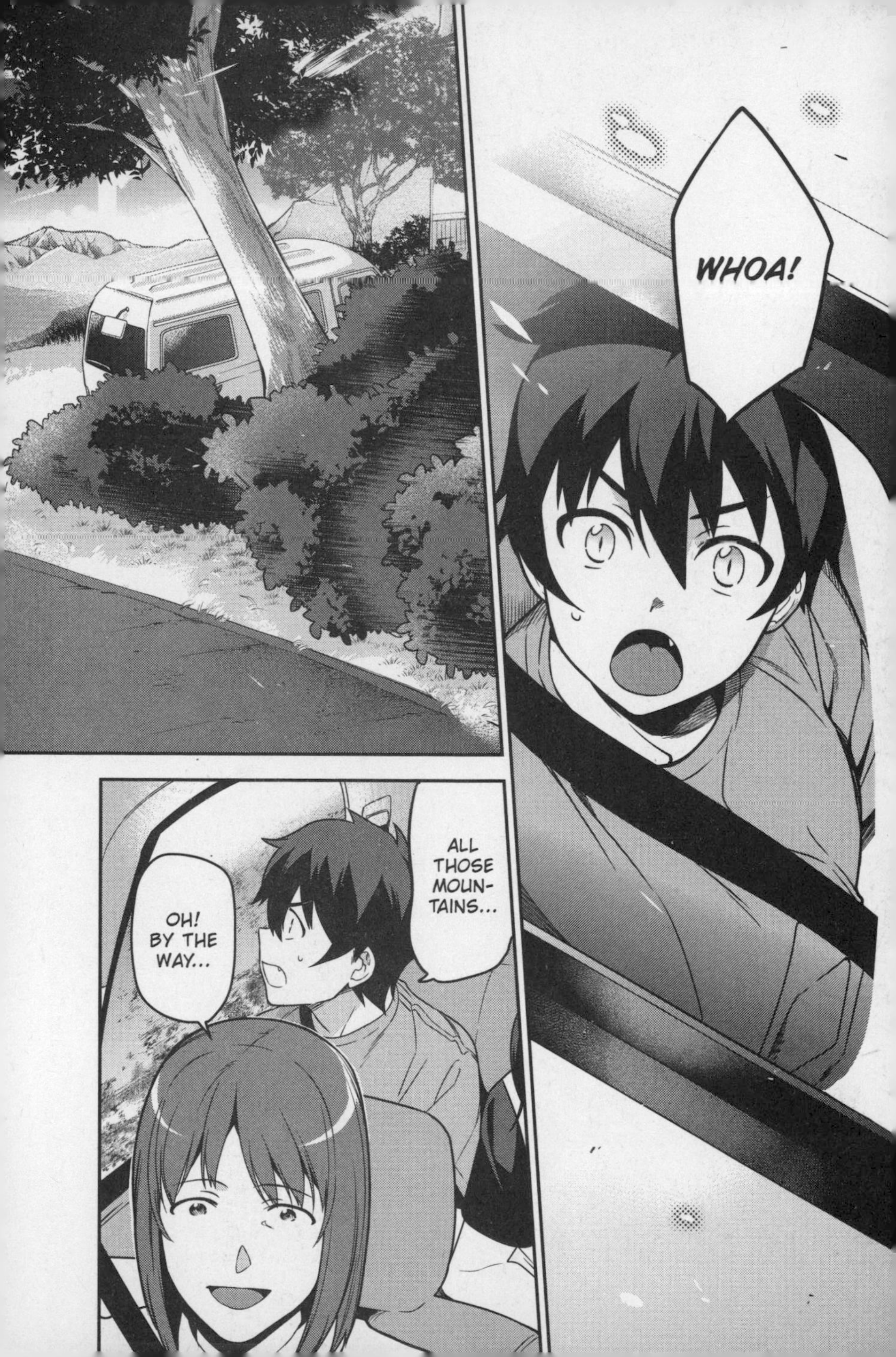
WHOA!
ALL THOSE MOUNTAINS...
OH! BY THE WAY...

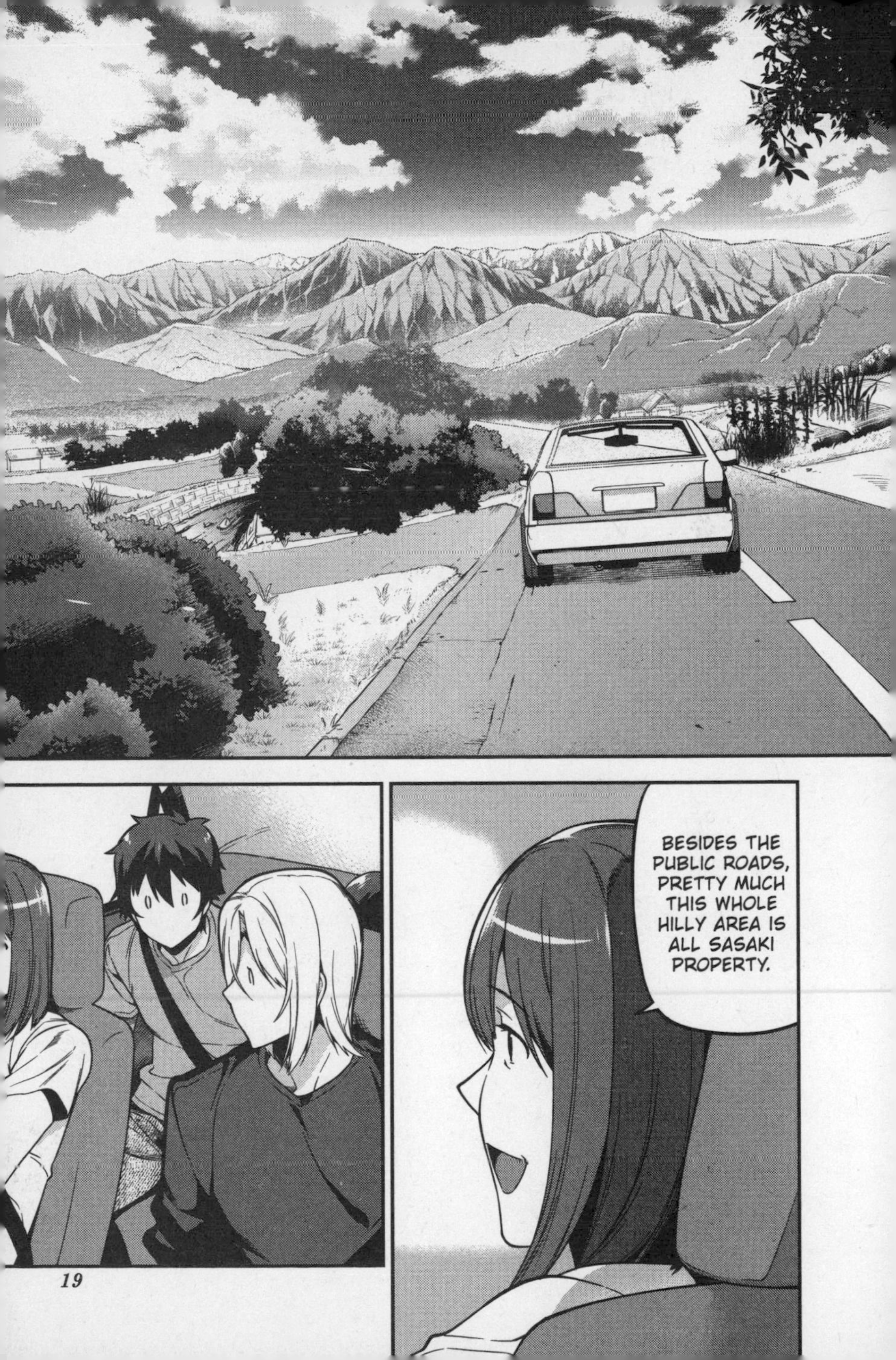
BESIDES THE PUBLIC ROADS, PRETTY MUCH THIS WHOLE HILLY AREA IS ALL SASAKI PROPERTY.

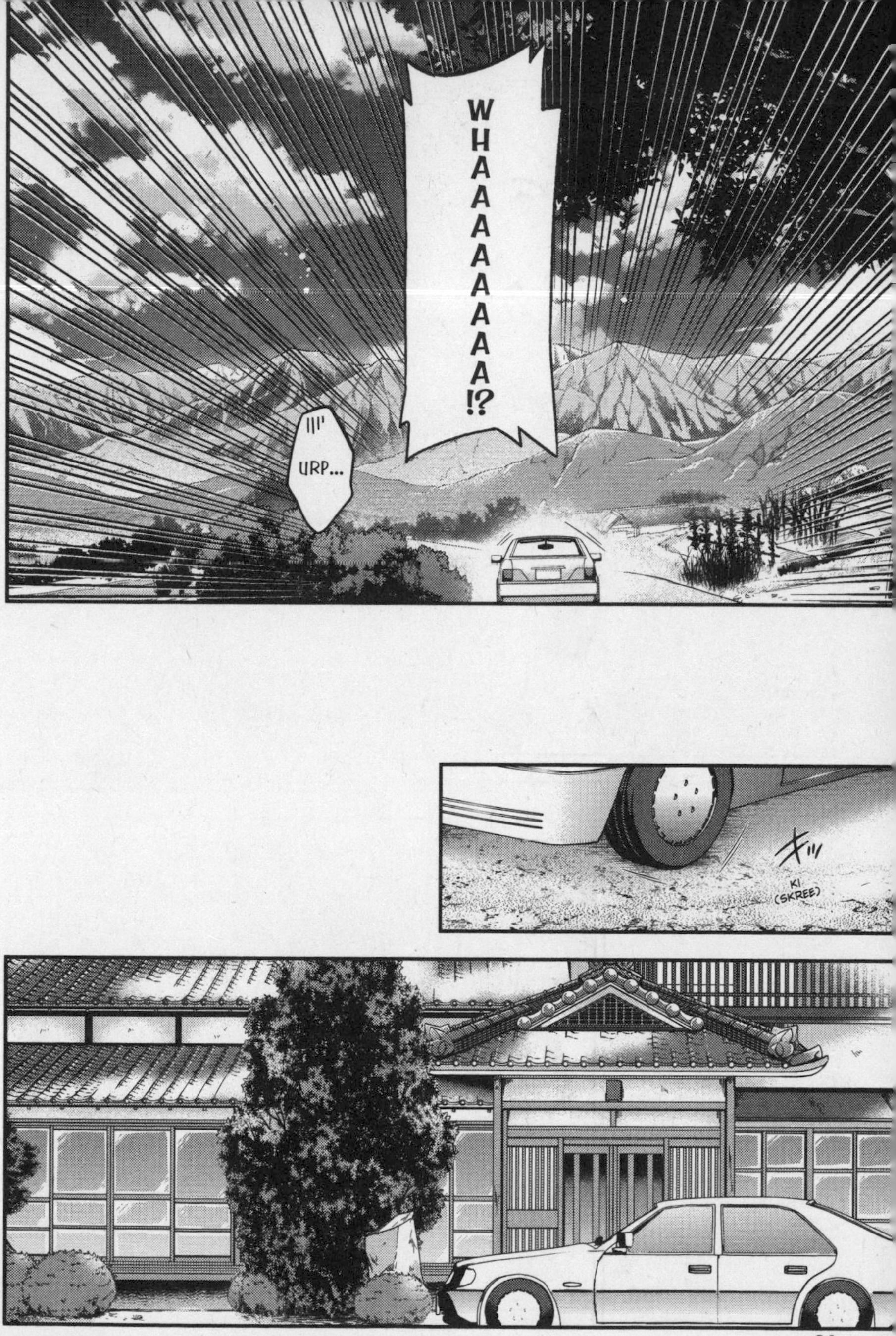
WHAAAAAAAA!?
URP...
KI (SKREE)

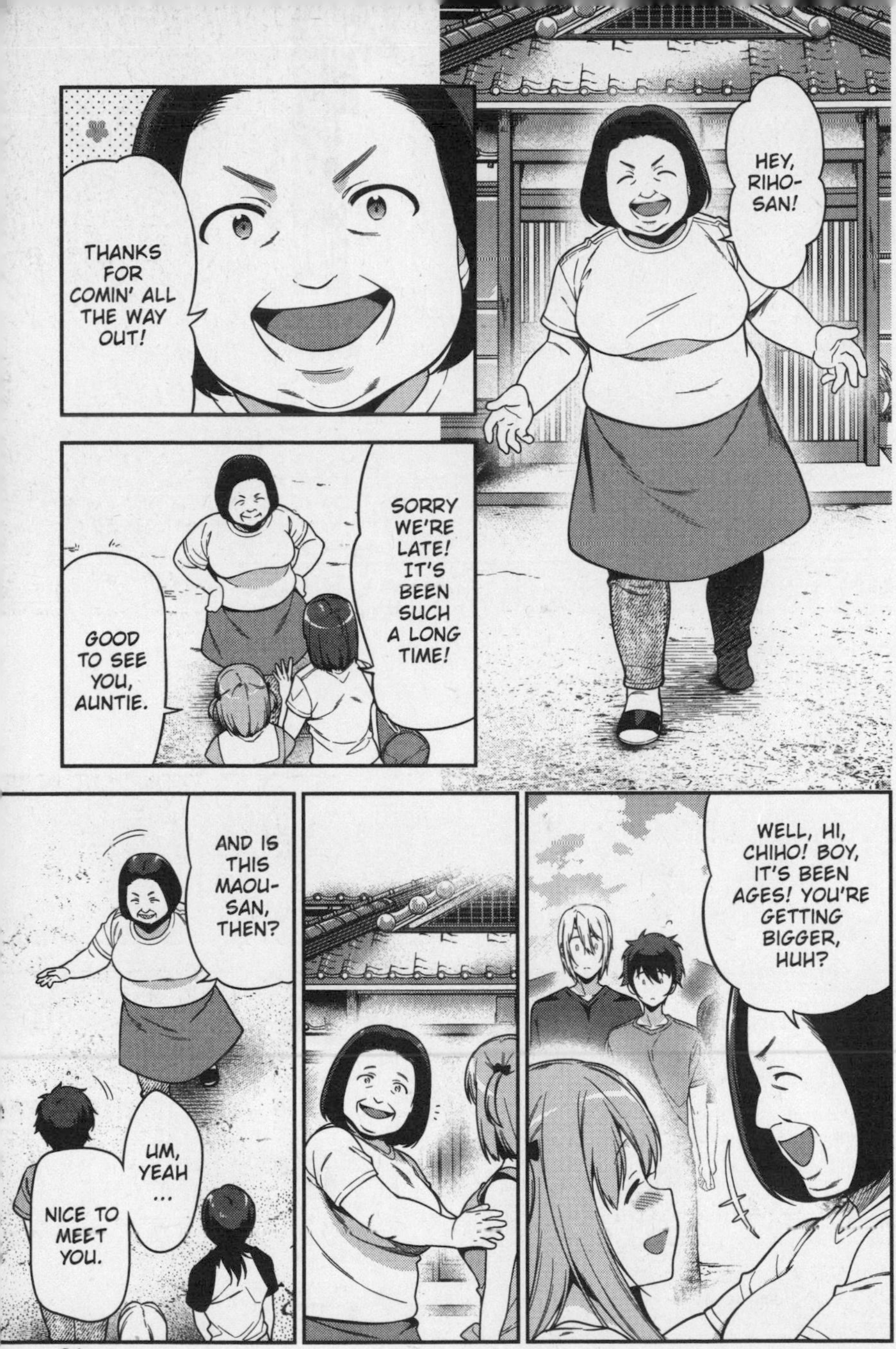
HEY, RIHO-SAN!
THANKS FOR COMIN' ALL THE WAY OUT!
SORRY WE'RE LATE! IT'S BEEN SUCH A LONG TIME!
GOOD TO SEE YOU, AUNTIE.
WELL, HI, CHIHO! BOY, IT'S BEEN AGES! YOU'RE GETTING BIGGER, HUH?
AND IS THIS MAOU-SAN, THEN?
UM, YEAH ...
NICE TO MEET YOU.

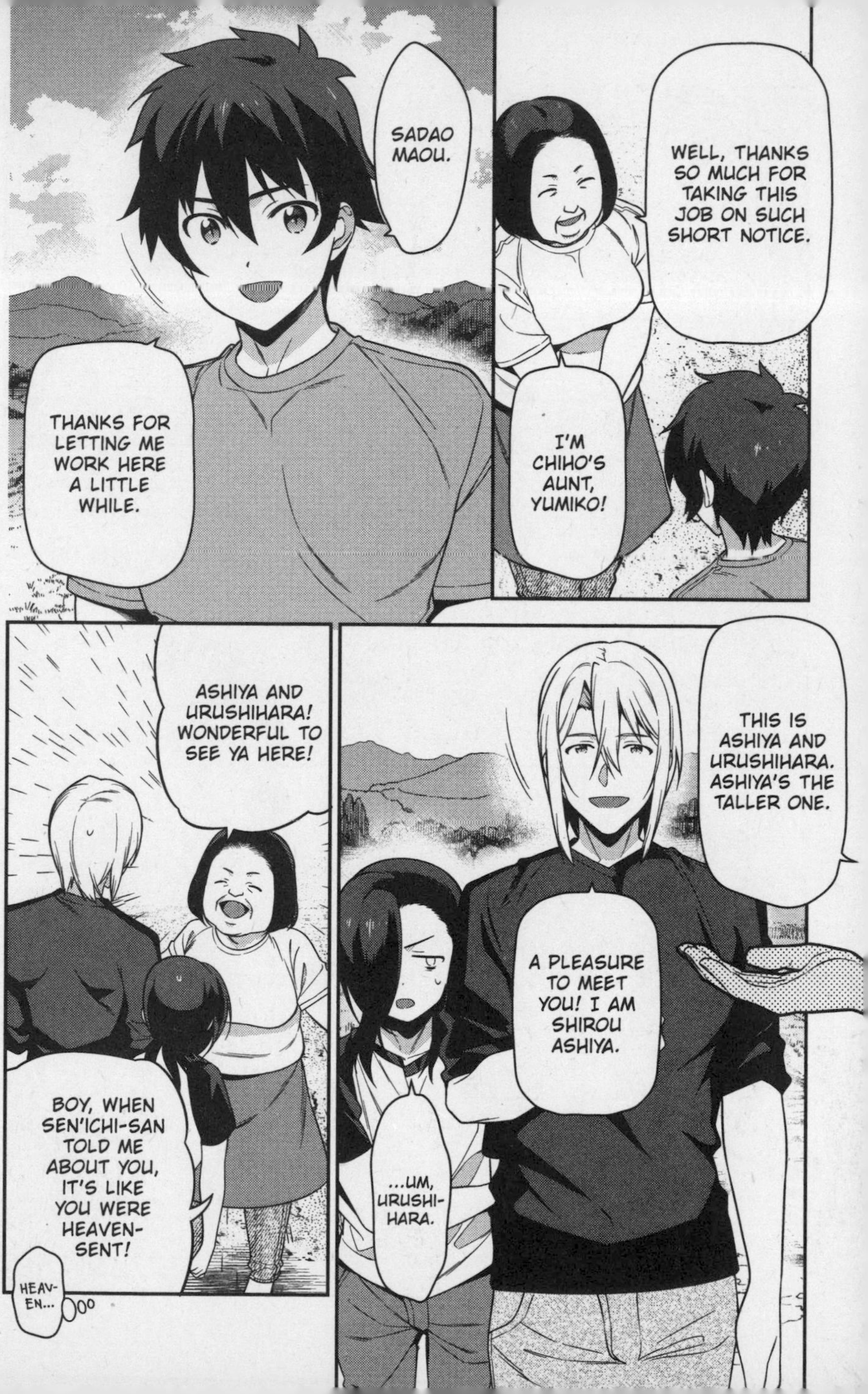
WELL, THANKS SO MUCH FOR TAKING THIS JOB ON SUCH SHORT NOTICE.
I'M CHIHO'S AUNT, YUMIKO!
SADAO MAOU.
THANKS FOR LETTING ME WORK HERE A LITTLE WHILE.
THIS IS ASHIYA AND URUSHIHARA. ASHIYA'S THE TALLER ONE.
A PLEASURE TO MEET YOU! I AM SHIROU ASHIYA.
...UM, URUSHIHARA.
ASHIYA AND URUSHIHARA! WONDERFUL TO SEE YA HERE!
BOY, WHEN SEN'ICHI-SAN TOLD ME ABOUT YOU, IT'S LIKE YOU WERE HEAVEN-SENT!
HEAV-EN...

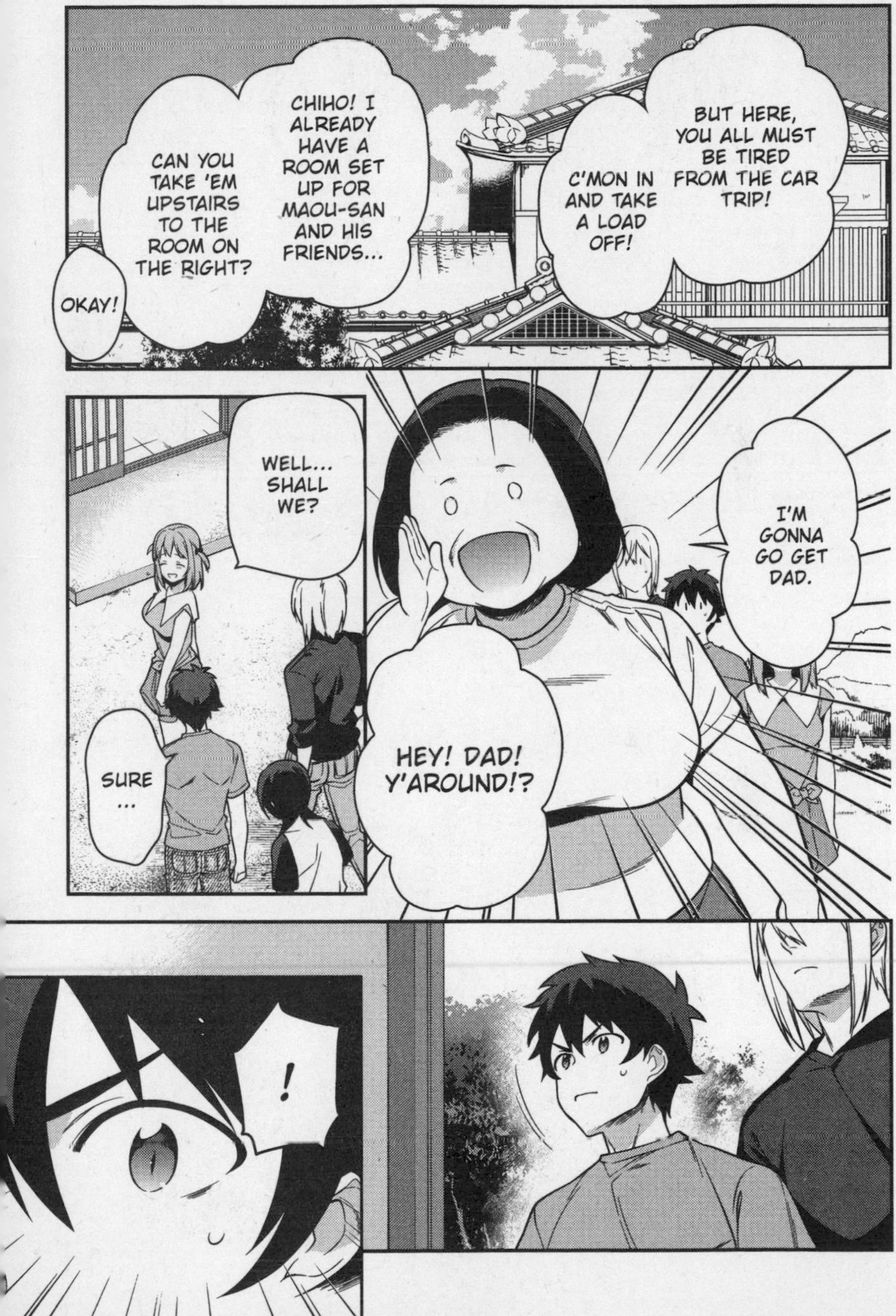
BUT HERE, YOU ALL MUST BE TIRED FROM THE CAR TRIP!
C'MON IN AND TAKE A LOAD OFF!
CHIHO! I ALREADY HAVE A ROOM SET UP FOR MAOU-SAN AND HIS FRIENDS...
CAN YOU TAKE 'EM UPSTAIRS TO THE ROOM ON THE RIGHT?
OKAY!
I'M GONNA GO GET DAD.
HEY! DAD! Y'AROUND!?
WELL... SHALL WE?
SURE...
!

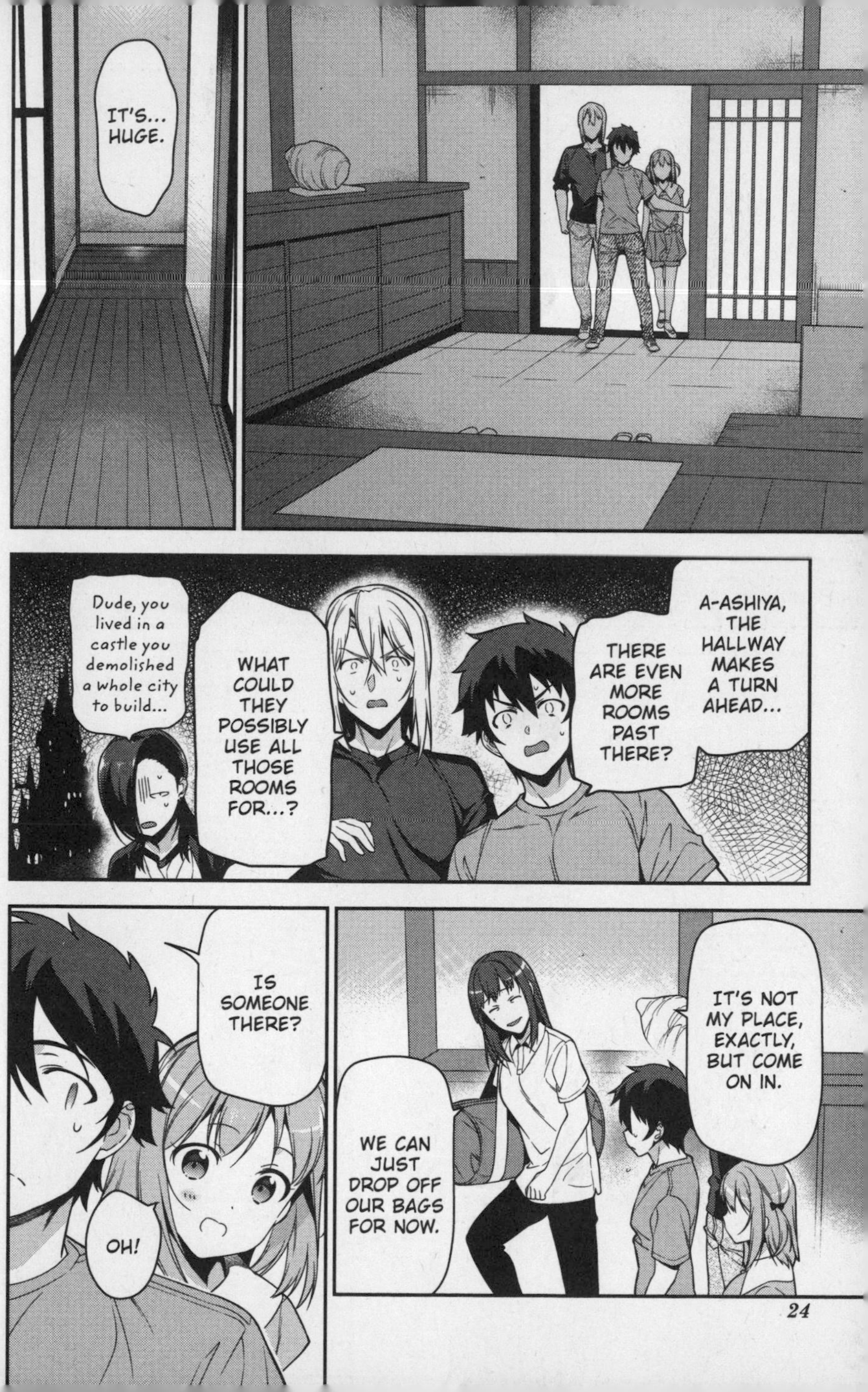
IT'S... HUGE.
A-ASHIYA, THE HALLWAY MAKES A TURN AHEAD...
THERE ARE EVEN MORE ROOMS PAST THERE?
WHAT COULD THEY POSSIBLY USE ALL THOSE ROOMS FOR...?
Dude, you lived in a castle you demolished a whole city to build...
IT'S NOT MY PLACE, EXACTLY, BUT COME ON IN.
WE CAN JUST DROP OFF OUR BAGS FOR NOW.
IS SOMEONE THERE?
OH!

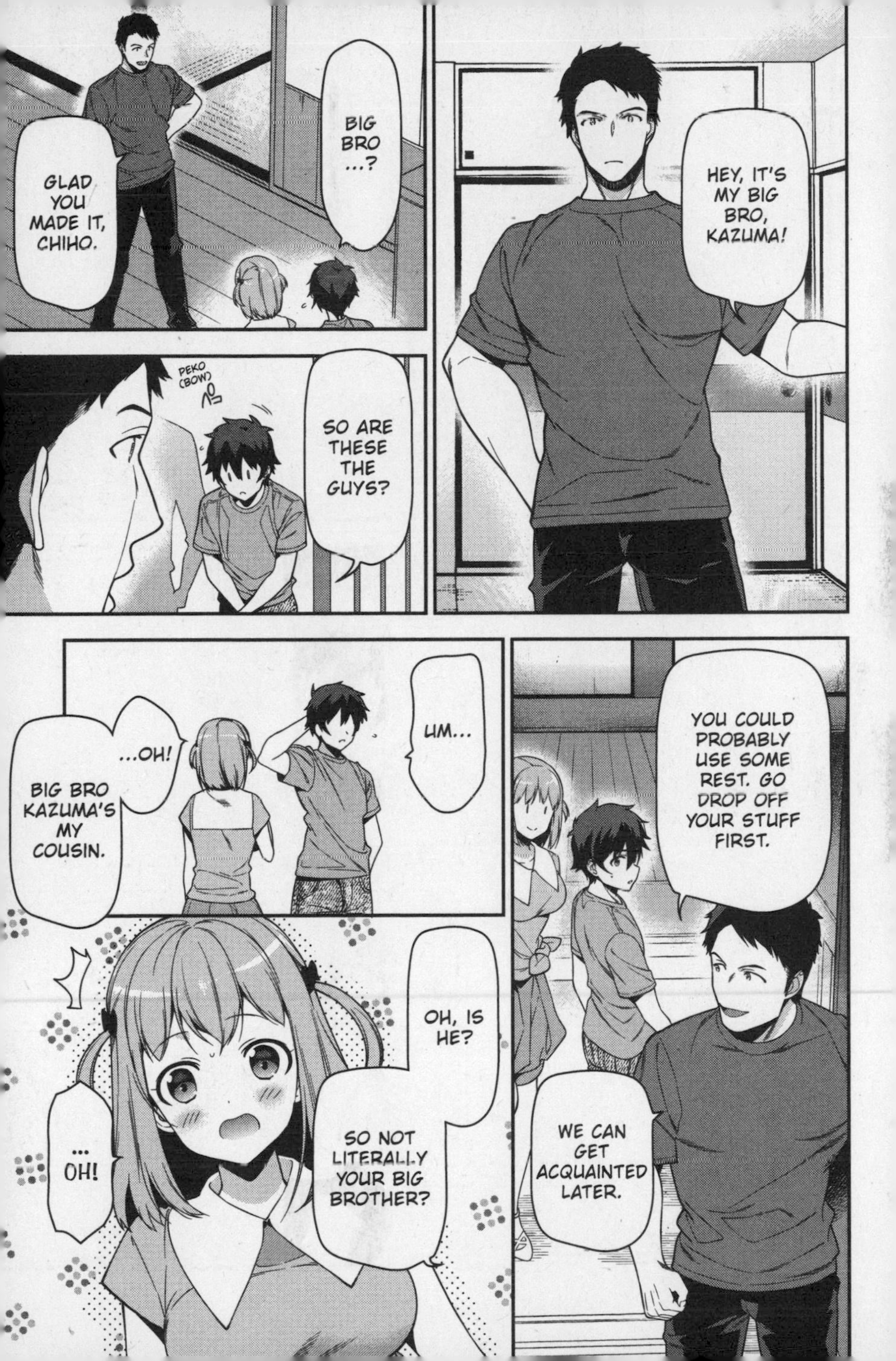
HEY, IT'S MY BIG BRO, KAZUMA!
BIG BRO ...?
GLAD YOU MADE IT, CHIHO.
SO ARE THESE THE GUYS?
PEKO (BOW)
YOU COULD PROBABLY USE SOME REST. GO DROP OFF YOUR STUFF FIRST.
WE CAN GET ACQUAINTED LATER.
UM...
...OH!
BIG BRO KAZUMA'S MY COUSIN.
OH, IS HE?
SO NOT LITERALLY YOUR BIG BROTHER?
... OH!

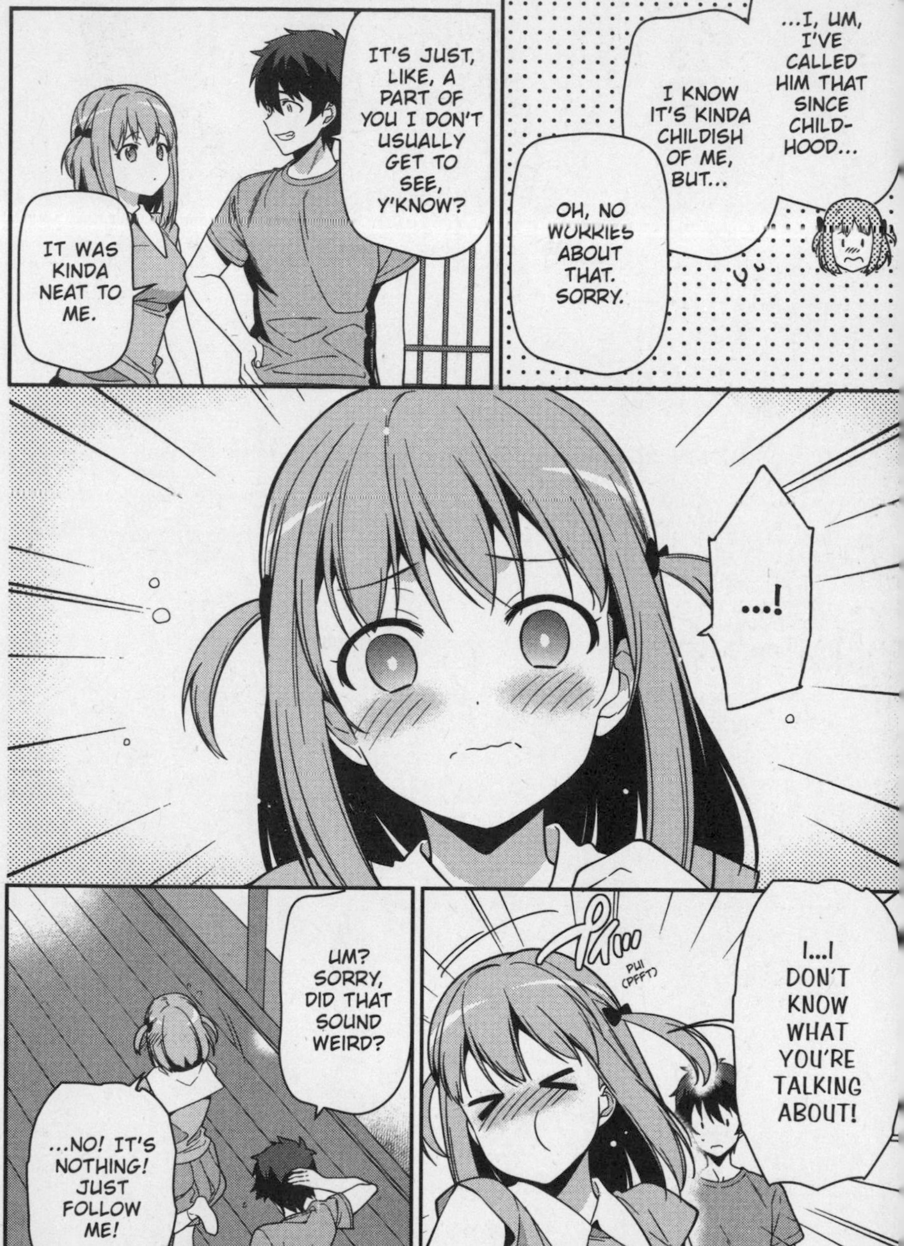
...I, UM, I'VE CALLED HIM THAT SINCE CHILD-HOOD...
I KNOW IT'S KINDA CHILDISH OF ME, BUT...
OH, NO WORRIES ABOUT THAT. SORRY.
IT'S JUST, LIKE, A PART OF YOU I DON'T USUALLY GET TO SEE, Y'KNOW?
IT WAS KINDA NEAT TO ME.
...!
PUI (PFFT)
I...I DON'T KNOW WHAT YOU'RE TALKING ABOUT!
UM? SORRY, DID THAT SOUND WEIRD?
...NO! IT'S NOTHING! JUST FOLLOW ME!

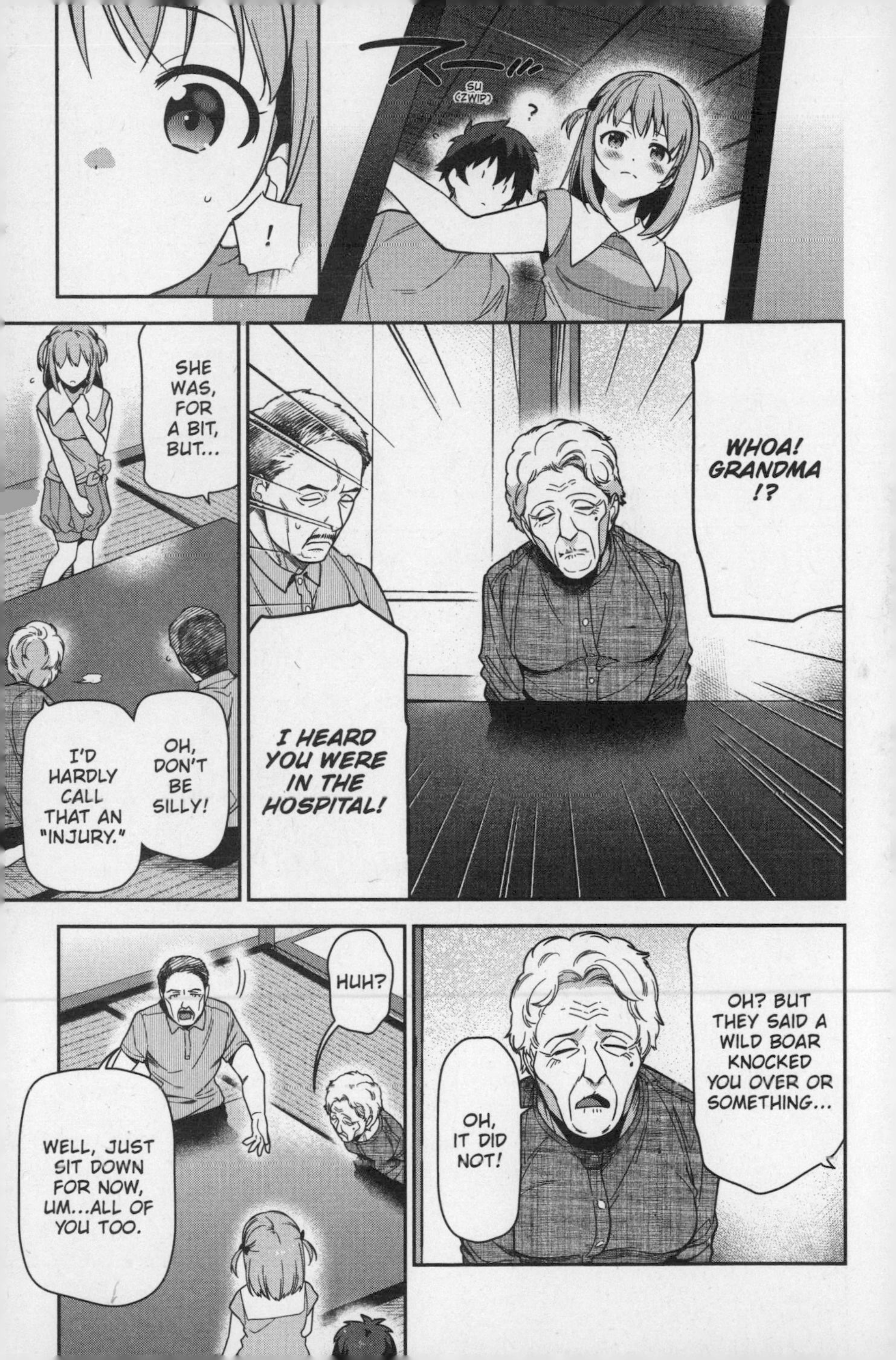
スーッ
SU (ZWIP)
?
!
WHOA! GRANDMA!?
I HEARD YOU WERE IN THE HOSPITAL!
SHE WAS, FOR A BIT, BUT...
OH, DON'T BE SILLY!
I'D HARDLY CALL THAT AN "INJURY."
OH? BUT THEY SAID A WILD BOAR KNOCKED YOU OVER OR SOMETHING...
OH, IT DID NOT!
HUH?
WELL, JUST SIT DOWN FOR NOW, UM...ALL OF YOU TOO.

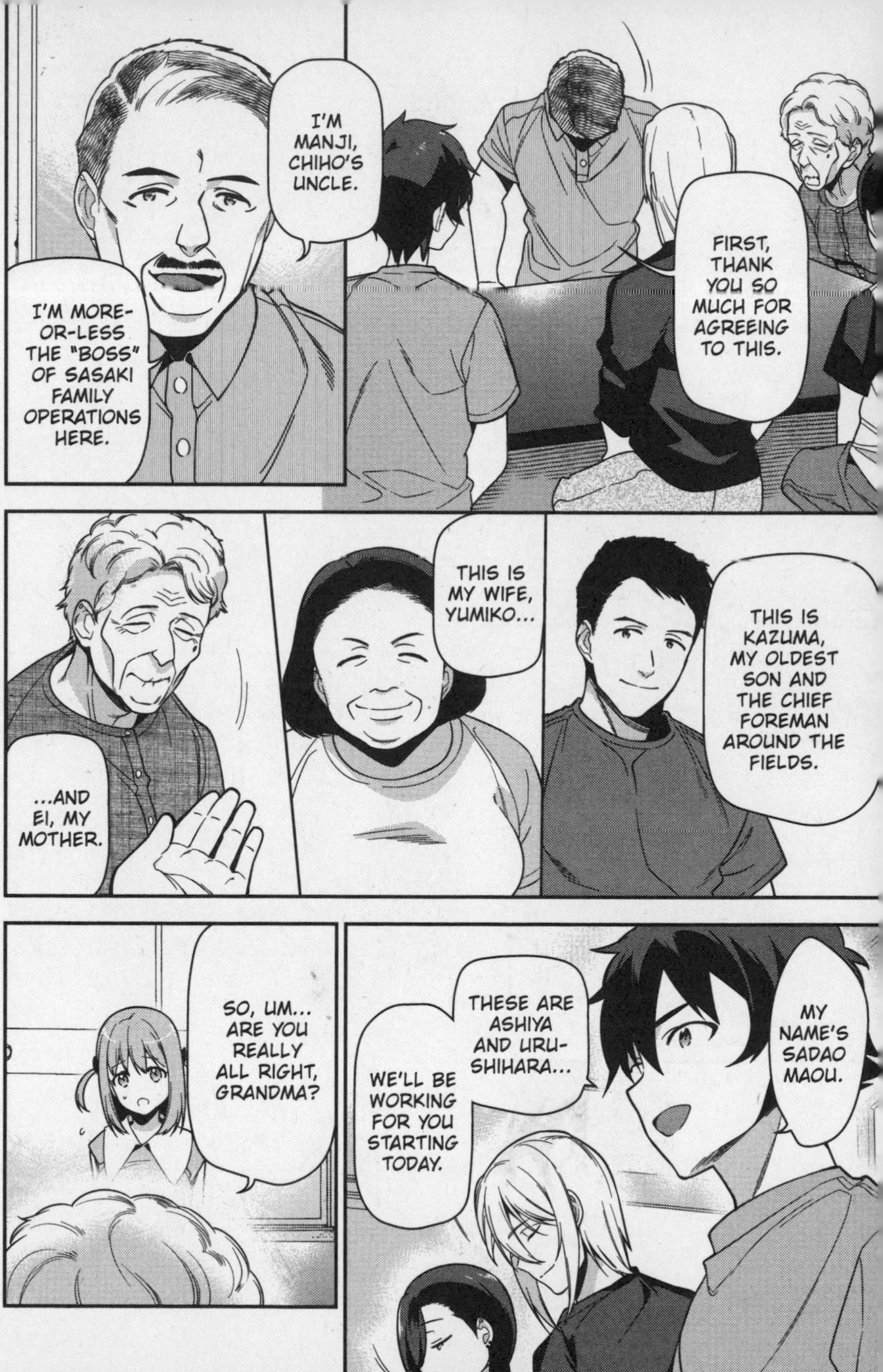
FIRST, THANK YOU SO MUCH FOR AGREEING TO THIS.
I'M MANJI, CHIHO'S UNCLE.
I'M MORE-OR-LESS THE "BOSS" OF SASAKI FAMILY OPERATIONS HERE.
THIS IS KAZUMA, MY OLDEST SON AND THE CHIEF FOREMAN AROUND THE FIELDS.
THIS IS MY WIFE, YUMIKO...
...AND EI, MY MOTHER.
MY NAME'S SADAO MAOU.
THESE ARE ASHIYA AND URU-SHIHARA...
WE'LL BE WORKING FOR YOU STARTING TODAY.
SO, UM... ARE YOU REALLY ALL RIGHT, GRANDMA?

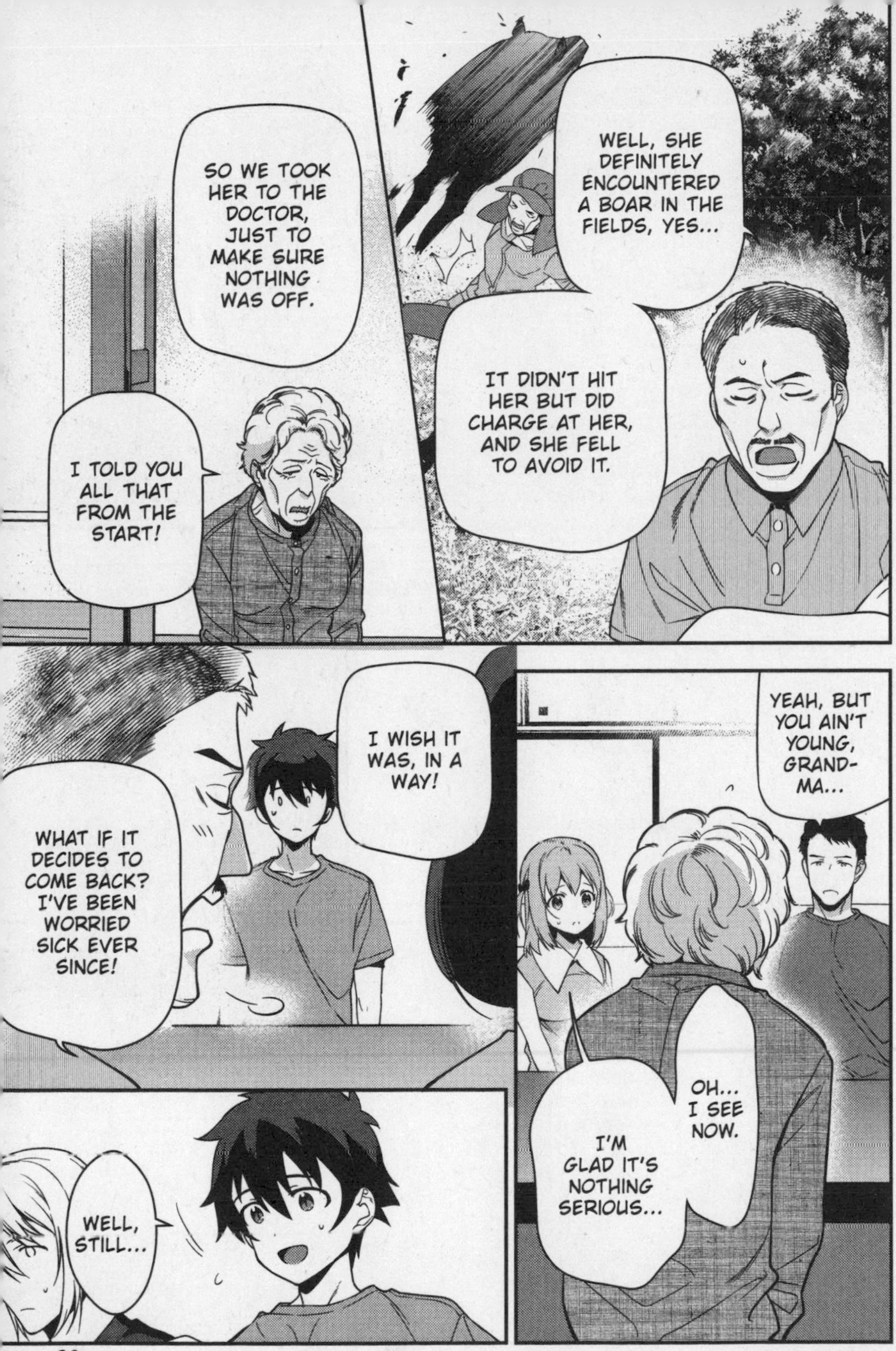
WELL, SHE DEFINITELY ENCOUNTERED A BOAR IN THE FIELDS, YES...
IT DIDN'T HIT HER BUT DID CHARGE AT HER, AND SHE FELL TO AVOID IT.
SO WE TOOK HER TO THE DOCTOR, JUST TO MAKE SURE NOTHING WAS OFF.
I TOLD YOU ALL THAT FROM THE START!
YEAH, BUT YOU AIN'T YOUNG, GRAND-MA...
OH... I SEE NOW.
I'M GLAD IT'S NOTHING SERIOUS...
I WISH IT WAS, IN A WAY!
WHAT IF IT DECIDES TO COME BACK? I'VE BEEN WORRIED SICK EVER SINCE!
WELL, STILL...

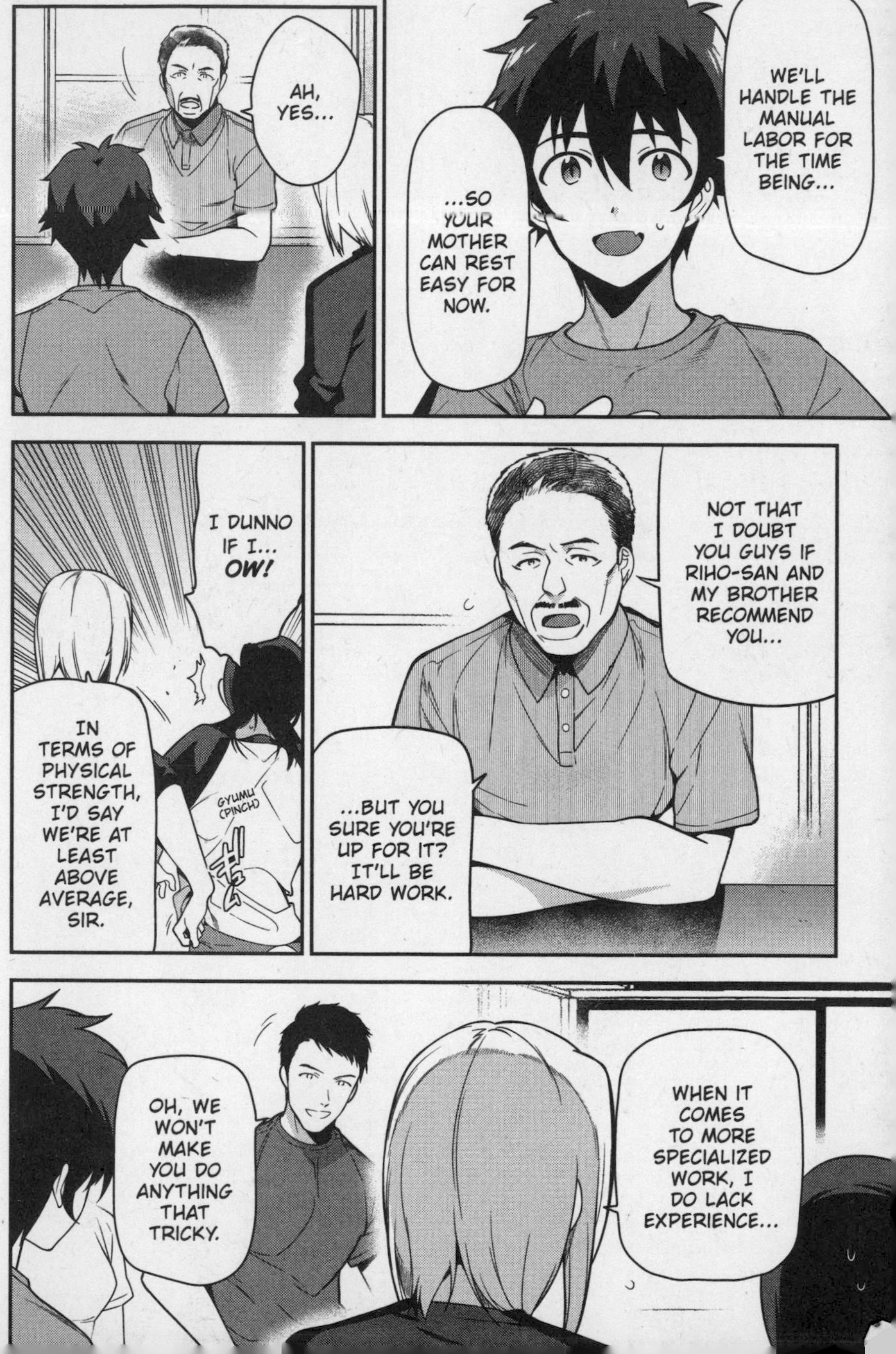
WE'LL HANDLE THE MANUAL LABOR FOR THE TIME BEING...
...SO YOUR MOTHER CAN REST EASY FOR NOW.
AH, YES...
NOT THAT I DOUBT YOU GUYS IF RIHO-SAN AND MY BROTHER RECOMMEND YOU...
...BUT YOU SURE YOU'RE UP FOR IT? IT'LL BE HARD WORK.
I DUNNO IF I... OW!
GYUMU (PINCH)
IN TERMS OF PHYSICAL STRENGTH, I'D SAY WE'RE AT LEAST ABOVE AVERAGE, SIR.
WHEN IT COMES TO MORE SPECIALIZED WORK, I DO LACK EXPERIENCE...
OH, WE WON'T MAKE YOU DO ANYTHING THAT TRICKY.

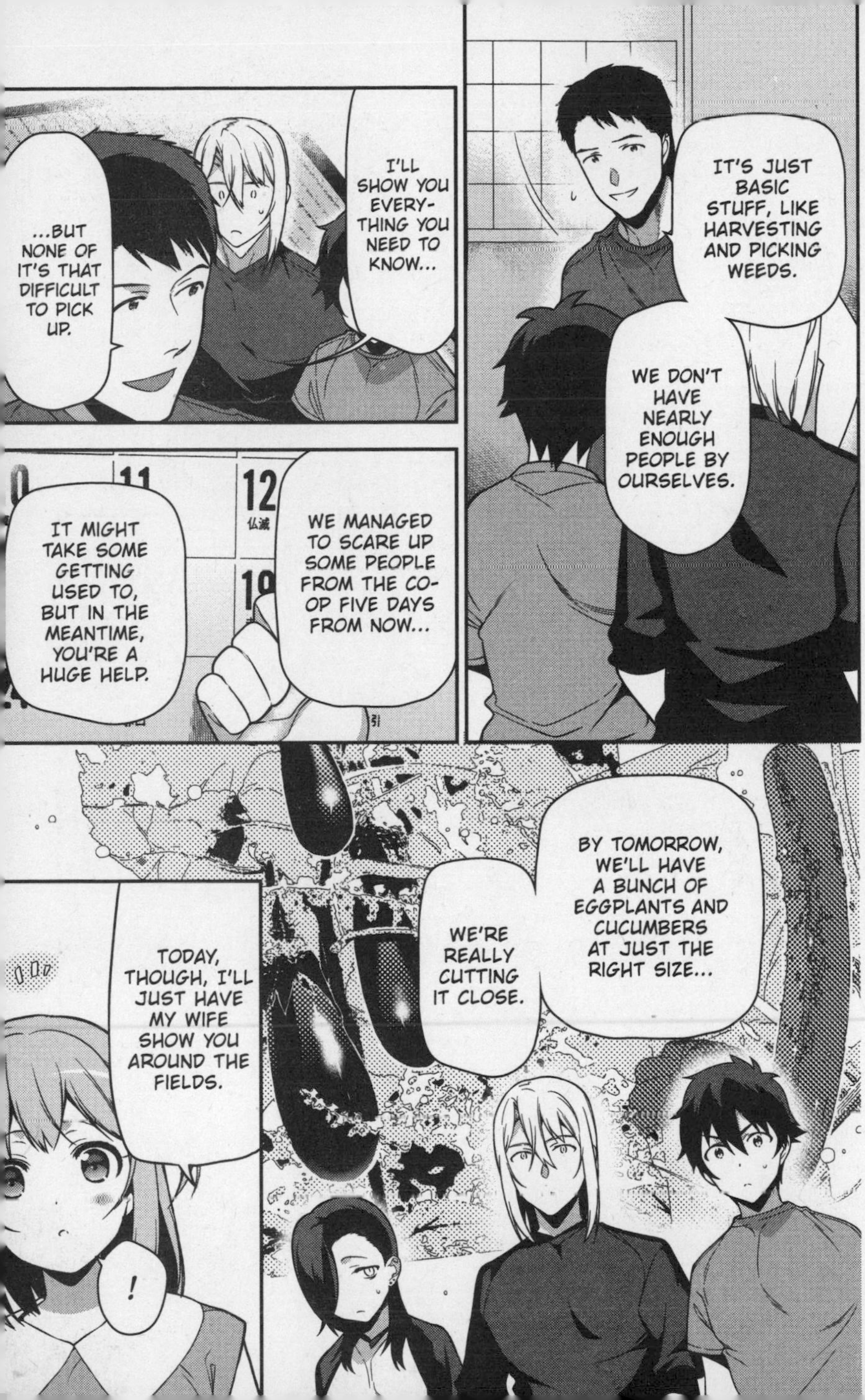
IT'S JUST BASIC STUFF, LIKE HARVESTING AND PICKING WEEDS.
WE DON'T HAVE NEARLY ENOUGH PEOPLE BY OURSELVES.
I'LL SHOW YOU EVERY-THING YOU NEED TO KNOW...
...BUT NONE OF IT'S THAT DIFFICULT TO PICK UP.
WE MANAGED TO SCARE UP SOME PEOPLE FROM THE CO-OP FIVE DAYS FROM NOW...
IT MIGHT TAKE SOME GETTING USED TO, BUT IN THE MEANTIME, YOU'RE A HUGE HELP.
BY TOMORROW, WE'LL HAVE A BUNCH OF EGGPLANTS AND CUCUMBERS AT JUST THE RIGHT SIZE...
WE'RE REALLY CUTTING IT CLOSE.
TODAY, THOUGH, I'LL JUST HAVE MY WIFE SHOW YOU AROUND THE FIELDS.
!

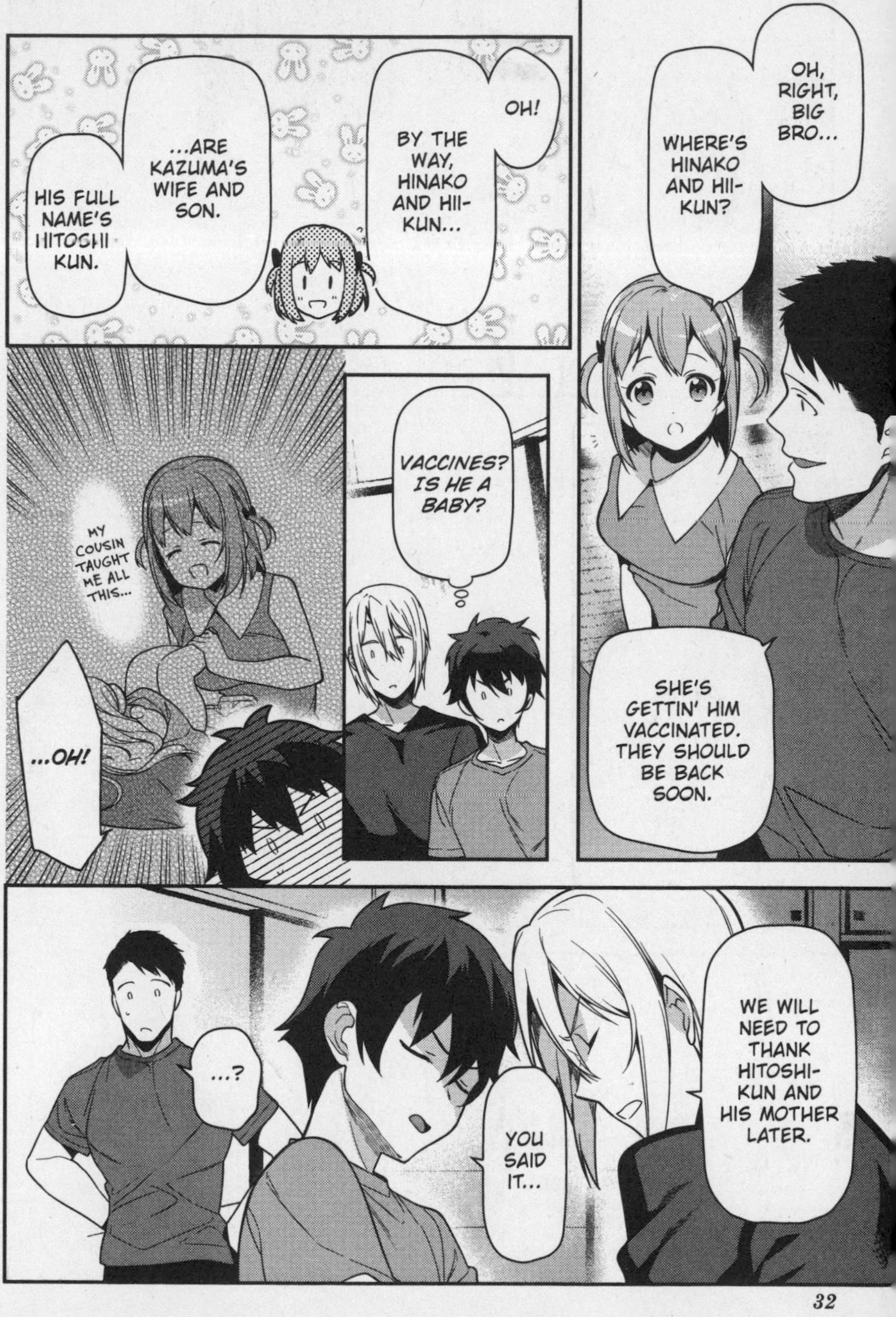
OH, RIGHT, BIG BRO...
WHERE'S HINAKO AND HII-KUN?
SHE'S GETTIN' HIM VACCINATED. THEY SHOULD BE BACK SOON.
OH!
BY THE WAY, HINAKO AND HII-KUN...
...ARE KAZUMA'S WIFE AND SON.
HIS FULL NAME'S HITOSHI KUN.
VACCINES? IS HE A BABY?
MY COUSIN TAUGHT ME ALL THIS...
...OH!
WE WILL NEED TO THANK HITOSHI-KUN AND HIS MOTHER LATER.
YOU SAID IT...
...?

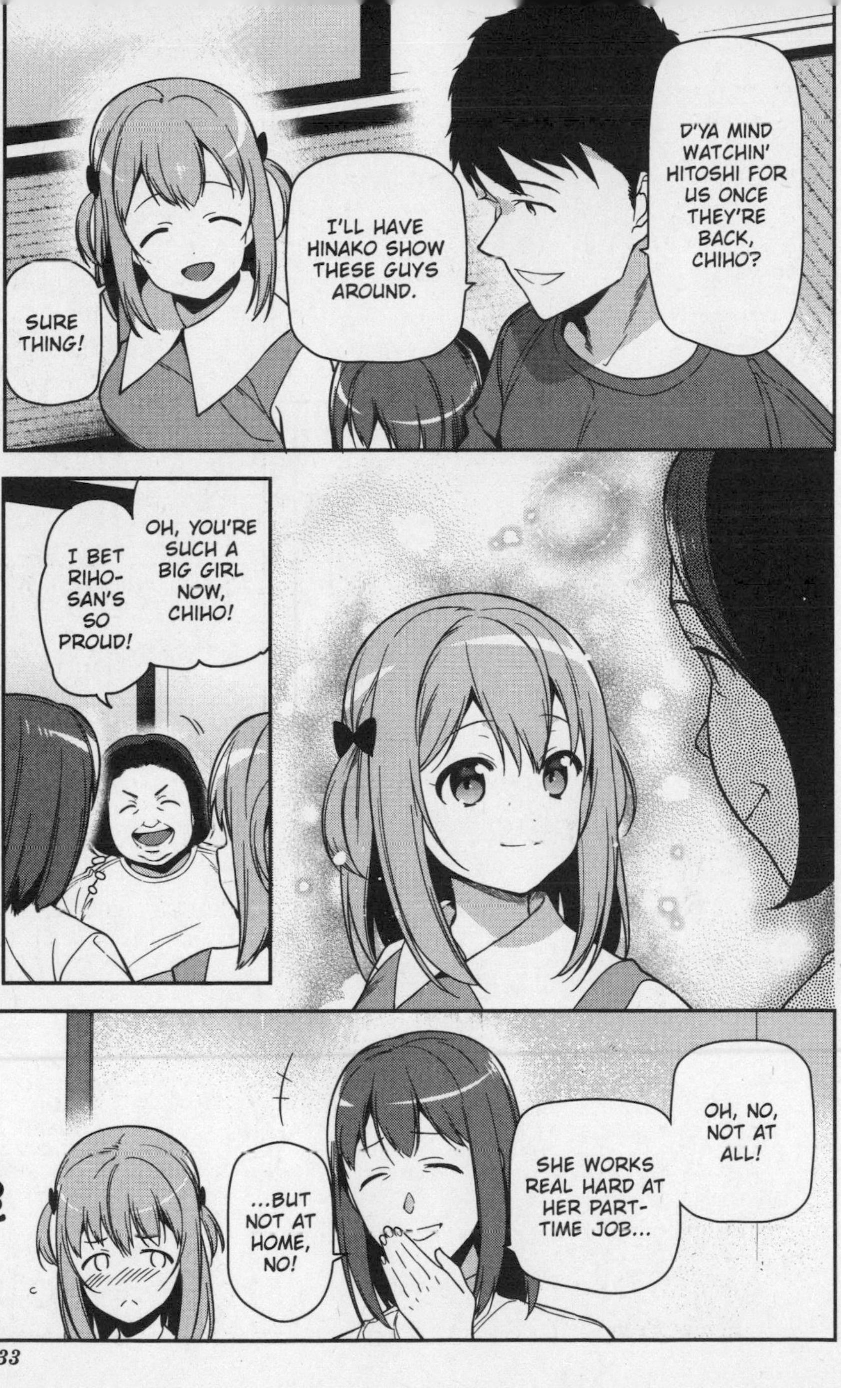

D'YA MIND WATCHIN' HITOSHI FOR US ONCE THEY'RE BACK, CHIHO?
I'LL HAVE HINAKO SHOW THESE GUYS AROUND.
SURE THING!
OH, YOU'RE SUCH A BIG GIRL NOW, CHIHO!
I BET RIHO-SAN'S SO PROUD!
OH, NO, NOT AT ALL!
SHE WORKS REAL HARD AT HER PART-TIME JOB...
...BUT NOT AT HOME, NO!

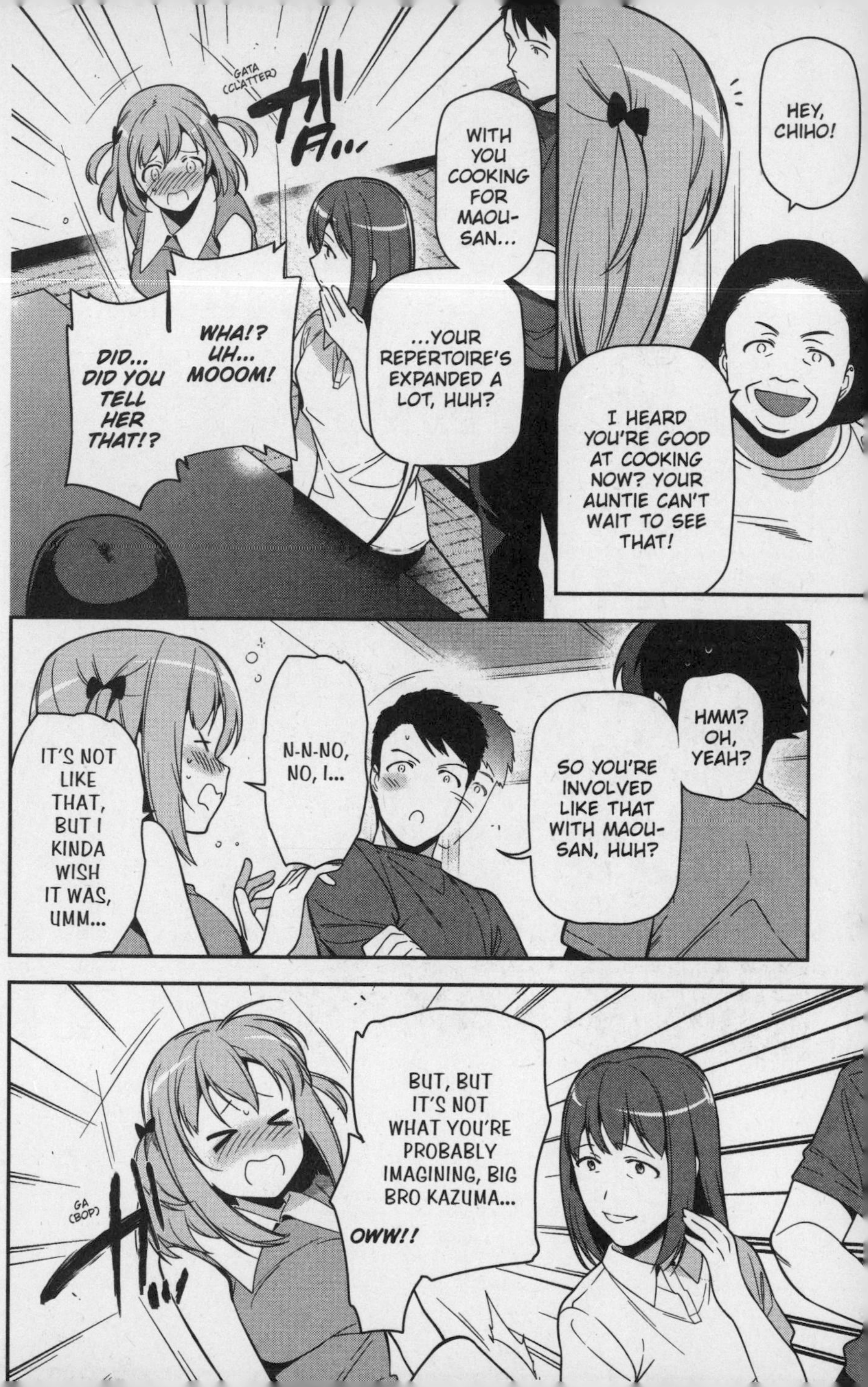
HEY, CHIHO!
I HEARD YOU'RE GOOD AT COOKING NOW? YOUR AUNTIE CAN'T WAIT TO SEE THAT!
WITH YOU COOKING FOR MAOU-SAN...
...YOUR REPERTOIRE'S EXPANDED A LOT, HUH?
GATA (CLATTER)
WHA!? UH... MOOOM!
DID... DID YOU TELL HER THAT!?
HMM? OH, YEAH?
SO YOU'RE INVOLVED LIKE THAT WITH MAOU-SAN, HUH?
N-N-NO, NO, I...
IT'S NOT LIKE THAT, BUT I KINDA WISH IT WAS, UMM...
BUT, BUT IT'S NOT WHAT YOU'RE PROBABLY IMAGINING, BIG BRO KAZUMA...
GA (BOP)
OWW!!

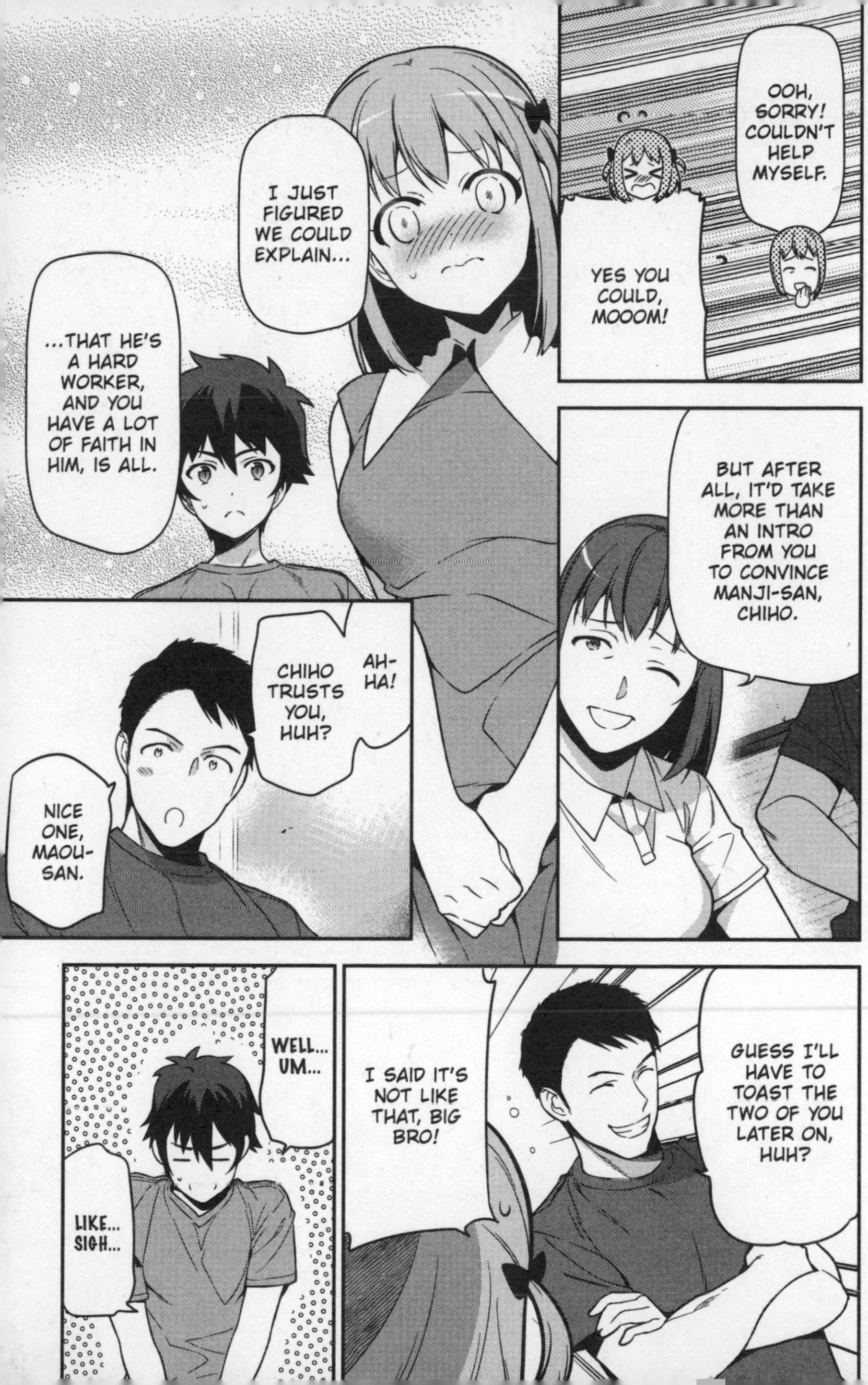
OOH, SORRY! COULDN'T HELP MYSELF.
YES YOU COULD, MOOOM!
I JUST FIGURED WE COULD EXPLAIN...
...THAT HE'S A HARD WORKER, AND YOU HAVE A LOT OF FAITH IN HIM, IS ALL.
BUT AFTER ALL, IT'D TAKE MORE THAN AN INTRO FROM YOU TO CONVINCE MANJI-SAN, CHIHO.
AH-HA! CHIHO TRUSTS YOU, HUH?
NICE ONE, MAOU-SAN.
GUESS I'LL HAVE TO TOAST THE TWO OF YOU LATER ON, HUH?
I SAID IT'S NOT LIKE THAT, BIG BRO!
WELL... UM...
LIKE... SIGH...

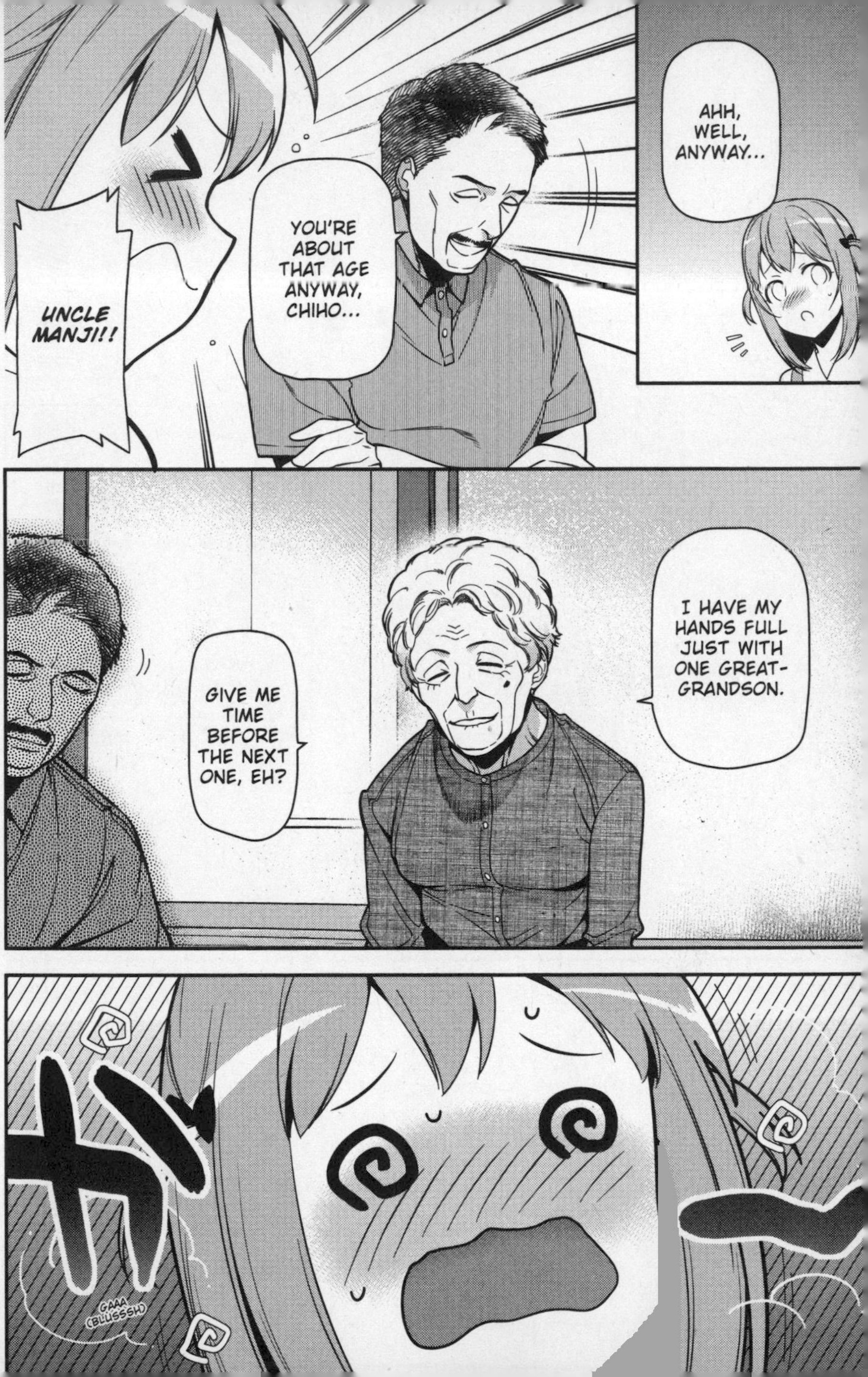
AHH, WELL, ANYWAY...
YOU'RE ABOUT THAT AGE ANYWAY, CHIHO...
UNCLE MANJI!!
I HAVE MY HANDS FULL JUST WITH ONE GREAT-GRANDSON.
GIVE ME TIME BEFORE THE NEXT ONE, EH?
GAAA (BLUSSSH)

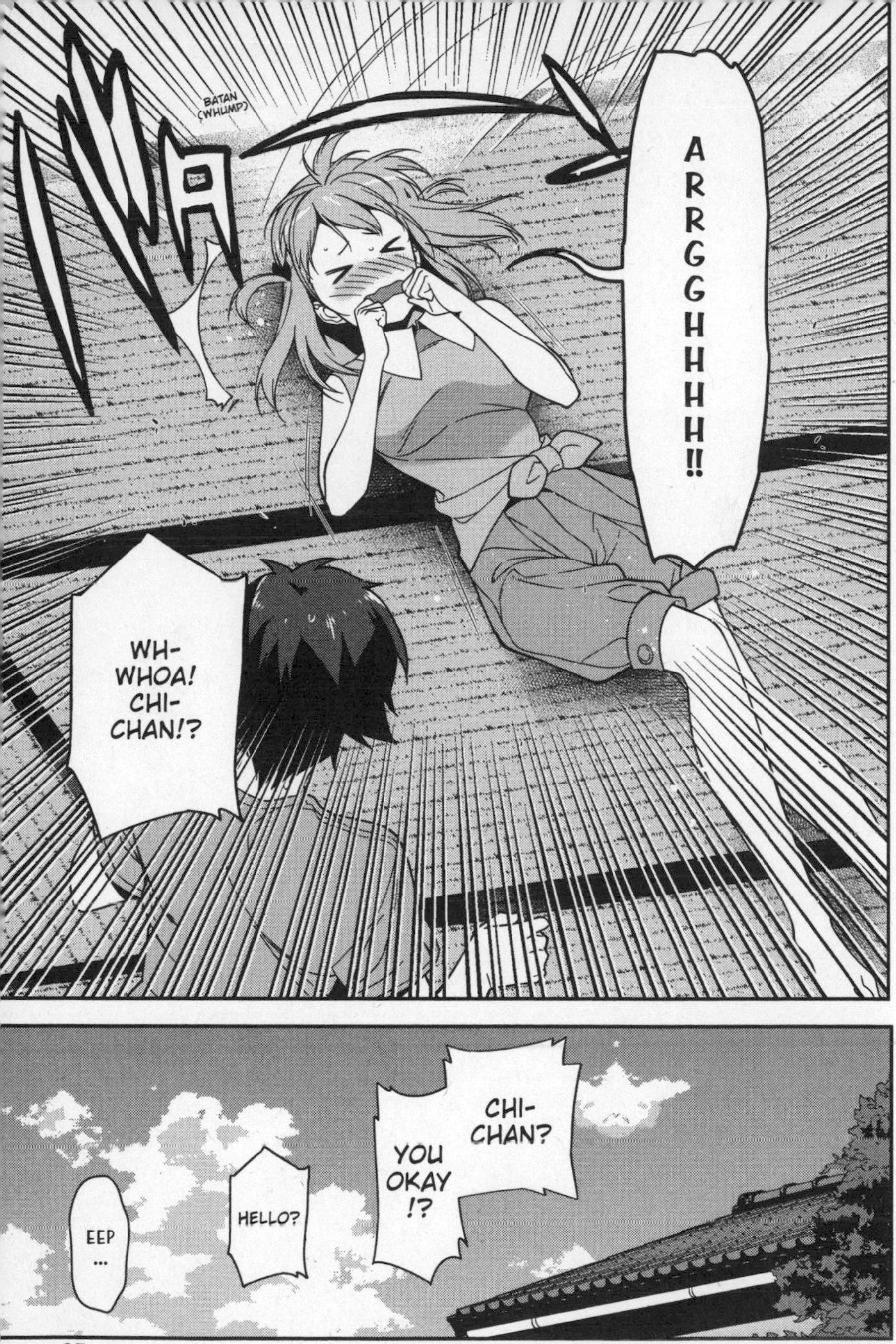
ARRGGHHHHH!!
BATAN (WHUMP)
WH-WHOA! CHI-CHAN!?
CHI-CHAN?
YOU OKAY!?
HELLO?
EEP...

THE DEVIL IS A PART-TIMER!

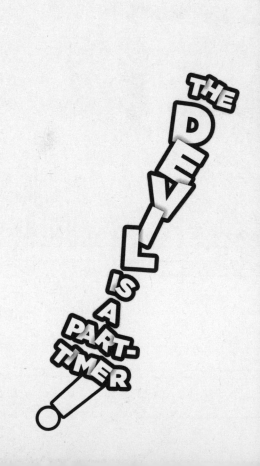

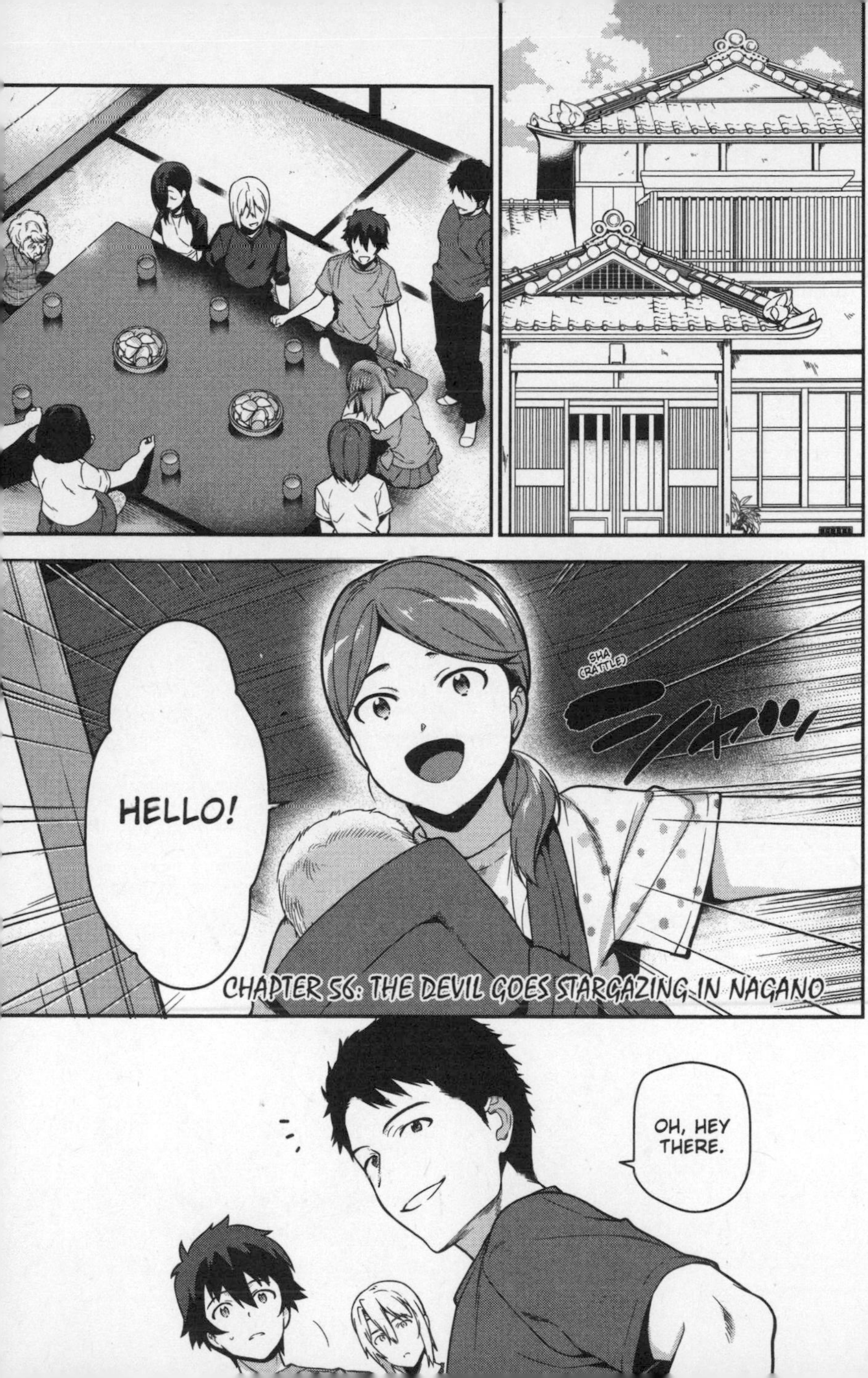
SHA (RATTLE)
HELLO!
CHAPTER 56: THE DEVIL GOES STARGAZING IN NAGANO
OH, HEY THERE.

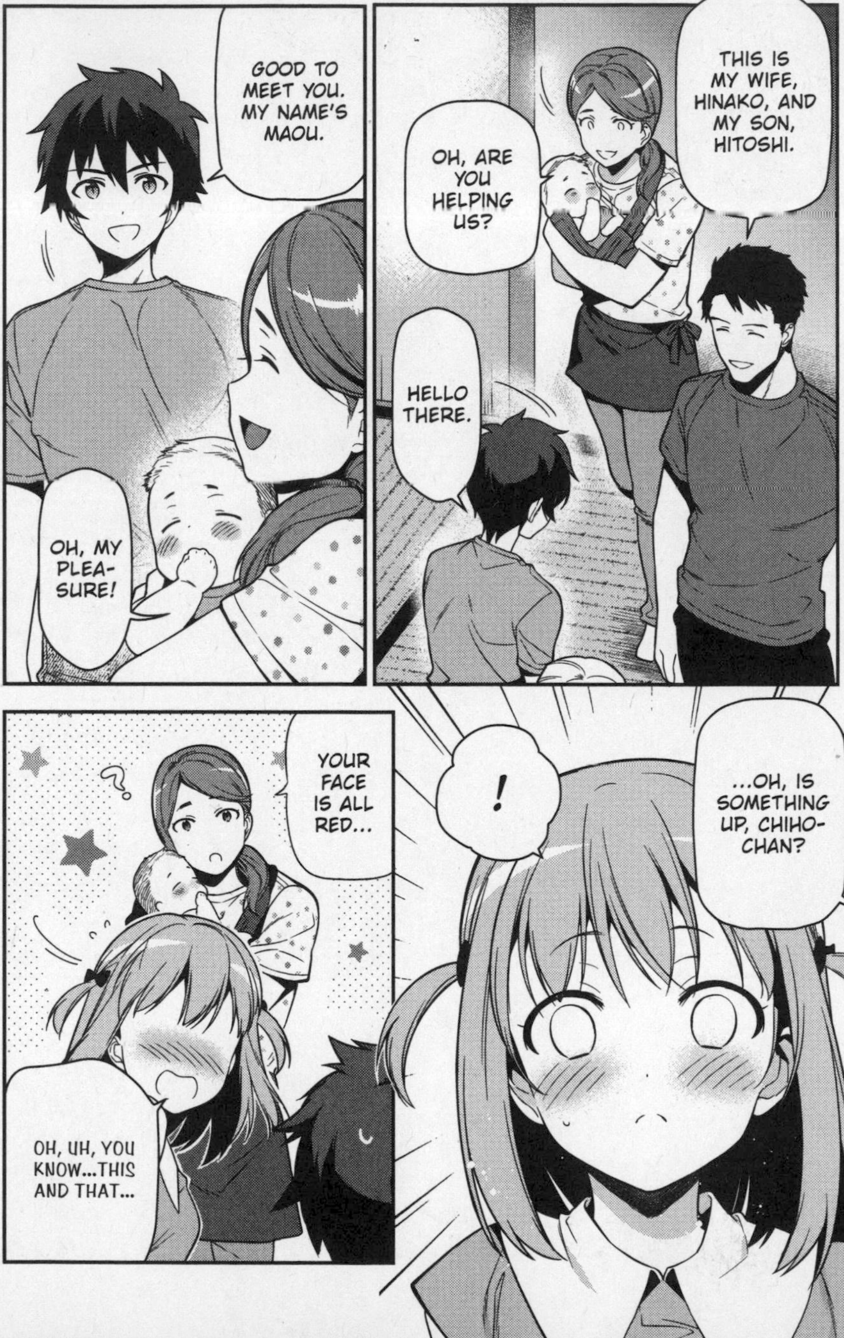
THIS IS MY WIFE, HINAKO, AND MY SON, HITOSHI.
OH, ARE YOU HELPING US?
HELLO THERE.
GOOD TO MEET YOU. MY NAME'S MAOU.
OH, MY PLEA-SURE!
...OH, IS SOMETHING UP, CHIHO-CHAN?
!
YOUR FACE IS ALL RED...
OH, UH, YOU KNOW...THIS AND THAT...

SO NOW THAT HINAKO'S BACK HOME...
...HOW 'BOUT WE GO CHECK OUT THE FIELDS?

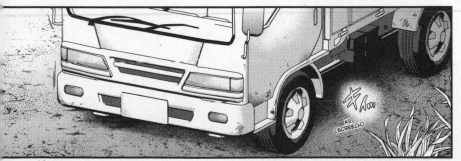

KII (SCREECH)

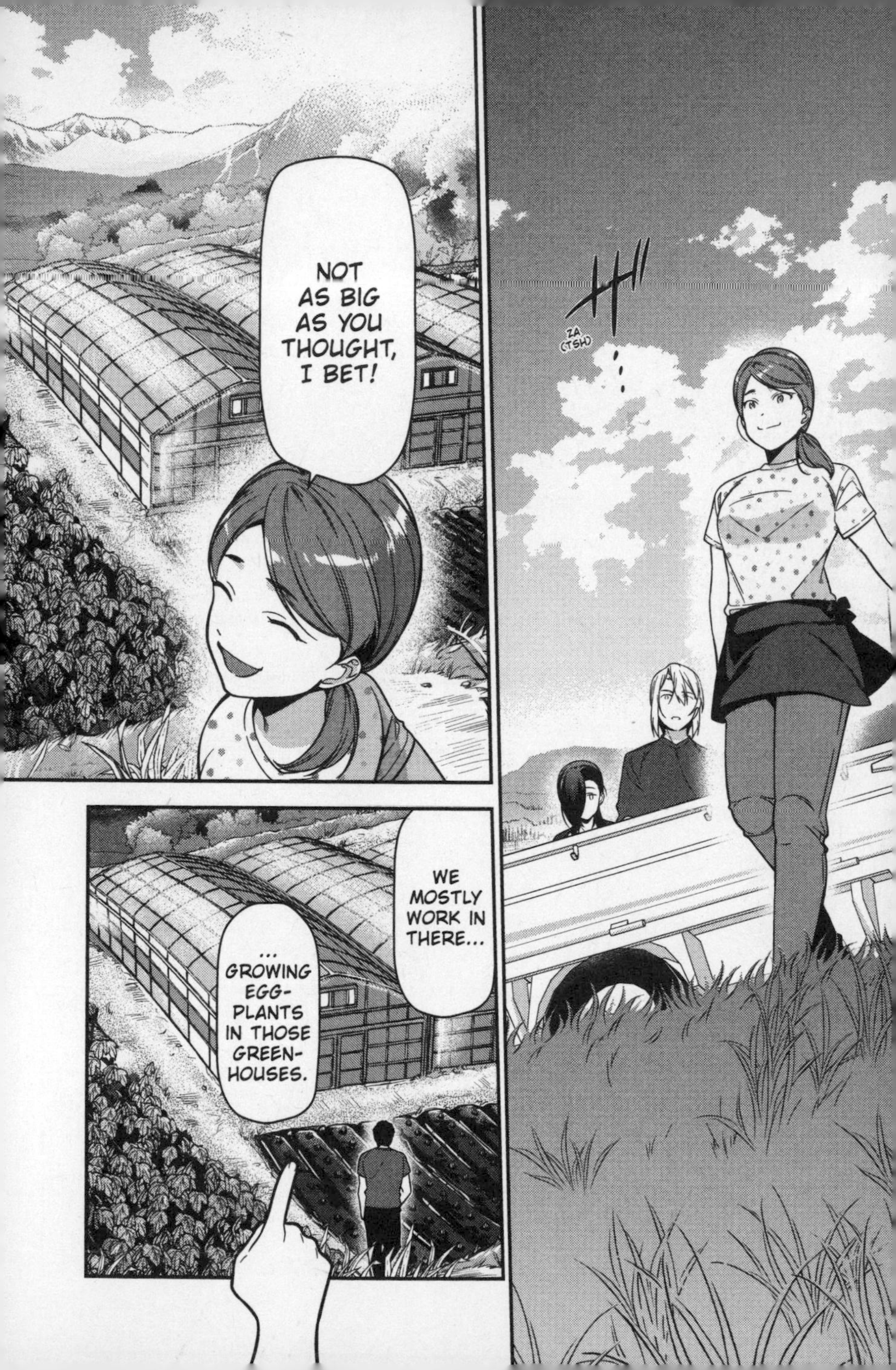
ZA (TSH)
NOT AS BIG AS YOU THOUGHT, I BET!
WE MOSTLY WORK IN THERE...
...GROWING EGG-PLANTS IN THOSE GREEN-HOUSES.

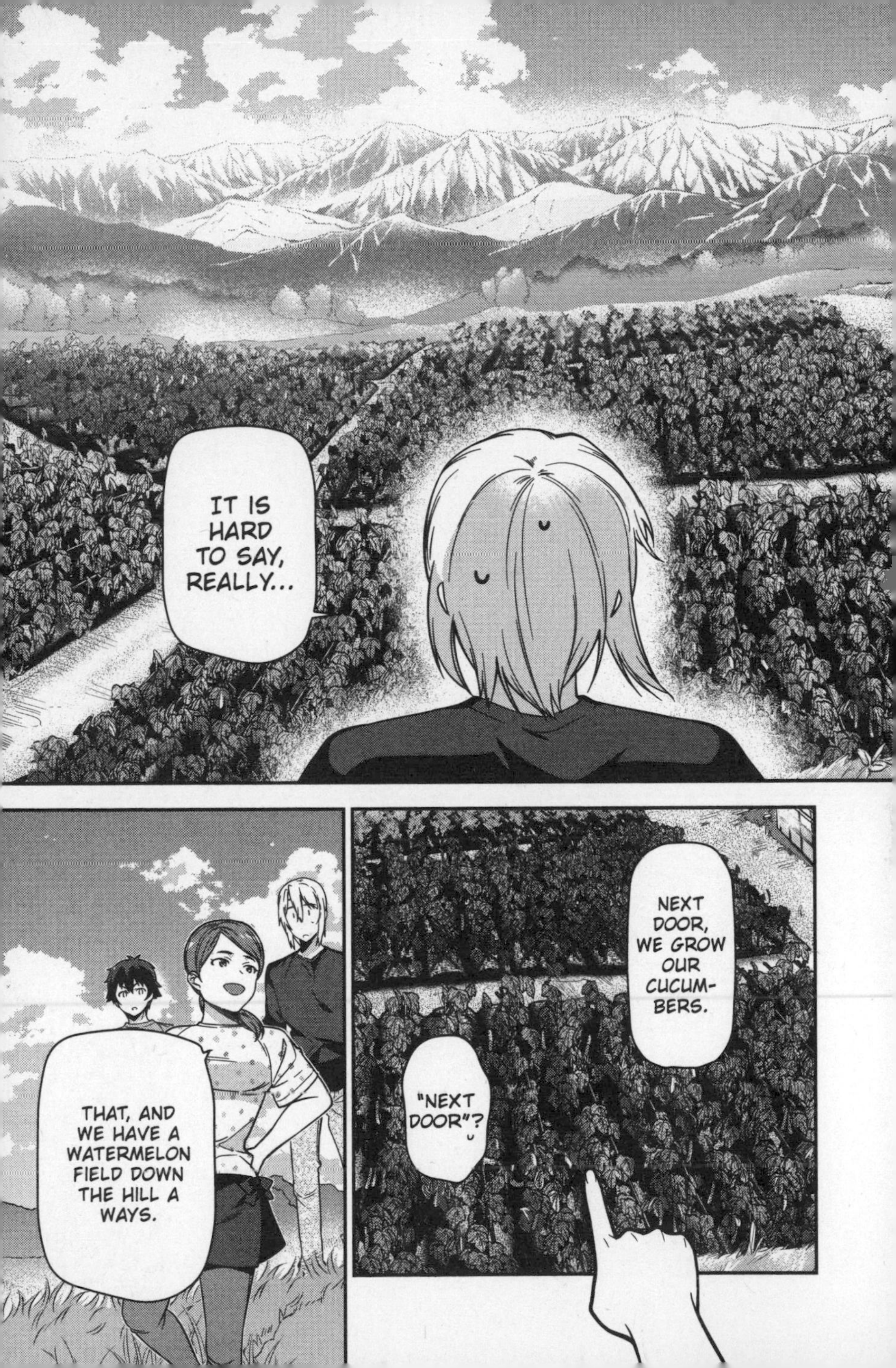
IT IS HARD TO SAY, REALLY...
NEXT DOOR, WE GROW OUR CUCUM-BERS.
"NEXT DOOR"?
THAT, AND WE HAVE A WATERMELON FIELD DOWN THE HILL A WAYS.

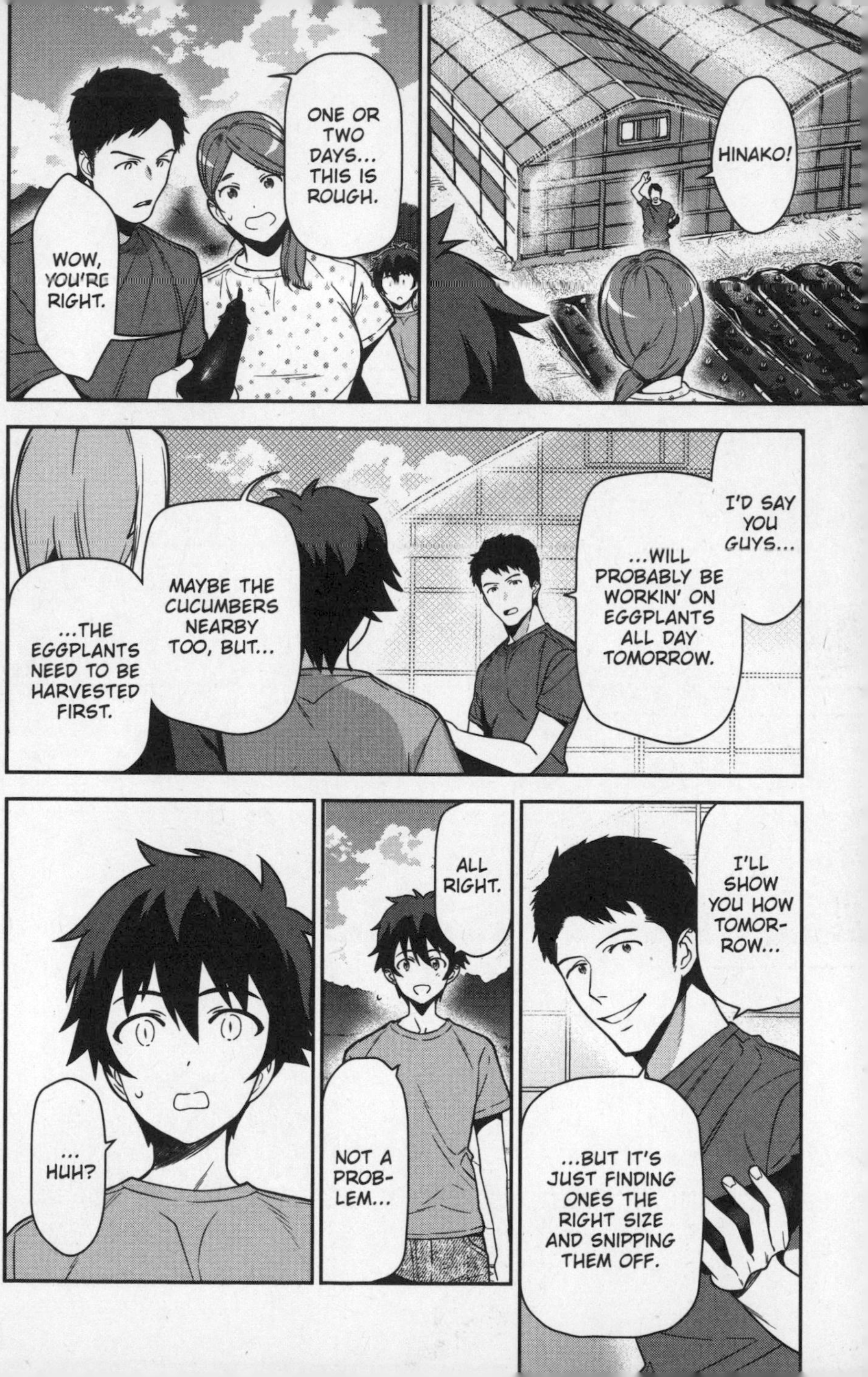
HINAKO!
ONE OR TWO DAYS... THIS IS ROUGH.
WOW, YOU'RE RIGHT.
I'D SAY YOU GUYS...
...WILL PROBABLY BE WORKIN' ON EGGPLANTS ALL DAY TOMORROW.
MAYBE THE CUCUMBERS NEARBY TOO, BUT...
...THE EGGPLANTS NEED TO BE HARVESTED FIRST.
I'LL SHOW YOU HOW TOMOR-ROW...
...BUT IT'S JUST FINDING ONES THE RIGHT SIZE AND SNIPPING THEM OFF.
ALL RIGHT.
NOT A PROB-LEM...
... HUH?

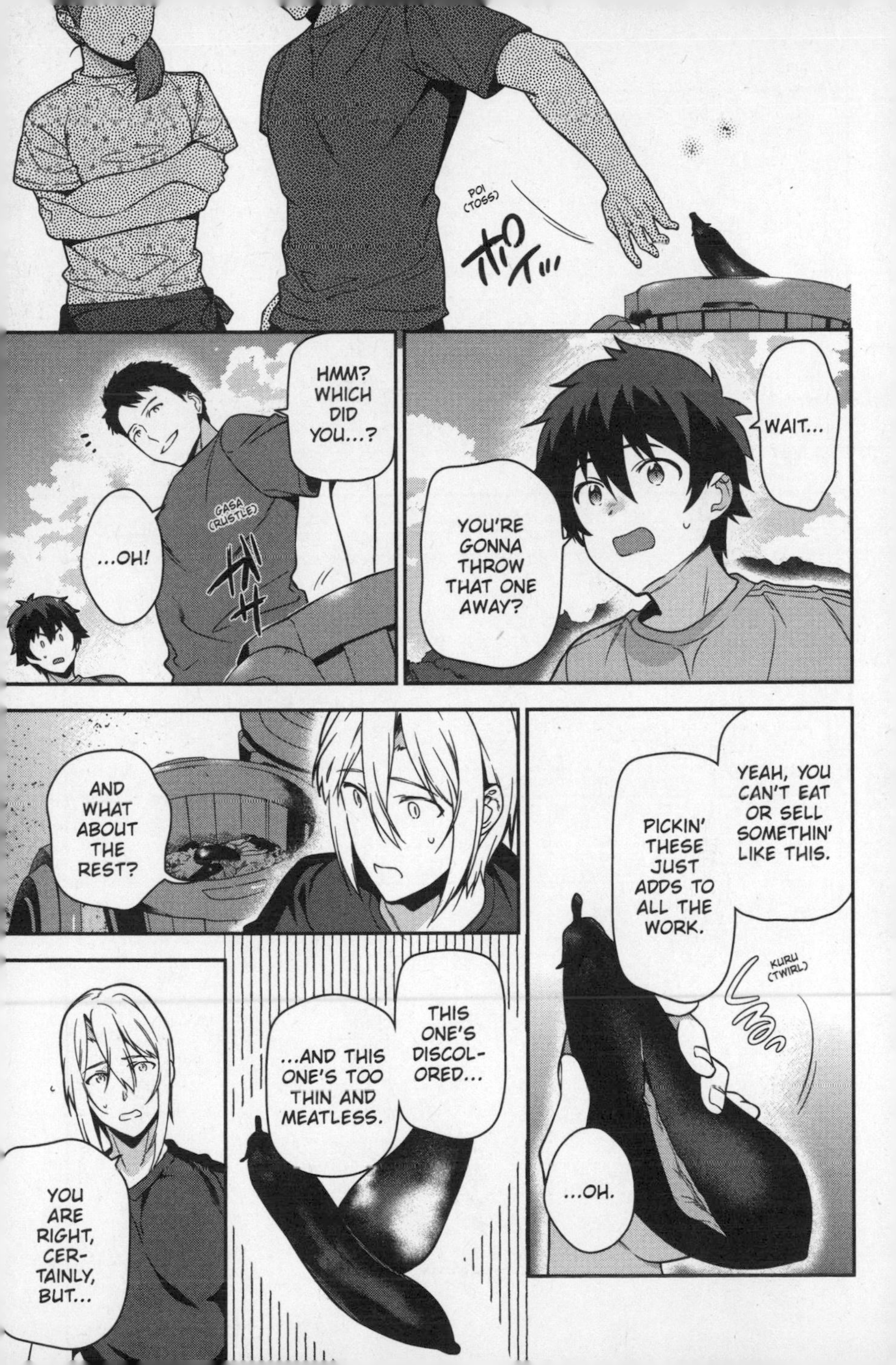

POI (TOSS)
WAIT...
YOU'RE GONNA THROW THAT ONE AWAY?
HMM? WHICH DID YOU...?
GASA (RUSTLE)
...OH!
YEAH, YOU CAN'T EAT OR SELL SOMETHIN' LIKE THIS.
PICKIN' THESE JUST ADDS TO ALL THE WORK.
AND WHAT ABOUT THE REST?
KURU (TWIRL)
...OH.
THIS ONE'S DISCOLORED...
...AND THIS ONE'S TOO THIN AND MEATLESS.
YOU ARE RIGHT, CERTAINLY, BUT...

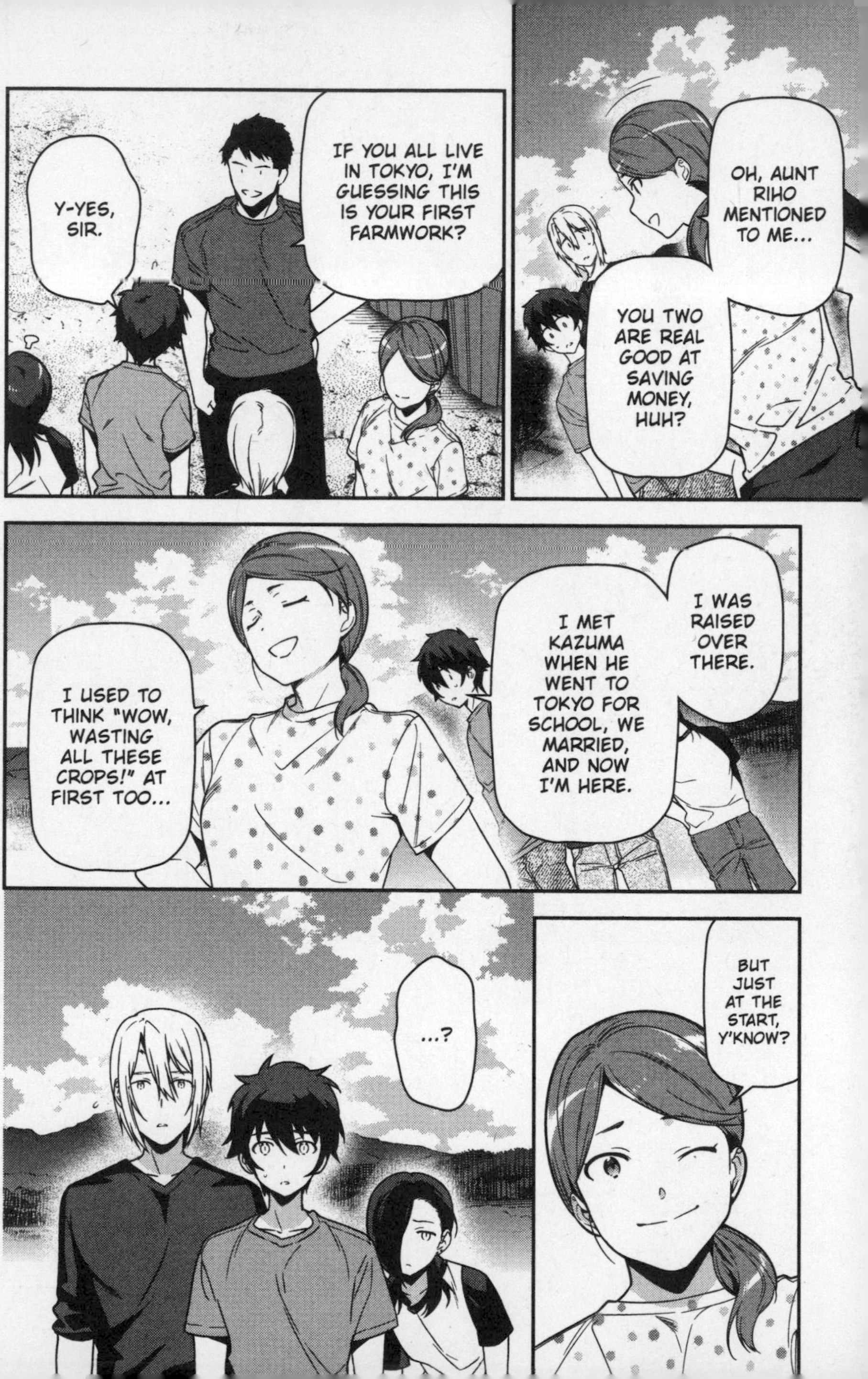
OH, AUNT RIHO MENTIONED TO ME...
YOU TWO ARE REAL GOOD AT SAVING MONEY, HUH?
IF YOU ALL LIVE IN TOKYO, I'M GUESSING THIS IS YOUR FIRST FARMWORK?
Y-YES, SIR.
I WAS RAISED OVER THERE.
I MET KAZUMA WHEN HE WENT TO TOKYO FOR SCHOOL, WE MARRIED, AND NOW I'M HERE.
I USED TO THINK "WOW, WASTING ALL THESE CROPS!" AT FIRST TOO...
BUT JUST AT THE START, Y'KNOW?
...?

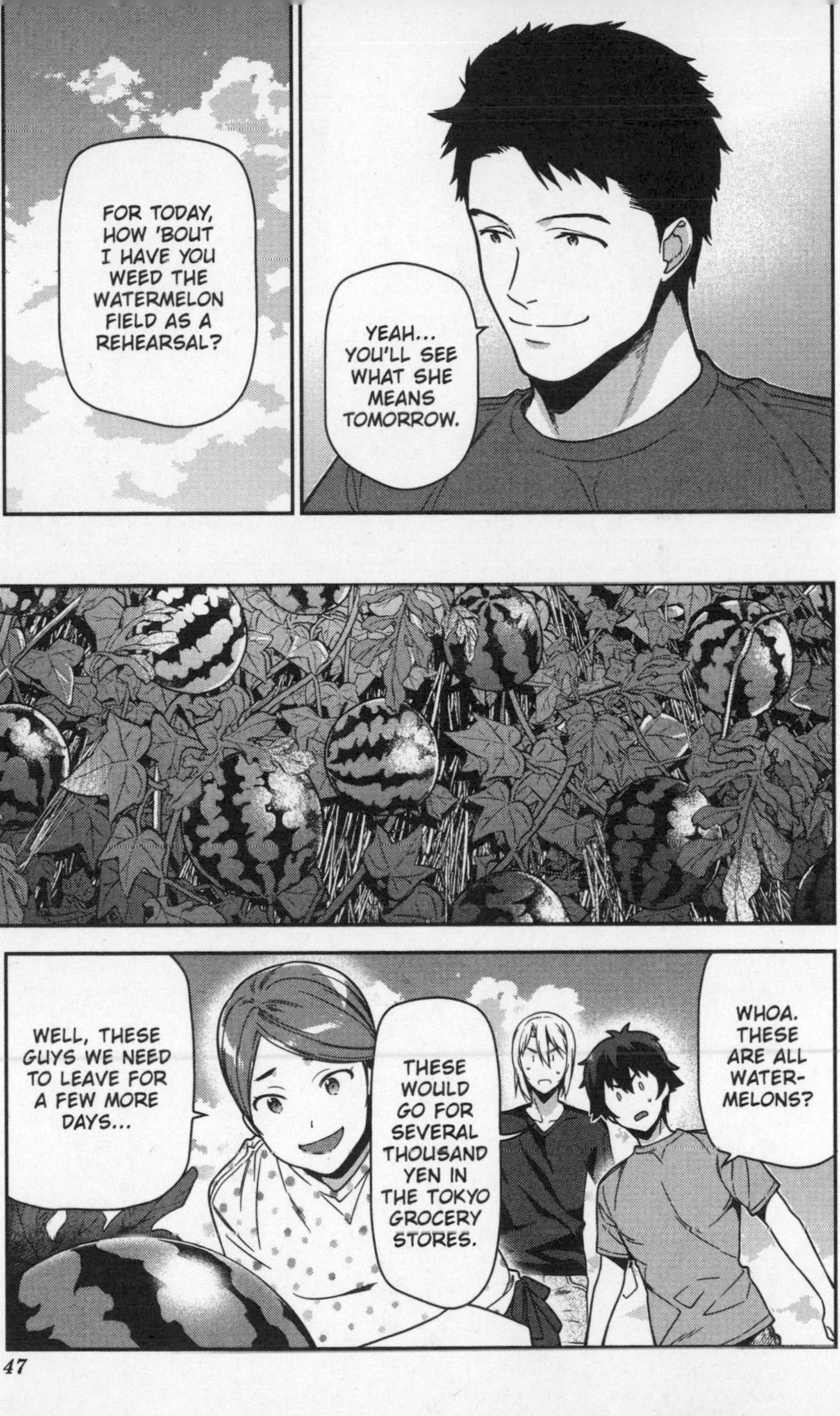
YEAH... YOU'LL SEE WHAT SHE MEANS TOMORROW.
FOR TODAY, HOW 'BOUT I HAVE YOU WEED THE WATERMELON FIELD AS A REHEARSAL?
WHOA. THESE ARE ALL WATER-MELONS?
THESE WOULD GO FOR SEVERAL THOUSAND YEN IN THE TOKYO GROCERY STORES.
WELL, THESE GUYS WE NEED TO LEAVE FOR A FEW MORE DAYS...

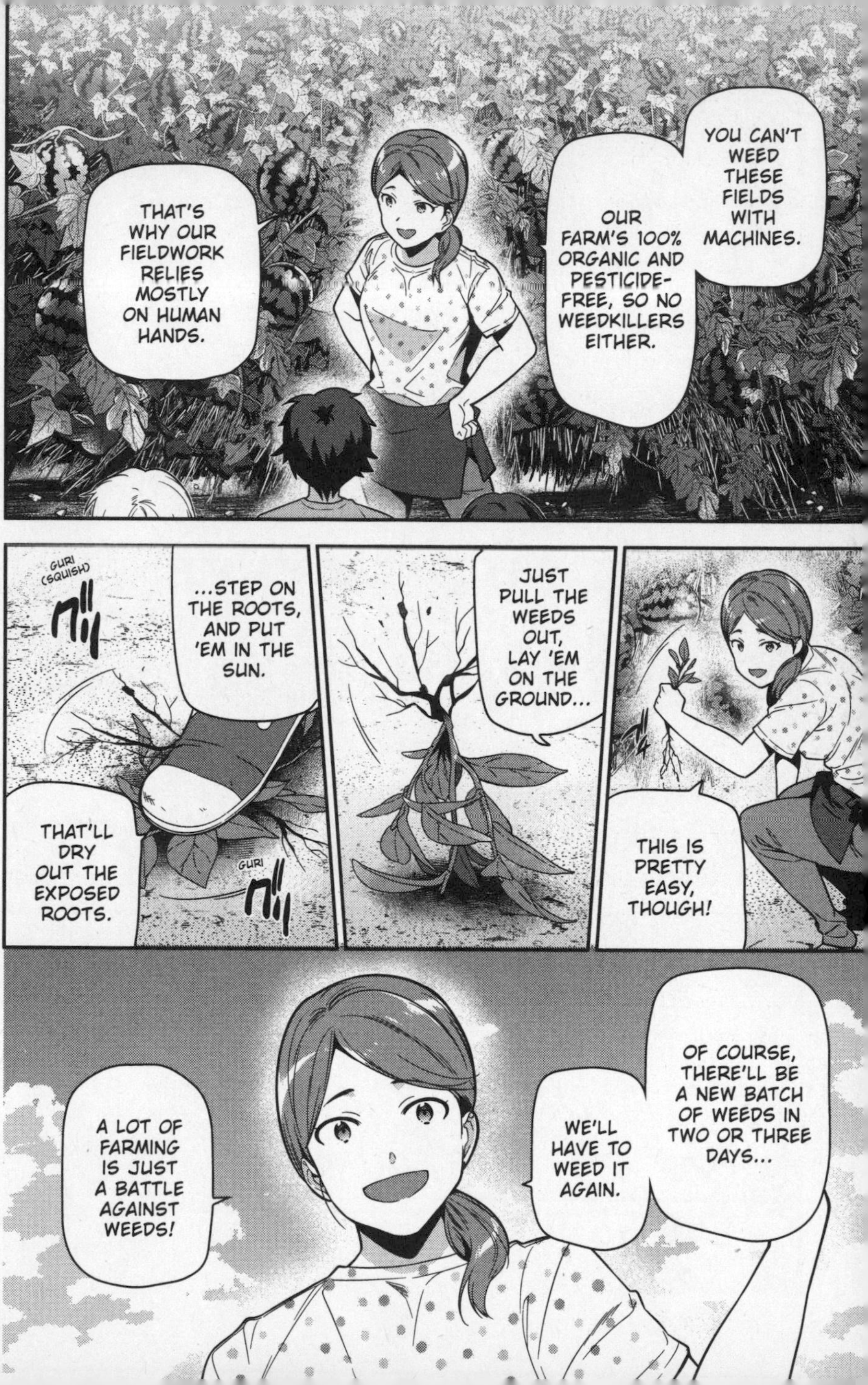
YOU CAN'T WEED THESE FIELDS WITH MACHINES.
OUR FARM'S 100% ORGANIC AND PESTICIDE-FREE, SO NO WEEDKILLERS EITHER.
THAT'S WHY OUR FIELDWORK RELIES MOSTLY ON HUMAN HANDS.
THIS IS PRETTY EASY, THOUGH!
JUST PULL THE WEEDS OUT, LAY 'EM ON THE GROUND...
...STEP ON THE ROOTS, AND PUT 'EM IN THE SUN.
GURI (SQUISH)
THAT'LL DRY OUT THE EXPOSED ROOTS.
GURI
OF COURSE, THERE'LL BE A NEW BATCH OF WEEDS IN TWO OR THREE DAYS...
WE'LL HAVE TO WEED IT AGAIN.
A LOT OF FARMING IS JUST A BATTLE AGAINST WEEDS!

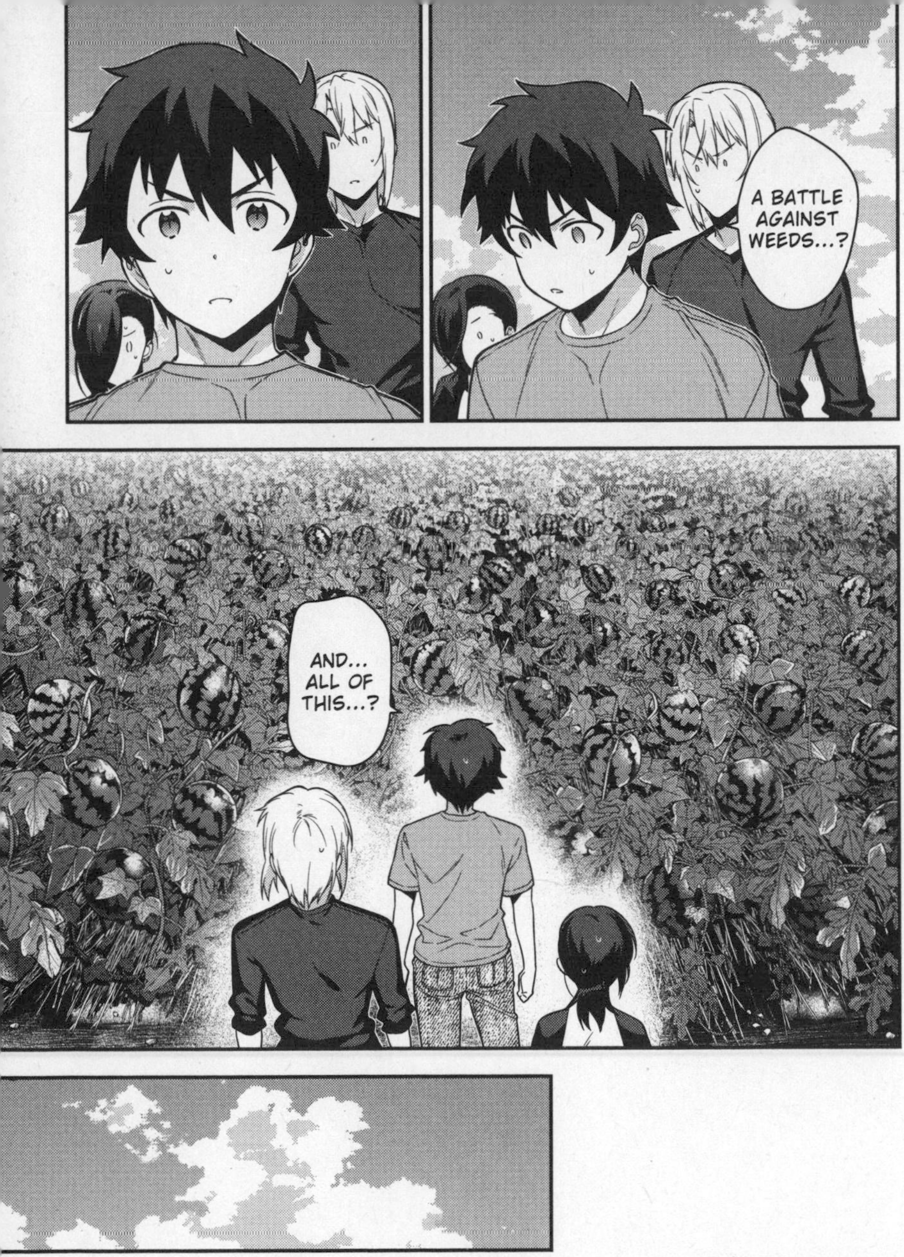
A BATTLE AGAINST WEEDS...?
AND... ALL OF THIS...?

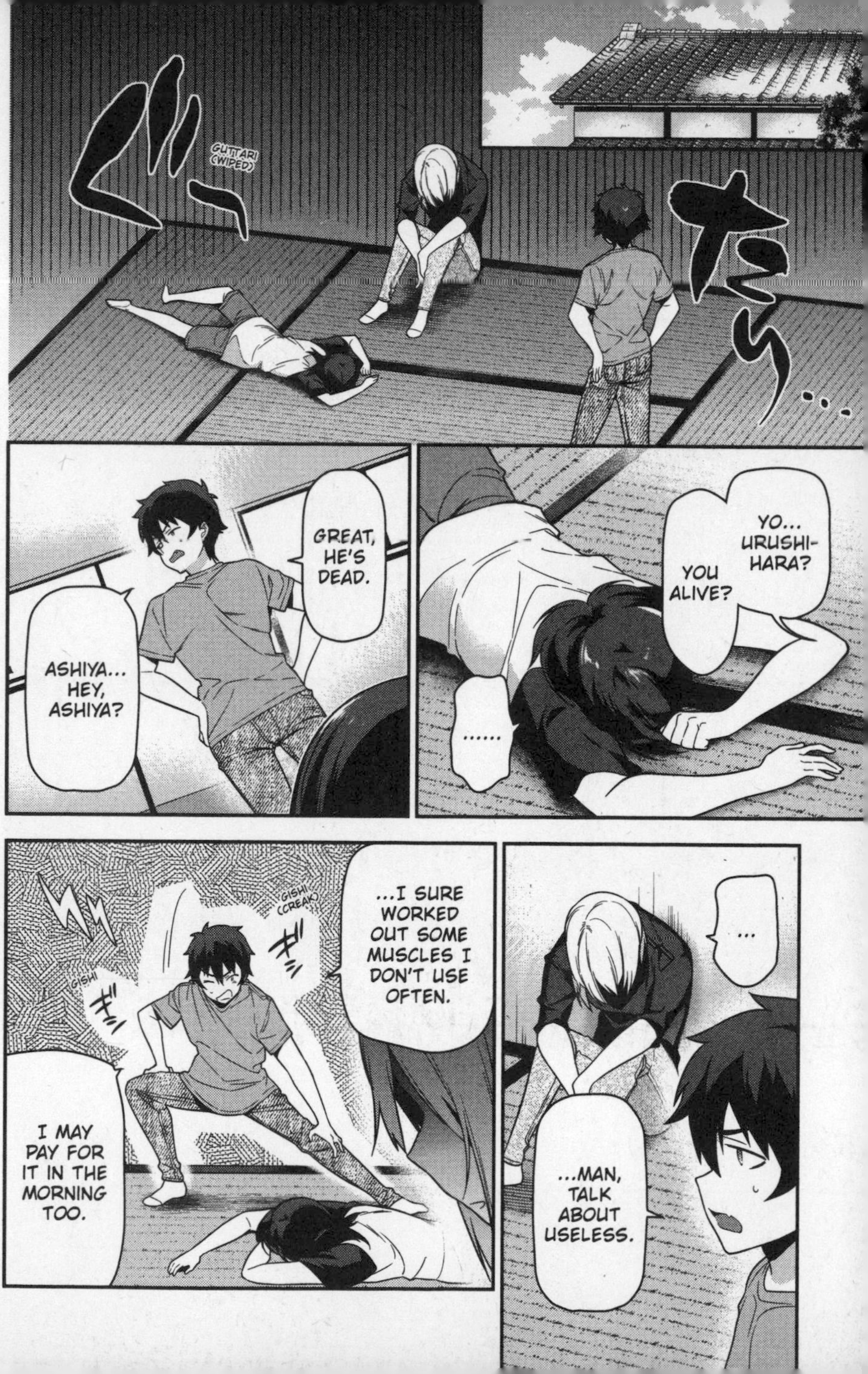
GUTTARI (WIPED)
YO... URUSHI-HARA? YOU ALIVE?
......
GREAT, HE'S DEAD.
ASHIYA... HEY, ASHIYA?
...
...MAN, TALK ABOUT USELESS.
GISHI (CREAK)
...I SURE WORKED OUT SOME MUSCLES I DON'T USE OFTEN.
GISHI
I MAY PAY FOR IT IN THE MORNING TOO.

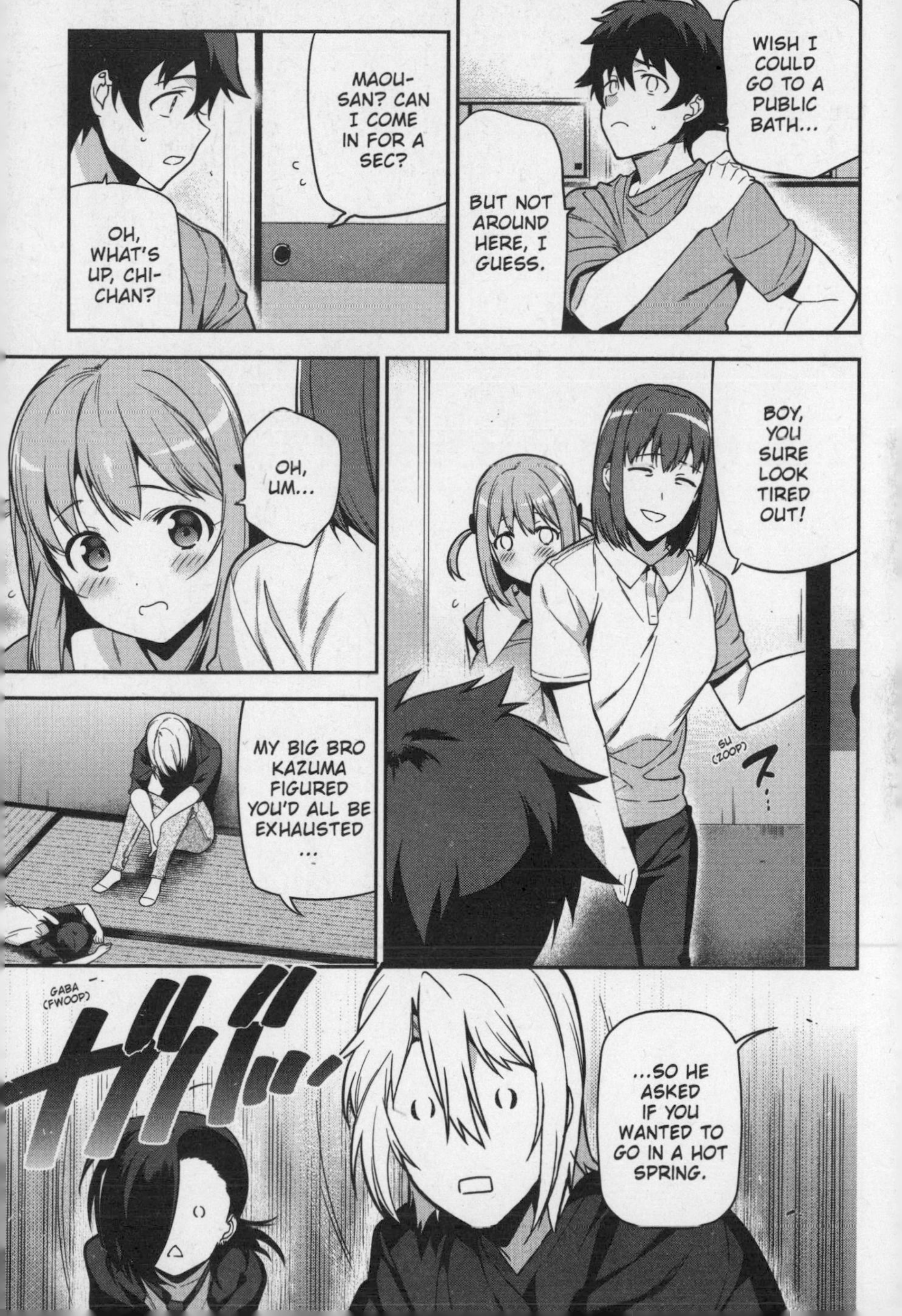
WISH I COULD GO TO A PUBLIC BATH...
BUT NOT AROUND HERE, I GUESS.
MAOU-SAN? CAN I COME IN FOR A SEC?
OH, WHAT'S UP, CHI-CHAN?
BOY, YOU SURE LOOK TIRED OUT!
SU (ZOOP)
OH, UM...
MY BIG BRO KAZUMA FIGURED YOU'D ALL BE EXHAUSTED ...
...SO HE ASKED IF YOU WANTED TO GO IN A HOT SPRING.
GABA (FWOOP)

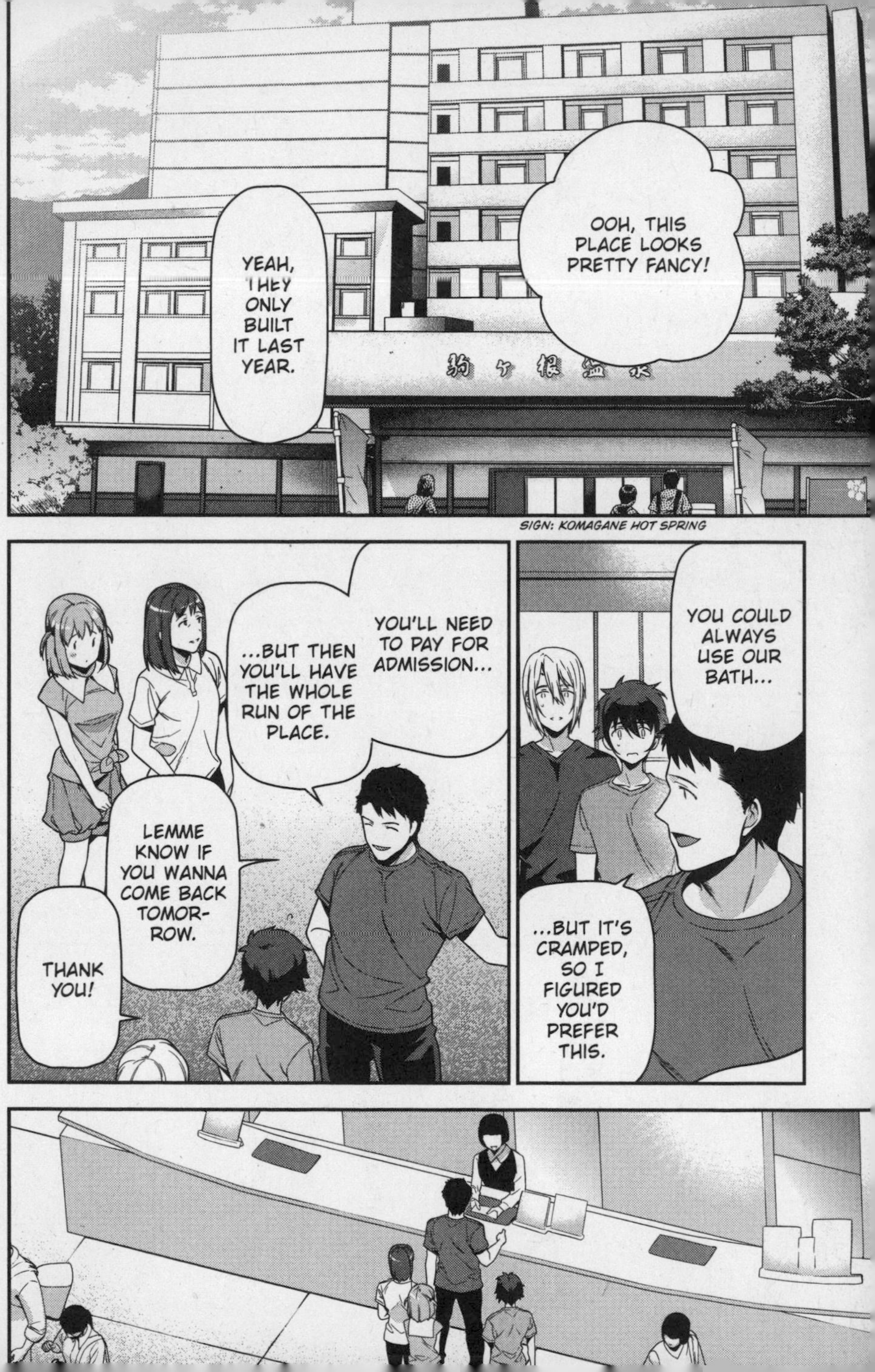
OOH, THIS PLACE LOOKS PRETTY FANCY!
YEAH, THEY ONLY BUILT IT LAST YEAR.
駒ヶ根温泉
SIGN: KOMAGANE HOT SPRING
YOU COULD ALWAYS USE OUR BATH...
...BUT IT'S CRAMPED, SO I FIGURED YOU'D PREFER THIS.
YOU'LL NEED TO PAY FOR ADMISSION...
...BUT THEN YOU'LL HAVE THE WHOLE RUN OF THE PLACE.
LEMME KNOW IF YOU WANNA COME BACK TOMOR-ROW.
THANK YOU!

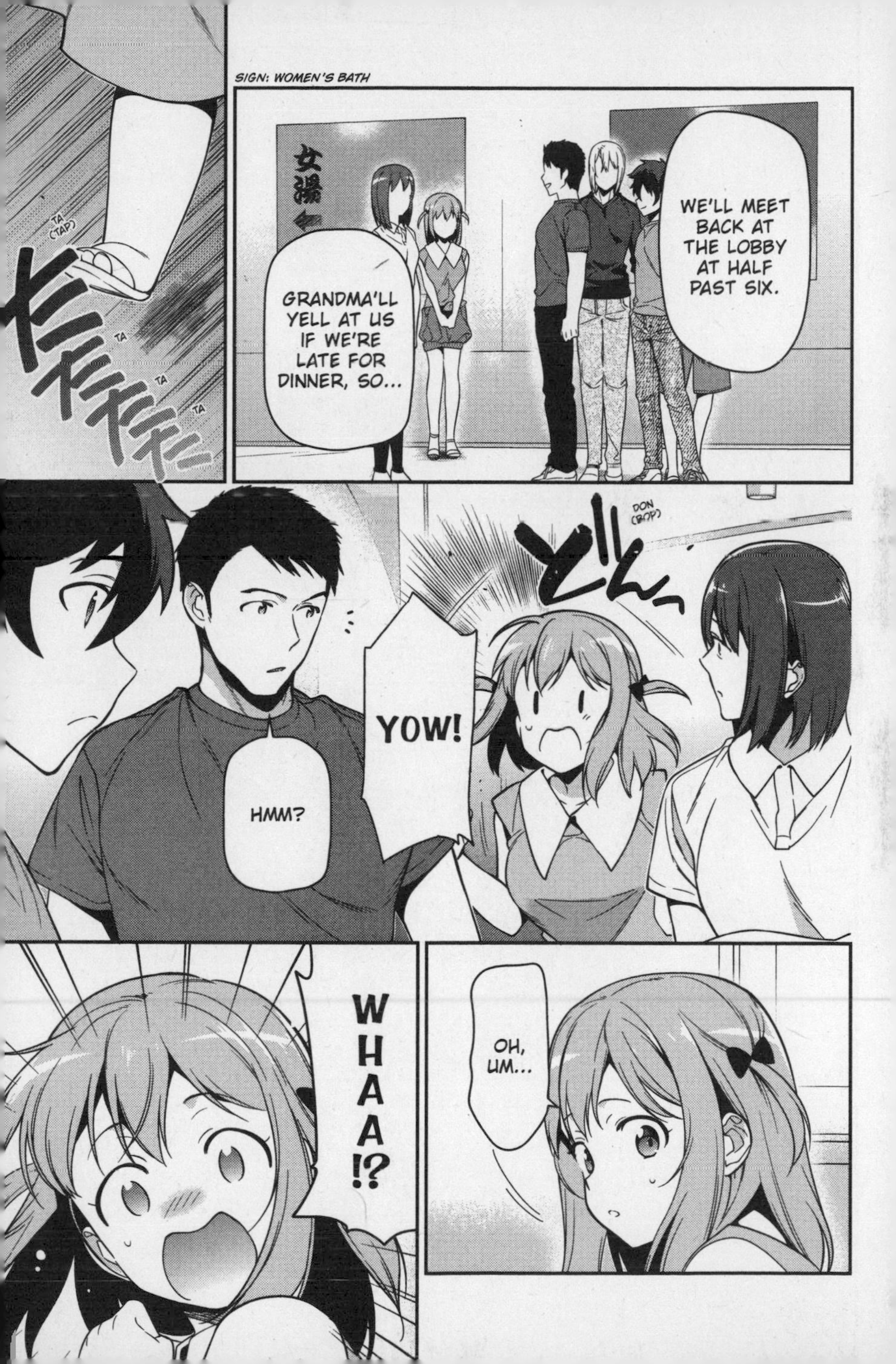
SIGN: WOMEN'S BATH
女湯
WE'LL MEET BACK AT THE LOBBY AT HALF PAST SIX.
GRANDMA'LL YELL AT US IF WE'RE LATE FOR DINNER, SO...
TA (TAP)
TA
TA
TA
DON (BOP)
どん
YOW!
HMM?
OH, UM...
WHAA!?

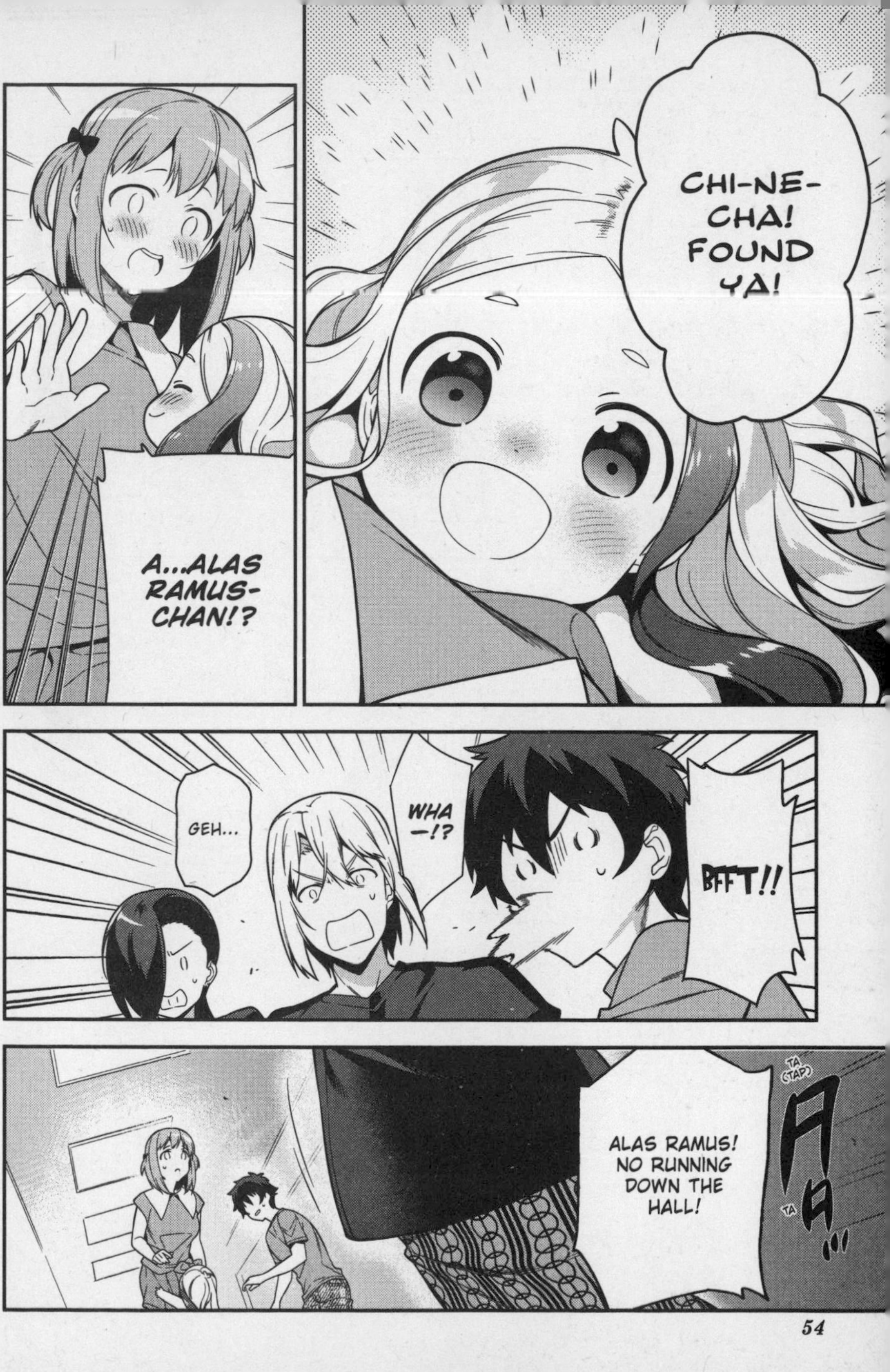
CHI-NE-CHA! FOUND YA!
A...ALAS RAMUS-CHAN!?
BFFT!!
WHA—!?
GEH...
TA (TAP)
ALAS RAMUS! NO RUNNING DOWN THE HALL!
TA

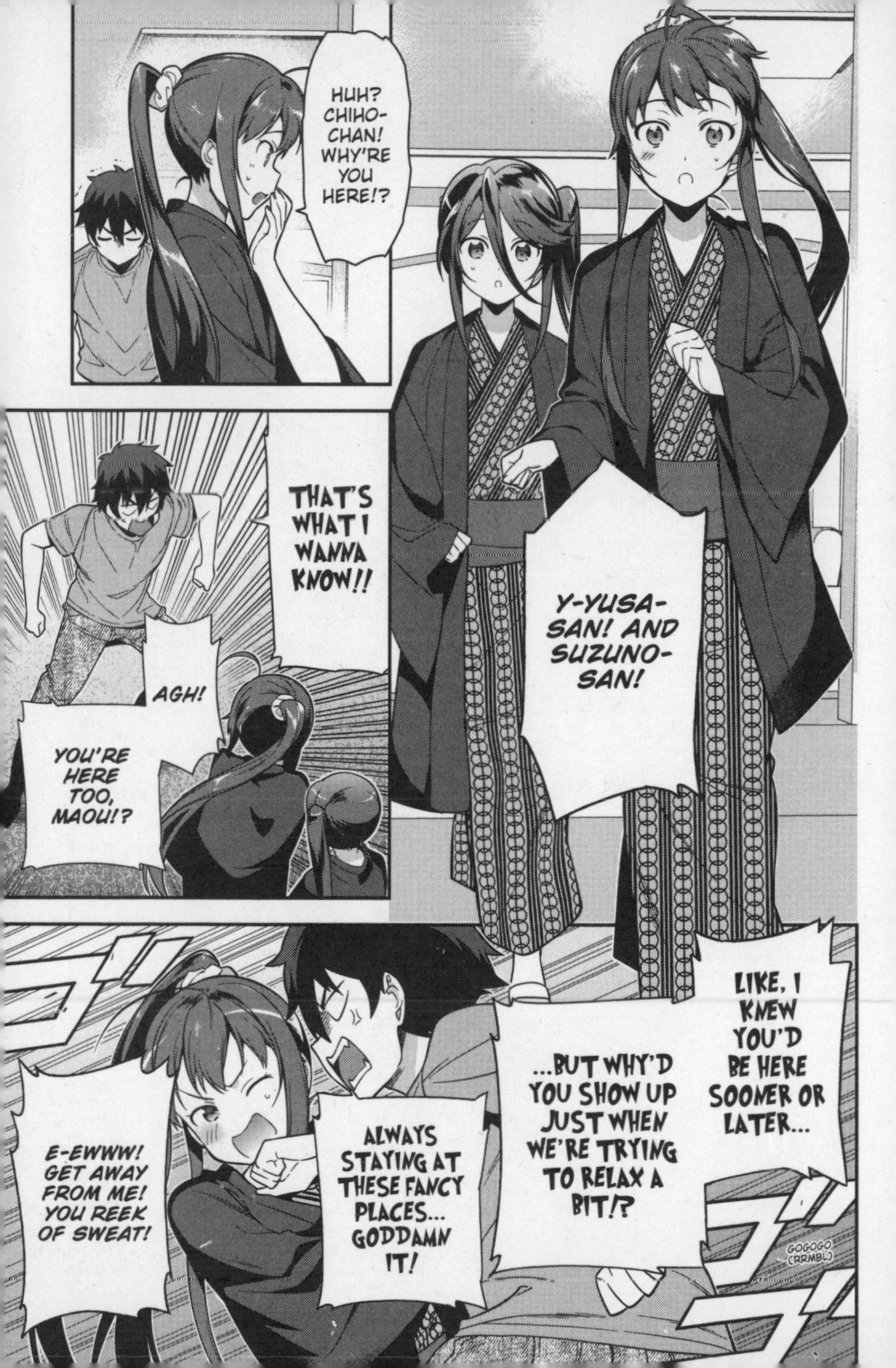
Y-YUSA-SAN! AND SUZUNO-SAN!
HUH? CHIHO-CHAN! WHY'RE YOU HERE!?
THAT'S WHAT I WANNA KNOW!!
AGH!
YOU'RE HERE TOO, MAOU!?
LIKE, I KNEW YOU'D BE HERE SOONER OR LATER...
...BUT WHY'D YOU SHOW UP JUST WHEN WE'RE TRYING TO RELAX A BIT!?
GOGOGO (RRMBL)
ALWAYS STAYING AT THESE FANCY PLACES... GODDAMN IT!
E-EWWW! GET AWAY FROM ME! YOU REEK OF SWEAT!

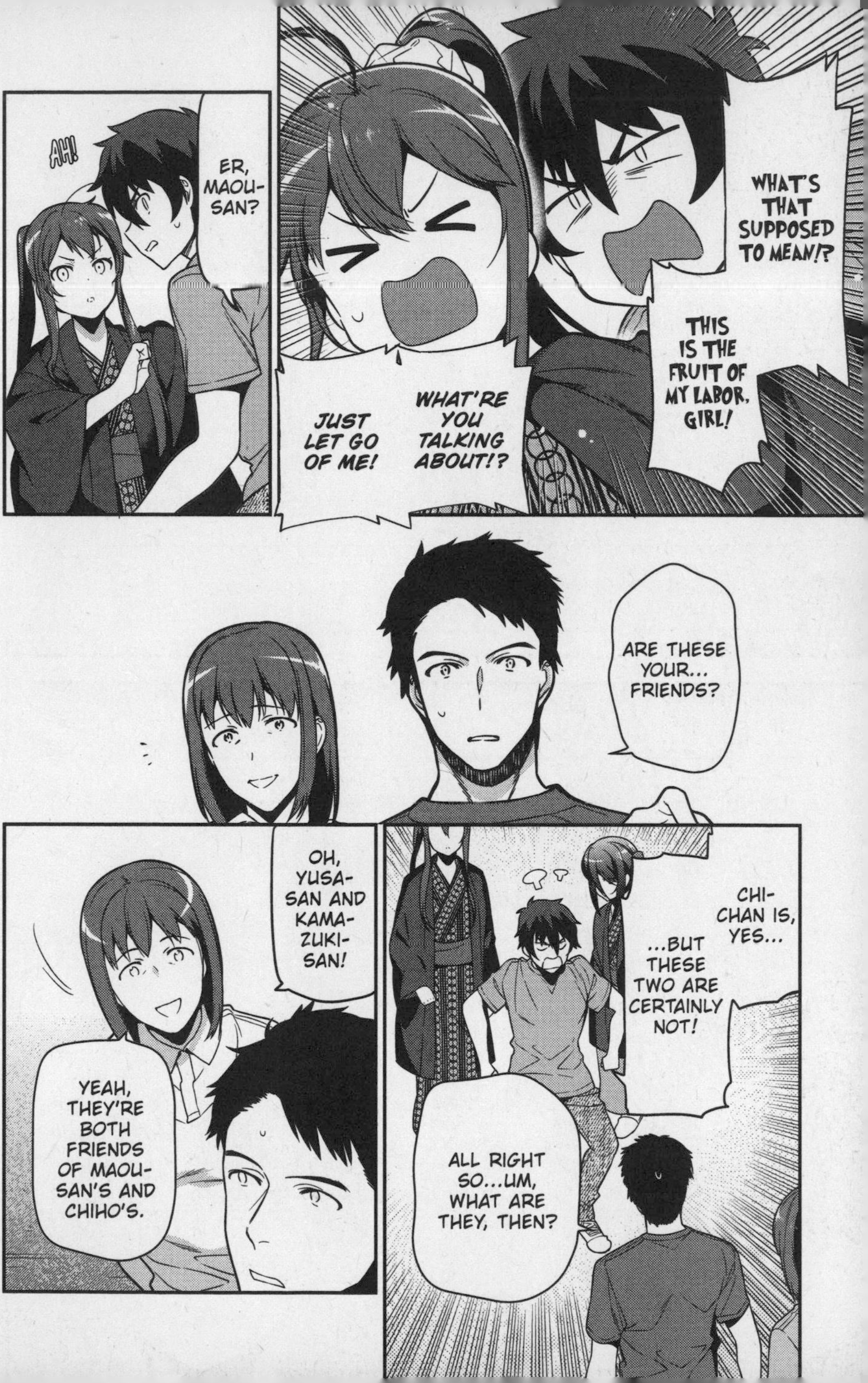
WHAT'S THAT SUPPOSED TO MEAN!?
THIS IS THE FRUIT OF MY LABOR, GIRL!
WHAT'RE YOU TALKING ABOUT!?
JUST LET GO OF ME!
ER, MAOU-SAN?
AH!
ARE THESE YOUR... FRIENDS?
CHI-CHAN IS, YES...
...BUT THESE TWO ARE CERTAINLY NOT!
ALL RIGHT SO...UM, WHAT ARE THEY, THEN?
OH, YUSA-SAN AND KAMAZUKI-SAN!
YEAH, THEY'RE BOTH FRIENDS OF MAOU-SAN'S AND CHIHO'S.

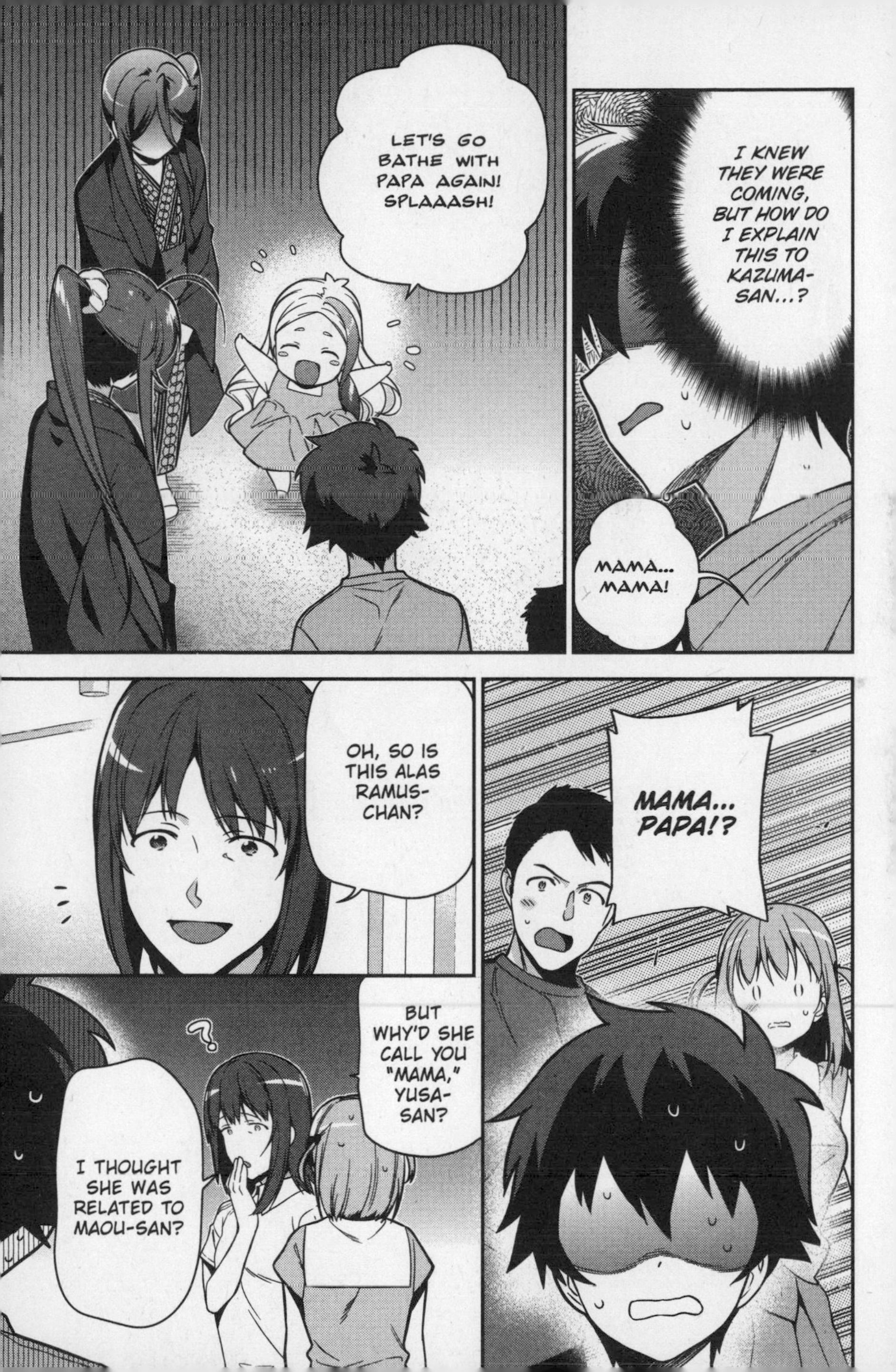
I KNEW THEY WERE COMING, BUT HOW DO I EXPLAIN THIS TO KAZUMA-SAN...?
MAMA... MAMA!
LET'S GO BATHE WITH PAPA AGAIN! SPLAAASH!
MAMA... PAPA!?
OH, SO IS THIS ALAS RAMUS-CHAN?
BUT WHY'D SHE CALL YOU "MAMA," YUSA-SAN?
I THOUGHT SHE WAS RELATED TO MAOU-SAN?

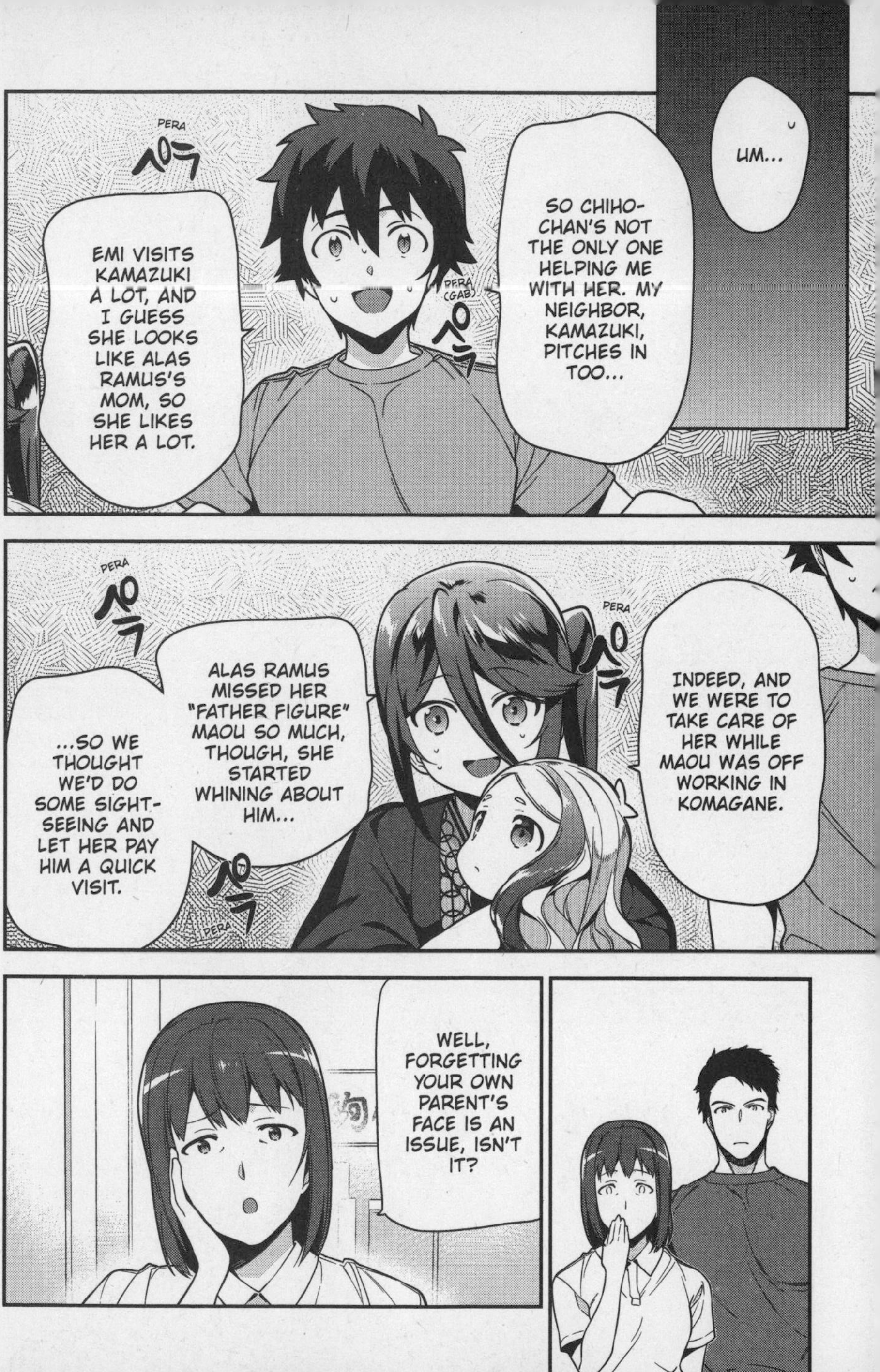
UM...
SO CHIHO-CHAN'S NOT THE ONLY ONE HELPING ME WITH HER. MY NEIGHBOR, KAMAZUKI, PITCHES IN TOO...
PERA (GAB)
PERA
EMI VISITS KAMAZUKI A LOT, AND I GUESS SHE LOOKS LIKE ALAS RAMUS'S MOM, SO SHE LIKES HER A LOT.
INDEED, AND WE WERE TO TAKE CARE OF HER WHILE MAOU WAS OFF WORKING IN KOMAGANE.
PERA
ALAS RAMUS MISSED HER "FATHER FIGURE" MAOU SO MUCH, THOUGH, SHE STARTED WHINING ABOUT HIM...
PERA
PERA
...SO WE THOUGHT WE'D DO SOME SIGHT-SEEING AND LET HER PAY HIM A QUICK VISIT.
WELL, FORGETTING YOUR OWN PARENT'S FACE IS AN ISSUE, ISN'T IT?

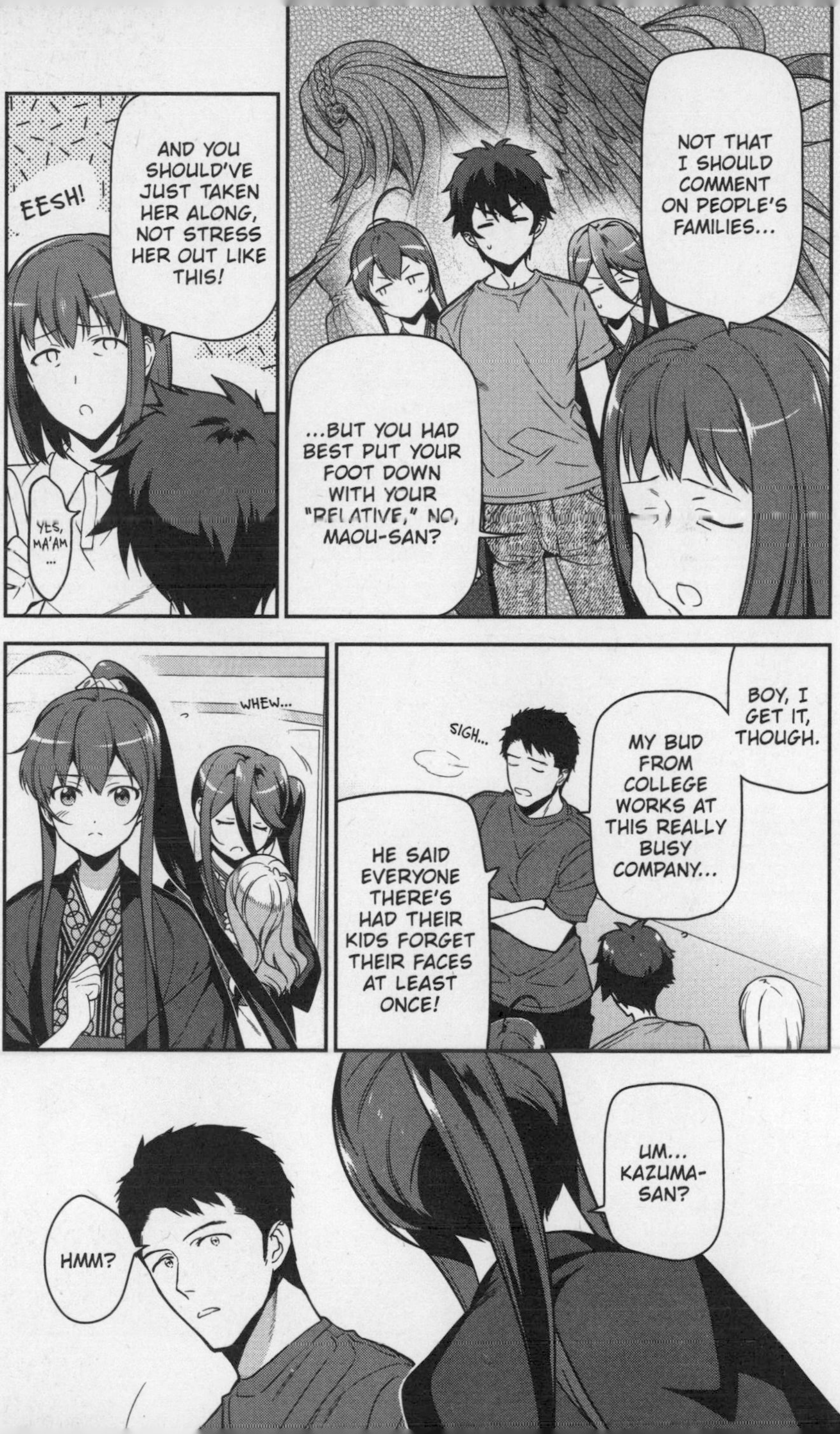
NOT THAT I SHOULD COMMENT ON PEOPLE'S FAMILIES...
...BUT YOU HAD BEST PUT YOUR FOOT DOWN WITH YOUR "RELATIVE," NO, MAOU-SAN?
AND YOU SHOULD'VE JUST TAKEN HER ALONG, NOT STRESS HER OUT LIKE THIS!
EESH!
YES, MA'AM...
BOY, I GET IT, THOUGH.
SIGH...
MY BUD FROM COLLEGE WORKS AT THIS REALLY BUSY COMPANY...
HE SAID EVERYONE THERE'S HAD THEIR KIDS FORGET THEIR FACES AT LEAST ONCE!
WHEW...
UM... KAZUMA-SAN?
HMM?

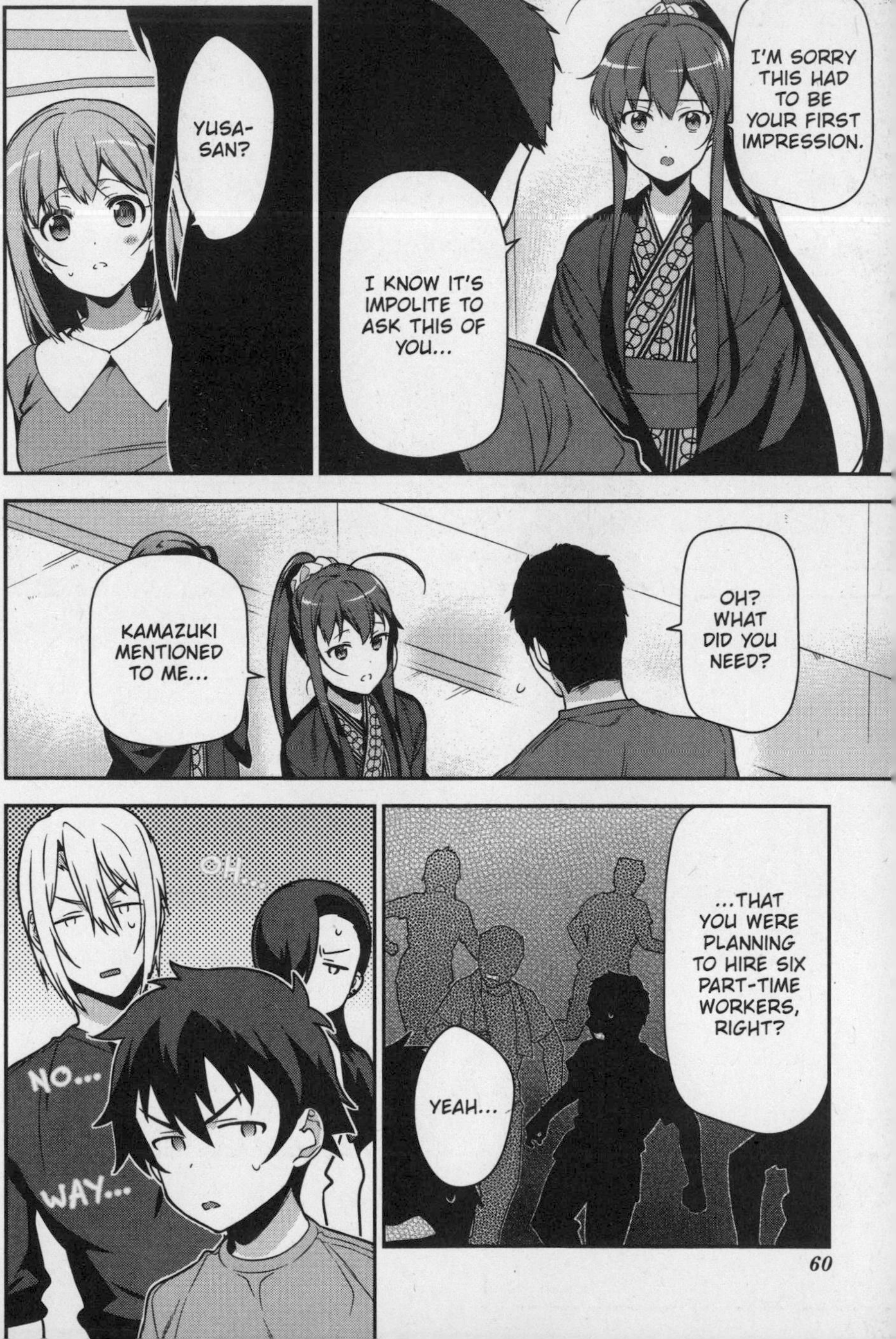
I'M SORRY THIS HAD TO BE YOUR FIRST IMPRESSION.
I KNOW IT'S IMPOLITE TO ASK THIS OF YOU...
YUSA-SAN?
OH? WHAT DID YOU NEED?
KAMAZUKI MENTIONED TO ME...
...THAT YOU WERE PLANNING TO HIRE SIX PART-TIME WORKERS, RIGHT?
YEAH...
OH...
NO... WAY...

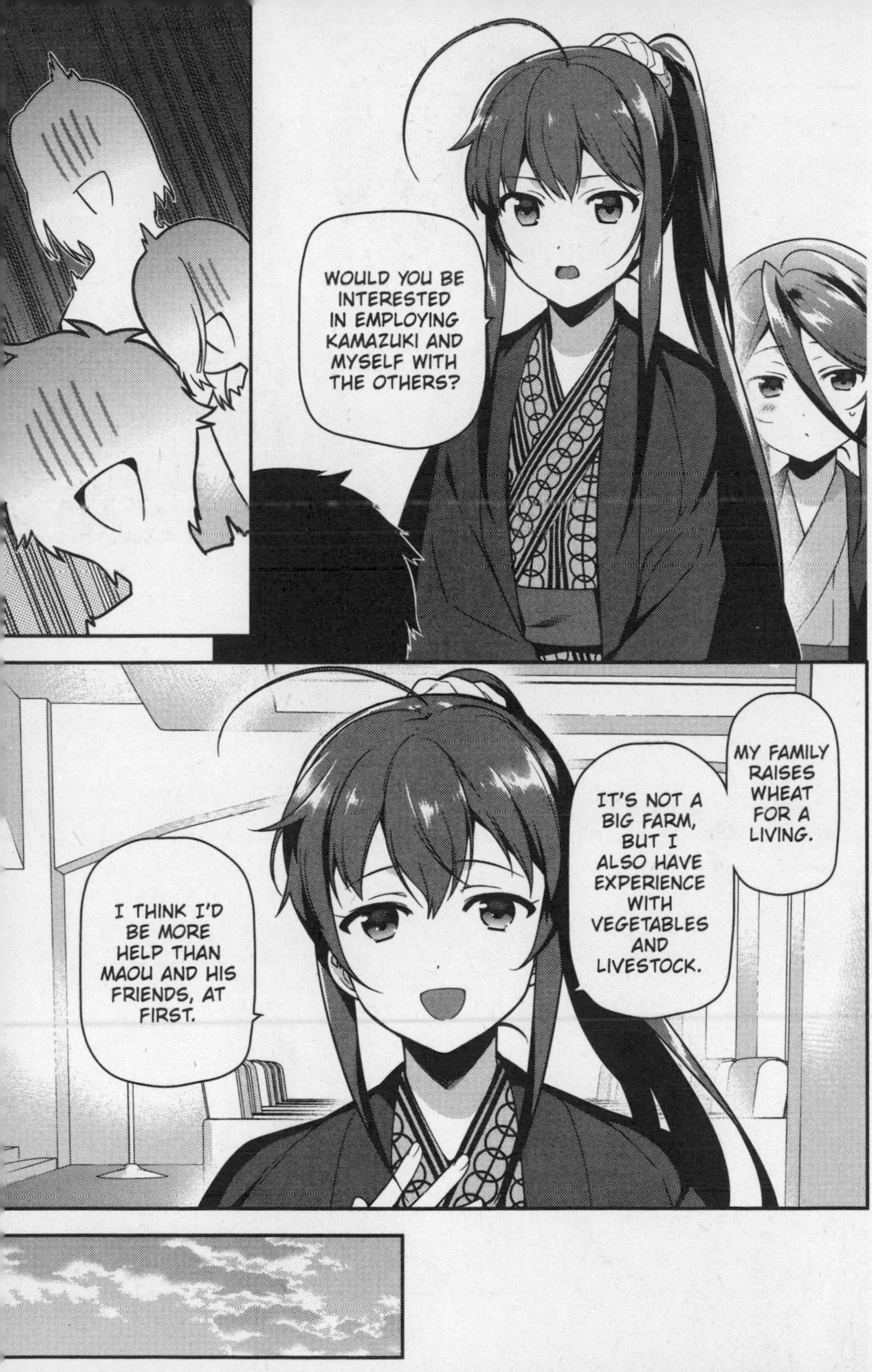
WOULD YOU BE INTERESTED IN EMPLOYING KAMAZUKI AND MYSELF WITH THE OTHERS?
MY FAMILY RAISES WHEAT FOR A LIVING.
IT'S NOT A BIG FARM, BUT I ALSO HAVE EXPERIENCE WITH VEGETABLES AND LIVESTOCK.
I THINK I'D BE MORE HELP THAN MAOU AND HIS FRIENDS, AT FIRST.

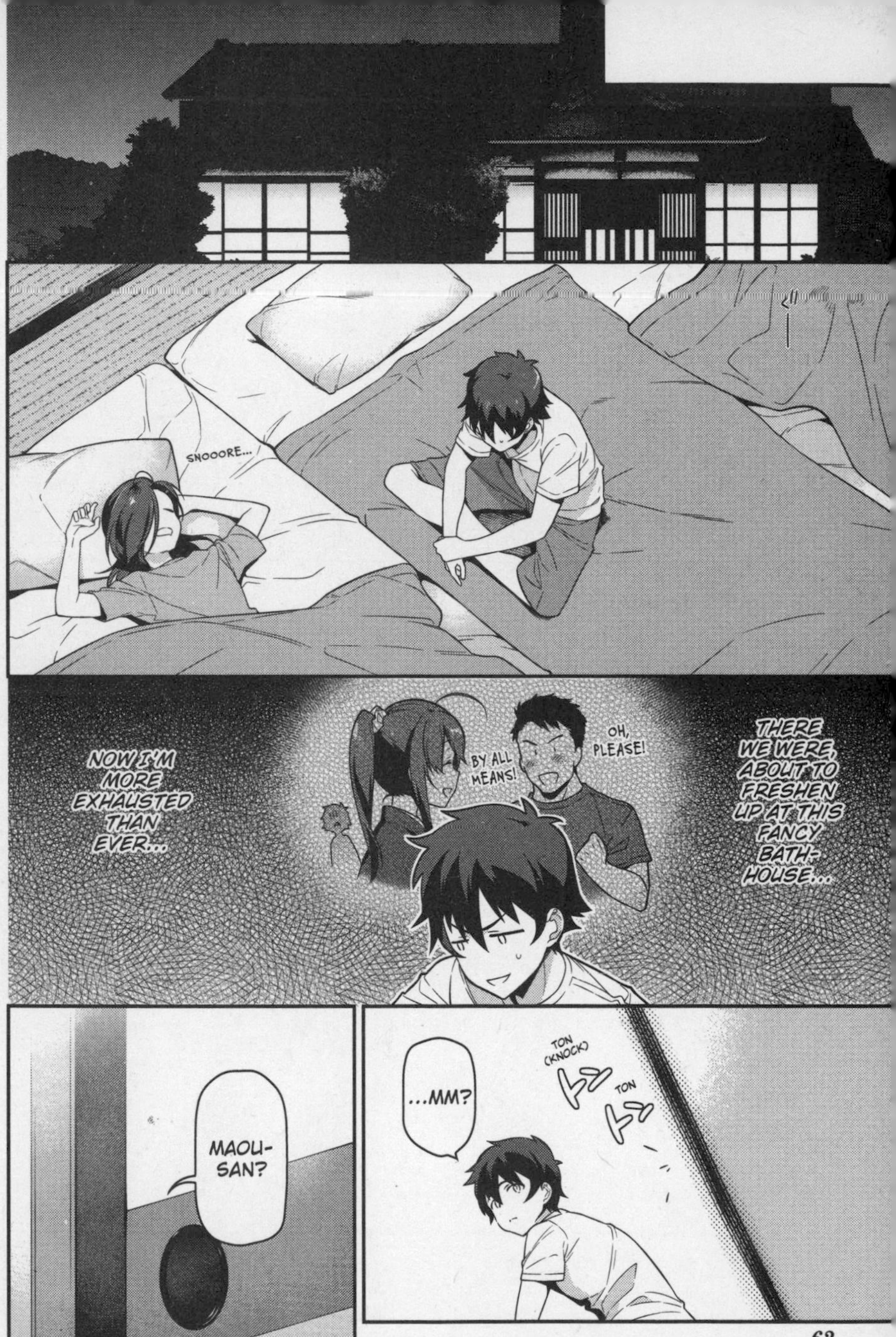

SNOOORE...
THERE WE WERE, ABOUT TO FRESHEN UP AT THIS FANCY BATH-HOUSE...
OH, PLEASE!
BY ALL MEANS!
NOW I'M MORE EXHAUSTED THAN EVER...
TON (KNOCK)
TON
...MM?
MAOU-SAN?

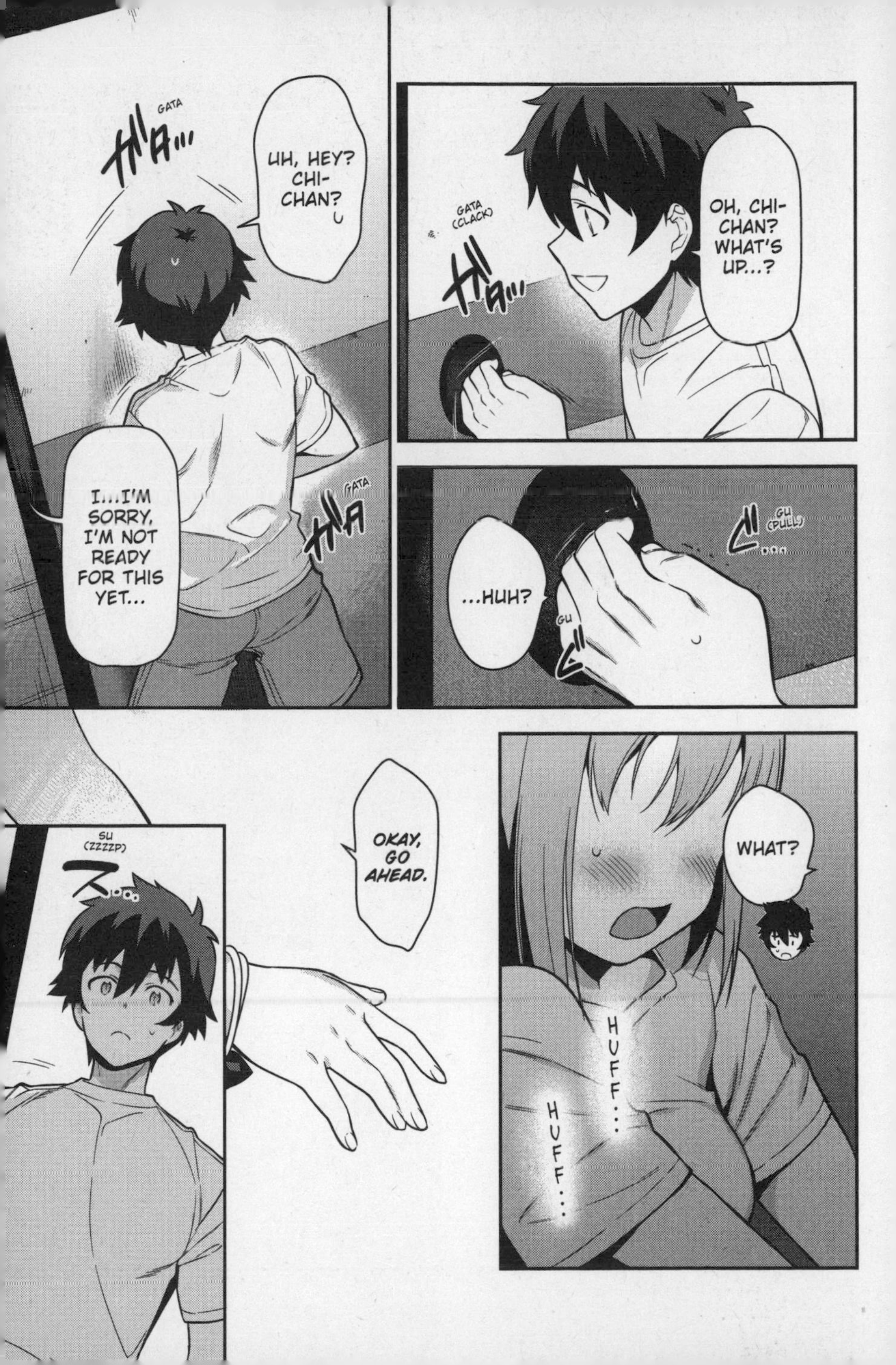
GATA (CLACK)
OH, CHI-CHAN? WHAT'S UP...?
GU (PULL)
GU
...HUH?
GATA
UH, HEY? CHI-CHAN?
GATA
I...I'M SORRY, I'M NOT READY FOR THIS YET...
WHAT?
HUFF...
HUFF...
OKAY, GO AHEAD.
SU (ZZZZP)

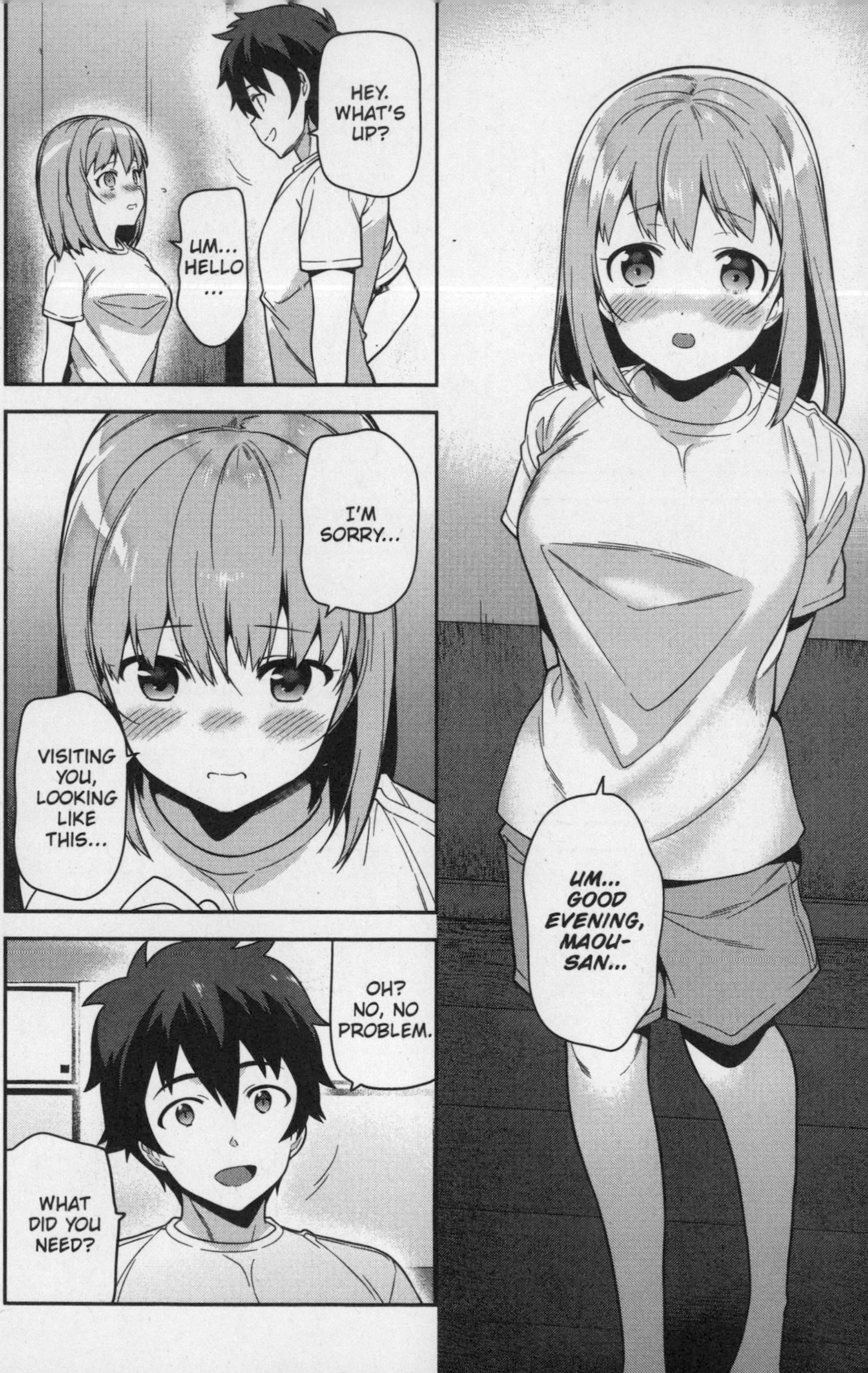
UM... GOOD EVENING, MAOU-SAN...
HEY. WHAT'S UP?
UM... HELLO ...
I'M SORRY...
VISITING YOU, LOOKING LIKE THIS...
OH? NO, NO PROBLEM.
WHAT DID YOU NEED?

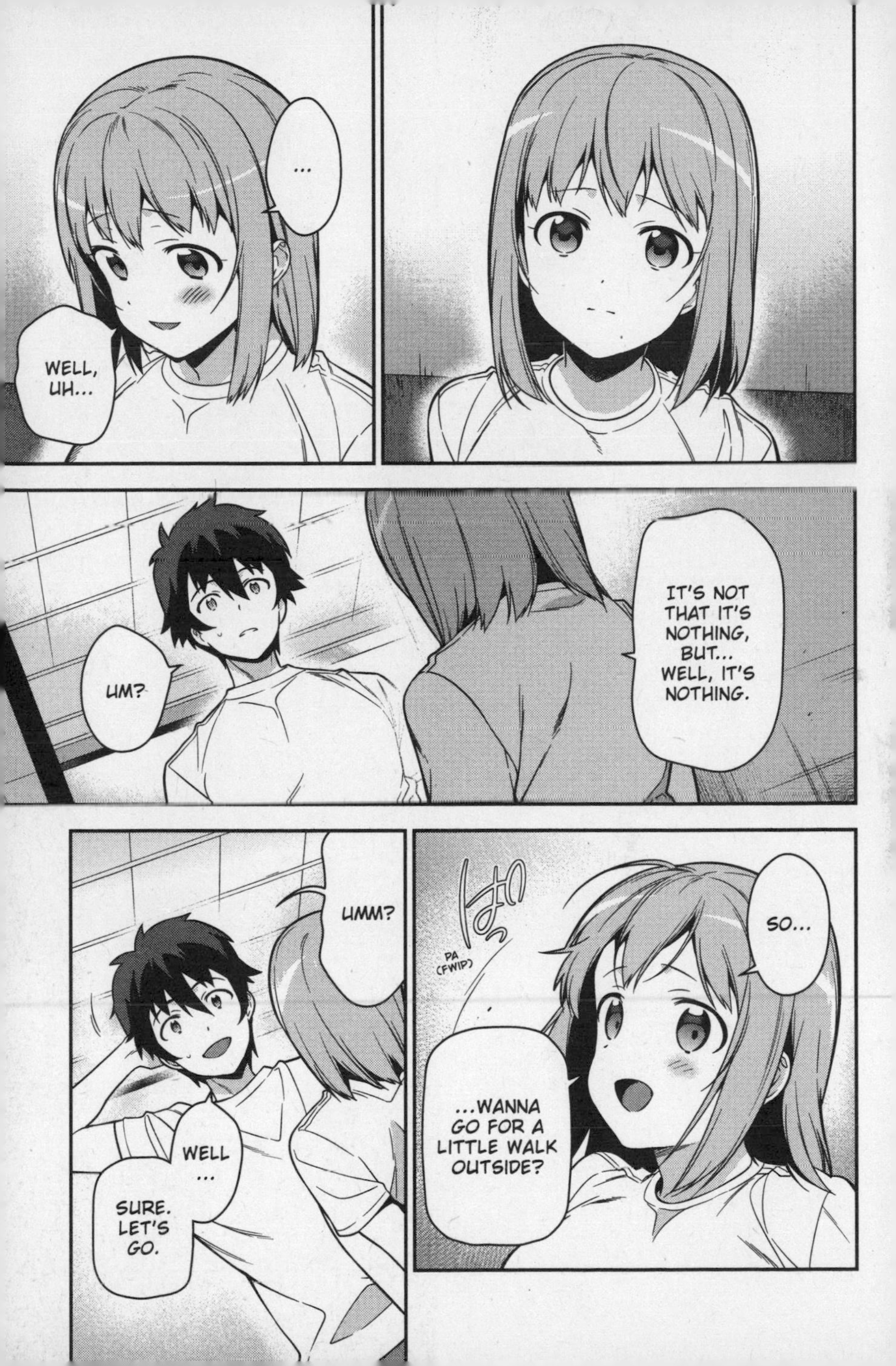
...
WELL, UH...
IT'S NOT THAT IT'S NOTHING, BUT... WELL, IT'S NOTHING.
UM?
SO...
PA (FWIP)
...WANNA GO FOR A LITTLE WALK OUTSIDE?
UMM?
WELL ...
SURE. LET'S GO.

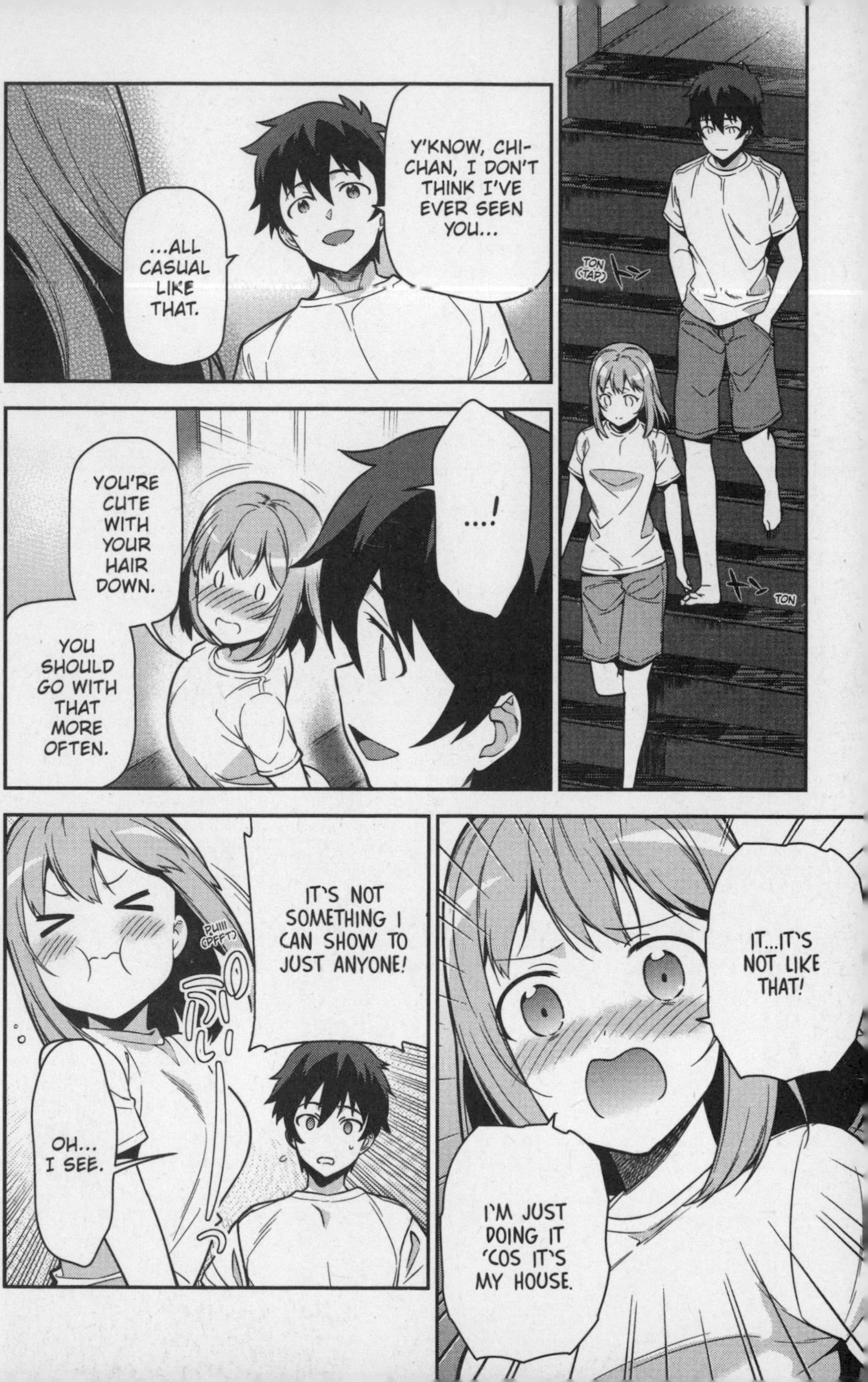
TON (TAP)
TON
Y'KNOW, CHI-CHAN, I DON'T THINK I'VE EVER SEEN YOU...
...ALL CASUAL LIKE THAT.
...!
YOU'RE CUTE WITH YOUR HAIR DOWN.
YOU SHOULD GO WITH THAT MORE OFTEN.
IT...IT'S NOT LIKE THAT!
I'M JUST DOING IT 'COS IT'S MY HOUSE.
IT'S NOT SOMETHING I CAN SHOW TO JUST ANYONE!
PUIIII (PFFT)
OH... I SEE.

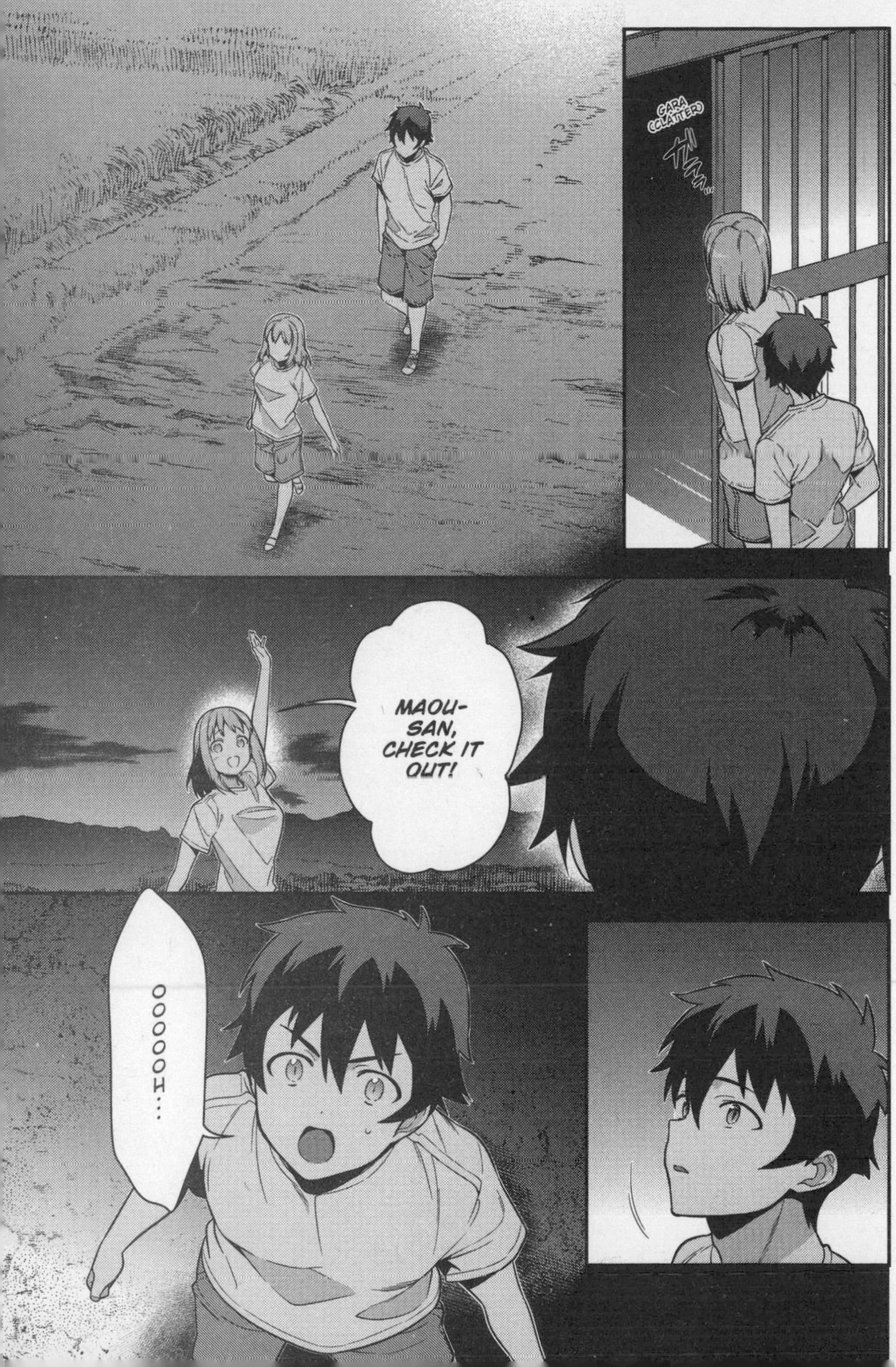
GARA (CLATTER)
MAOU-SAN, CHECK IT OUT!
OOOOOH...

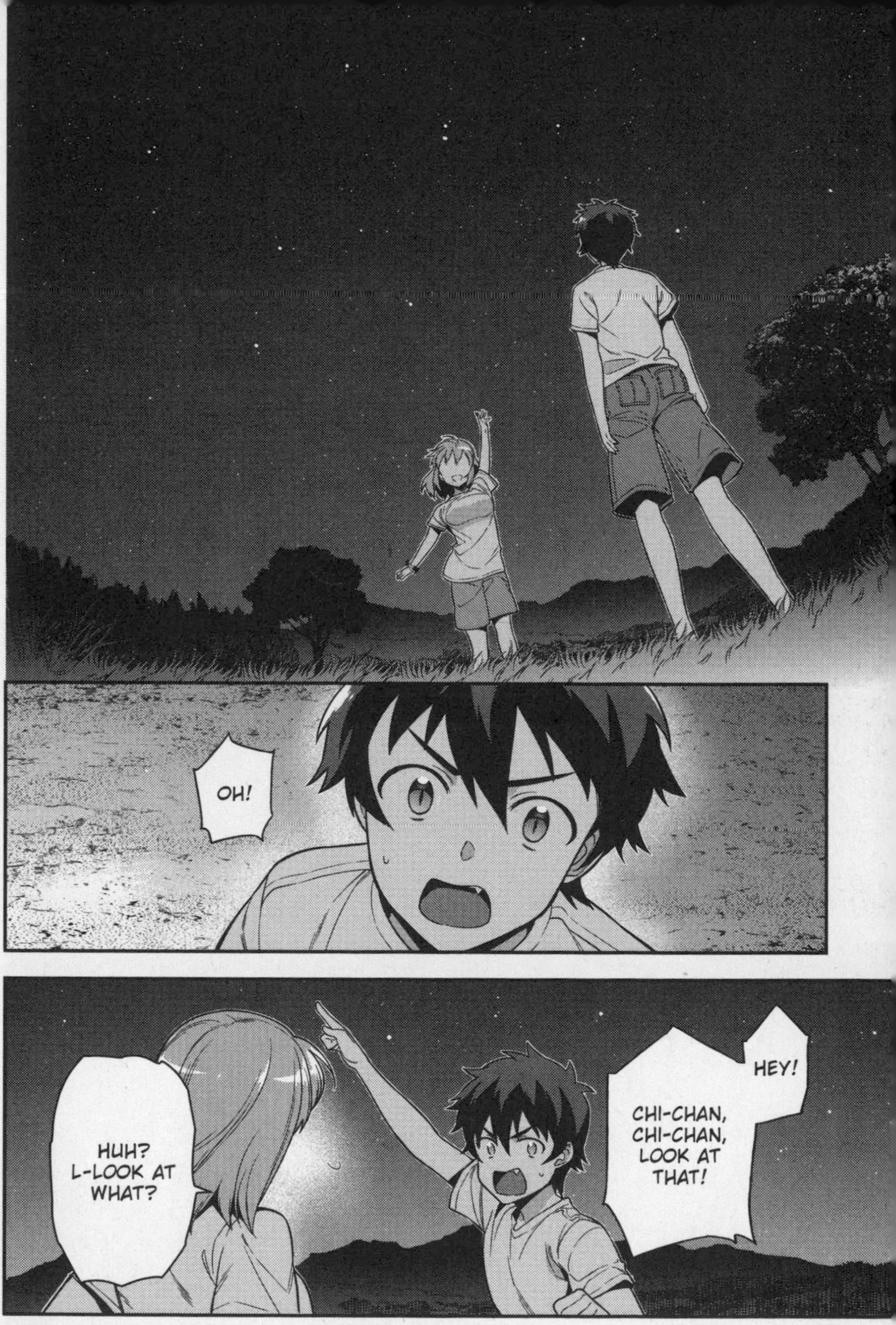
OH!
HEY!
CHI-CHAN, CHI-CHAN, LOOK AT THAT!
HUH? L-LOOK AT WHAT?

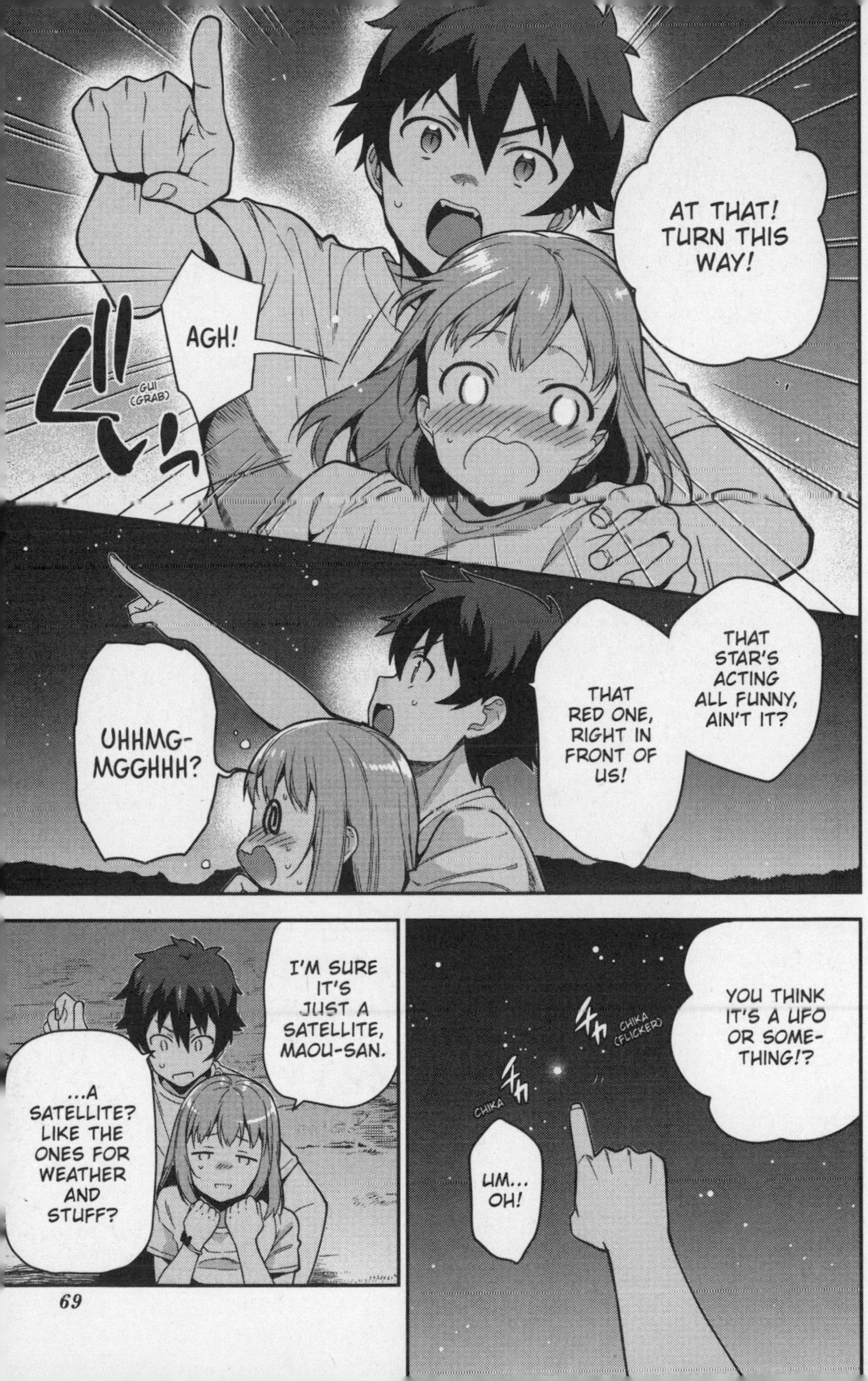
AT THAT! TURN THIS WAY!
AGH!
GUI (GRAB)
THAT STAR'S ACTING ALL FUNNY, AIN'T IT?
THAT RED ONE, RIGHT IN FRONT OF US!
UHHMG-MGGHHH?
YOU THINK IT'S A UFO OR SOME-THING!?
CHIKA (FLICKER)
CHIKA
UM... OH!
I'M SURE IT'S JUST A SATELLITE, MAOU-SAN.
...A SATELLITE? LIKE THE ONES FOR WEATHER AND STUFF?

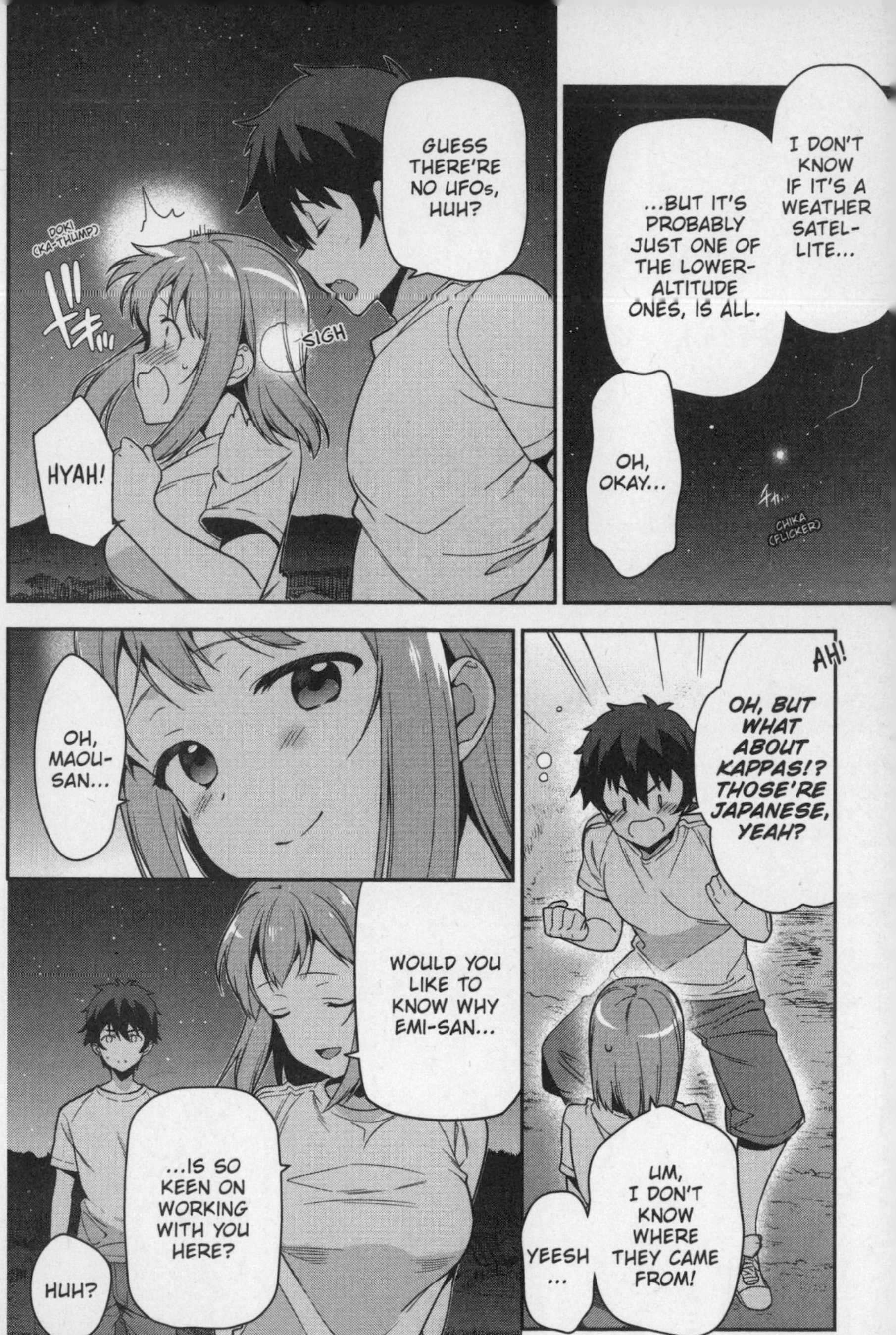
I DON'T KNOW IF IT'S A WEATHER SATEL-LITE...
...BUT IT'S PROBABLY JUST ONE OF THE LOWER-ALTITUDE ONES, IS ALL.
OH, OKAY...
CHIKA (FLICKER)
GUESS THERE'RE NO UFOs, HUH?
DOKI (KA-THUMP)
SIGH
HYAH!
AH!
OH, BUT WHAT ABOUT KAPPAS!? THOSE'RE JAPANESE, YEAH?
UM, I DON'T KNOW WHERE THEY CAME FROM!
YEESH...
OH, MAOU-SAN...
WOULD YOU LIKE TO KNOW WHY EMI-SAN...
...IS SO KEEN ON WORKING WITH YOU HERE?
HUH?

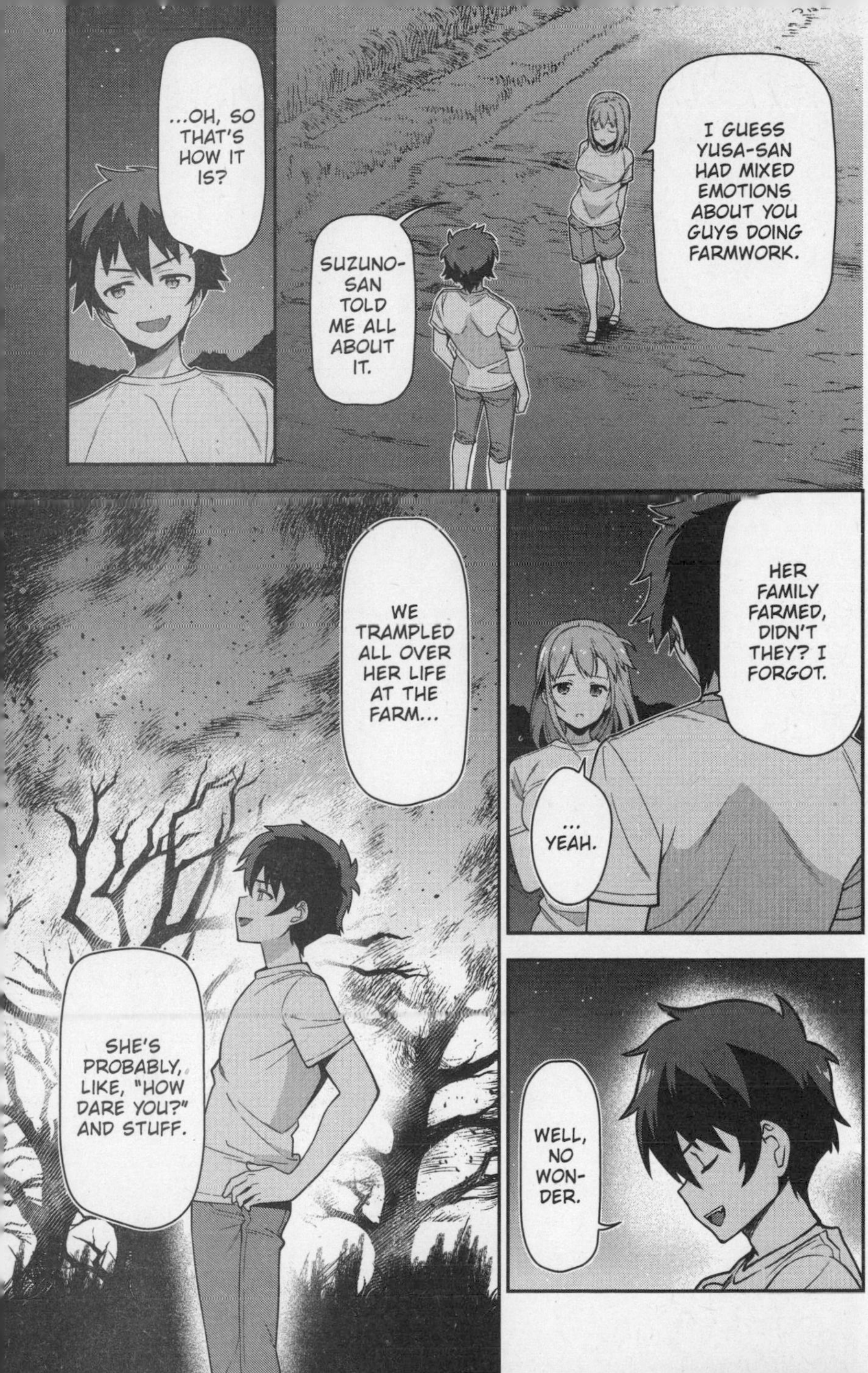
I GUESS YUSA-SAN HAD MIXED EMOTIONS ABOUT YOU GUYS DOING FARMWORK.
SUZUNO-SAN TOLD ME ALL ABOUT IT.
...OH, SO THAT'S HOW IT IS?
HER FAMILY FARMED, DIDN'T THEY? I FORGOT.
...YEAH.
WELL, NO WON-DER.
WE TRAMPLED ALL OVER HER LIFE AT THE FARM...
SHE'S PROBABLY, LIKE, "HOW DARE YOU?" AND STUFF.

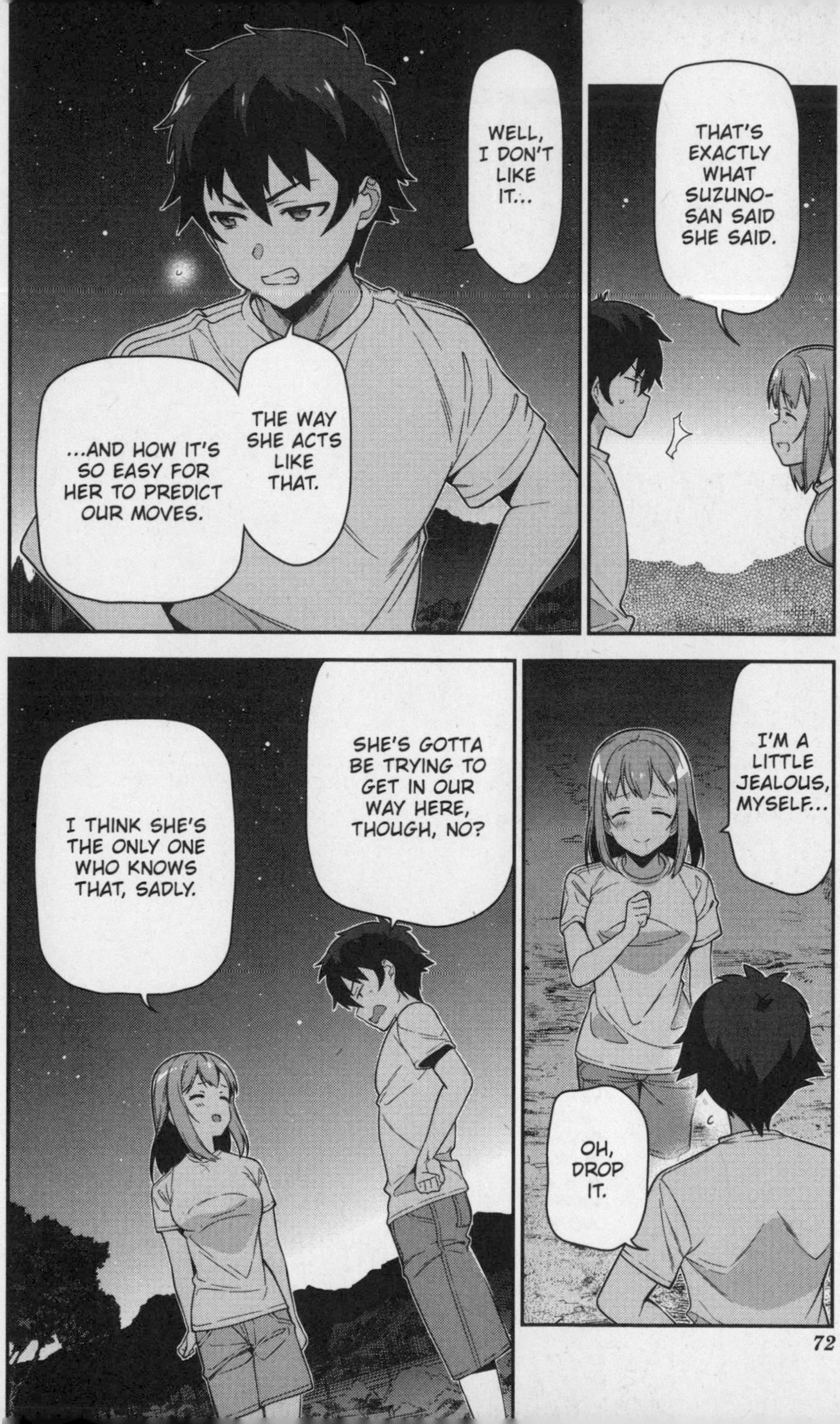
THAT'S EXACTLY WHAT SUZUNO-SAN SAID SHE SAID.
WELL, I DON'T LIKE IT...
THE WAY SHE ACTS LIKE THAT.
...AND HOW IT'S SO EASY FOR HER TO PREDICT OUR MOVES.
I'M A LITTLE JEALOUS, MYSELF...
OH, DROP IT.
SHE'S GOTTA BE TRYING TO GET IN OUR WAY HERE, THOUGH, NO?
I THINK SHE'S THE ONLY ONE WHO KNOWS THAT, SADLY.

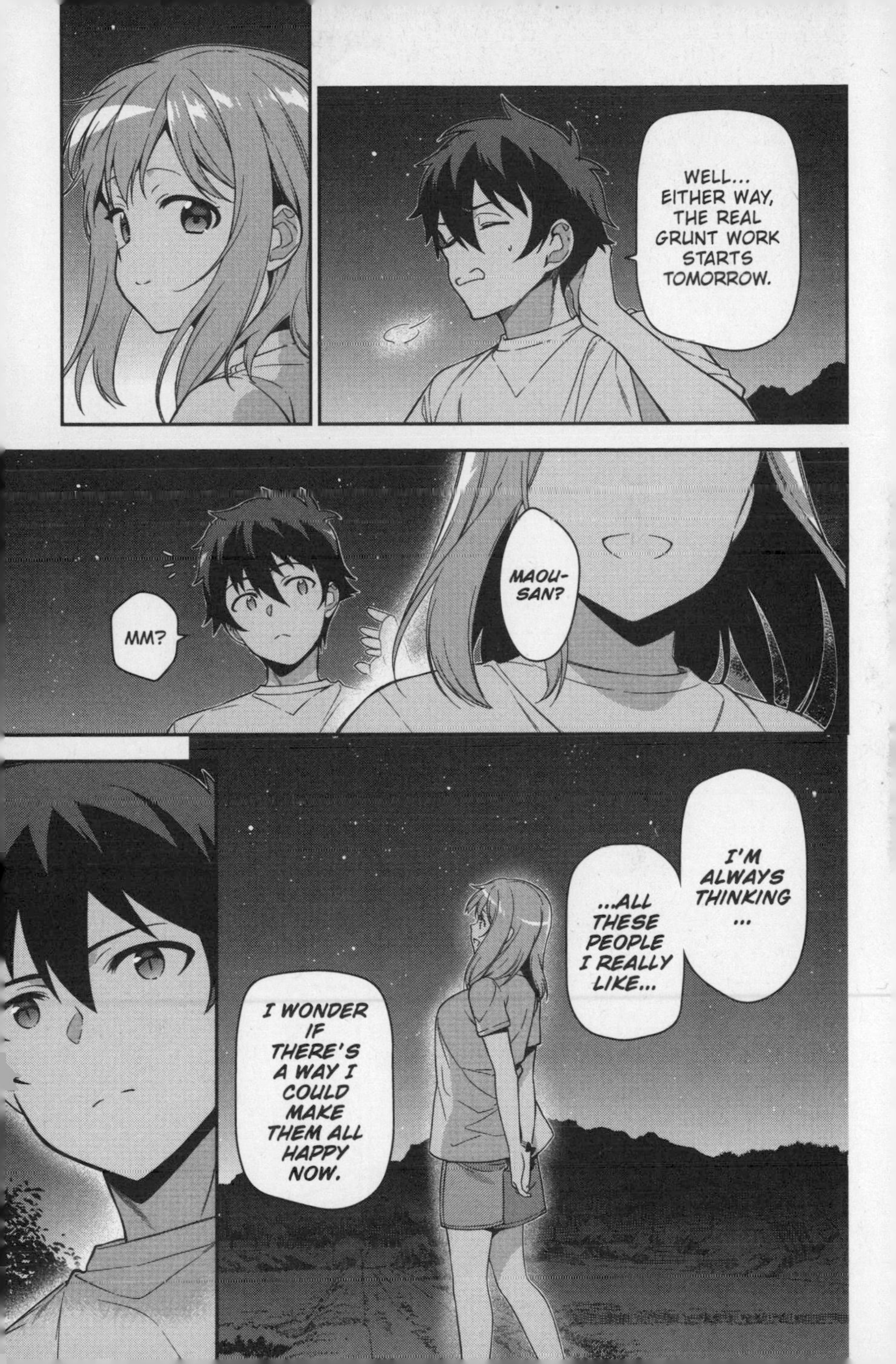
WELL... EITHER WAY, THE REAL GRUNT WORK STARTS TOMORROW.
MAOU-SAN?
MM?
I'M ALWAYS THINKING ...
...ALL THESE PEOPLE I REALLY LIKE...
I WONDER IF THERE'S A WAY I COULD MAKE THEM ALL HAPPY NOW.

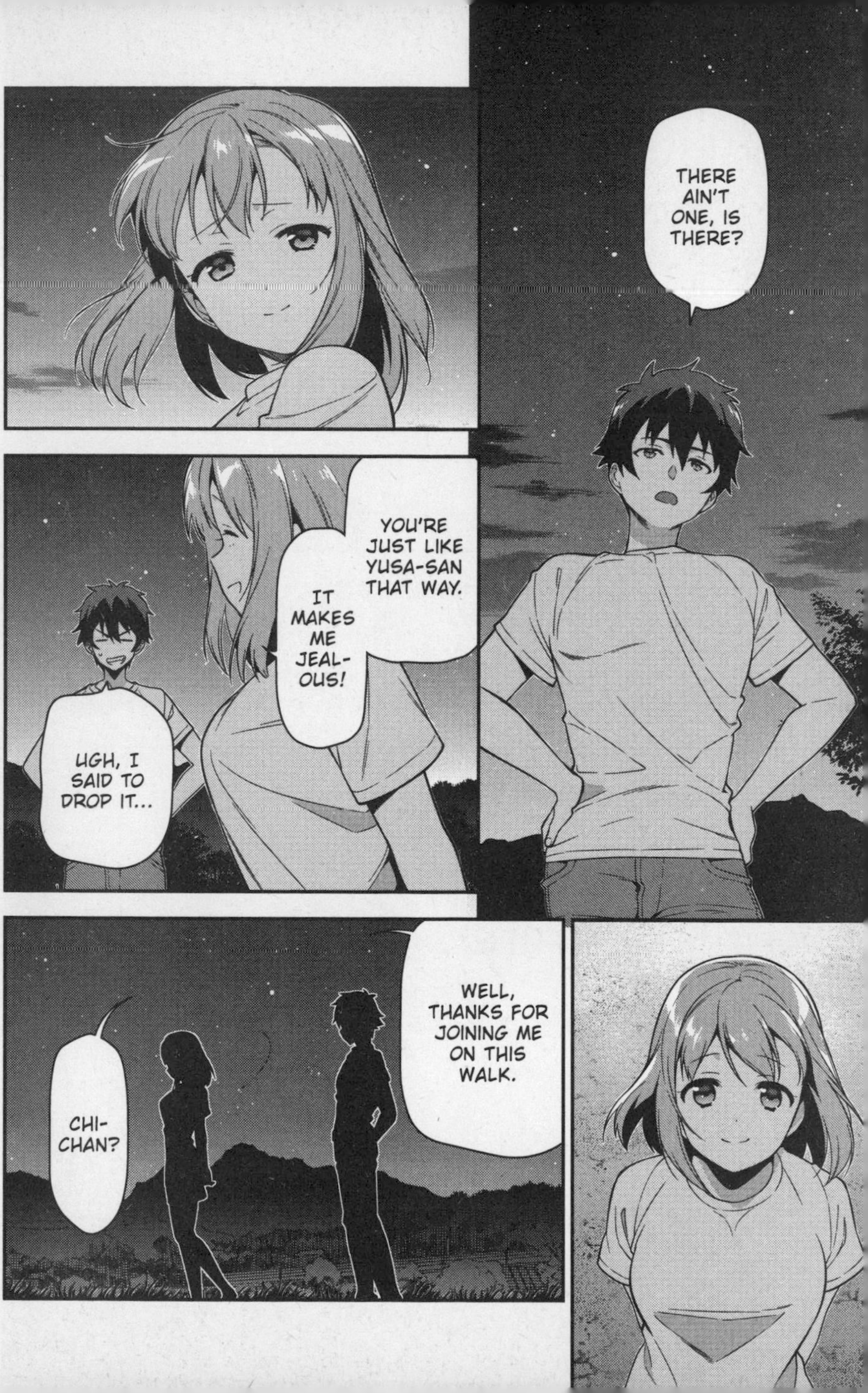
THERE AIN'T ONE, IS THERE?
YOU'RE JUST LIKE YUSA-SAN THAT WAY.
IT MAKES ME JEAL-OUS!
UGH, I SAID TO DROP IT...
WELL, THANKS FOR JOINING ME ON THIS WALK.
CHI-CHAN?

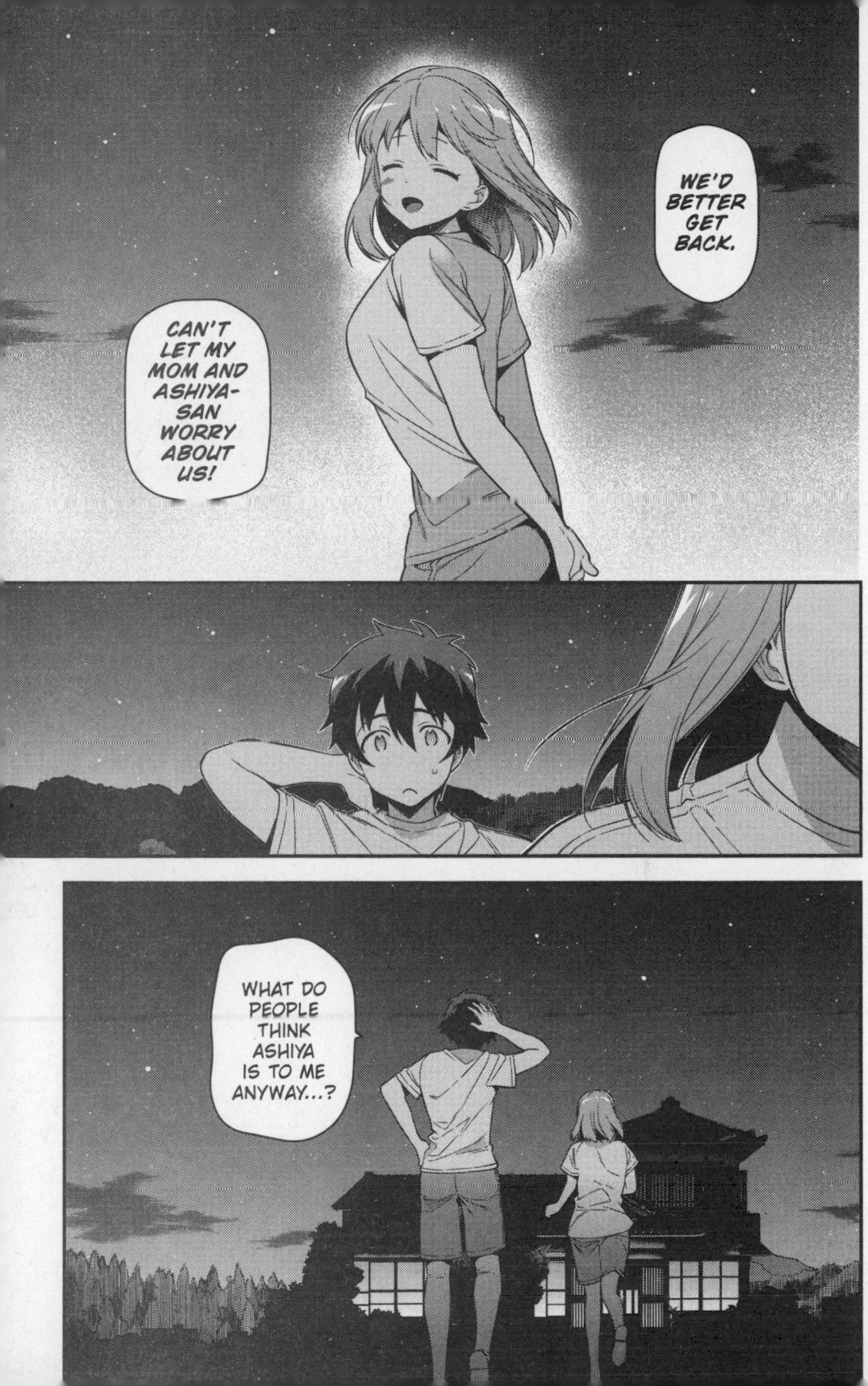
WE'D BETTER GET BACK.
CAN'T LET MY MOM AND ASHIYA-SAN WORRY ABOUT US!
WHAT DO PEOPLE THINK ASHIYA IS TO ME ANYWAY...?

THE DEVIL IS A PART-TIMER!

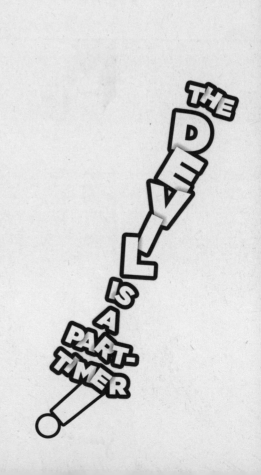

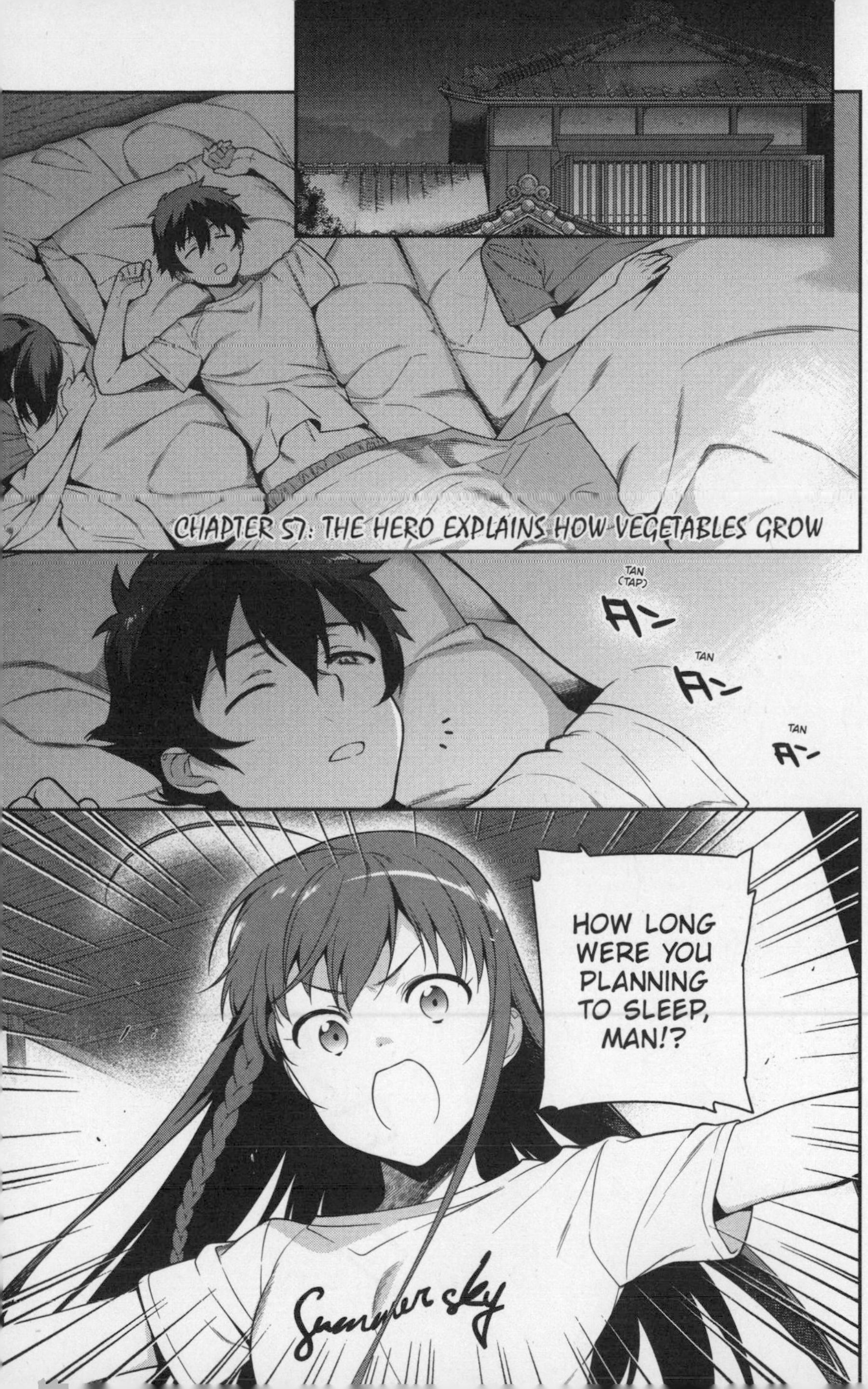
CHAPTER 57: THE HERO EXPLAINS HOW VEGETABLES GROW
TAN (TAP)
TAN
TAN
HOW LONG WERE YOU PLANNING TO SLEEP, MAN!?
Summer sky

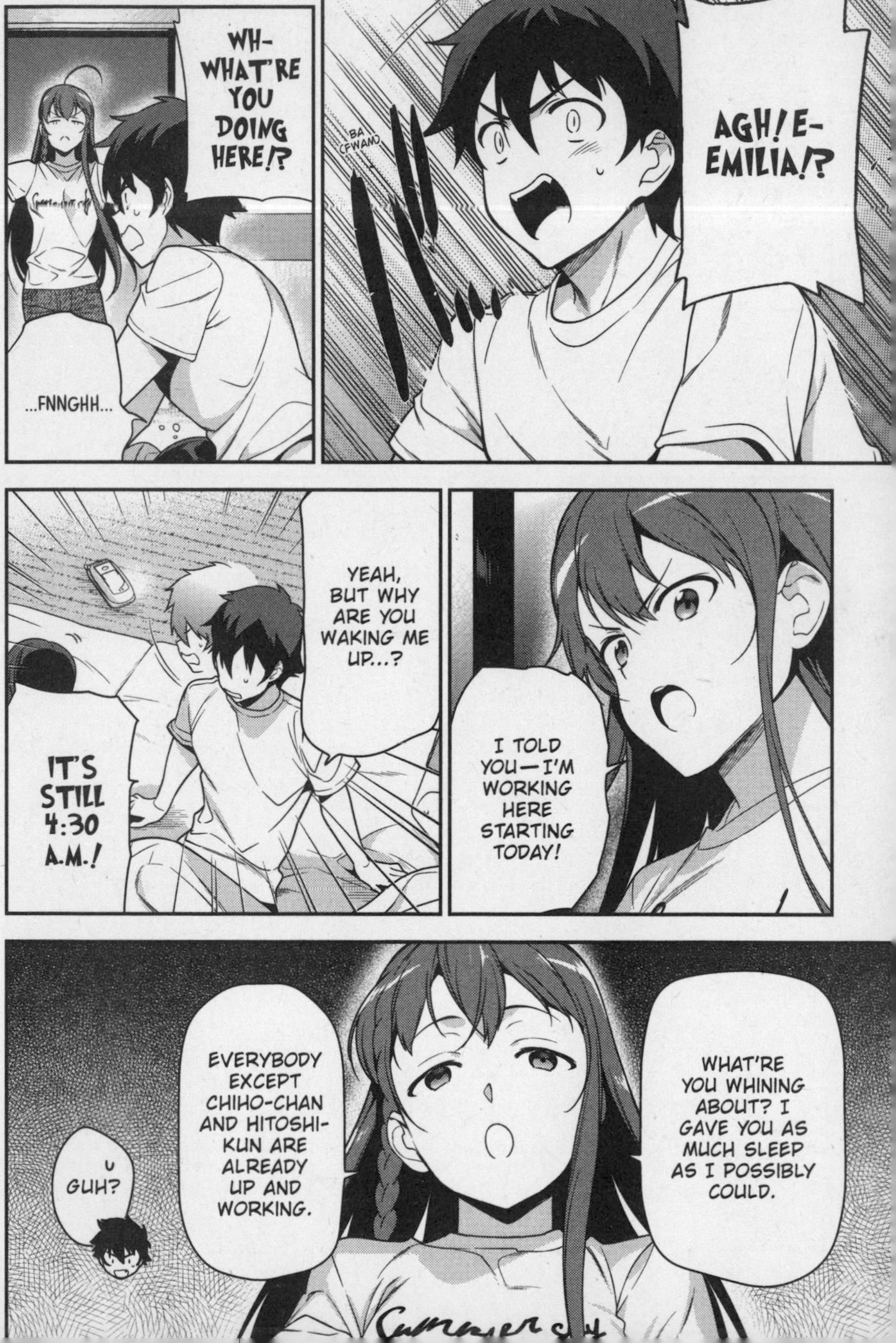
AGH! E-EMILIA!?
BA (FWAM)
WH-WHAT'RE YOU DOING HERE!?
...FNNGHH...
I TOLD YOU—I'M WORKING HERE STARTING TODAY!
YEAH, BUT WHY ARE YOU WAKING ME UP...?
IT'S STILL 4:30 A.M.!
WHAT'RE YOU WHINING ABOUT? I GAVE YOU AS MUCH SLEEP AS I POSSIBLY COULD.
EVERYBODY EXCEPT CHIHO-CHAN AND HITOSHI-KUN ARE ALREADY UP AND WORKING.
GUH?

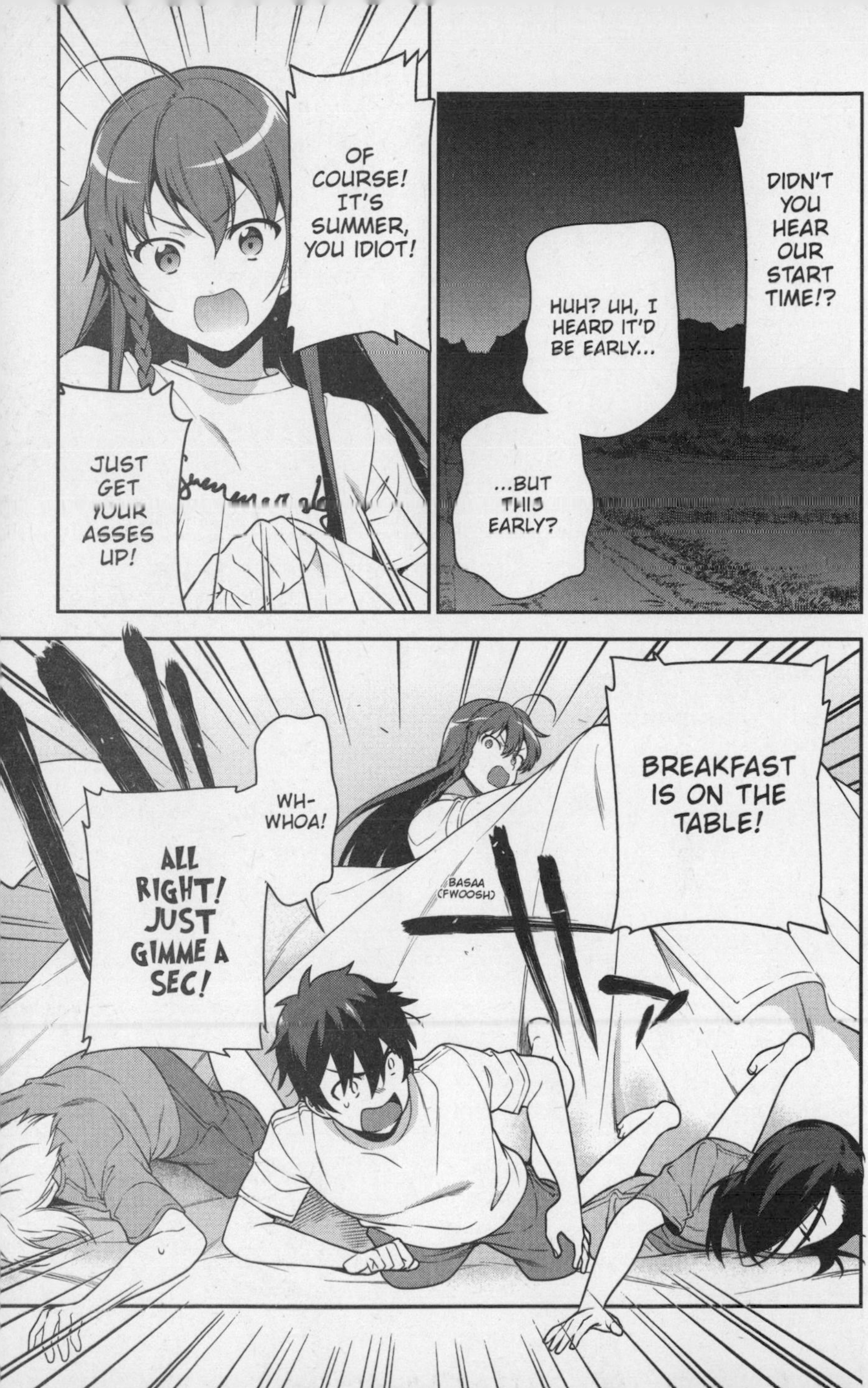
DIDN'T YOU HEAR OUR START TIME!?
HUH? UH, I HEARD IT'D BE EARLY...
...BUT THIS EARLY?
OF COURSE! IT'S SUMMER, YOU IDIOT!
JUST GET YOUR ASSES UP!
BREAKFAST IS ON THE TABLE!
BASAA (FWOOSH)
WH- WHOA!
ALL RIGHT! JUST GIMME A SEC!

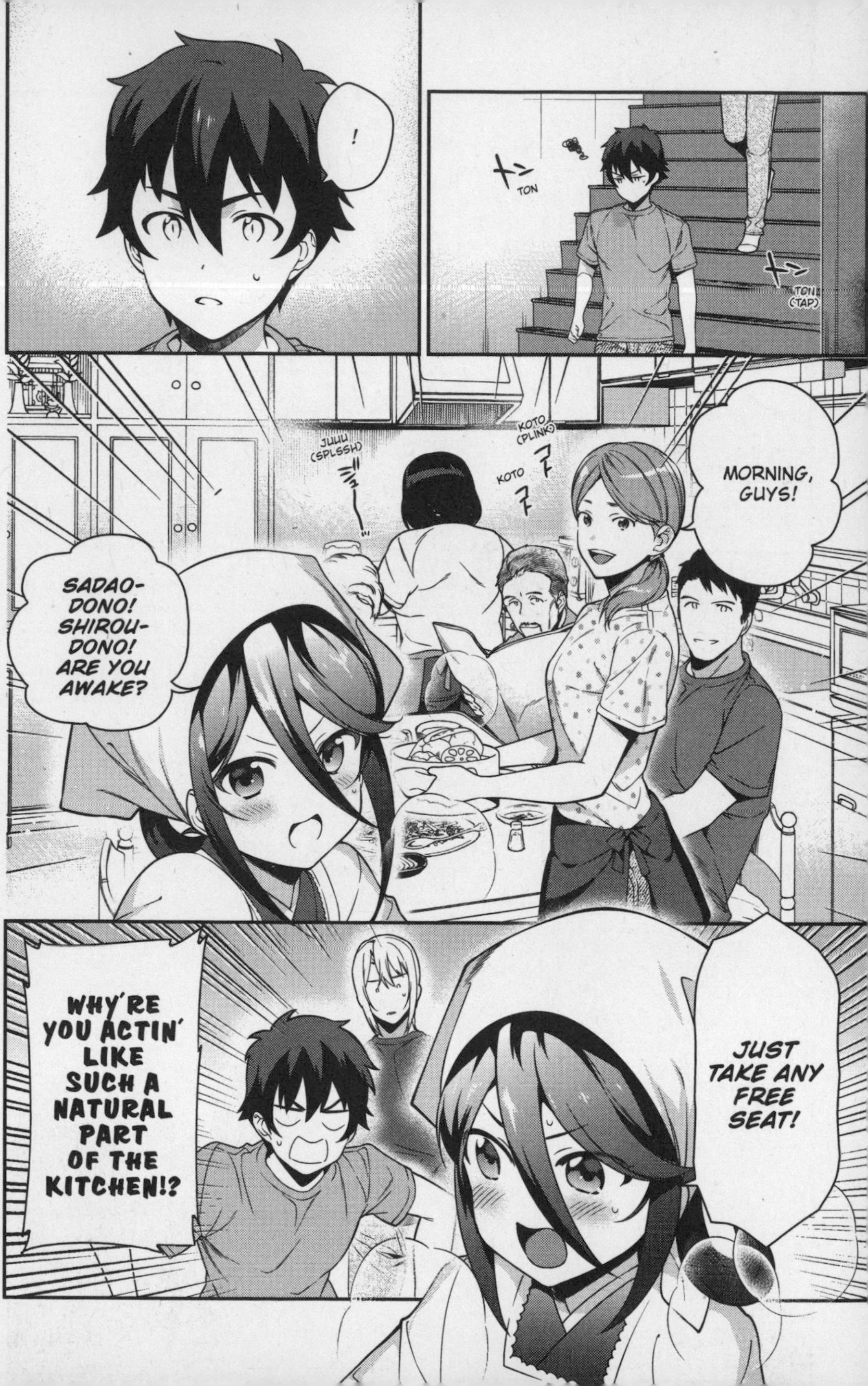
TON
TON (TAP)
!
MORNING, GUYS!
KOTO (PLINK)
KOTO
JUUU (SPLSSH)
SADAO-DONO! SHIROU-DONO! ARE YOU AWAKE?
JUST TAKE ANY FREE SEAT!
WHY'RE YOU ACTIN' LIKE SUCH A NATURAL PART OF THE KITCHEN!?

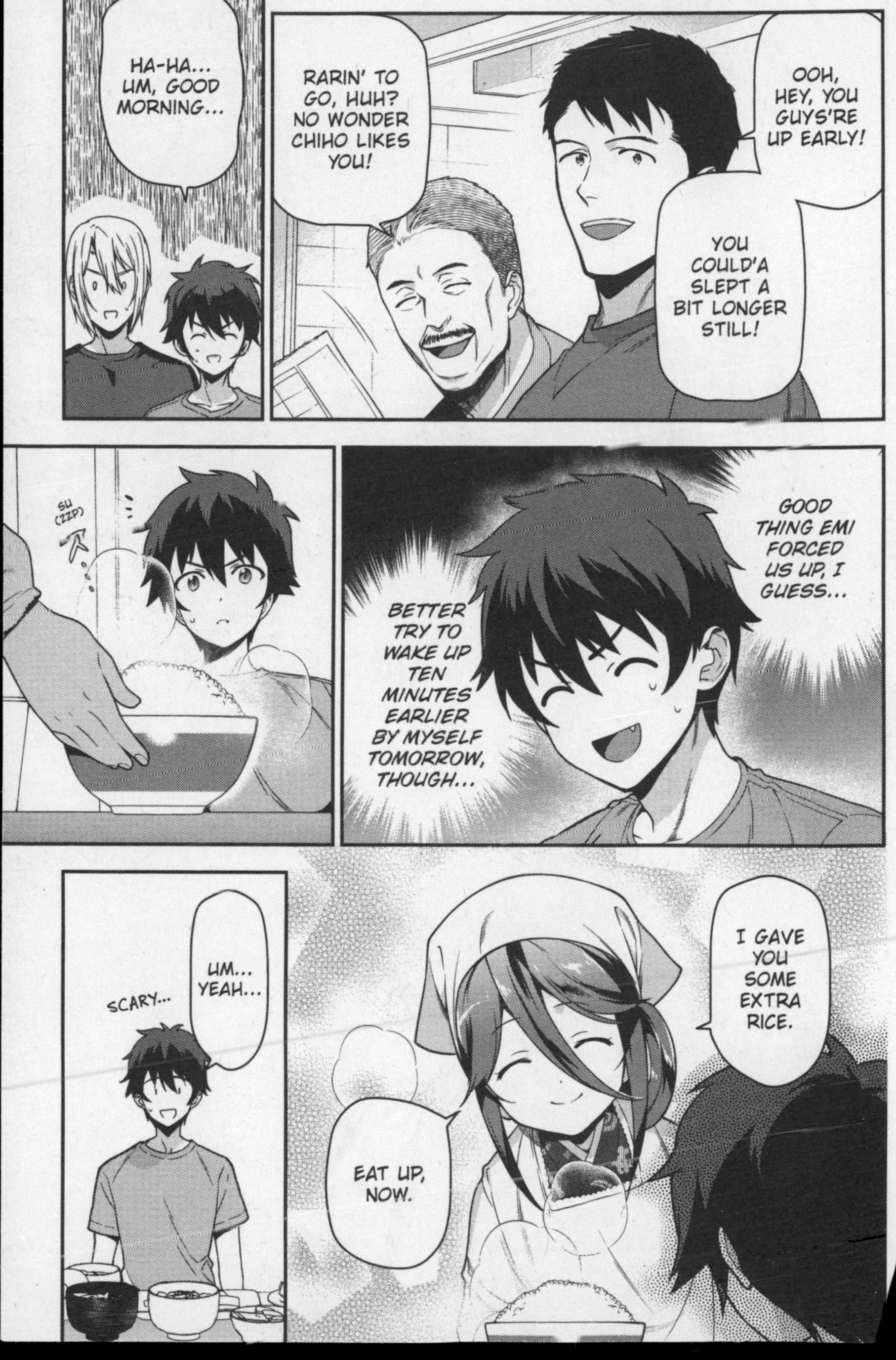
OOH, HEY, YOU GUYS'RE UP EARLY!
YOU COULD'A SLEPT A BIT LONGER STILL!
RARIN' TO GO, HUH? NO WONDER CHIHO LIKES YOU!
HA-HA... UM, GOOD MORNING...
GOOD THING EMI FORCED US UP, I GUESS...
BETTER TRY TO WAKE UP TEN MINUTES EARLIER BY MYSELF TOMORROW, THOUGH...
SU (ZZP)
I GAVE YOU SOME EXTRA RICE.
EAT UP, NOW.
UM... YEAH...
SCARY...

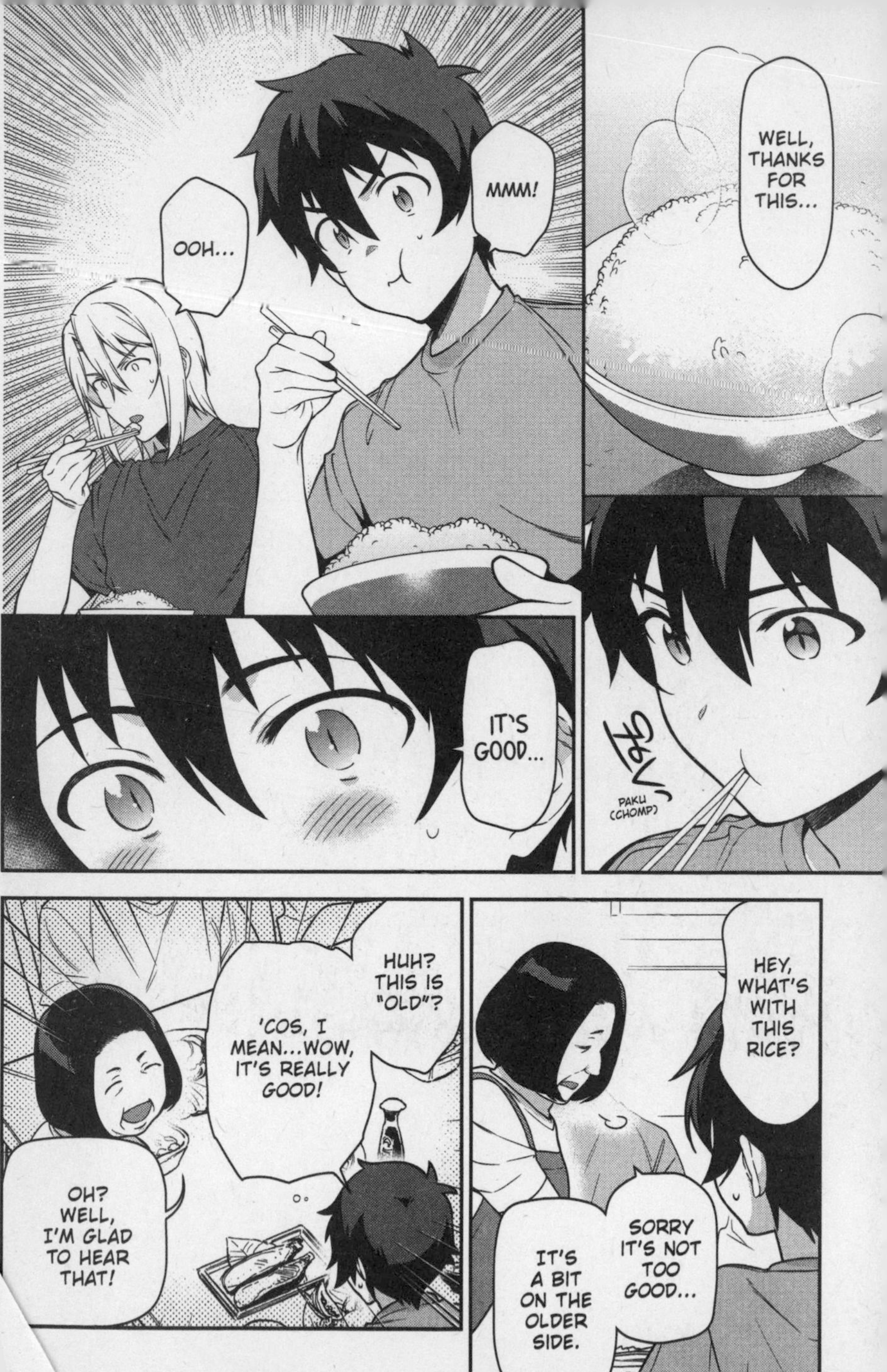
WELL, THANKS FOR THIS...
MMM!
OOH...
PAKU (CHOMP)
IT'S GOOD...
HEY, WHAT'S WITH THIS RICE?
SORRY IT'S NOT TOO GOOD...
IT'S A BIT ON THE OLDER SIDE.
HUH? THIS IS "OLD"?
'COS, I MEAN...WOW, IT'S REALLY GOOD!
OH? WELL, I'M GLAD TO HEAR THAT!

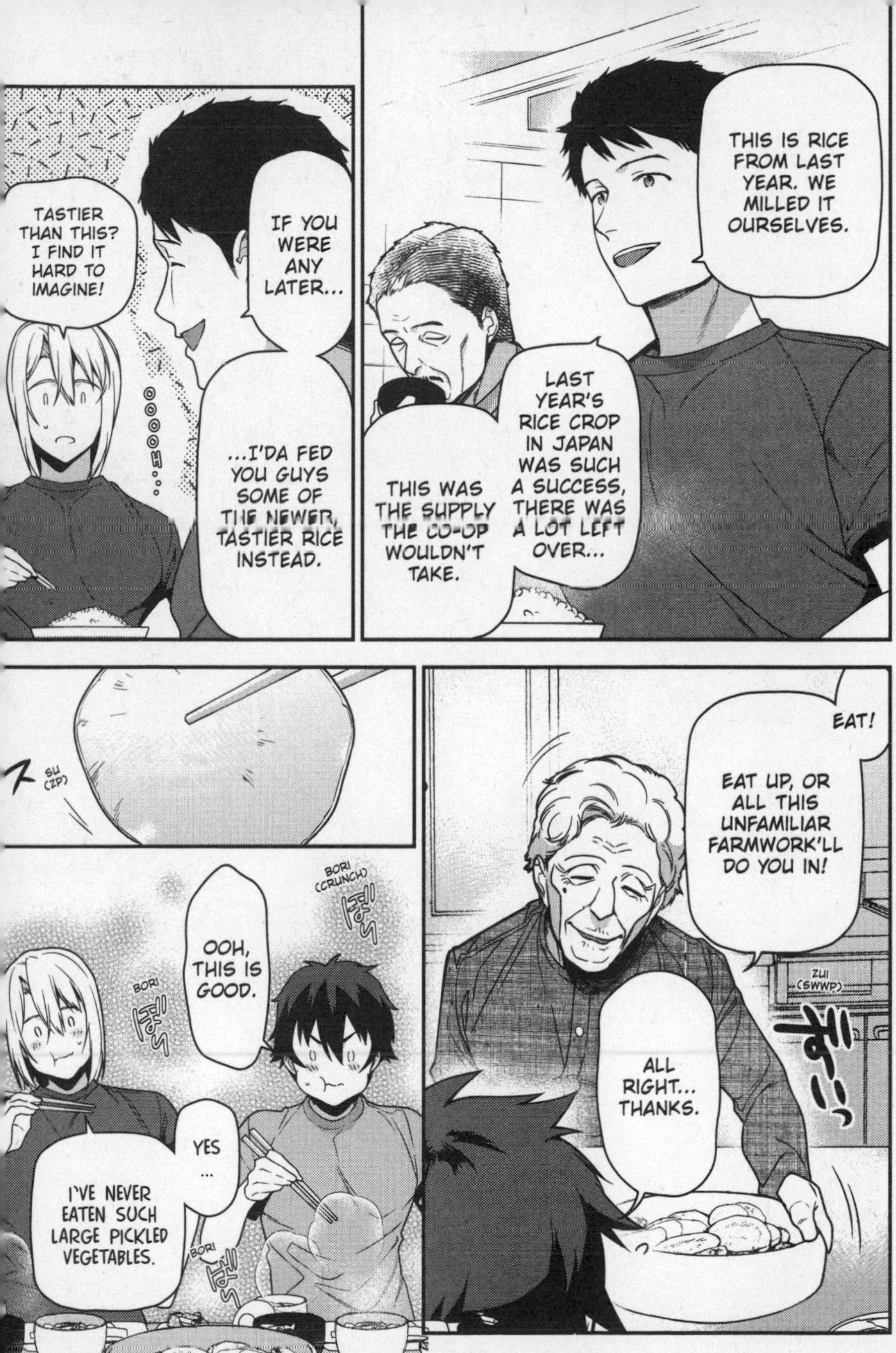
THIS IS RICE FROM LAST YEAR. WE MILLED IT OURSELVES.
LAST YEAR'S RICE CROP IN JAPAN WAS SUCH A SUCCESS, THERE WAS A LOT LEFT OVER...
THIS WAS THE SUPPLY THE CO-OP WOULDN'T TAKE.
IF YOU WERE ANY LATER...
...I'DA FED YOU GUYS SOME OF THE NEWER, TASTIER RICE INSTEAD.
TASTIER THAN THIS? I FIND IT HARD TO IMAGINE!
OOOOH...
EAT!
EAT UP, OR ALL THIS UNFAMILIAR FARMWORK'LL DO YOU IN!
ZUI (SWWP)
ALL RIGHT... THANKS.
SU (ZP)
BORI (CRUNCH)
OOH, THIS IS GOOD.
BORI
YES ...
I'VE NEVER EATEN SUCH LARGE PICKLED VEGETABLES.
BORI

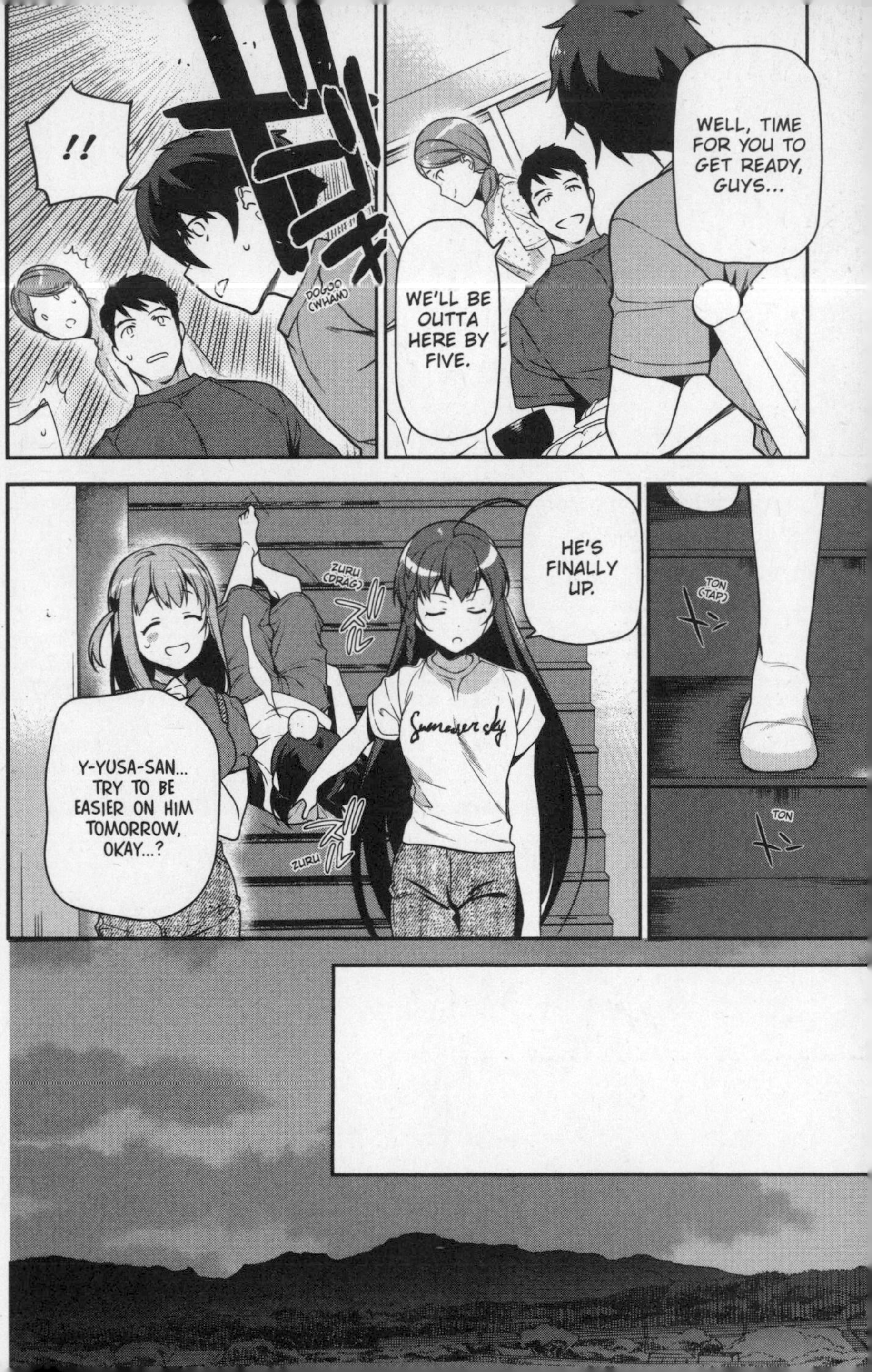
WELL, TIME FOR YOU TO GET READY, GUYS...
WE'LL BE OUTTA HERE BY FIVE.
DOGOO (WHAM)
!!
TON (TAP)
TON
HE'S FINALLY UP.
ZURU (DRAG)
Y-YUSA-SAN... TRY TO BE EASIER ON HIM TOMORROW, OKAY...?
ZURU

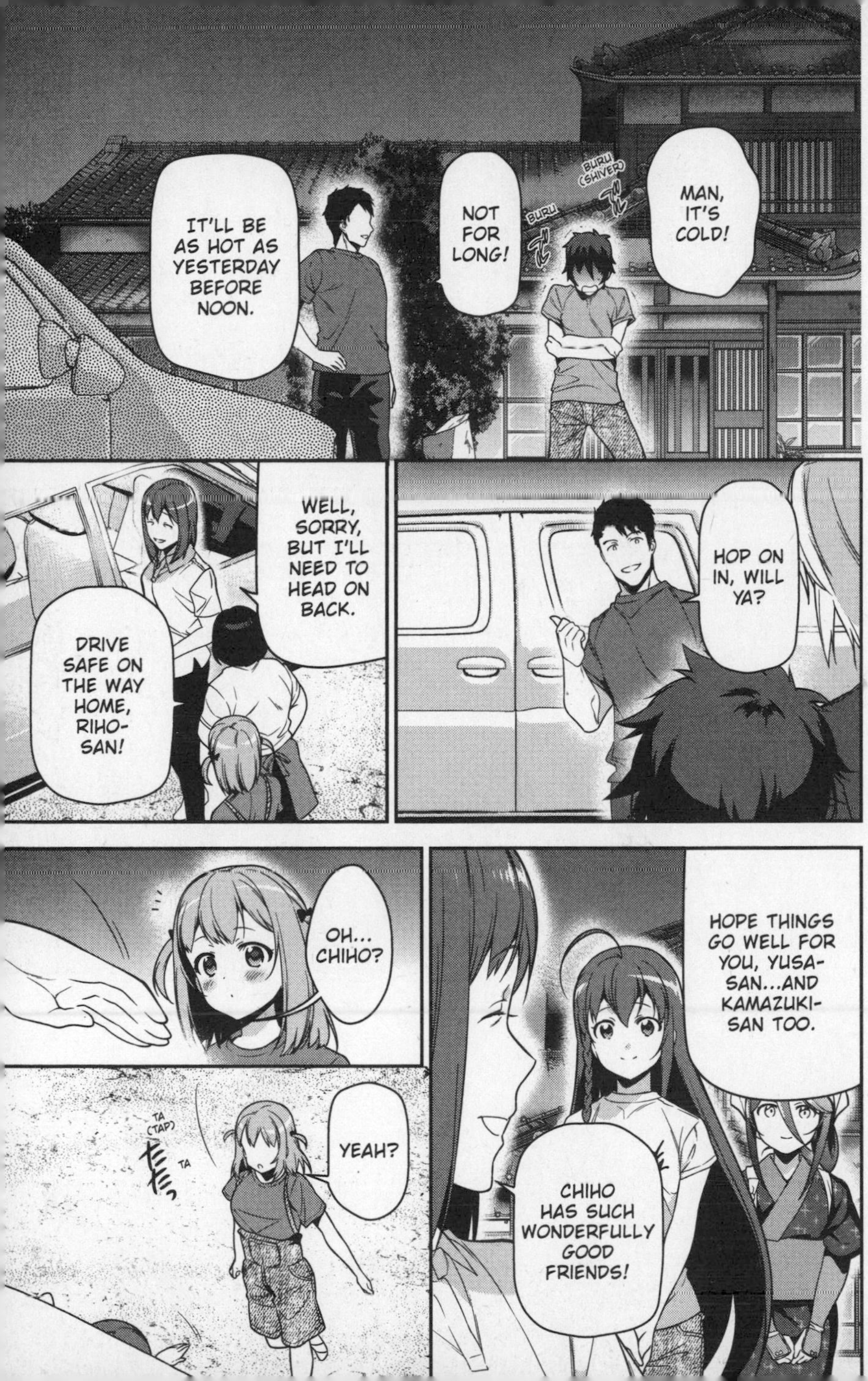
MAN, IT'S COLD!
BURU (SHIVER)
BURU
NOT FOR LONG!
IT'LL BE AS HOT AS YESTERDAY BEFORE NOON.
HOP ON IN, WILL YA?
WELL, SORRY, BUT I'LL NEED TO HEAD ON BACK.
DRIVE SAFE ON THE WAY HOME, RIHO-SAN!
HOPE THINGS GO WELL FOR YOU, YUSA-SAN...AND KAMAZUKI-SAN TOO.
OH... CHIHO?
TA (TAP)
TA
YEAH?
CHIHO HAS SUCH WONDERFULLY GOOD FRIENDS!

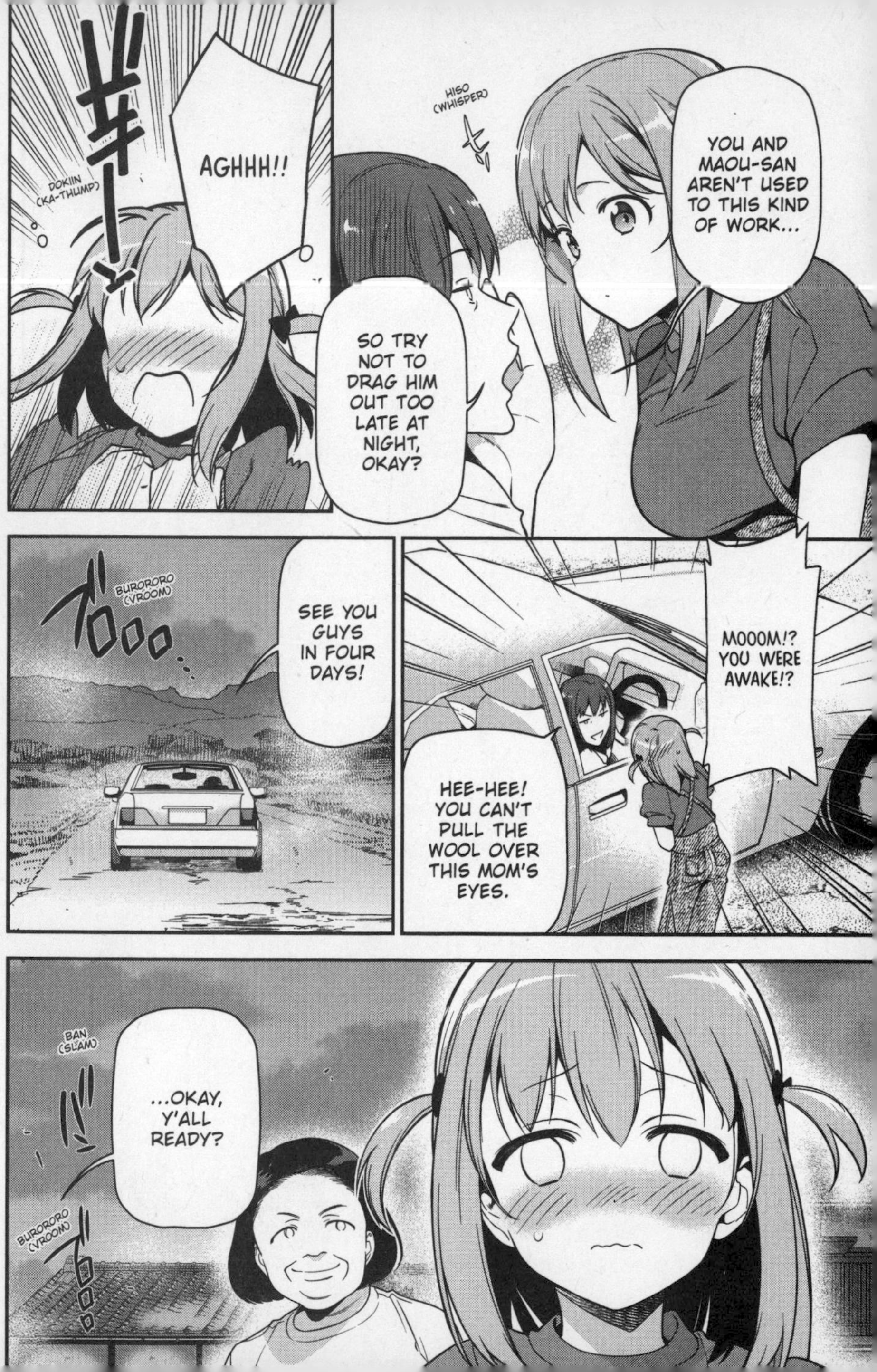
HISO (WHISPER)
YOU AND MAOU-SAN AREN'T USED TO THIS KIND OF WORK...
SO TRY NOT TO DRAG HIM OUT TOO LATE AT NIGHT, OKAY?
AGHHH!!
DOKIIN (KA-THUMP)
MOOOM!? YOU WERE AWAKE!?
HEE-HEE! YOU CAN'T PULL THE WOOL OVER THIS MOM'S EYES.
SEE YOU GUYS IN FOUR DAYS!
BURORORO (VROOM)
BAN (SLAM)
...OKAY, Y'ALL READY?
BURORORO (VROOM)

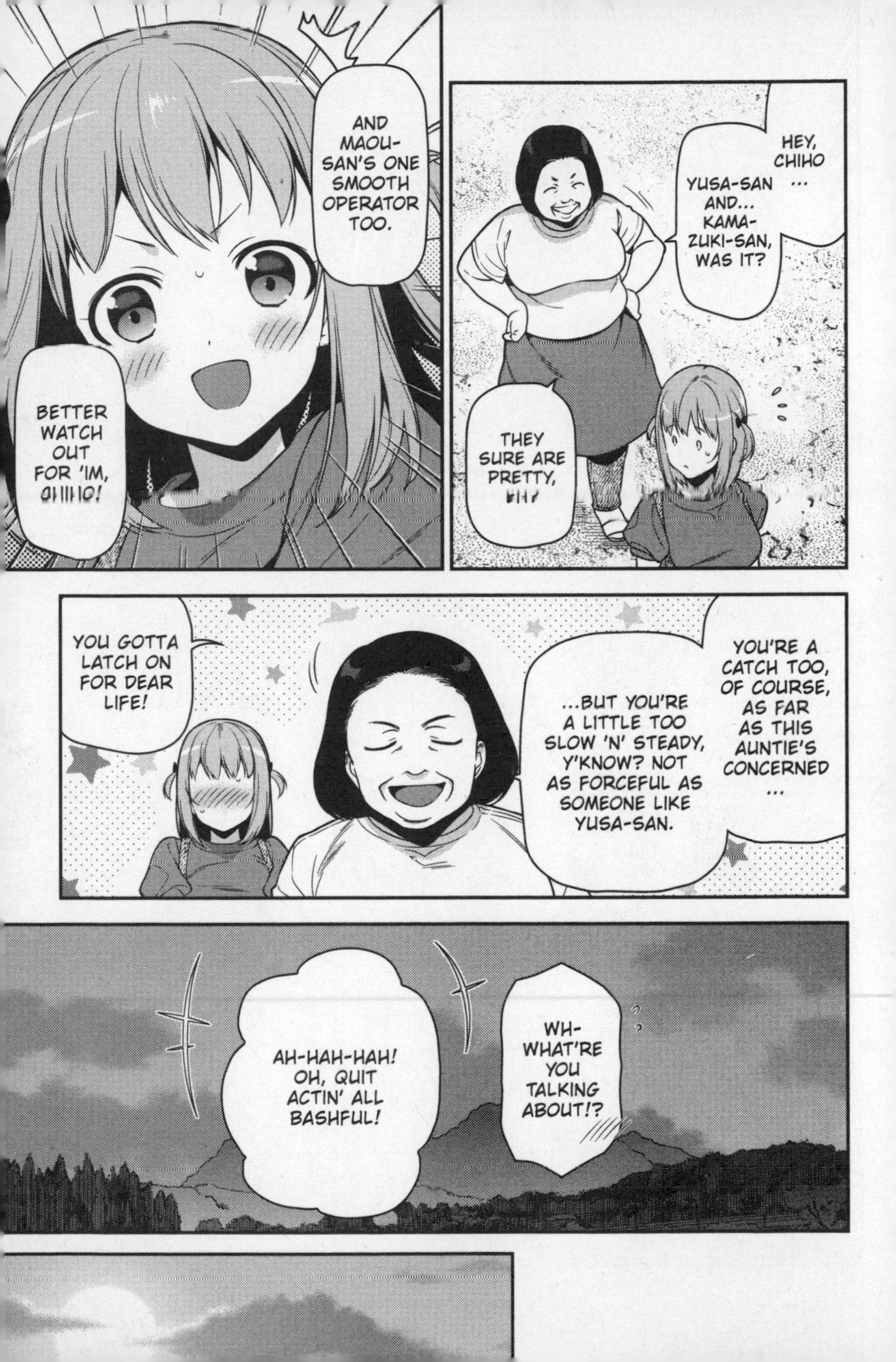
HEY, CHIHO ... YUSA-SAN AND... KAMA-ZUKI-SAN, WAS IT?
THEY SURE ARE PRETTY,
AND MAOU-SAN'S ONE SMOOTH OPERATOR TOO.
BETTER WATCH OUT FOR 'IM,
YOU'RE A CATCH TOO, OF COURSE, AS FAR AS THIS AUNTIE'S CONCERNED ...
...BUT YOU'RE A LITTLE TOO SLOW 'N' STEADY, Y'KNOW? NOT AS FORCEFUL AS SOMEONE LIKE YUSA-SAN.
YOU GOTTA LATCH ON FOR DEAR LIFE!
WH-WHAT'RE YOU TALKING ABOUT!?
AH-HAH-HAH! OH, QUIT ACTIN' ALL BASHFUL!

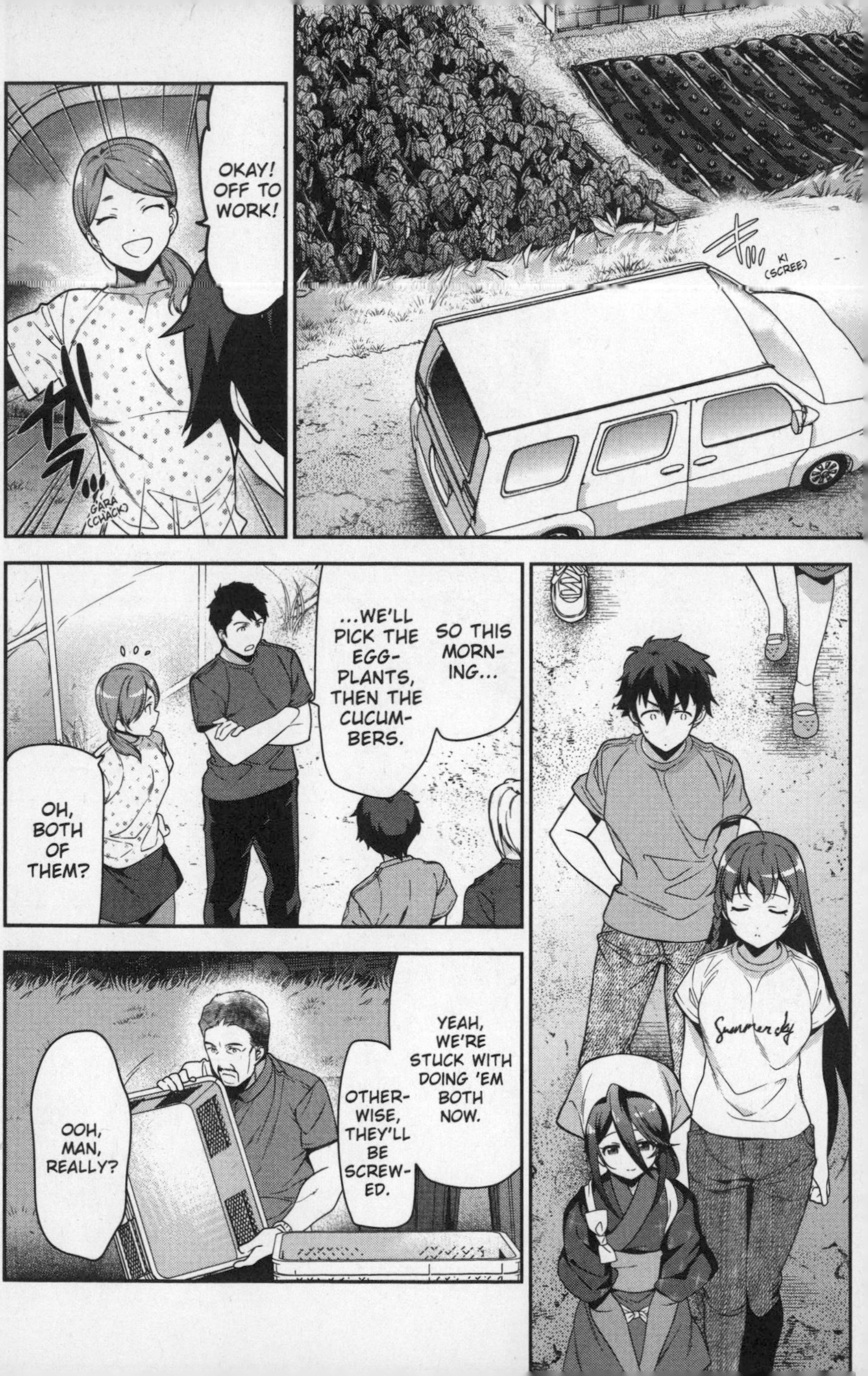
KI (SCREE)
OKAY! OFF TO WORK!
GARA (CHACK)
Summer sky
SO THIS MORNING...
...WE'LL PICK THE EGGPLANTS, THEN THE CUCUMBERS.
OH, BOTH OF THEM?
YEAH, WE'RE STUCK WITH DOING 'EM BOTH NOW.
OTHERWISE, THEY'LL BE SCREWED.
OOH, MAN, REALLY?

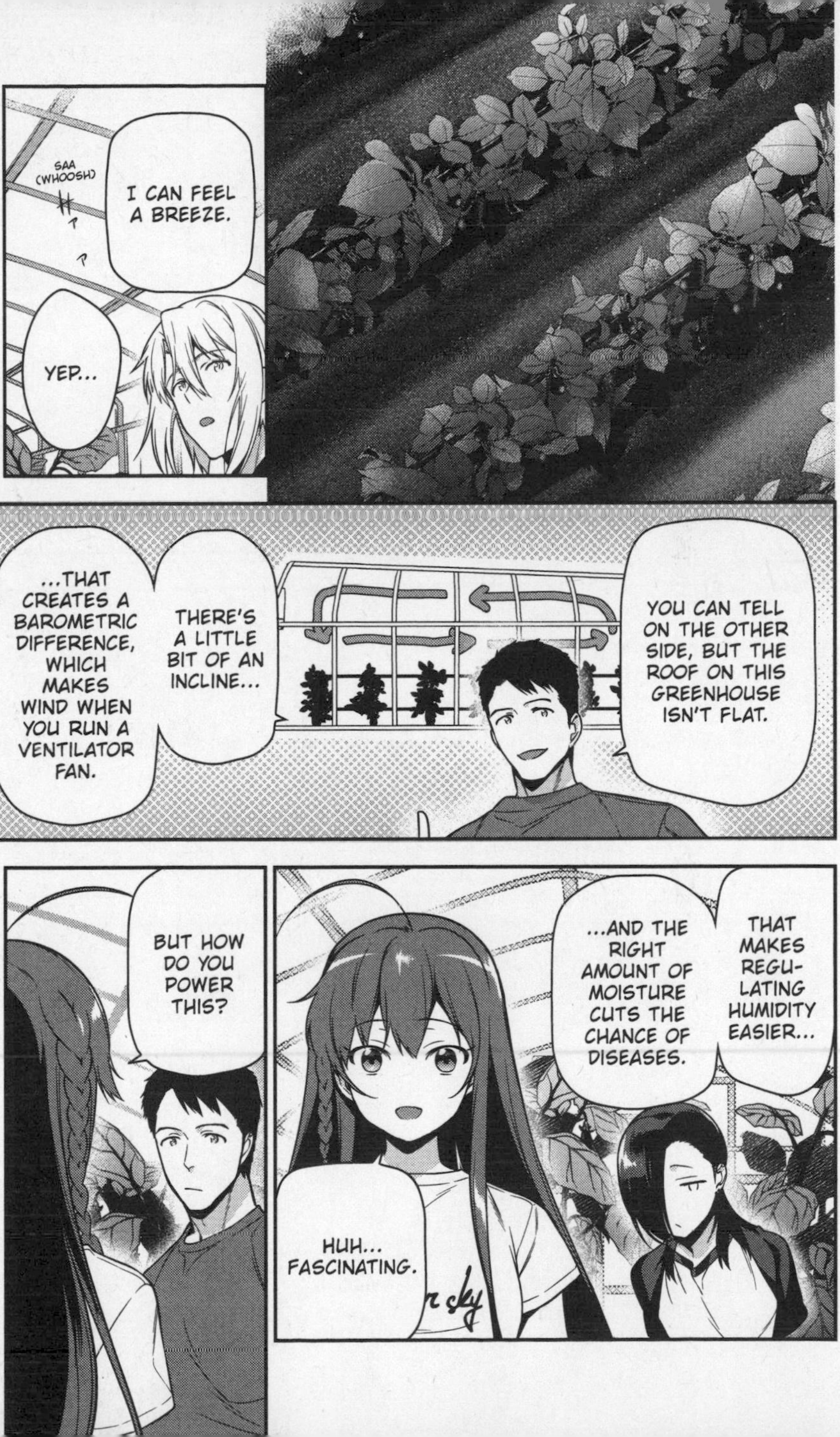
SAA (WHOOSH)
I CAN FEEL A BREEZE.
YEP...
YOU CAN TELL ON THE OTHER SIDE, BUT THE ROOF ON THIS GREENHOUSE ISN'T FLAT.
THERE'S A LITTLE BIT OF AN INCLINE...
...THAT CREATES A BAROMETRIC DIFFERENCE, WHICH MAKES WIND WHEN YOU RUN A VENTILATOR FAN.
THAT MAKES REGU-LATING HUMIDITY EASIER...
...AND THE RIGHT AMOUNT OF MOISTURE CUTS THE CHANCE OF DISEASES.
HUH... FASCINATING.
BUT HOW DO YOU POWER THIS?

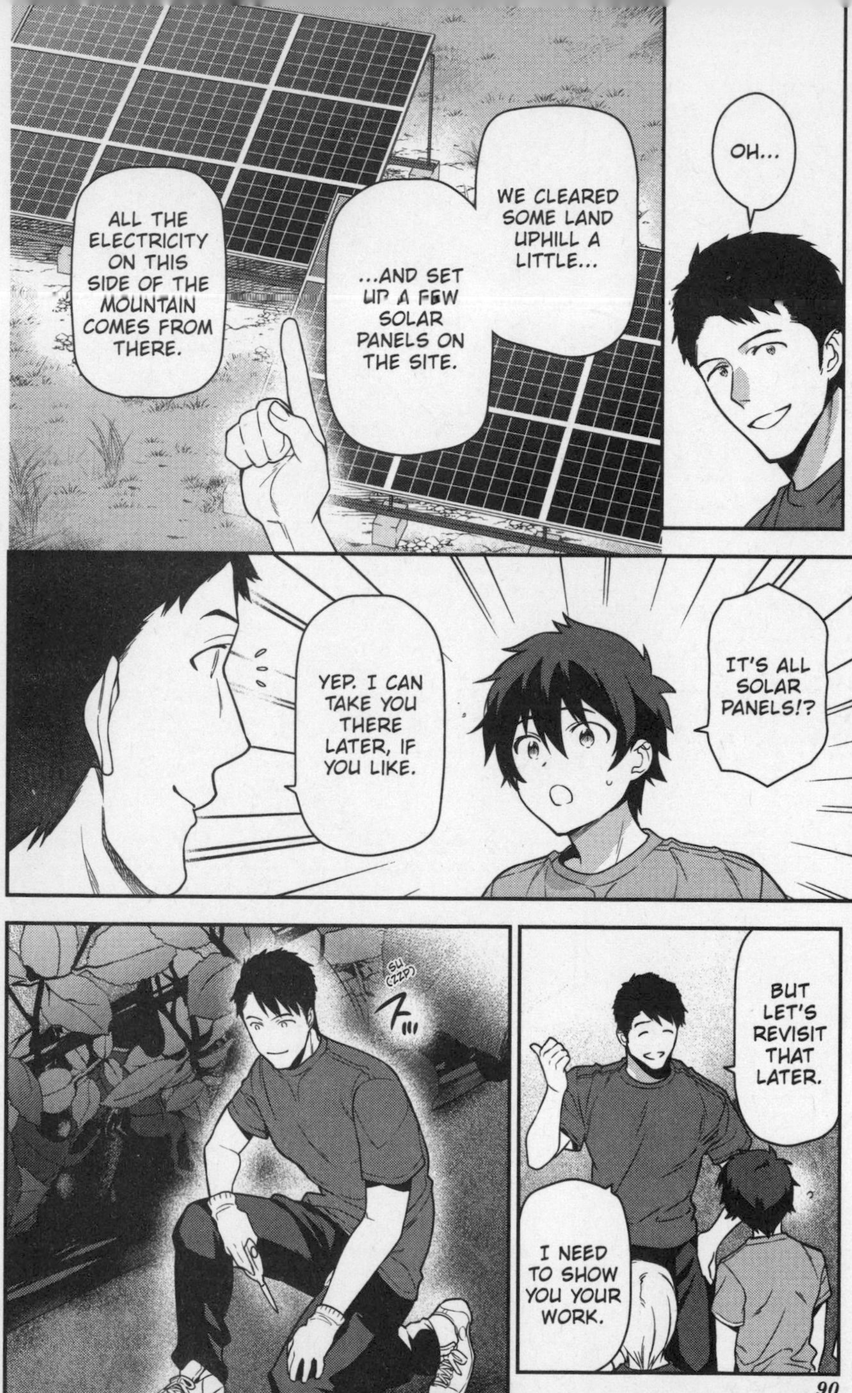
OH...
WE CLEARED SOME LAND UPHILL A LITTLE...
...AND SET UP A FEW SOLAR PANELS ON THE SITE.
ALL THE ELECTRICITY ON THIS SIDE OF THE MOUNTAIN COMES FROM THERE.
IT'S ALL SOLAR PANELS!?
YEP. I CAN TAKE YOU THERE LATER, IF YOU LIKE.
BUT LET'S REVISIT THAT LATER.
I NEED TO SHOW YOU YOUR WORK.
SU (ZZZP)
ス

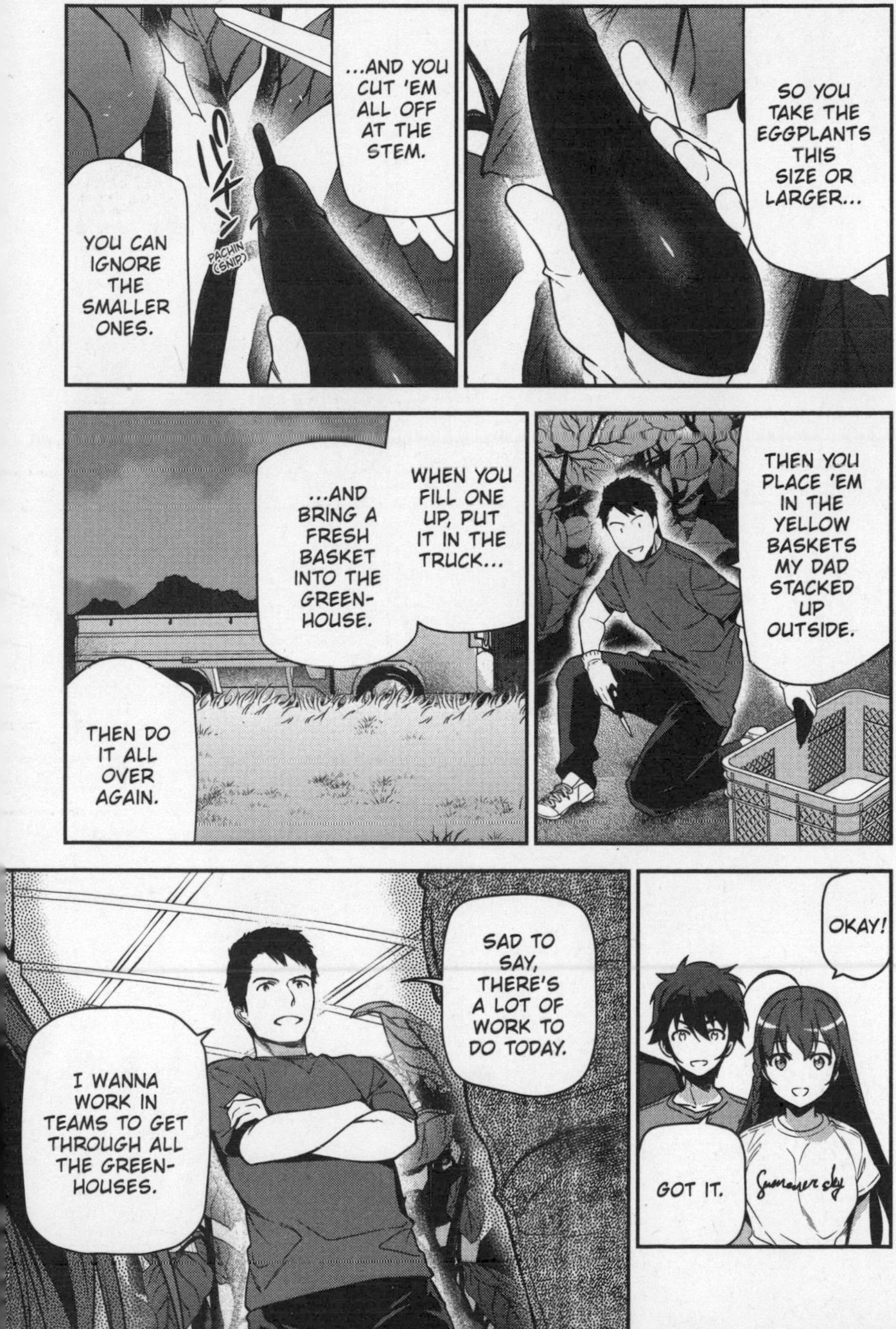
SO YOU TAKE THE EGGPLANTS THIS SIZE OR LARGER...
...AND YOU CUT 'EM ALL OFF AT THE STEM.
PACHIN (SNIP)
YOU CAN IGNORE THE SMALLER ONES.
THEN YOU PLACE 'EM IN THE YELLOW BASKETS MY DAD STACKED UP OUTSIDE.
WHEN YOU FILL ONE UP, PUT IT IN THE TRUCK...
...AND BRING A FRESH BASKET INTO THE GREEN-HOUSE.
THEN DO IT ALL OVER AGAIN.
OKAY!
GOT IT.
SAD TO SAY, THERE'S A LOT OF WORK TO DO TODAY.
I WANNA WORK IN TEAMS TO GET THROUGH ALL THE GREEN-HOUSES.

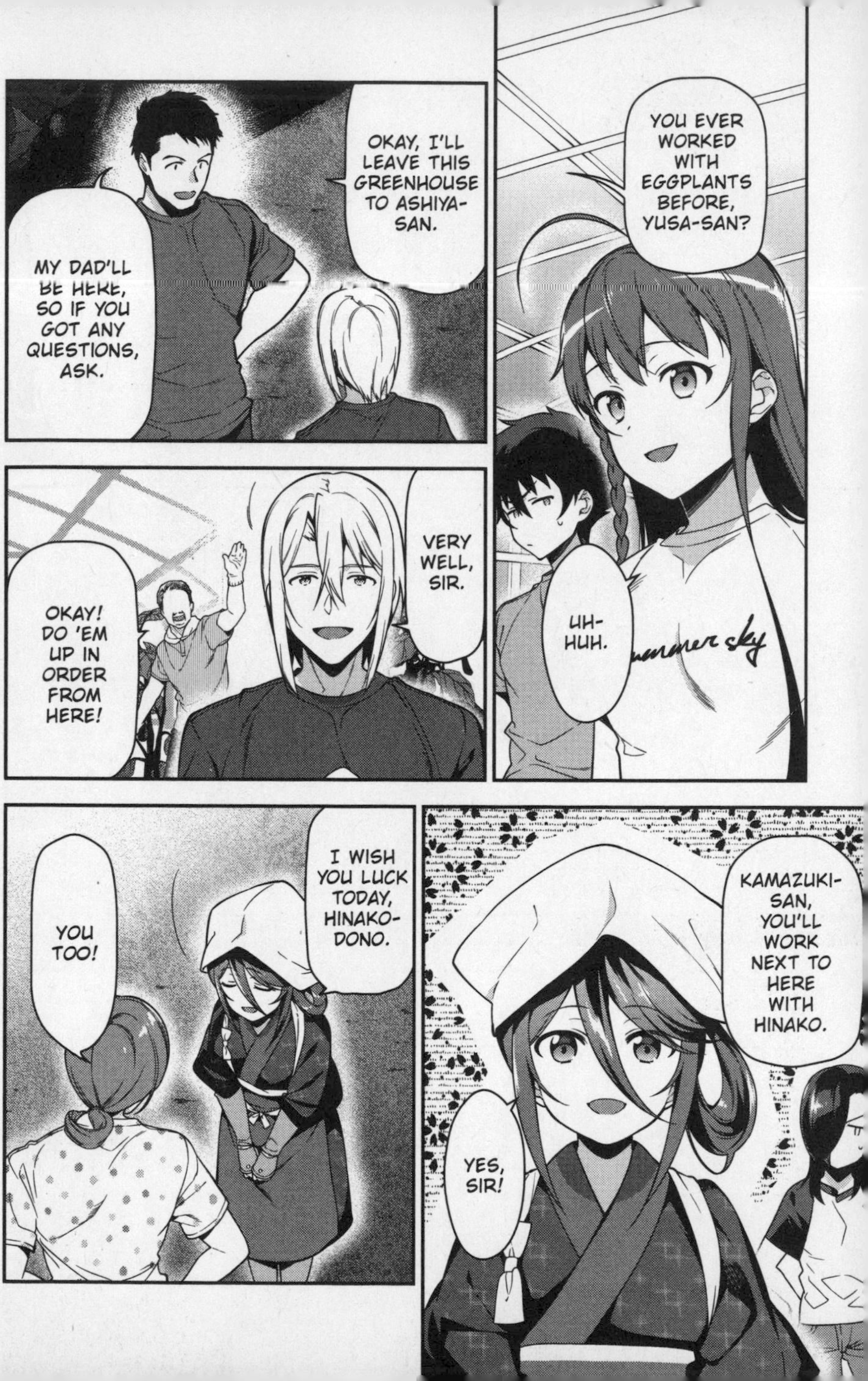
YOU EVER WORKED WITH EGGPLANTS BEFORE, YUSA-SAN?
UH-HUH.
OKAY, I'LL LEAVE THIS GREENHOUSE TO ASHIYA-SAN.
MY DAD'LL BE HERE, SO IF YOU GOT ANY QUESTIONS, ASK.
VERY WELL, SIR.
OKAY! DO 'EM UP IN ORDER FROM HERE!
KAMAZUKI-SAN, YOU'LL WORK NEXT TO HERE WITH HINAKO.
YES, SIR!
I WISH YOU LUCK TODAY, HINAKO-DONO.
YOU TOO!

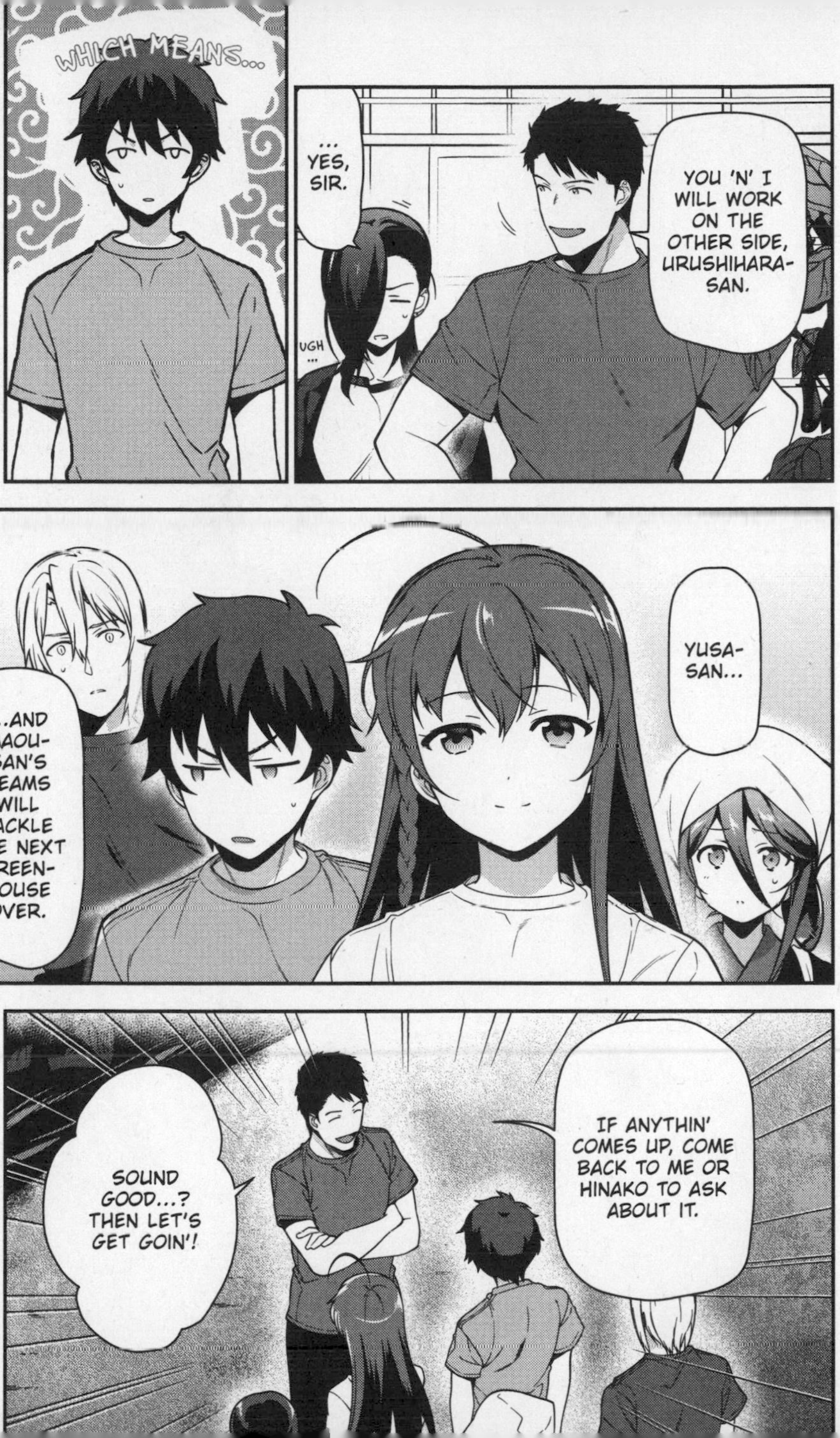
YOU 'N' I WILL WORK ON THE OTHER SIDE, URUSHIHARA-SAN.
...YES, SIR.
UGH...
WHICH MEANS...
YUSA-SAN...
...AND MAOU-SAN'S TEAMS WILL TACKLE THE NEXT GREENHOUSE OVER.
IF ANYTHIN' COMES UP, COME BACK TO ME OR HINAKO TO ASK ABOUT IT.
SOUND GOOD...? THEN LET'S GET GOIN'!

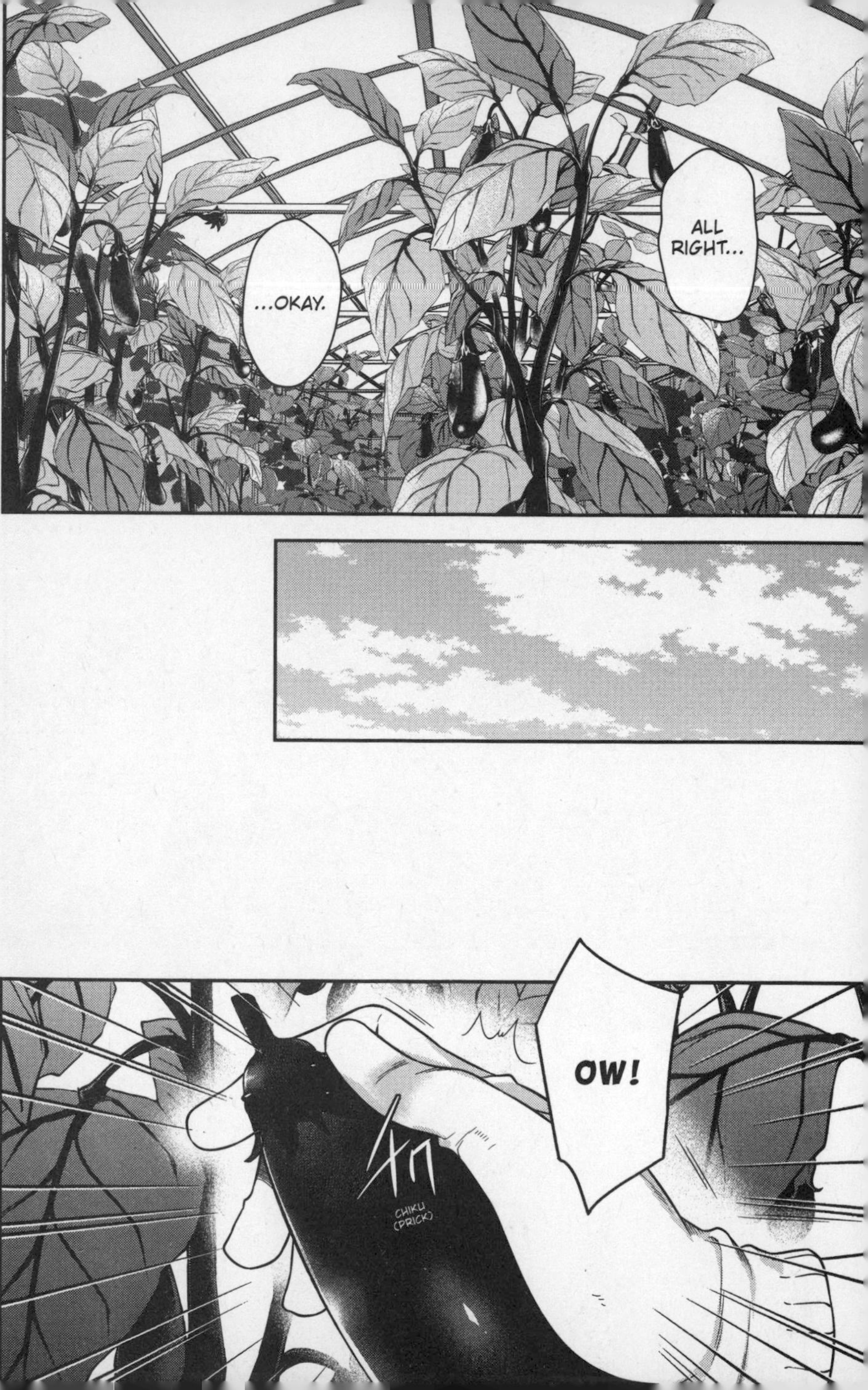
ALL RIGHT...
...OKAY.
OW!
CHIKU (PRICK)

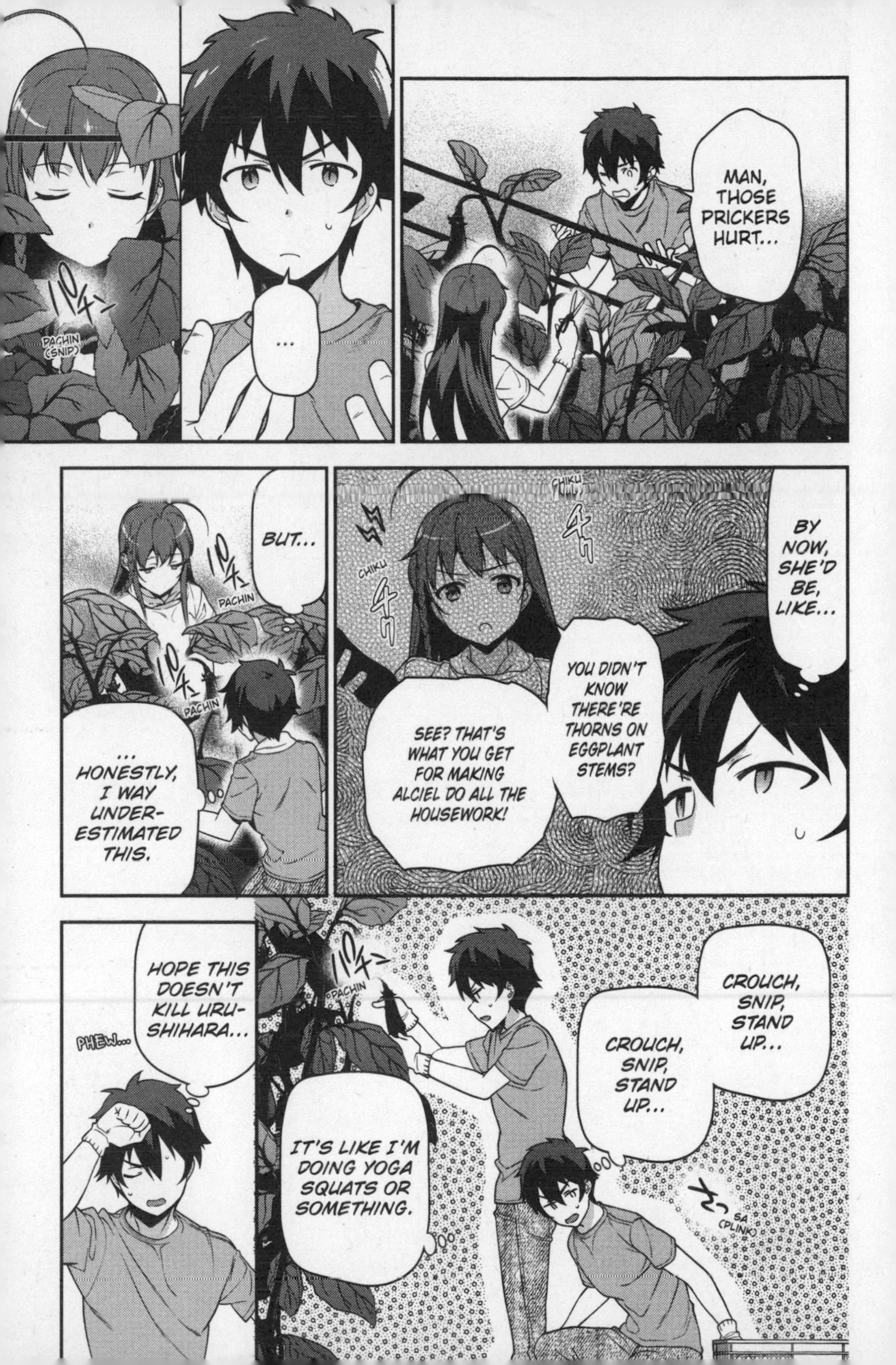
MAN, THOSE PRICKERS HURT...
...
PACHIN (SNIP)
BY NOW, SHE'D BE, LIKE...
CHIKU
CHIKU
YOU DIDN'T KNOW THERE'RE THORNS ON EGGPLANT STEMS?
SEE? THAT'S WHAT YOU GET FOR MAKING ALCIEL DO ALL THE HOUSEWORK!
BUT...
PACHIN
PACHIN
...HONESTLY, I WAY UNDER-ESTIMATED THIS.
CROUCH, SNIP, STAND UP...
CROUCH, SNIP, STAND UP...
PACHIN
IT'S LIKE I'M DOING YOGA SQUATS OR SOMETHING.
SA (PLINK)
HOPE THIS DOESN'T KILL URU-SHIHARA...
PHEW...

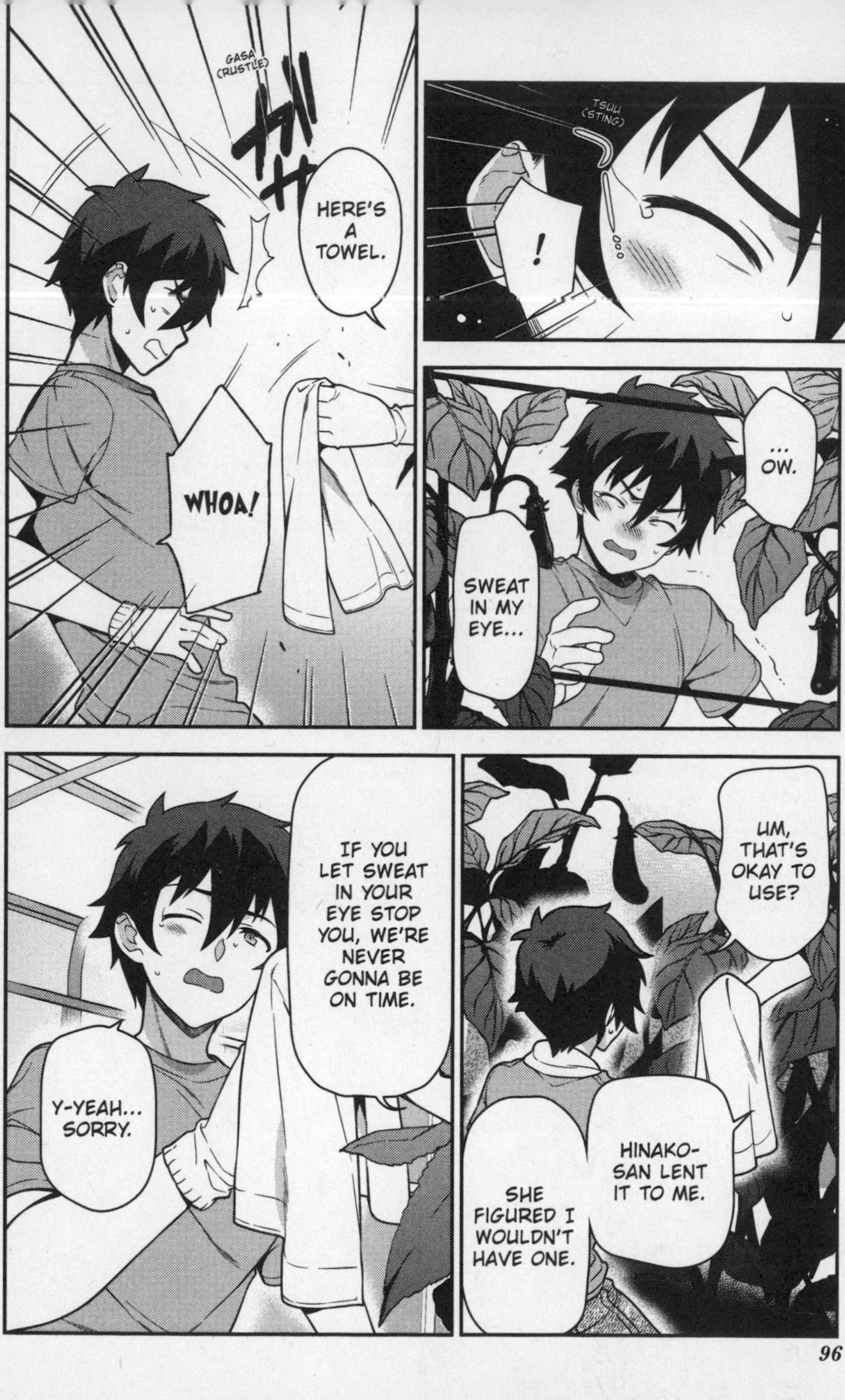

TSUU (STING)
!
... OW.
SWEAT IN MY EYE...
GASA (RUSTLE)
HERE'S A TOWEL.
WHOA!
UM, THAT'S OKAY TO USE?
HINAKO-SAN LENT IT TO ME.
SHE FIGURED I WOULDN'T HAVE ONE.
IF YOU LET SWEAT IN YOUR EYE STOP YOU, WE'RE NEVER GONNA BE ON TIME.
Y-YEAH... SORRY.

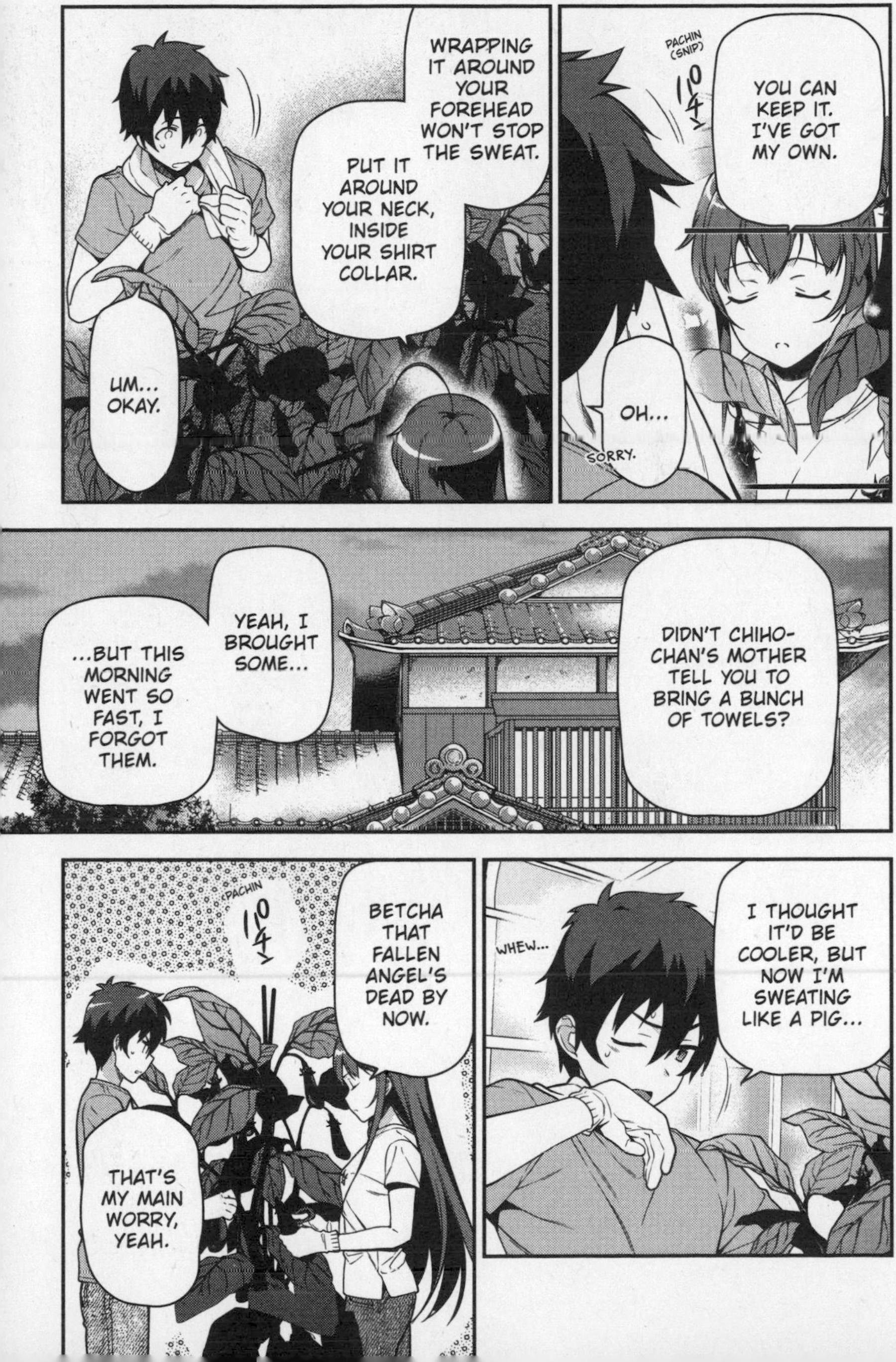
PACHIN (SNIP)
YOU CAN KEEP IT. I'VE GOT MY OWN.
OH...
SORRY.
WRAPPING IT AROUND YOUR FOREHEAD WON'T STOP THE SWEAT.
PUT IT AROUND YOUR NECK, INSIDE YOUR SHIRT COLLAR.
UM... OKAY.
DIDN'T CHIHO-CHAN'S MOTHER TELL YOU TO BRING A BUNCH OF TOWELS?
YEAH, I BROUGHT SOME...
...BUT THIS MORNING WENT SO FAST, I FORGOT THEM.
I THOUGHT IT'D BE COOLER, BUT NOW I'M SWEATING LIKE A PIG...
WHEW...
BETCHA THAT FALLEN ANGEL'S DEAD BY NOW.
PACHIN
THAT'S MY MAIN WORRY, YEAH.

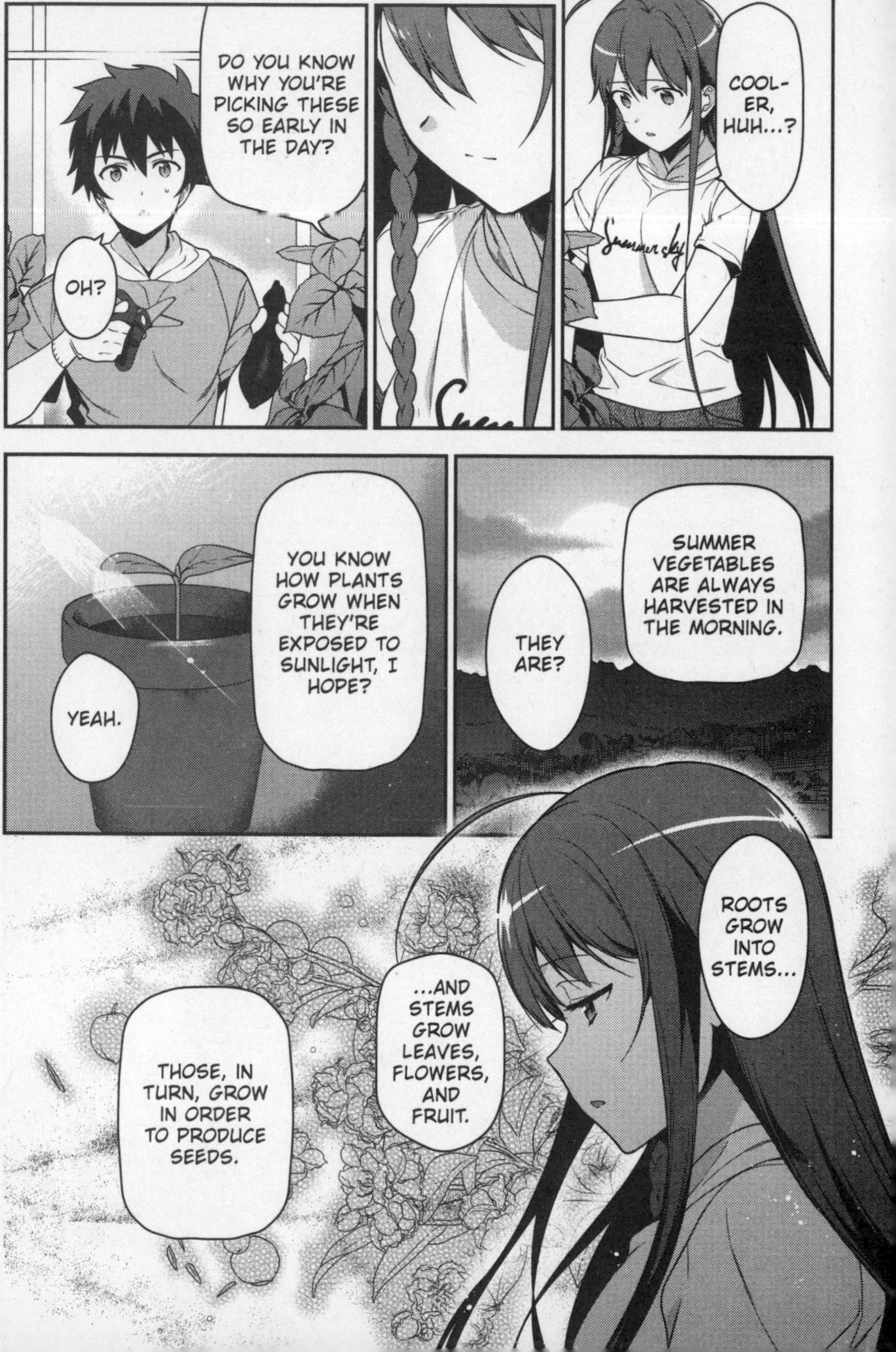
COOL-ER, HUH...?
DO YOU KNOW WHY YOU'RE PICKING THESE SO EARLY IN THE DAY?
OH?
SUMMER VEGETABLES ARE ALWAYS HARVESTED IN THE MORNING.
THEY ARE?
YOU KNOW HOW PLANTS GROW WHEN THEY'RE EXPOSED TO SUNLIGHT, I HOPE?
YEAH.
ROOTS GROW INTO STEMS...
...AND STEMS GROW LEAVES, FLOWERS, AND FRUIT.
THOSE, IN TURN, GROW IN ORDER TO PRODUCE SEEDS.

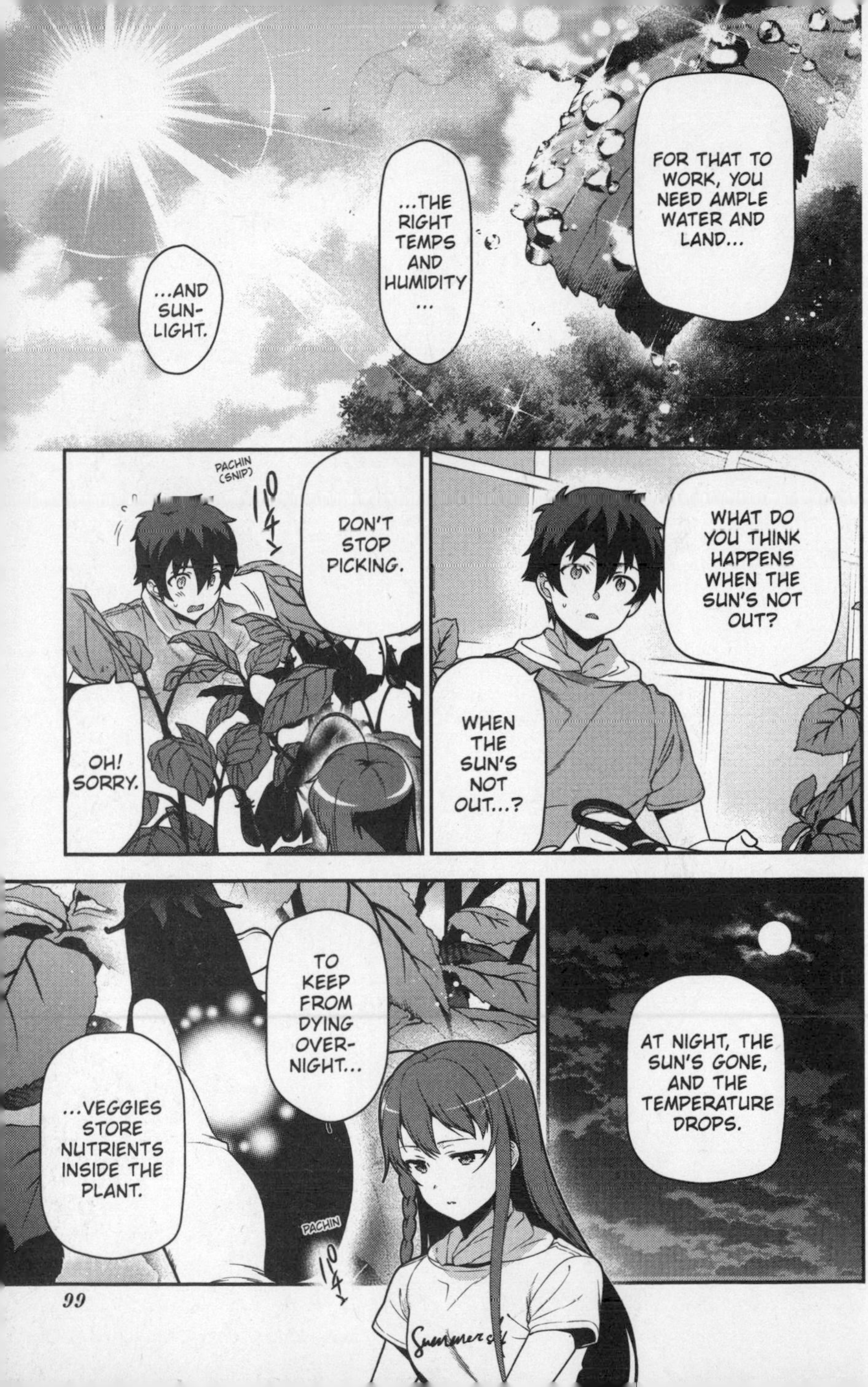
FOR THAT TO WORK, YOU NEED AMPLE WATER AND LAND...
...THE RIGHT TEMPS AND HUMIDITY...
...AND SUN-LIGHT.
WHAT DO YOU THINK HAPPENS WHEN THE SUN'S NOT OUT?
WHEN THE SUN'S NOT OUT...?
PACHIN (SNIP)
DON'T STOP PICKING.
OH! SORRY.
AT NIGHT, THE SUN'S GONE, AND THE TEMPERATURE DROPS.
TO KEEP FROM DYING OVER-NIGHT...
...VEGGIES STORE NUTRIENTS INSIDE THE PLANT.
PACHIN

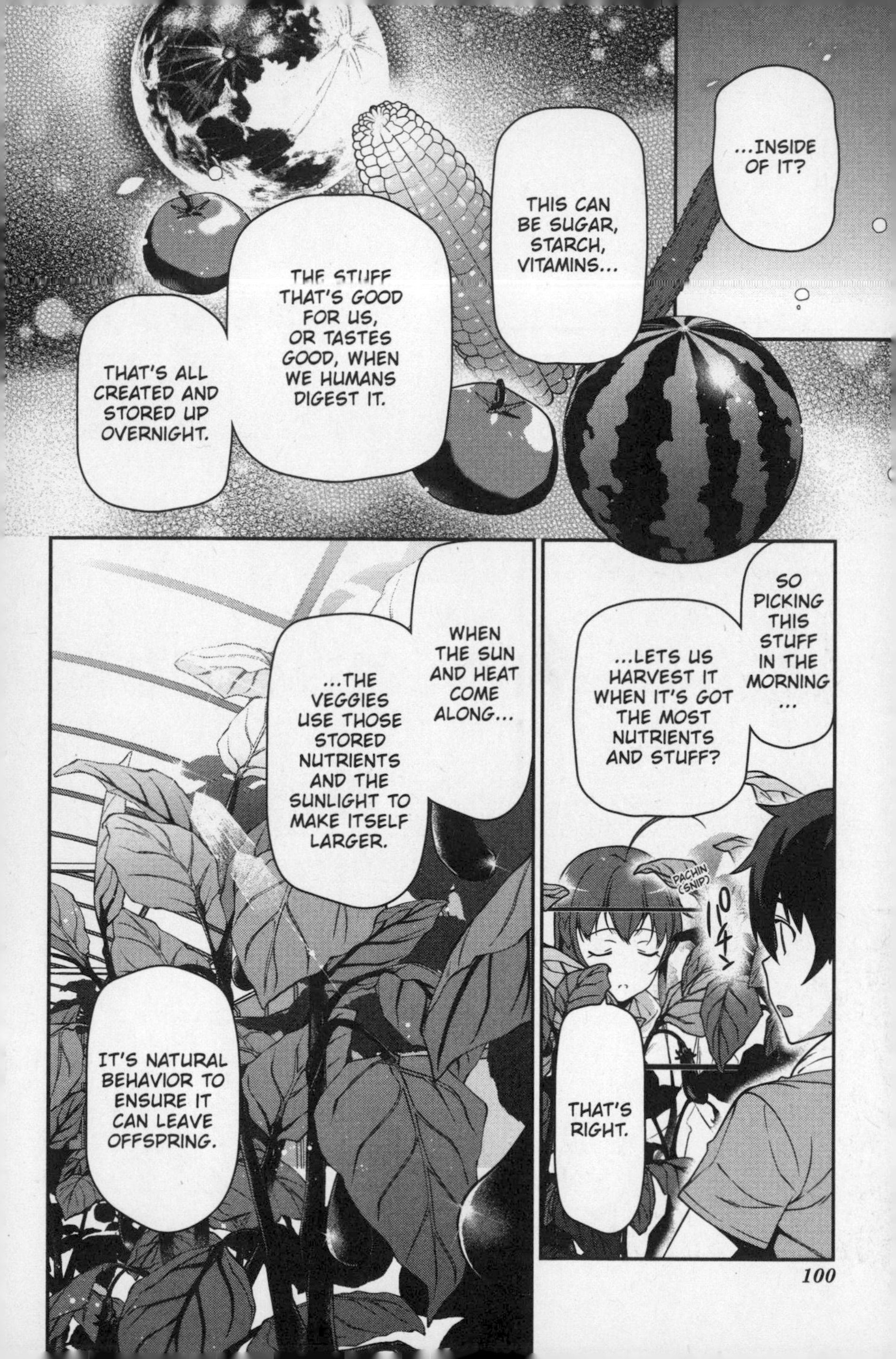

...INSIDE OF IT?
THIS CAN BE SUGAR, STARCH, VITAMINS...
THE STUFF THAT'S GOOD FOR US, OR TASTES GOOD, WHEN WE HUMANS DIGEST IT.
THAT'S ALL CREATED AND STORED UP OVERNIGHT.
SO PICKING THIS STUFF IN THE MORNING...
...LETS US HARVEST IT WHEN IT'S GOT THE MOST NUTRIENTS AND STUFF?
PACHIN (SNIP)
THAT'S RIGHT.
WHEN THE SUN AND HEAT COME ALONG...
...THE VEGGIES USE THOSE STORED NUTRIENTS AND THE SUNLIGHT TO MAKE ITSELF LARGER.
IT'S NATURAL BEHAVIOR TO ENSURE IT CAN LEAVE OFFSPRING.

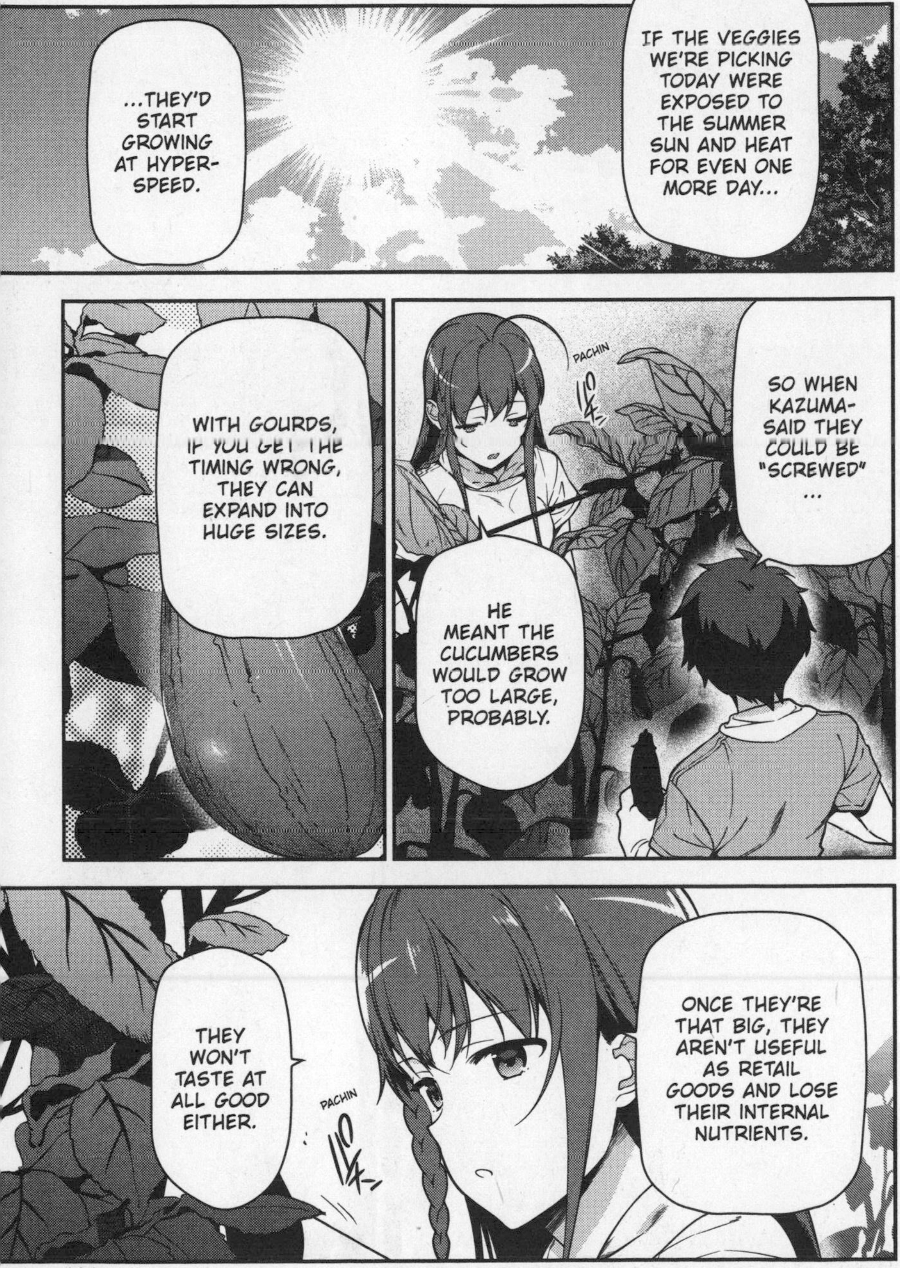
IF THE VEGGIES WE'RE PICKING TODAY WERE EXPOSED TO THE SUMMER SUN AND HEAT FOR EVEN ONE MORE DAY...
...THEY'D START GROWING AT HYPER-SPEED.
SO WHEN KAZUMA- SAID THEY COULD BE "SCREWED" ...
PACHIN
HE MEANT THE CUCUMBERS WOULD GROW TOO LARGE, PROBABLY.
WITH GOURDS, IF YOU GET THE TIMING WRONG, THEY CAN EXPAND INTO HUGE SIZES.
ONCE THEY'RE THAT BIG, THEY AREN'T USEFUL AS RETAIL GOODS AND LOSE THEIR INTERNAL NUTRIENTS.
PACHIN
THEY WON'T TASTE AT ALL GOOD EITHER.

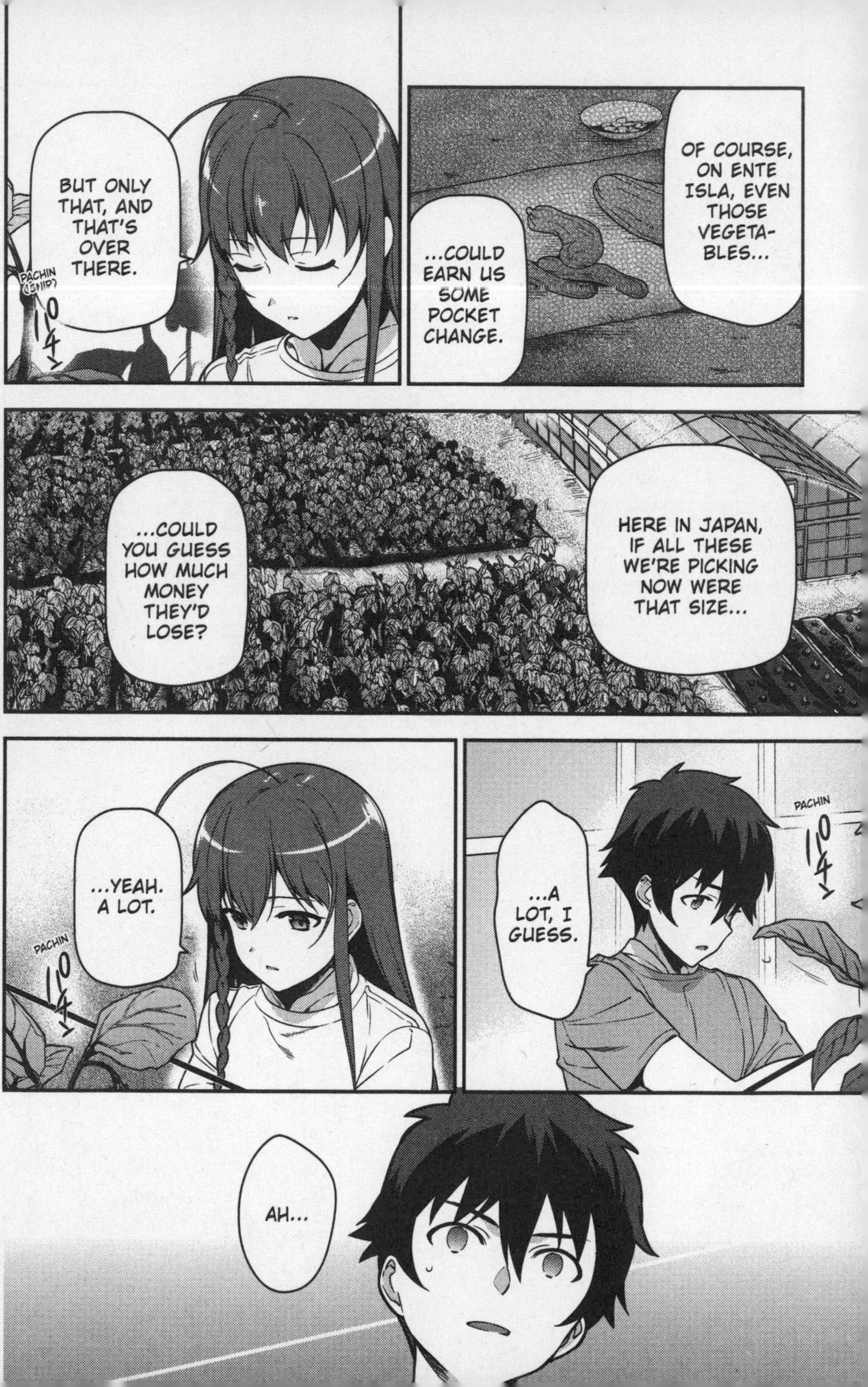
OF COURSE, ON ENTE ISLA, EVEN THOSE VEGETA-BLES...
...COULD EARN US SOME POCKET CHANGE.
BUT ONLY THAT, AND THAT'S OVER THERE.
PACHIN (SNIP)
HERE IN JAPAN, IF ALL THESE WE'RE PICKING NOW WERE THAT SIZE...
...COULD YOU GUESS HOW MUCH MONEY THEY'D LOSE?
PACHIN
...A LOT, I GUESS.
...YEAH. A LOT.
PACHIN
AH...

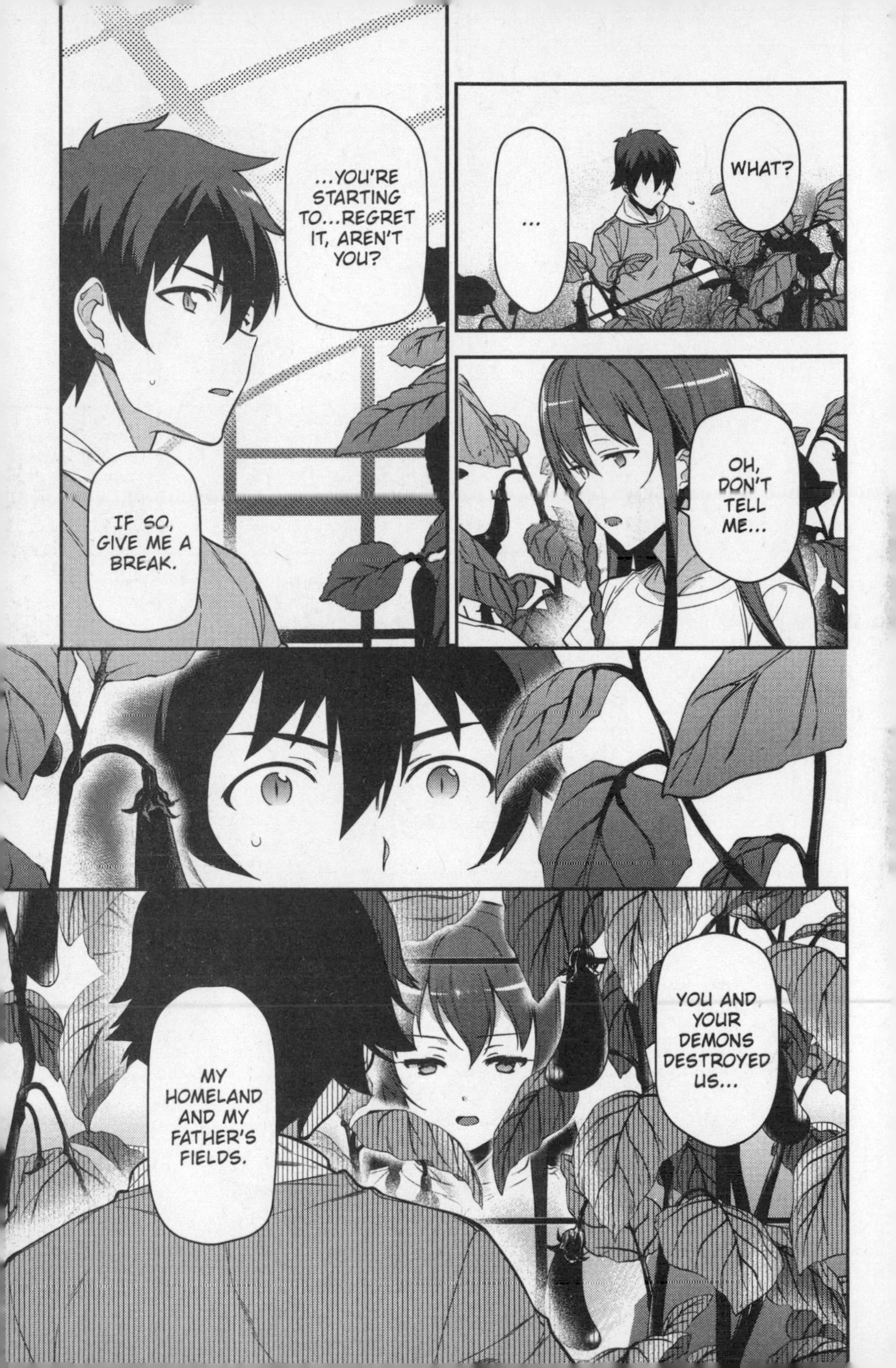
WHAT?
...
OH, DON'T TELL ME...
...YOU'RE STARTING TO...REGRET IT, AREN'T YOU?
IF SO, GIVE ME A BREAK.
YOU AND YOUR DEMONS DESTROYED US...
MY HOMELAND AND MY FATHER'S FIELDS.

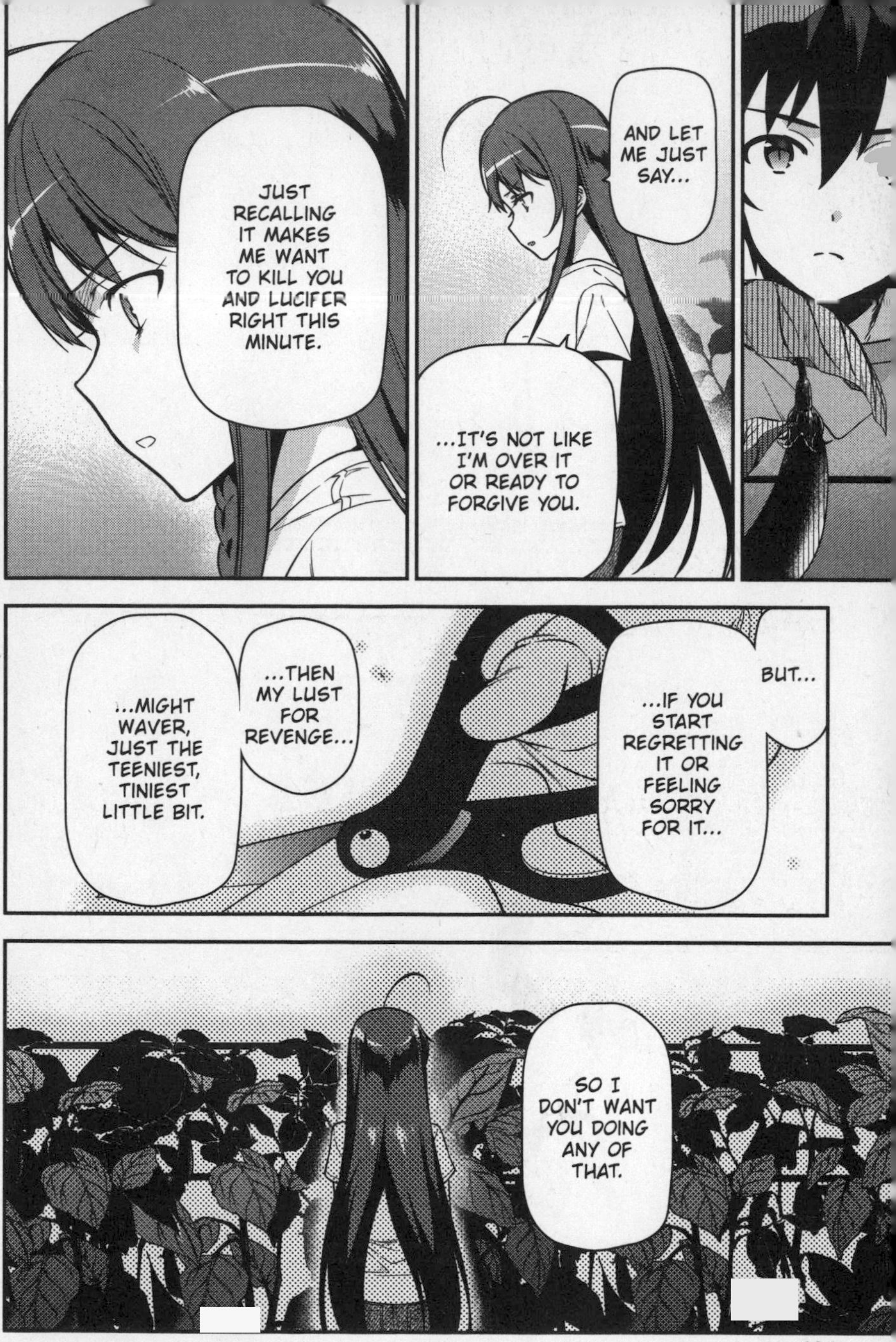
AND LET ME JUST SAY...
...IT'S NOT LIKE I'M OVER IT OR READY TO FORGIVE YOU.
JUST RECALLING IT MAKES ME WANT TO KILL YOU AND LUCIFER RIGHT THIS MINUTE.
BUT...
...IF YOU START REGRETTING IT OR FEELING SORRY FOR IT...
...THEN MY LUST FOR REVENGE...
...MIGHT WAVER, JUST THE TEENIEST, TINIEST LITTLE BIT.
SO I DON'T WANT YOU DOING ANY OF THAT.

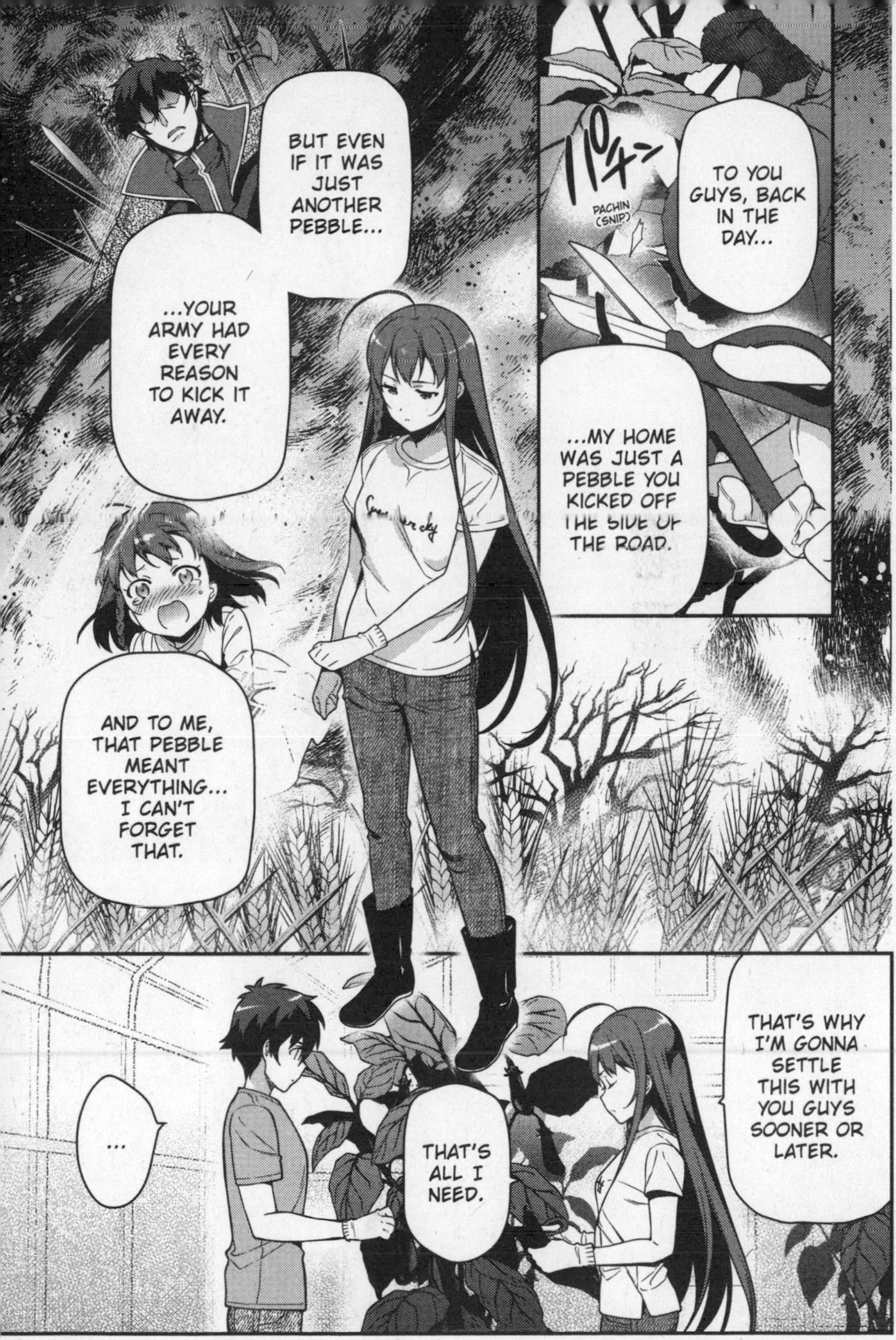
パチン
PACHIN (SNIP)
TO YOU GUYS, BACK IN THE DAY...
...MY HOME WAS JUST A PEBBLE YOU KICKED OFF THE SIDE OF THE ROAD.
BUT EVEN IF IT WAS JUST ANOTHER PEBBLE...
...YOUR ARMY HAD EVERY REASON TO KICK IT AWAY.
AND TO ME, THAT PEBBLE MEANT EVERYTHING... I CAN'T FORGET THAT.
THAT'S WHY I'M GONNA SETTLE THIS WITH YOU GUYS SOONER OR LATER.
THAT'S ALL I NEED.
...

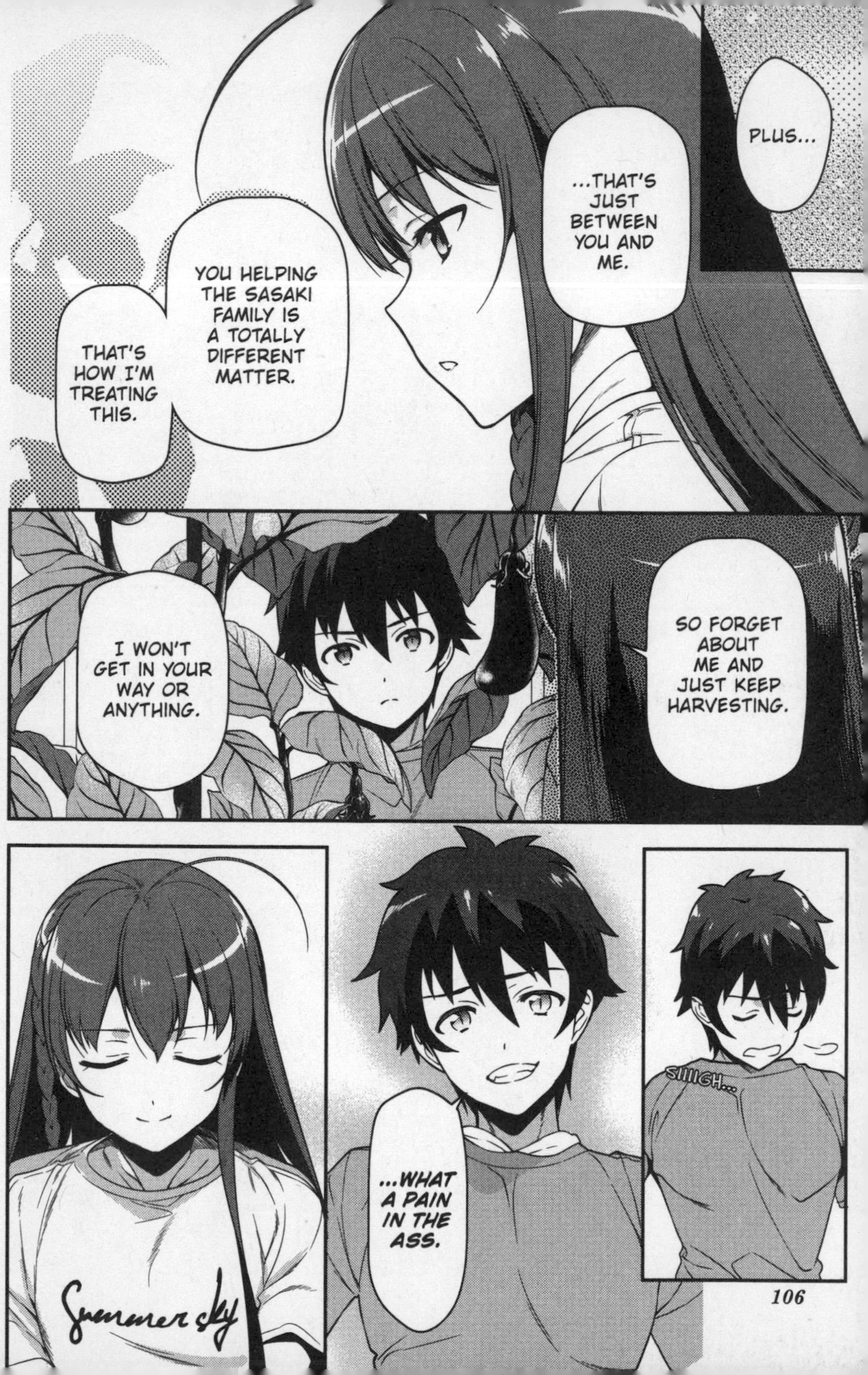
PLUS...
...THAT'S JUST BETWEEN YOU AND ME.
YOU HELPING THE SASAKI FAMILY IS A TOTALLY DIFFERENT MATTER.
THAT'S HOW I'M TREATING THIS.
SO FORGET ABOUT ME AND JUST KEEP HARVESTING.
I WON'T GET IN YOUR WAY OR ANYTHING.
SIIIGH...
...WHAT A PAIN IN THE ASS.
Summer sky

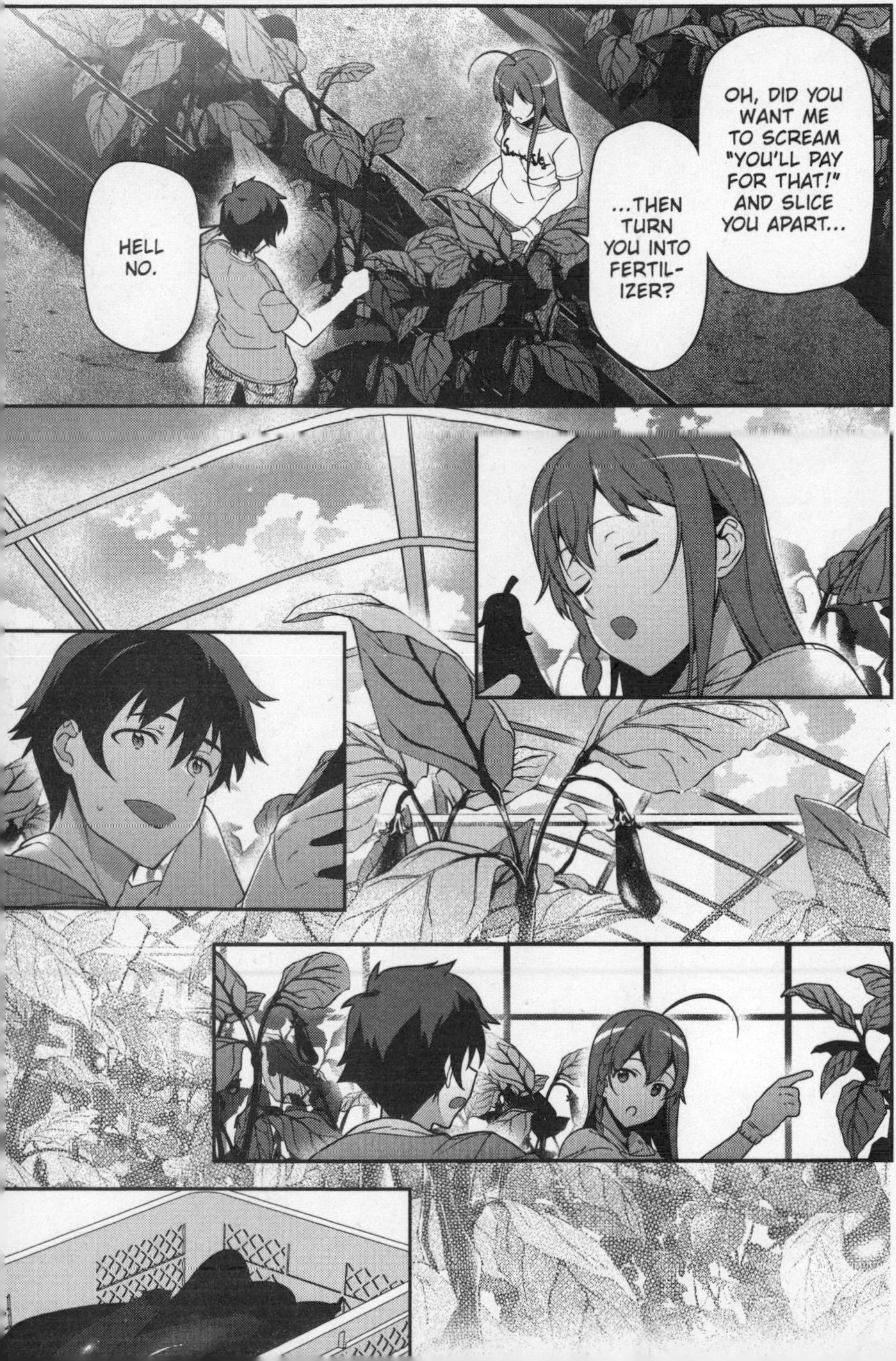
OH, DID YOU WANT ME TO SCREAM "YOU'LL PAY FOR THAT!" AND SLICE YOU APART...
...THEN TURN YOU INTO FERTIL-IZER?
HELL NO.

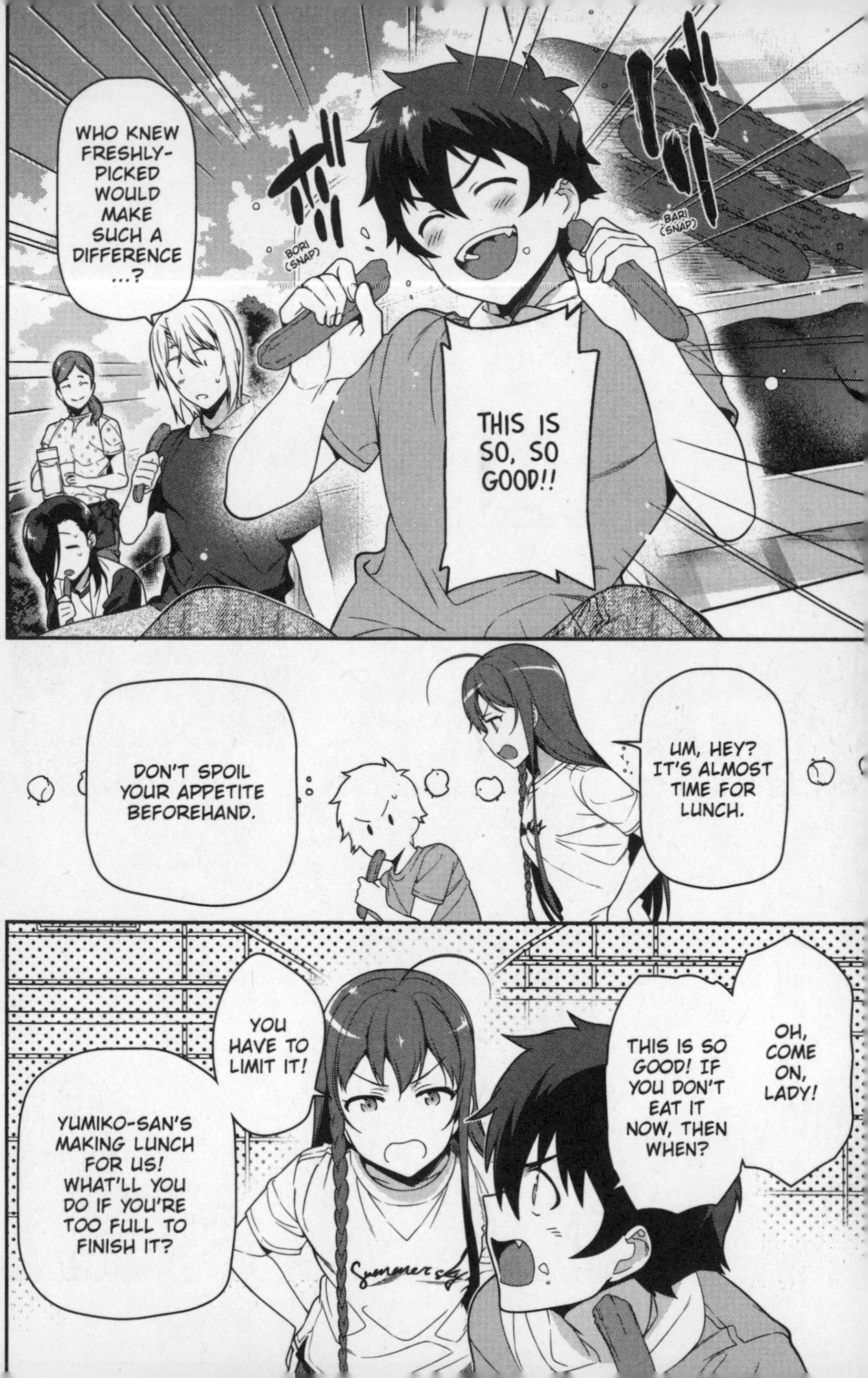
BARI (SNAP)
THIS IS SO, SO GOOD!!
BORI (SNAP)
WHO KNEW FRESHLY-PICKED WOULD MAKE SUCH A DIFFERENCE ...?
UM, HEY? IT'S ALMOST TIME FOR LUNCH.
DON'T SPOIL YOUR APPETITE BEFOREHAND.
OH, COME ON, LADY!
THIS IS SO GOOD! IF YOU DON'T EAT IT NOW, THEN WHEN?
YOU HAVE TO LIMIT IT!
YUMIKO-SAN'S MAKING LUNCH FOR US! WHAT'LL YOU DO IF YOU'RE TOO FULL TO FINISH IT?
Summer sky

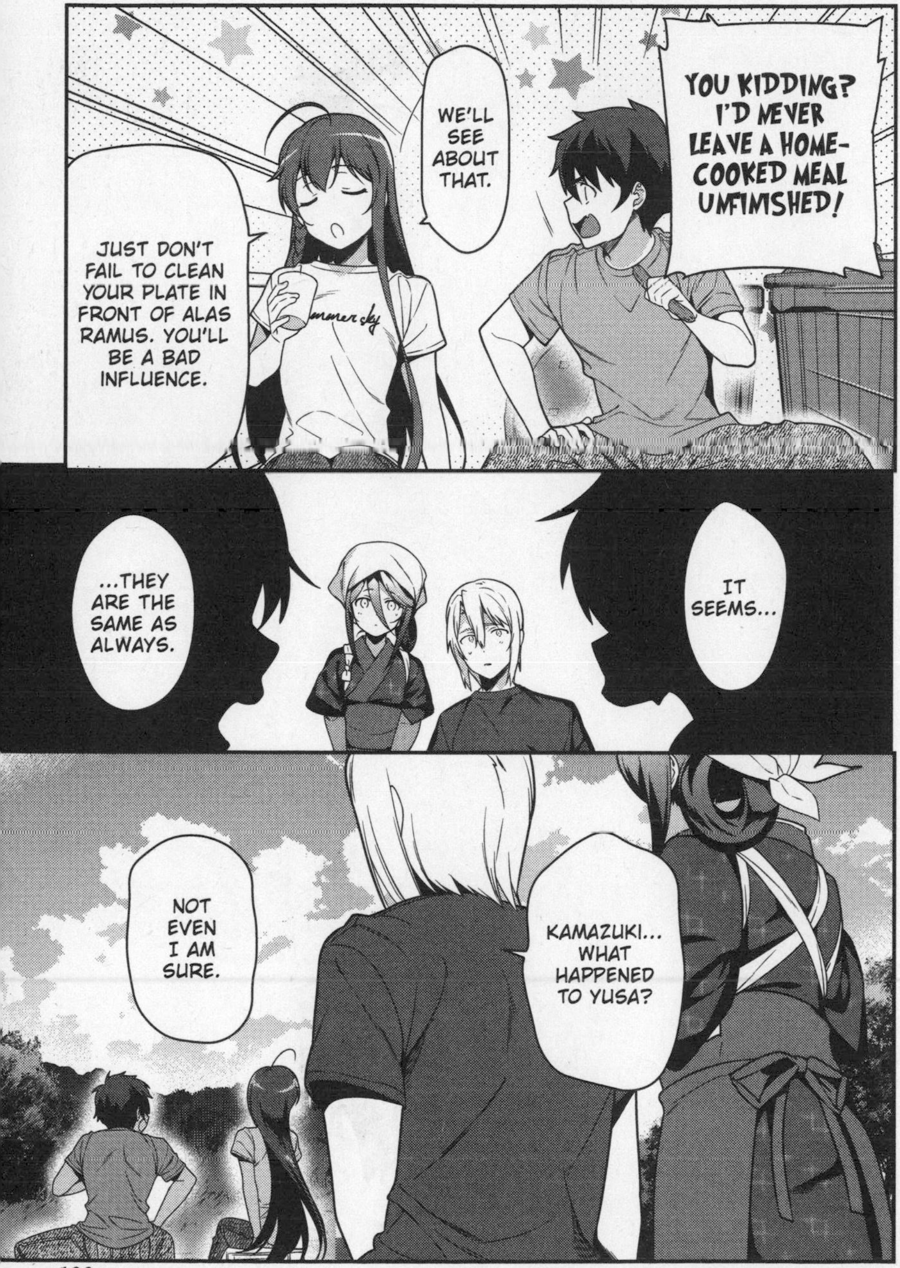
YOU KIDDING? I'D NEVER LEAVE A HOME-COOKED MEAL UNFINISHED!
WE'LL SEE ABOUT THAT.
JUST DON'T FAIL TO CLEAN YOUR PLATE IN FRONT OF ALAS RAMUS. YOU'LL BE A BAD INFLUENCE.
IT SEEMS...
...THEY ARE THE SAME AS ALWAYS.
KAMAZUKI... WHAT HAPPENED TO YUSA?
NOT EVEN I AM SURE.

THE DEVIL IS A PART-TIMER!

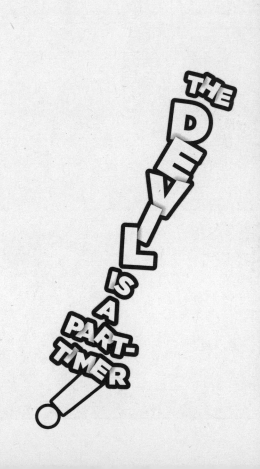

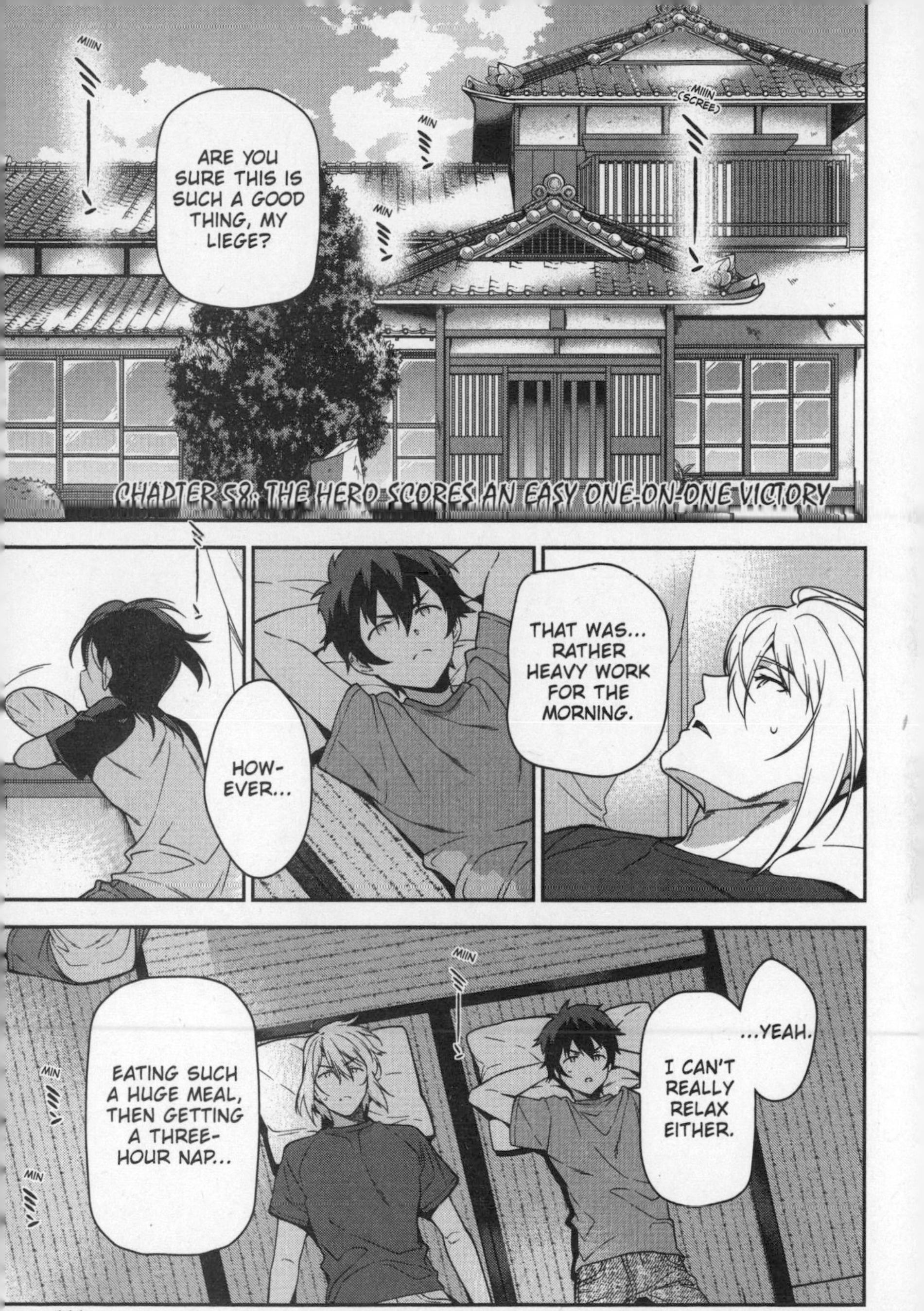
MIIN (SCREE)
MIN
MIN
ARE YOU SURE THIS IS SUCH A GOOD THING, MY LIEGE?
MIIN
CHAPTER 58: THE HERO SCORES AN EASY ONE-ON-ONE VICTORY
THAT WAS... RATHER HEAVY WORK FOR THE MORNING.
HOW-EVER...
...YEAH.
I CAN'T REALLY RELAX EITHER.
MIIN
EATING SUCH A HUGE MEAL, THEN GETTING A THREE-HOUR NAP...
MIN
MIN

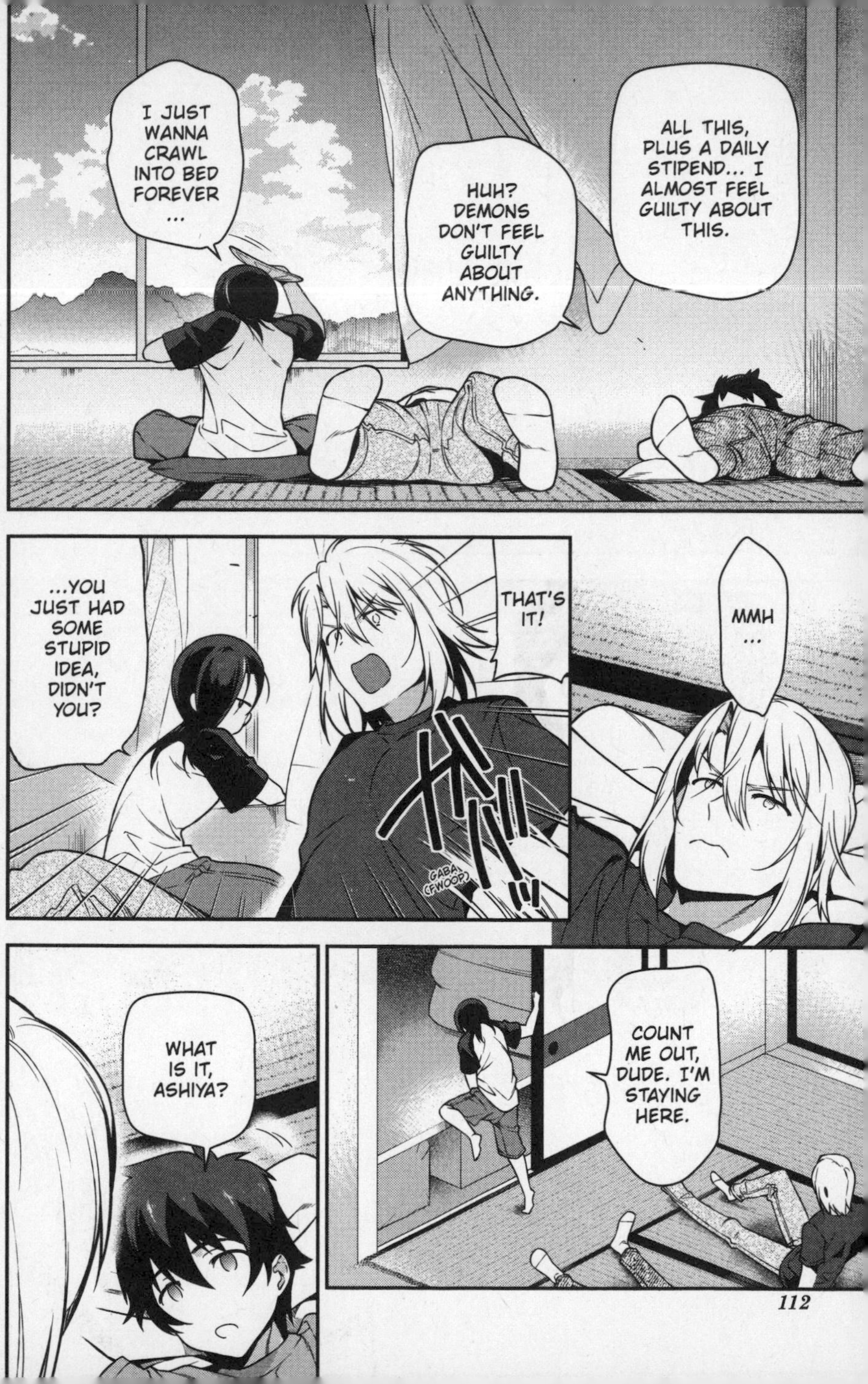
ALL THIS, PLUS A DAILY STIPEND... I ALMOST FEEL GUILTY ABOUT THIS.
HUH? DEMONS DON'T FEEL GUILTY ABOUT ANYTHING.
I JUST WANNA CRAWL INTO BED FOREVER ...
MMH ...
THAT'S IT!
GABA (FWOOP)
...YOU JUST HAD SOME STUPID IDEA, DIDN'T YOU?
COUNT ME OUT, DUDE. I'M STAYING HERE.
WHAT IS IT, ASHIYA?

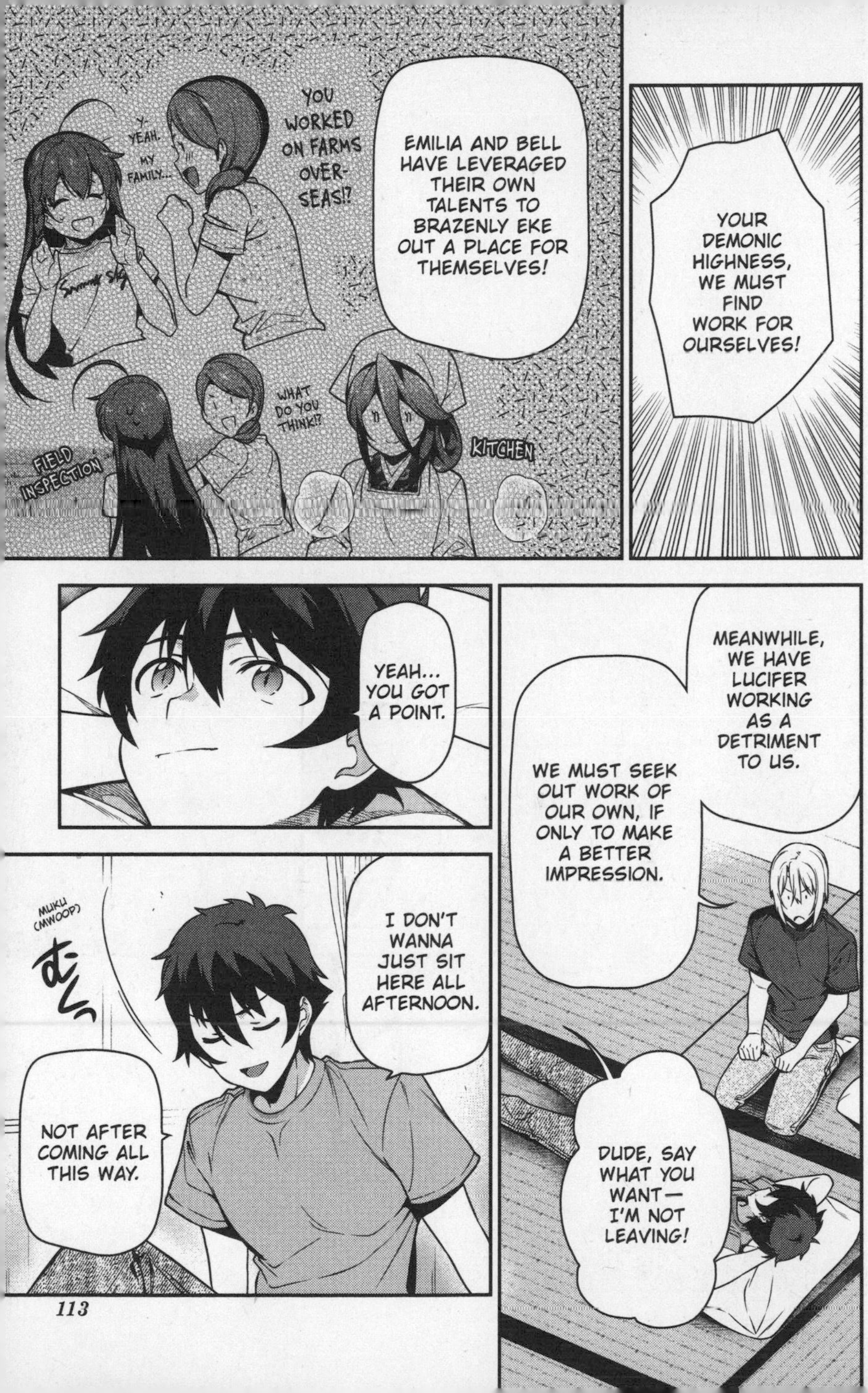
YOUR DEMONIC HIGHNESS, WE MUST FIND WORK FOR OURSELVES!
EMILIA AND BELL HAVE LEVERAGED THEIR OWN TALENTS TO BRAZENLY EKE OUT A PLACE FOR THEMSELVES!
YOU WORKED ON FARMS OVER-SEAS!?
Y-YEAH. MY FAMILY...
WHAT DO YOU THINK!?
KITCHEN
FIELD INSPECTION
MEANWHILE, WE HAVE LUCIFER WORKING AS A DETRIMENT TO US.
WE MUST SEEK OUT WORK OF OUR OWN, IF ONLY TO MAKE A BETTER IMPRESSION.
DUDE, SAY WHAT YOU WANT— I'M NOT LEAVING!
YEAH... YOU GOT A POINT.
I DON'T WANNA JUST SIT HERE ALL AFTERNOON.
MUKU (MWOOP)
むくっ
NOT AFTER COMING ALL THIS WAY.

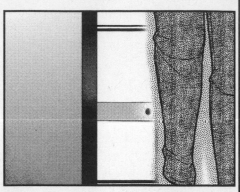

BUT IS THERE ANY WORK SUITED FOR US?

IF THERE IS NOT, WE COULD AT LEAST DO SOME CLEANING, MY LIEGE.

WHOA, THEY REALLY LEFT.

AT LEAST THE NET MAKES IT OUT THIS FAR...

GOSO (RUSTLE)
GOSO

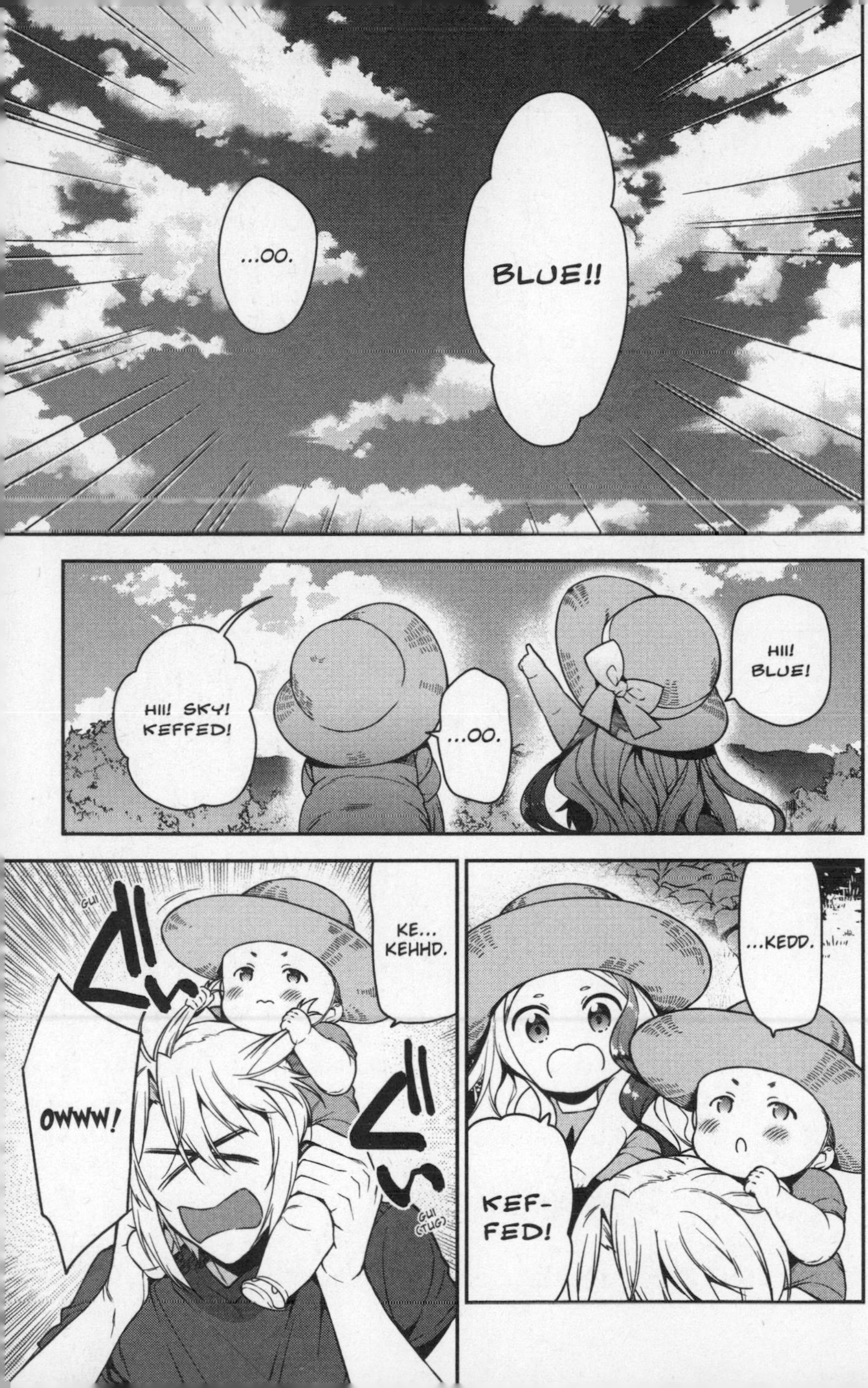
BLUE!!
...OO.
HII! BLUE!
...OO.
HII! SKY! KEFFED!
...KEDD.
KEF-FED!
KE... KEHHD.
GUI
OWWW!
GUI (TUG)

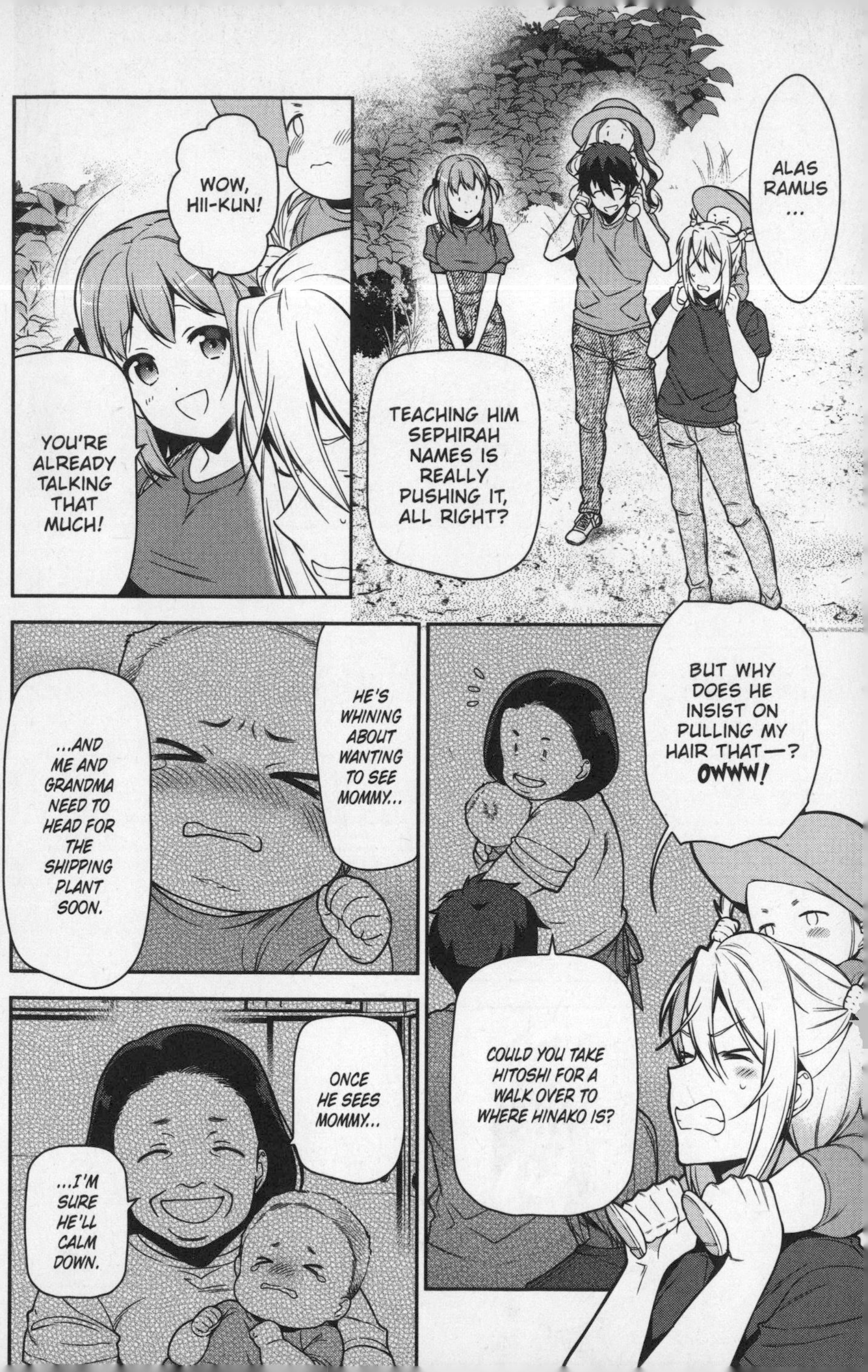

ALAS RAMUS ...
TEACHING HIM SEPHIRAH NAMES IS REALLY PUSHING IT, ALL RIGHT?
WOW, HII-KUN!
YOU'RE ALREADY TALKING THAT MUCH!
BUT WHY DOES HE INSIST ON PULLING MY HAIR THAT—? OWWW!
COULD YOU TAKE HITOSHI FOR A WALK OVER TO WHERE HINAKO IS?
HE'S WHINING ABOUT WANTING TO SEE MOMMY...
...AND ME AND GRANDMA NEED TO HEAD FOR THE SHIPPING PLANT SOON.
ONCE HE SEES MOMMY...
...I'M SURE HE'LL CALM DOWN.

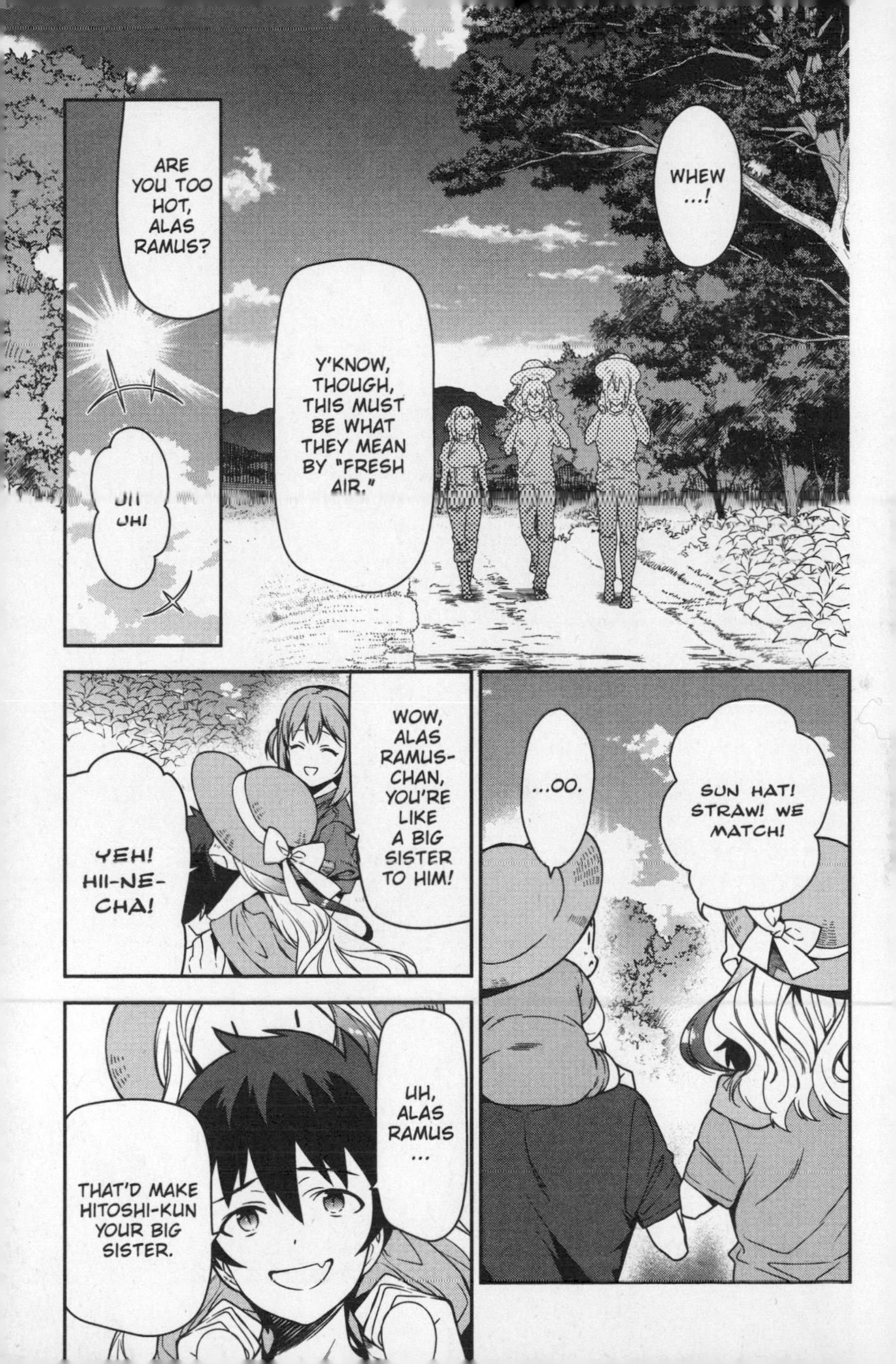
WHEW ...!
Y'KNOW, THOUGH, THIS MUST BE WHAT THEY MEAN BY "FRESH AIR."
ARE YOU TOO HOT, ALAS RAMUS?
SUN HAT! STRAW! WE MATCH!
...OO.
WOW, ALAS RAMUS-CHAN, YOU'RE LIKE A BIG SISTER TO HIM!
YEH! HII-NE-CHA!
UH, ALAS RAMUS ...
THAT'D MAKE HITOSHI-KUN YOUR BIG SISTER.

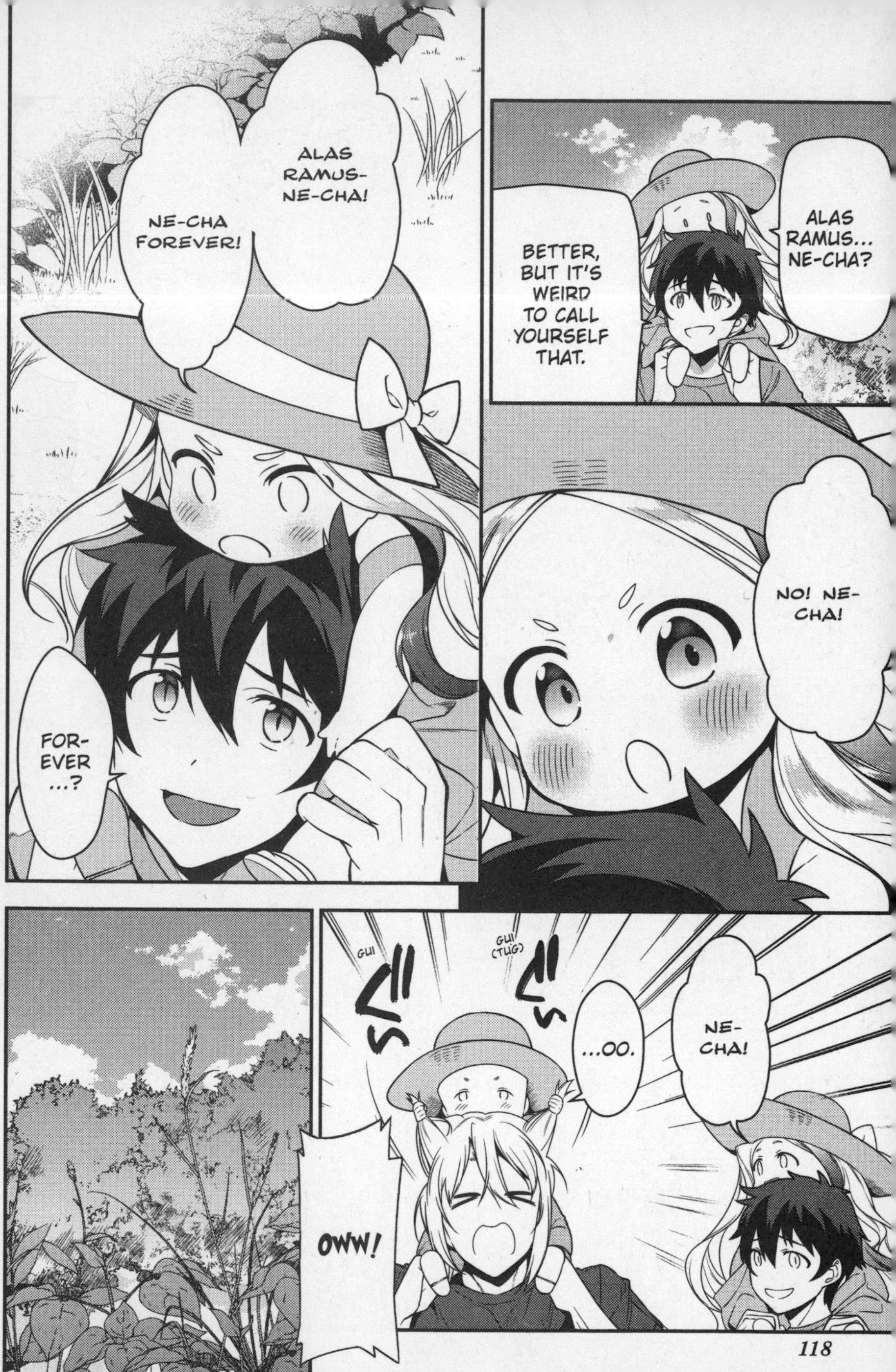
ALAS RAMUS... NE-CHA?
BETTER, BUT IT'S WEIRD TO CALL YOURSELF THAT.
NO! NE-CHA!
ALAS RAMUS-NE-CHA!
NE-CHA FOREVER!
FOR-EVER ...?
NE-CHA!
...OO.
GUI (TUG)
GUI
OWW!

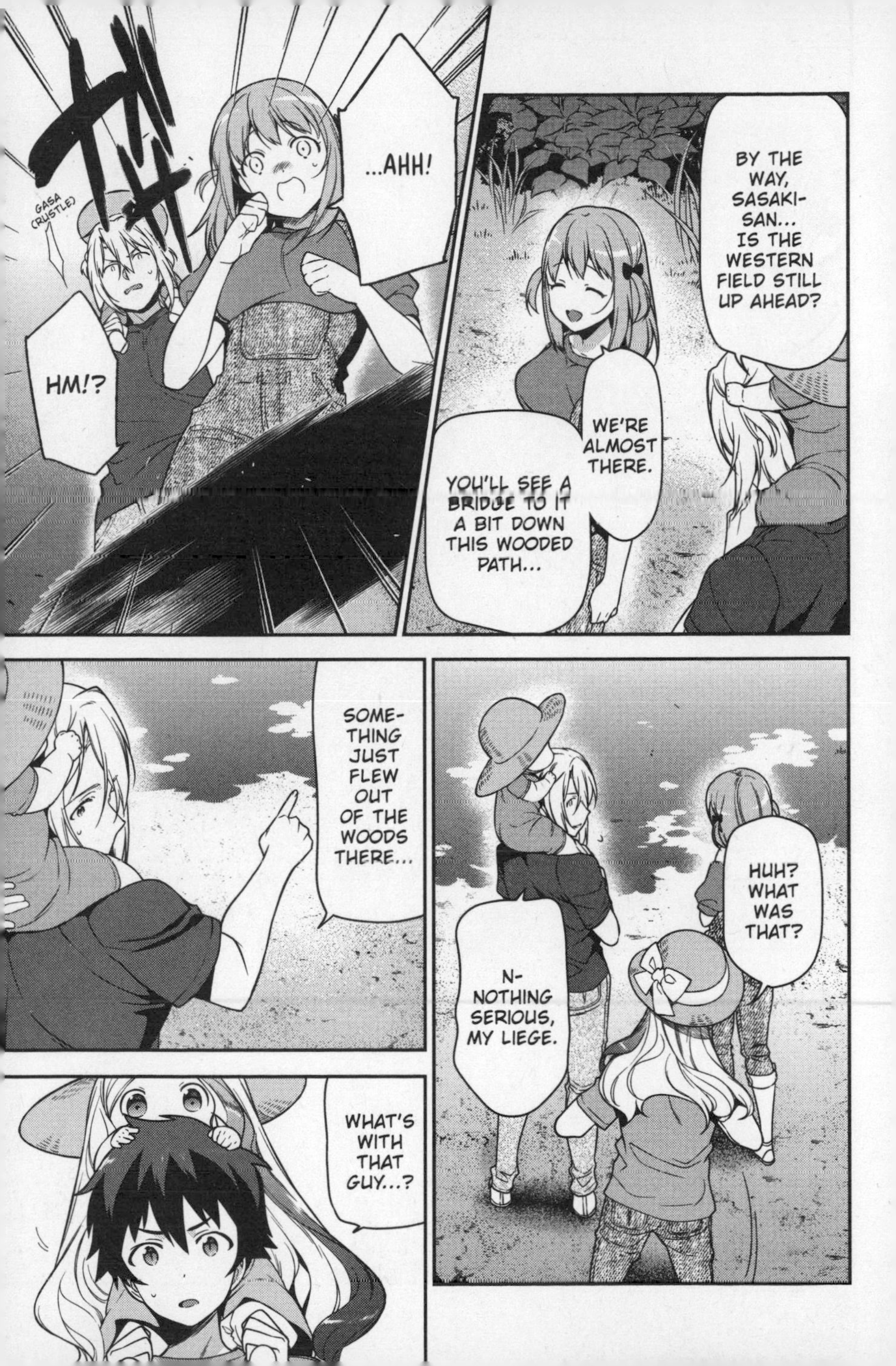
BY THE WAY, SASAKI-SAN... IS THE WESTERN FIELD STILL UP AHEAD?
WE'RE ALMOST THERE.
YOU'LL SEE A BRIDGE TO IT A BIT DOWN THIS WOODED PATH...
...AHH!
GASA (RUSTLE)
HM!?
HUH? WHAT WAS THAT?
N-NOTHING SERIOUS, MY LIEGE.
SOME-THING JUST FLEW OUT OF THE WOODS THERE...
WHAT'S WITH THAT GUY...?

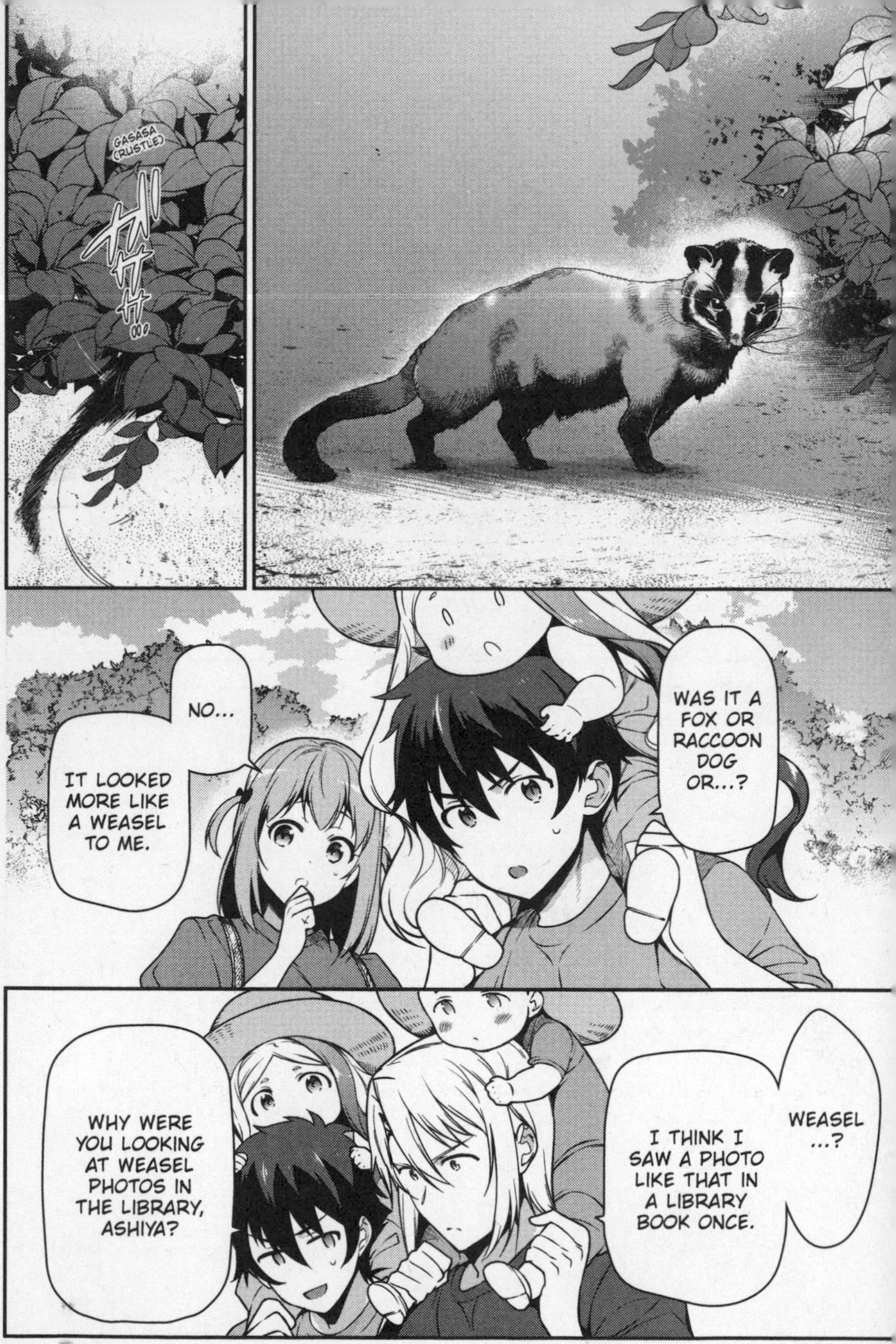
GASASA (RUSTLE)
WAS IT A FOX OR RACCOON DOG OR...?
NO...
IT LOOKED MORE LIKE A WEASEL TO ME.
WEASEL ...?
I THINK I SAW A PHOTO LIKE THAT IN A LIBRARY BOOK ONCE.
WHY WERE YOU LOOKING AT WEASEL PHOTOS IN THE LIBRARY, ASHIYA?

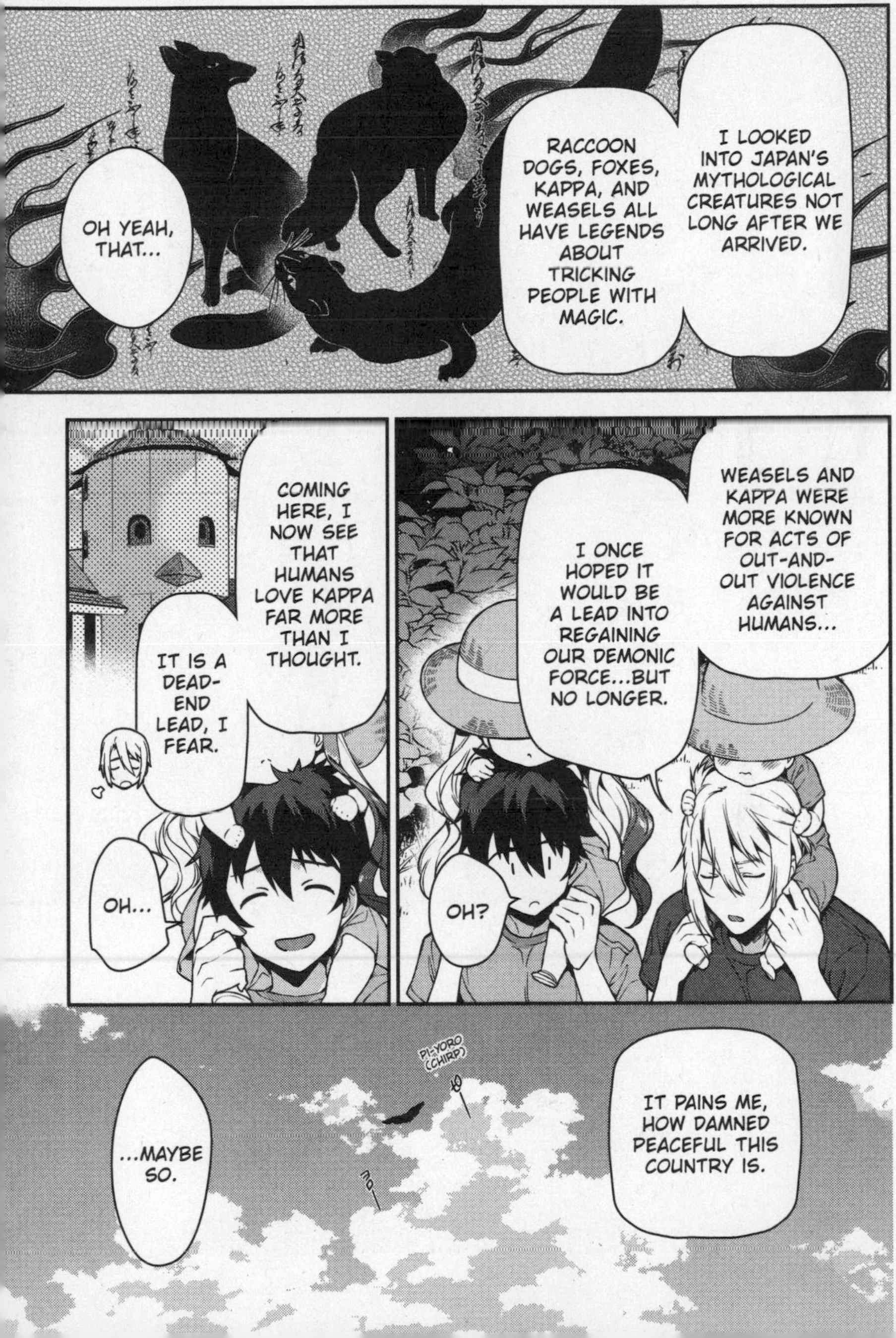
I LOOKED INTO JAPAN'S MYTHOLOGICAL CREATURES NOT LONG AFTER WE ARRIVED.
RACCOON DOGS, FOXES, KAPPA, AND WEASELS ALL HAVE LEGENDS ABOUT TRICKING PEOPLE WITH MAGIC.
OH YEAH, THAT...
WEASELS AND KAPPA WERE MORE KNOWN FOR ACTS OF OUT-AND-OUT VIOLENCE AGAINST HUMANS...
I ONCE HOPED IT WOULD BE A LEAD INTO REGAINING OUR DEMONIC FORCE...BUT NO LONGER.
OH?
COMING HERE, I NOW SEE THAT HUMANS LOVE KAPPA FAR MORE THAN I THOUGHT.
IT IS A DEAD-END LEAD, I FEAR.
OH...
PI-YORO (CHIRP)
IT PAINS ME, HOW DAMNED PEACEFUL THIS COUNTRY IS.
...MAYBE SO.

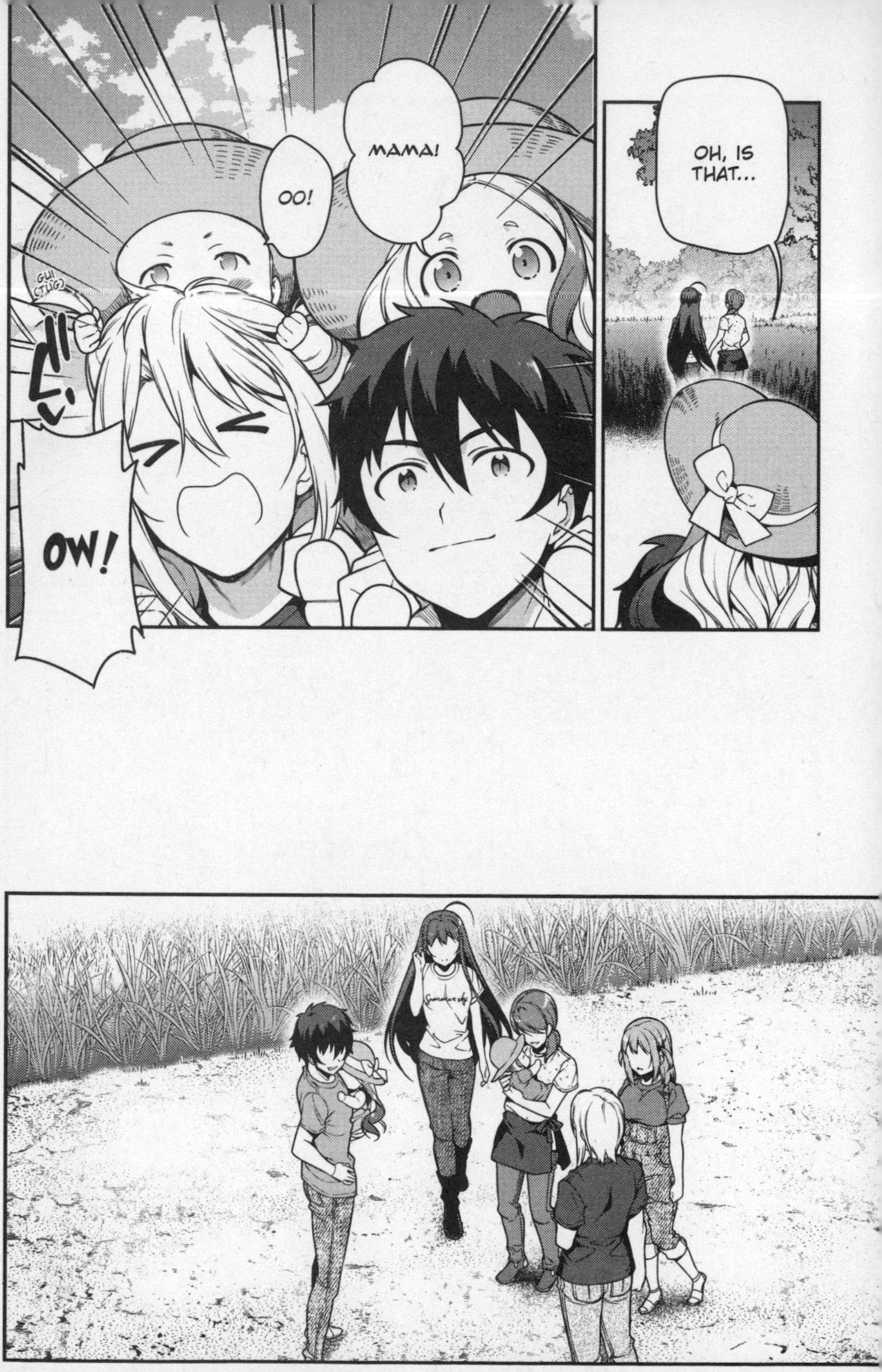
OH, IS THAT...
MAMA!
OO!
GUI (TUG)
OW!

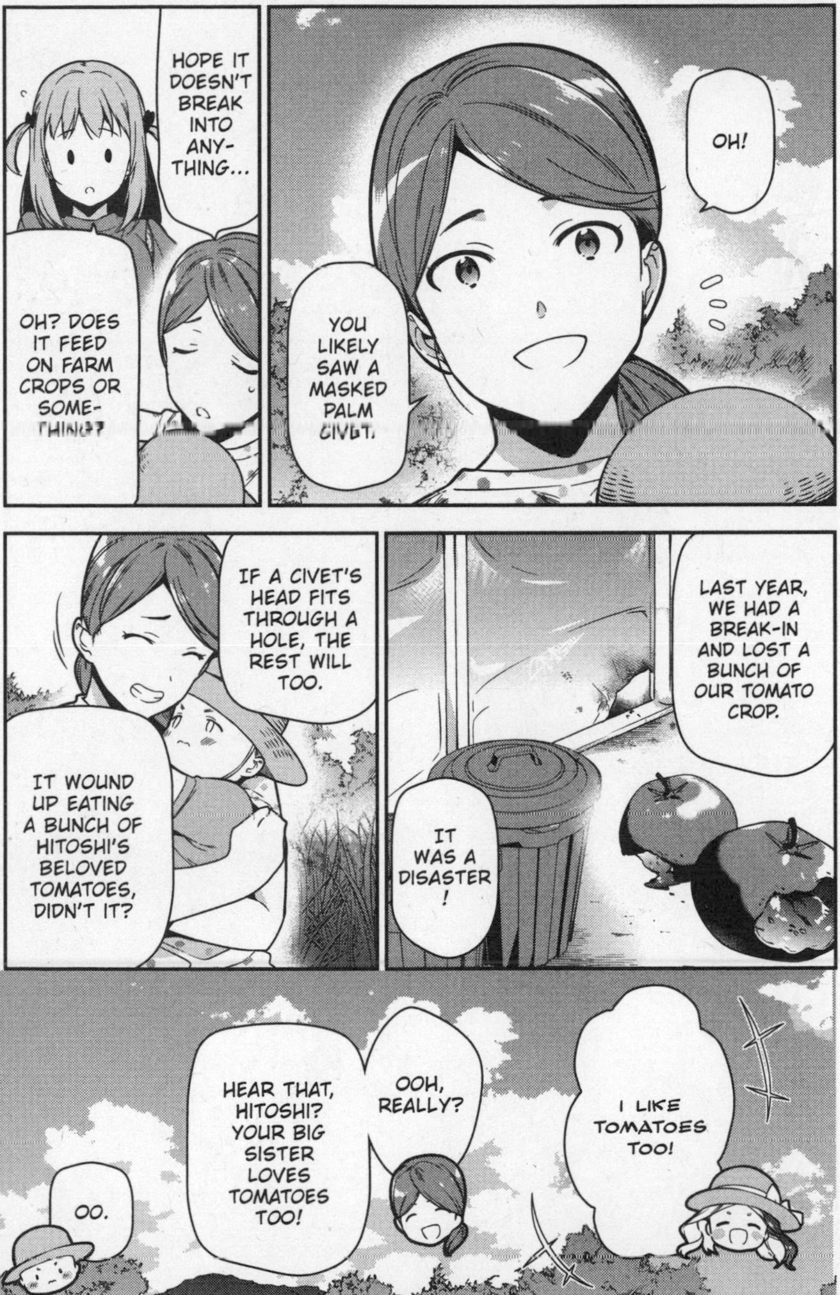
OH!
YOU LIKELY SAW A MASKED PALM CIVET.
HOPE IT DOESN'T BREAK INTO ANY-THING...
OH? DOES IT FEED ON FARM CROPS OR SOME-THING?
LAST YEAR, WE HAD A BREAK-IN AND LOST A BUNCH OF OUR TOMATO CROP.
IT WAS A DISASTER!
IF A CIVET'S HEAD FITS THROUGH A HOLE, THE REST WILL TOO.
IT WOUND UP EATING A BUNCH OF HITOSHI'S BELOVED TOMATOES, DIDN'T IT?
I LIKE TOMATOES TOO!
OOH, REALLY?
HEAR THAT, HITOSHI? YOUR BIG SISTER LOVES TOMATOES TOO!
OO.

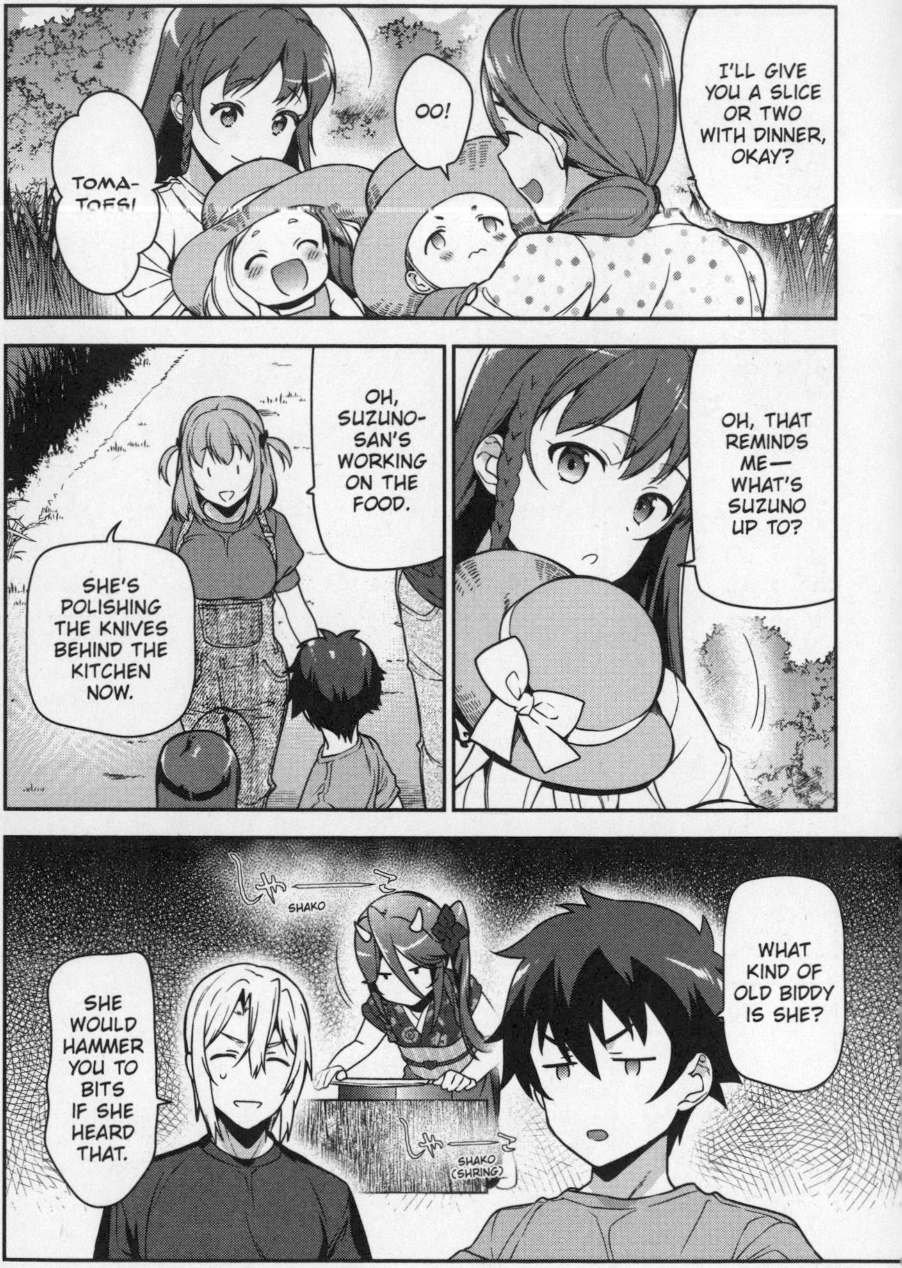
I'LL GIVE YOU A SLICE OR TWO WITH DINNER, OKAY?
OO!
TOMA-TOES!
OH, THAT REMINDS ME—WHAT'S SUZUNO UP TO?
OH, SUZUNO-SAN'S WORKING ON THE FOOD.
SHE'S POLISHING THE KNIVES BEHIND THE KITCHEN NOW.
WHAT KIND OF OLD BIDDY IS SHE?
SHAKO
SHE WOULD HAMMER YOU TO BITS IF SHE HEARD THAT.
SHAKO (SHRING)

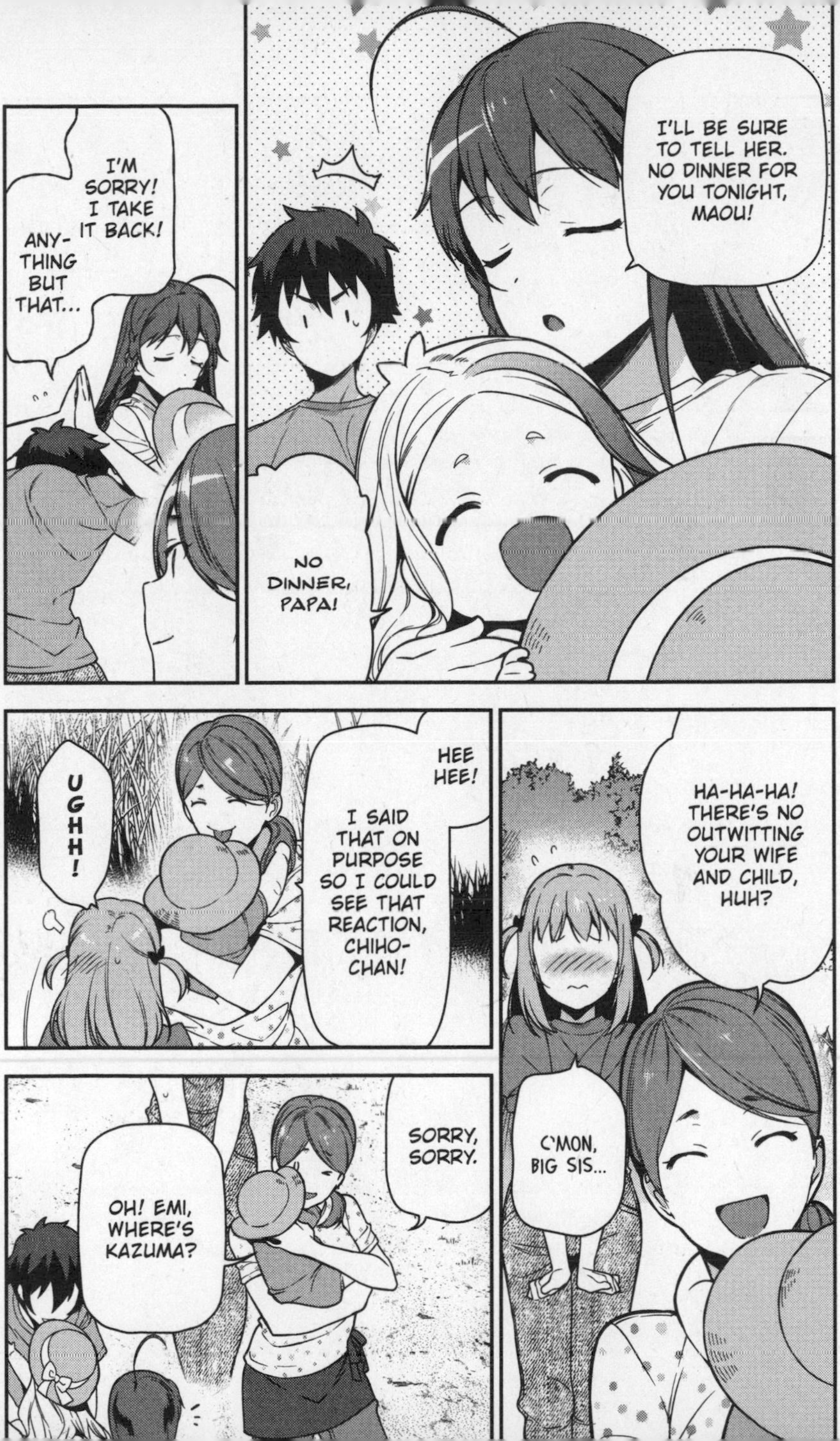
I'LL BE SURE TO TELL HER. NO DINNER FOR YOU TONIGHT, MAOU!
NO DINNER, PAPA!
I'M SORRY! I TAKE IT BACK!
ANY-THING BUT THAT...
HA-HA-HA! THERE'S NO OUTWITTING YOUR WIFE AND CHILD, HUH?
C'MON, BIG SIS...
HEE HEE!
I SAID THAT ON PURPOSE SO I COULD SEE THAT REACTION, CHIHO-CHAN!
UGHH!
SORRY, SORRY.
OH! EMI, WHERE'S KAZUMA?

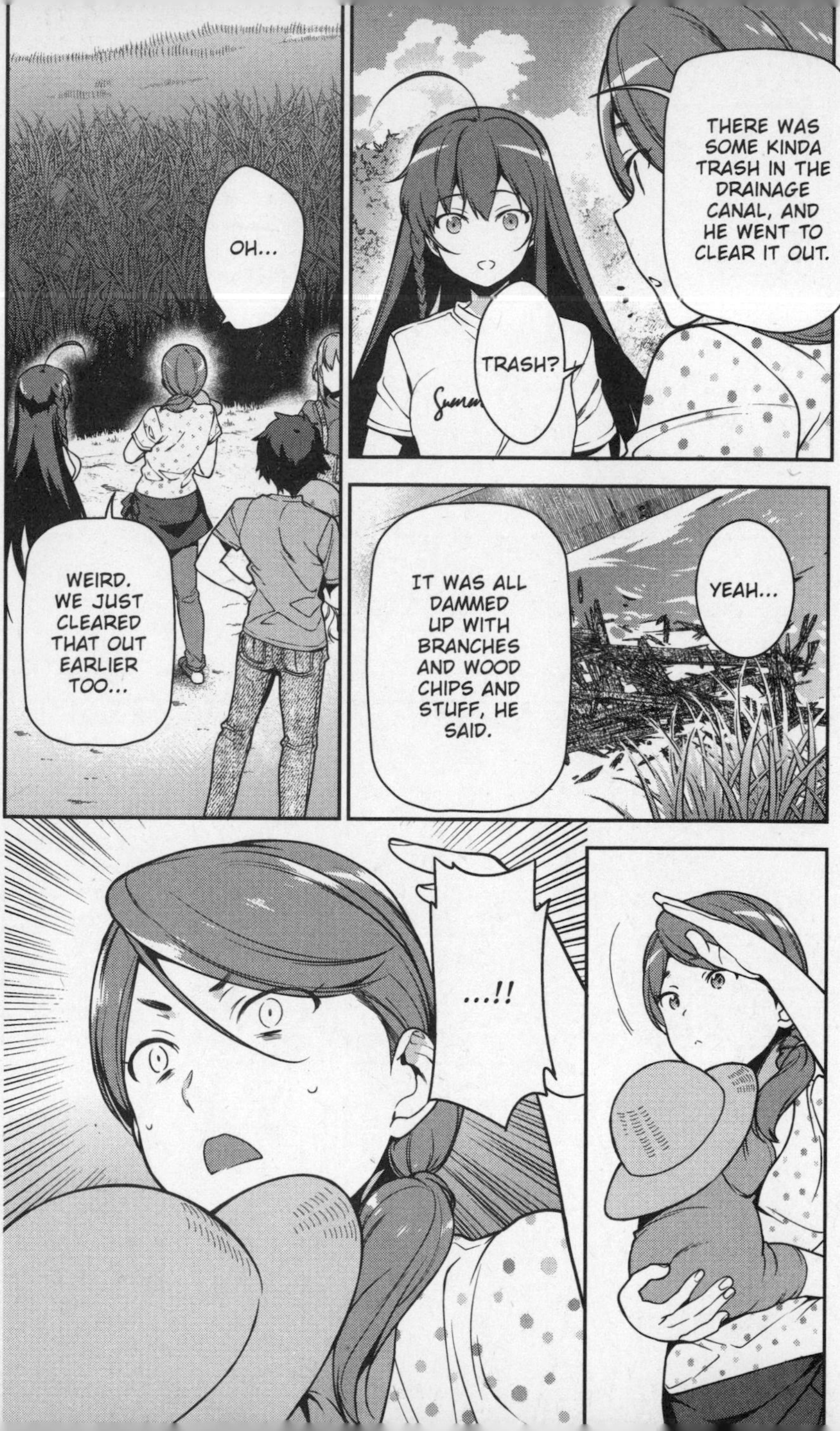
THERE WAS SOME KINDA TRASH IN THE DRAINAGE CANAL, AND HE WENT TO CLEAR IT OUT.
TRASH?
YEAH...
IT WAS ALL DAMMED UP WITH BRANCHES AND WOOD CHIPS AND STUFF, HE SAID.
OH...
WEIRD. WE JUST CLEARED THAT OUT EARLIER TOO...
...!!

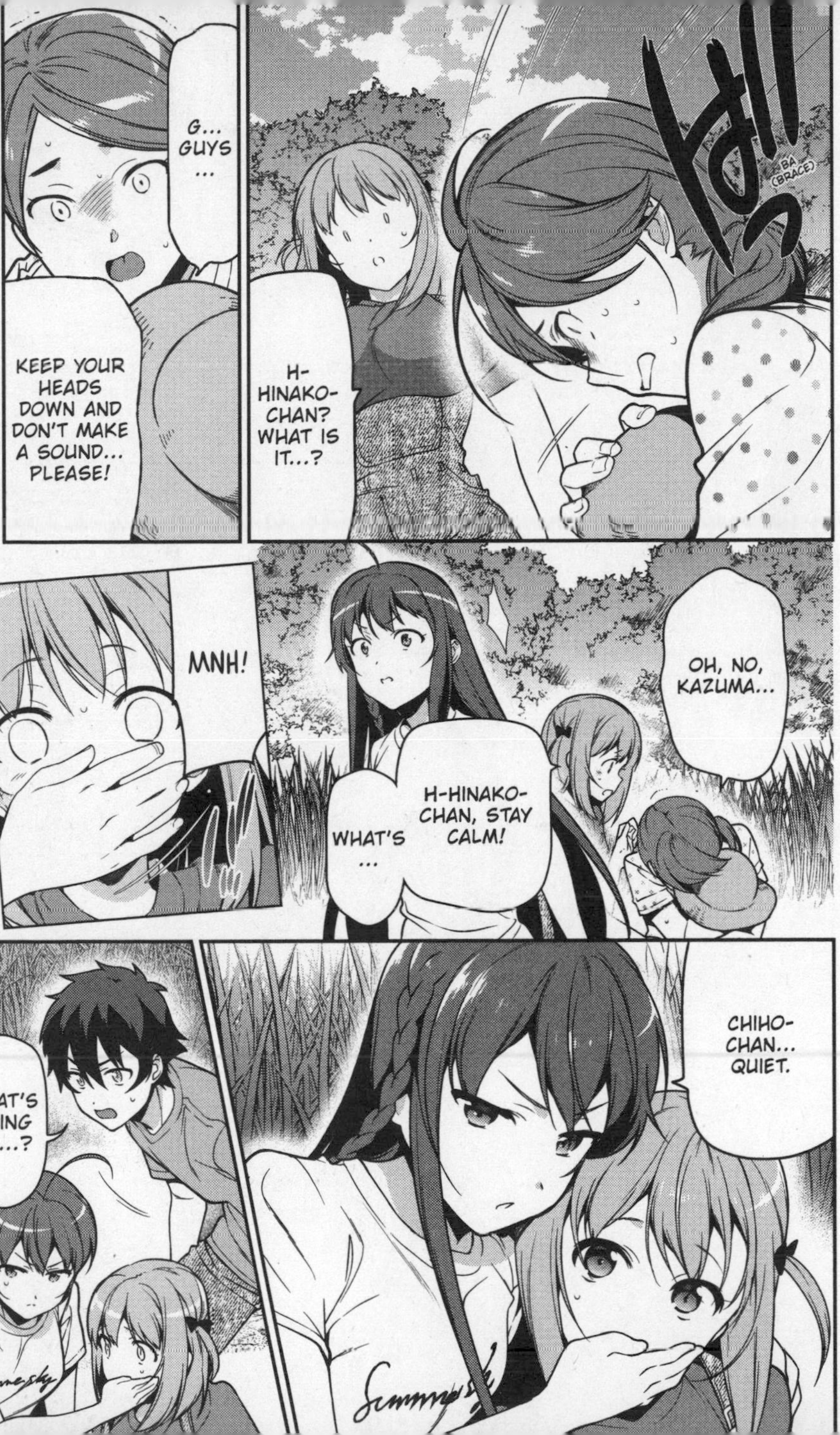
BA (BRACE)
H-HINAKO-CHAN? WHAT IS IT...?
G... GUYS ...
KEEP YOUR HEADS DOWN AND DON'T MAKE A SOUND... PLEASE!
OH, NO, KAZUMA...
H-HINAKO-CHAN, STAY CALM!
WHAT'S ...
MNH!
CHIHO-CHAN... QUIET.
WHAT'S GOING ON...?

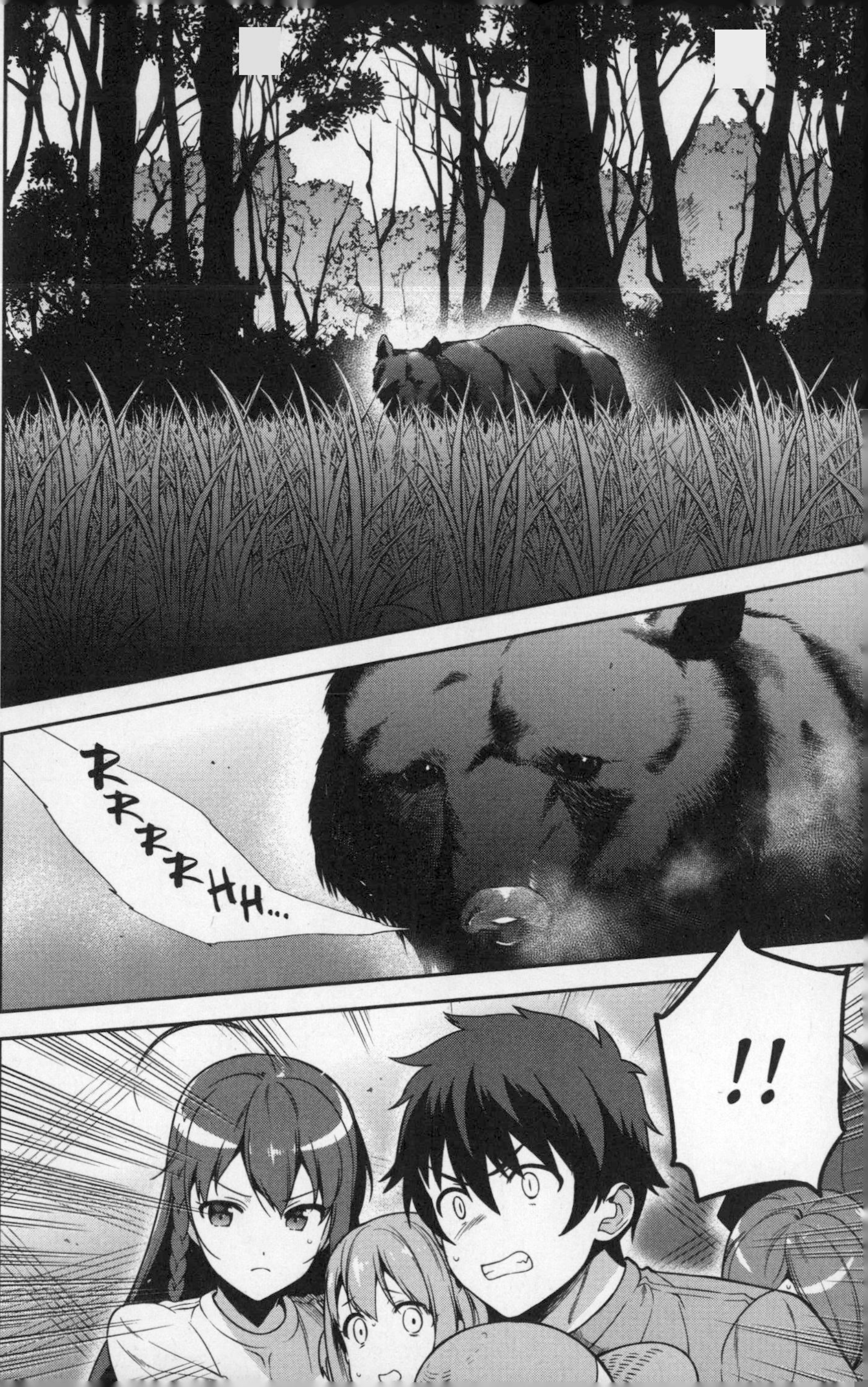
RRRRRHH...
!!

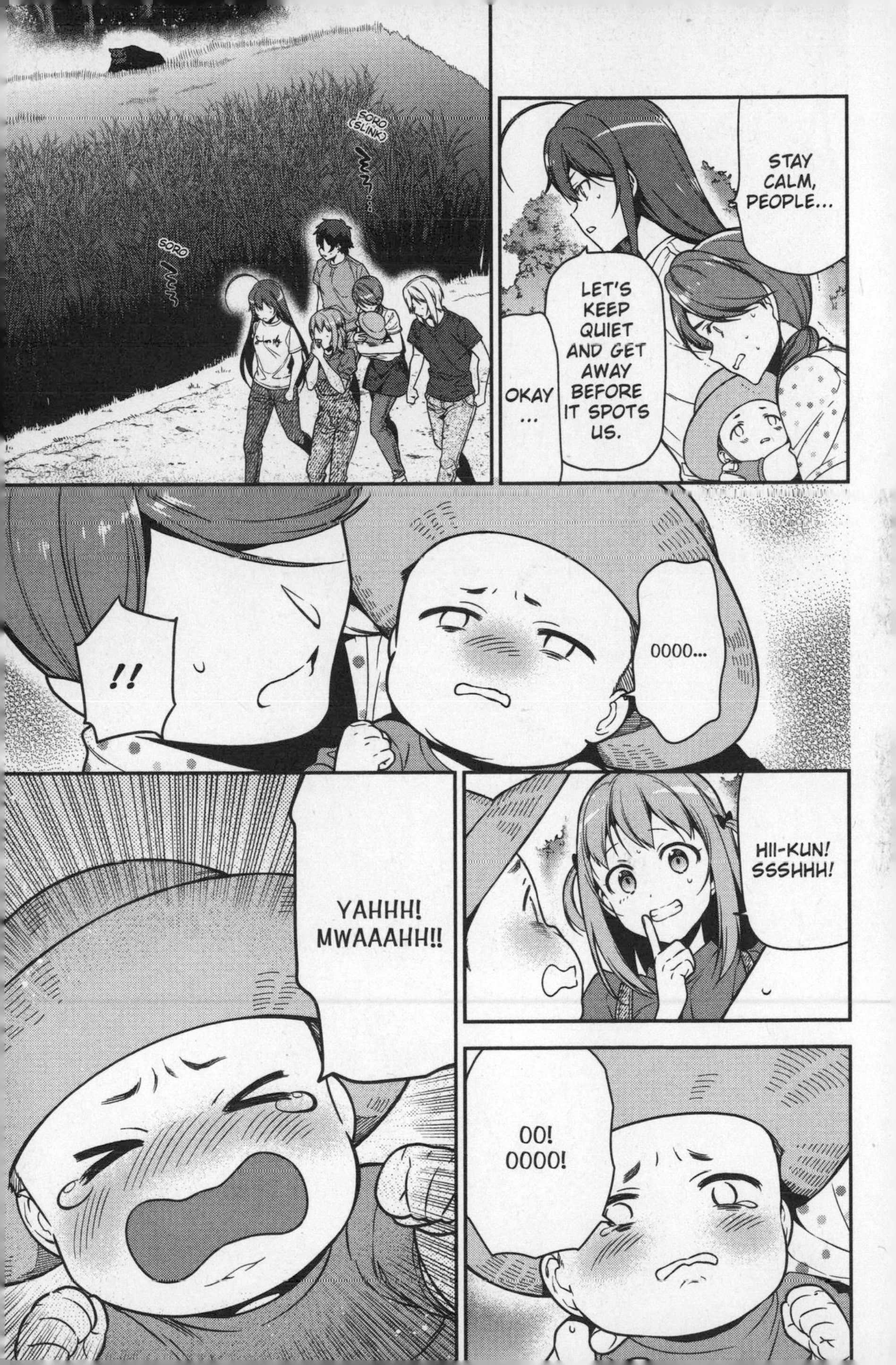
STAY CALM, PEOPLE...
LET'S KEEP QUIET AND GET AWAY BEFORE IT SPOTS US.
OKAY...
SORO (SLINK)
SORO
OOOO...
!!
HII-KUN! SSSHHH!
OO! OOOO!
YAHHH! MWAAAHH!!

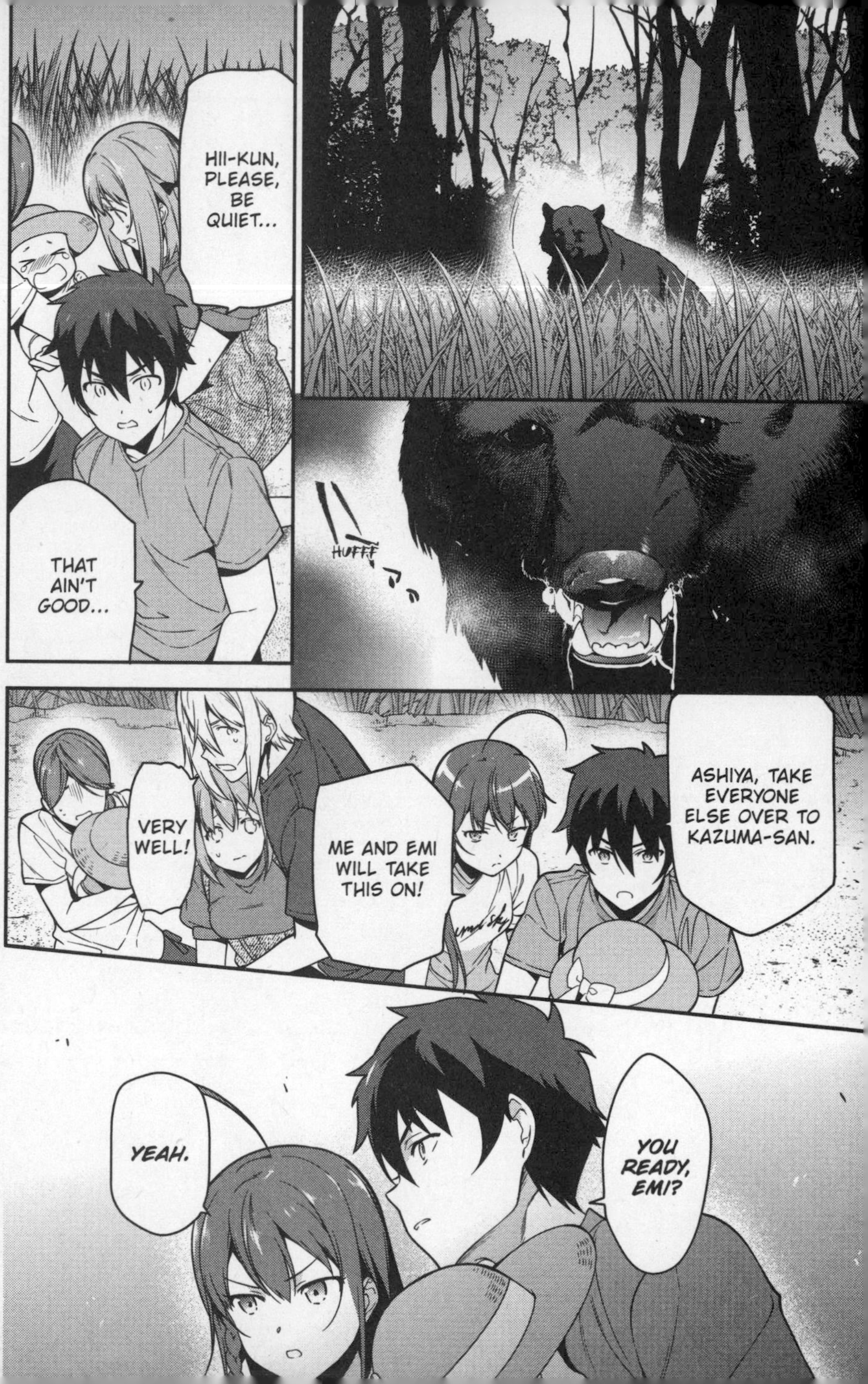
HUFFF
HII-KUN, PLEASE, BE QUIET...
THAT AIN'T GOOD...
ASHIYA, TAKE EVERYONE ELSE OVER TO KAZUMA-SAN.
ME AND EMI WILL TAKE THIS ON!
VERY WELL!
YOU READY, EMI?
YEAH.

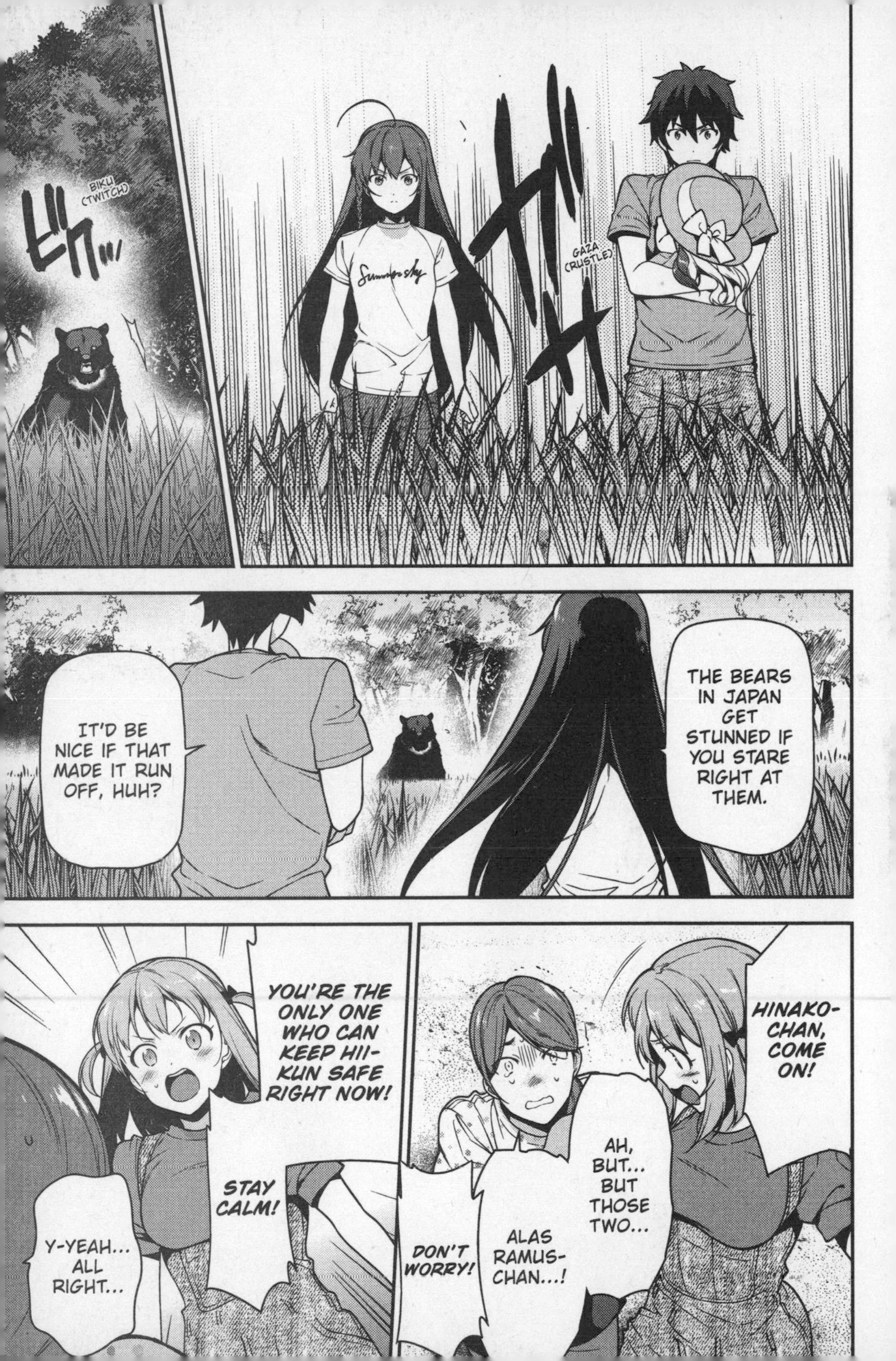
GAZA (RUSTLE)
BIKU (TWITCH)
THE BEARS IN JAPAN GET STUNNED IF YOU STARE RIGHT AT THEM.
IT'D BE NICE IF THAT MADE IT RUN OFF, HUH?
HINAKO-CHAN, COME ON!
AH, BUT... BUT THOSE TWO...
ALAS RAMUS-CHAN...!
DON'T WORRY!
YOU'RE THE ONLY ONE WHO CAN KEEP HII-KUN SAFE RIGHT NOW!
STAY CALM!
Y-YEAH... ALL RIGHT...

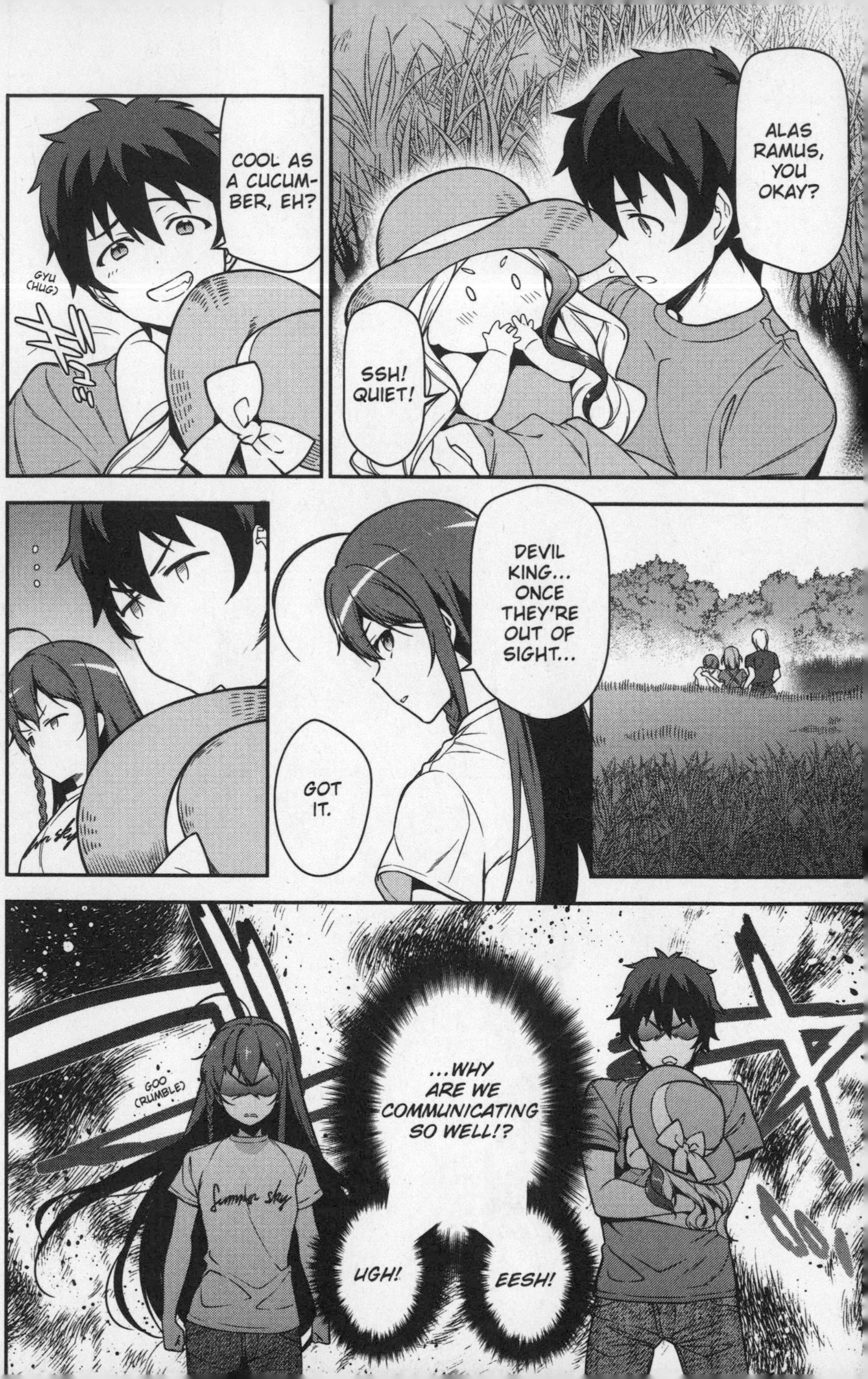
ALAS RAMUS, YOU OKAY?
SSH! QUIET!
COOL AS A CUCUMBER, EH?
GYU (HUG)
DEVIL KING... ONCE THEY'RE OUT OF SIGHT...
GOT IT.
...WHY ARE WE COMMUNICATING SO WELL!?
EESH!
UGH!
GOO (RUMBLE)

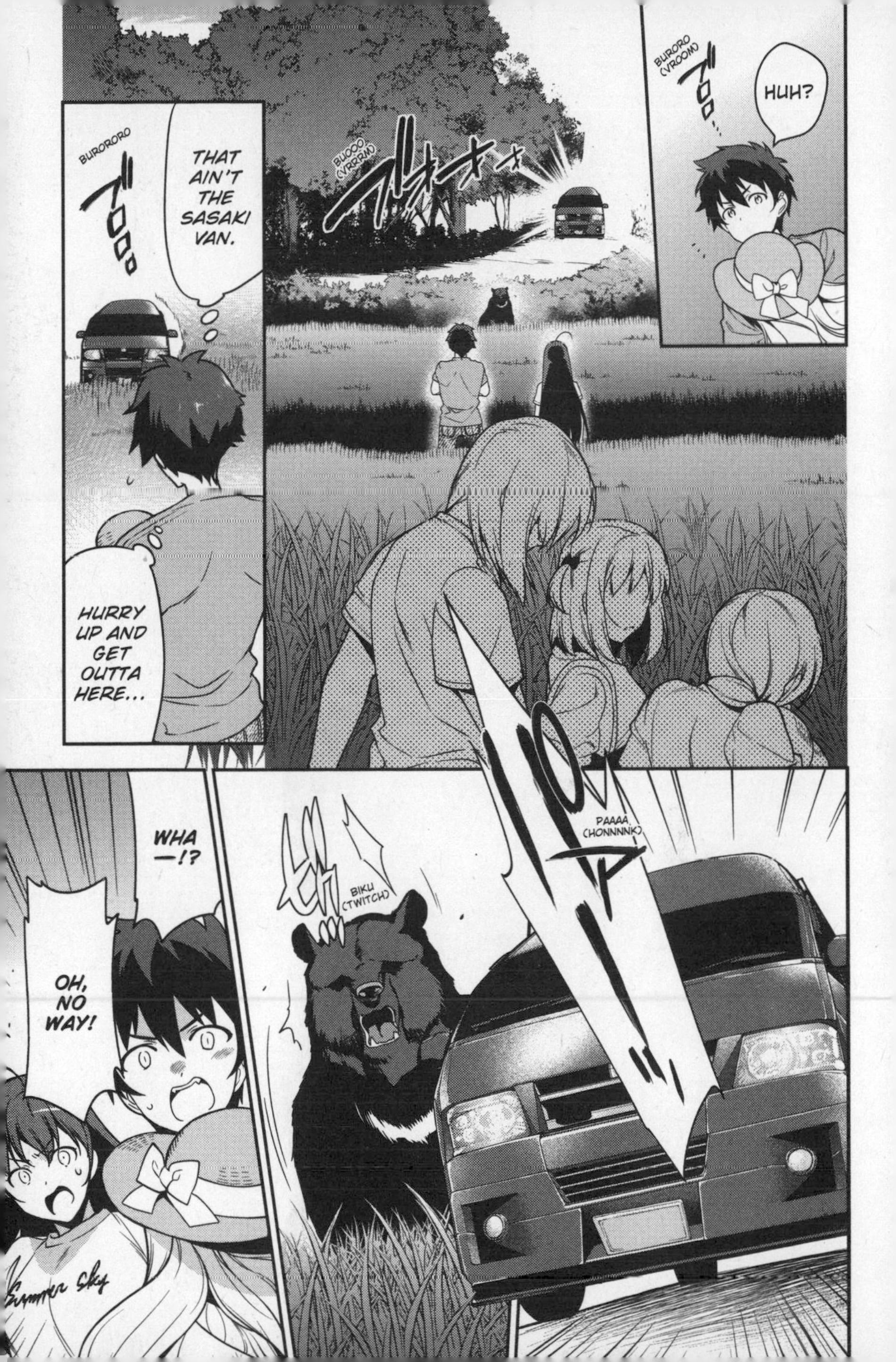
BURORO (VROOM)
HUH?
BUOOO (VRRRM)
BURORORO
THAT AIN'T THE SASAKI VAN.
HURRY UP AND GET OUTTA HERE...
PAAAA (HONNNNK)
BIKU (TWITCH)
WHA—!?
OH, NO WAY!
Summer sky

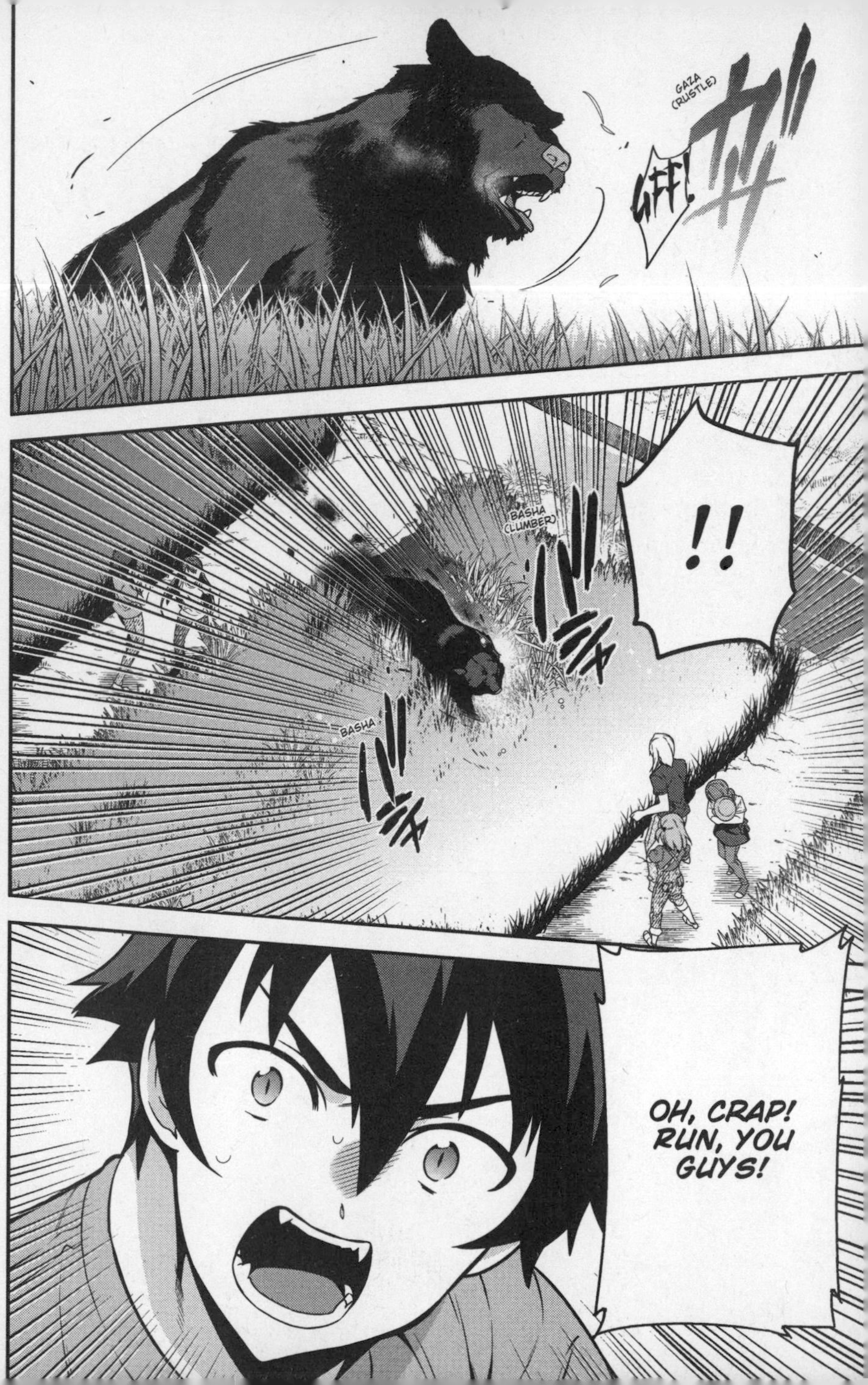
GAZA
(RUSTLE)
GFF!
!!
BASHA
(LUMBER)
BASHA
OH, CRAP! RUN, YOU GUYS!

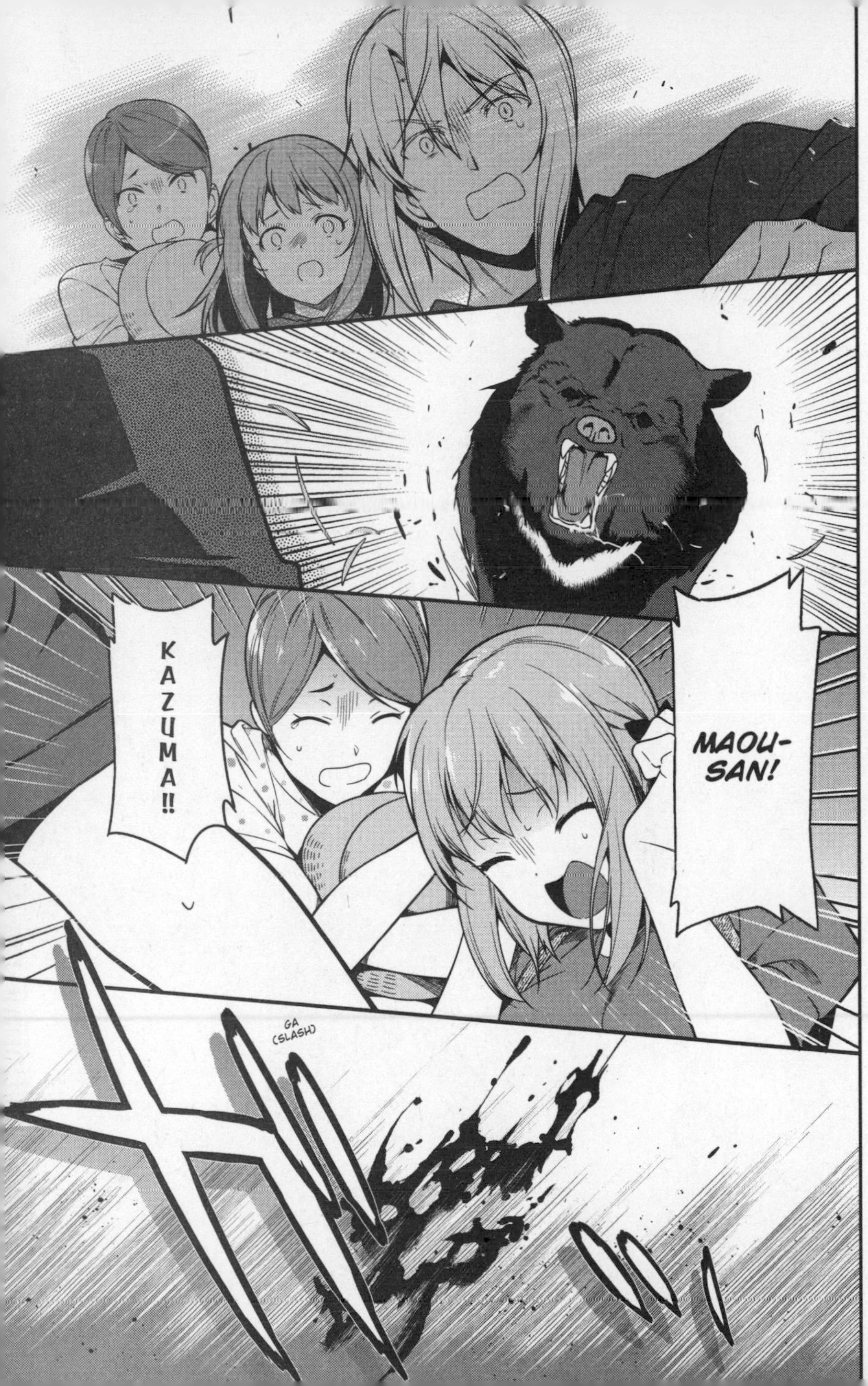
MAOU-SAN!
KAZUMA!!
GA (SLASH)

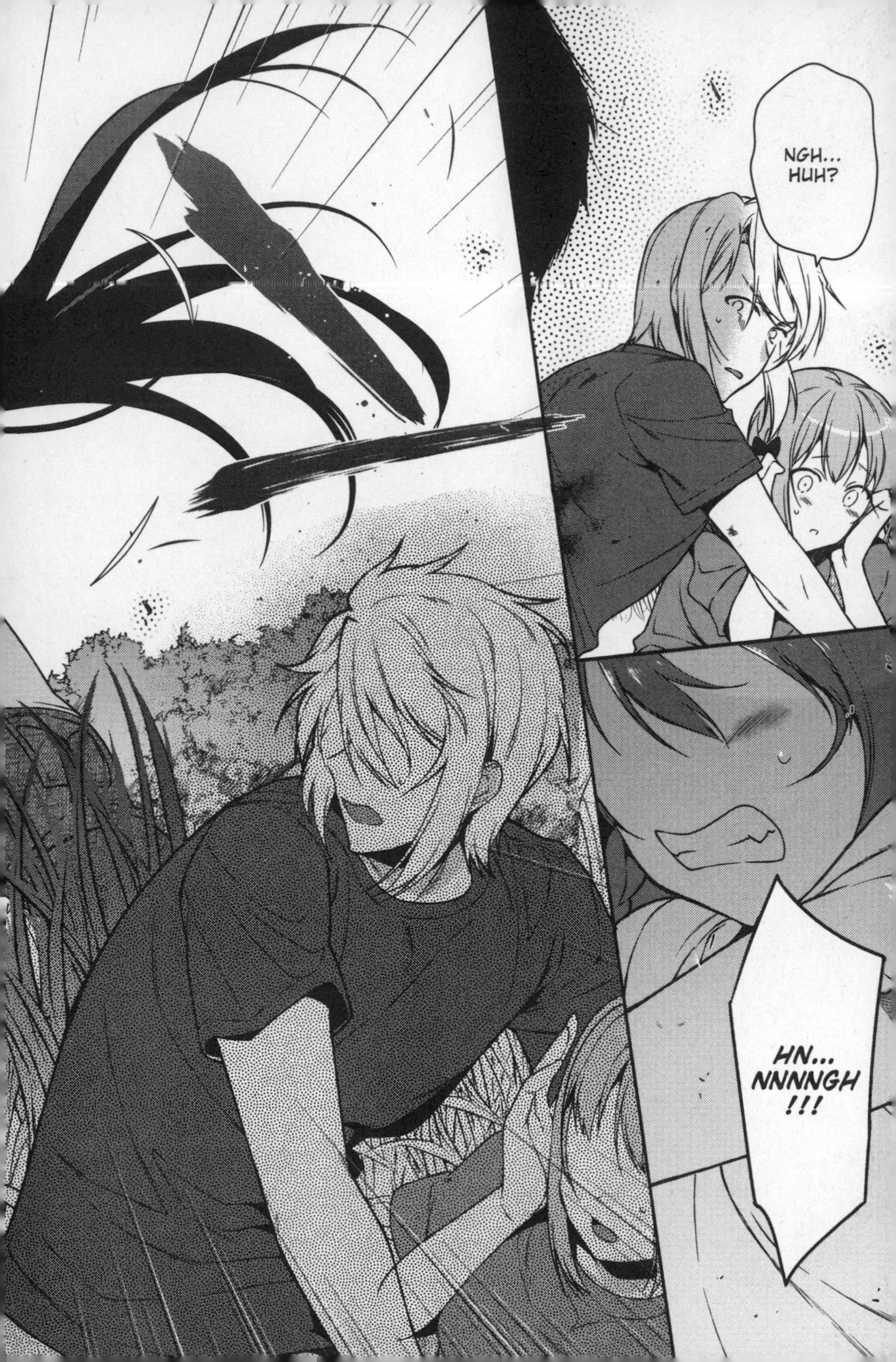
NGH... HUH?
HN... NNNNGH !!!

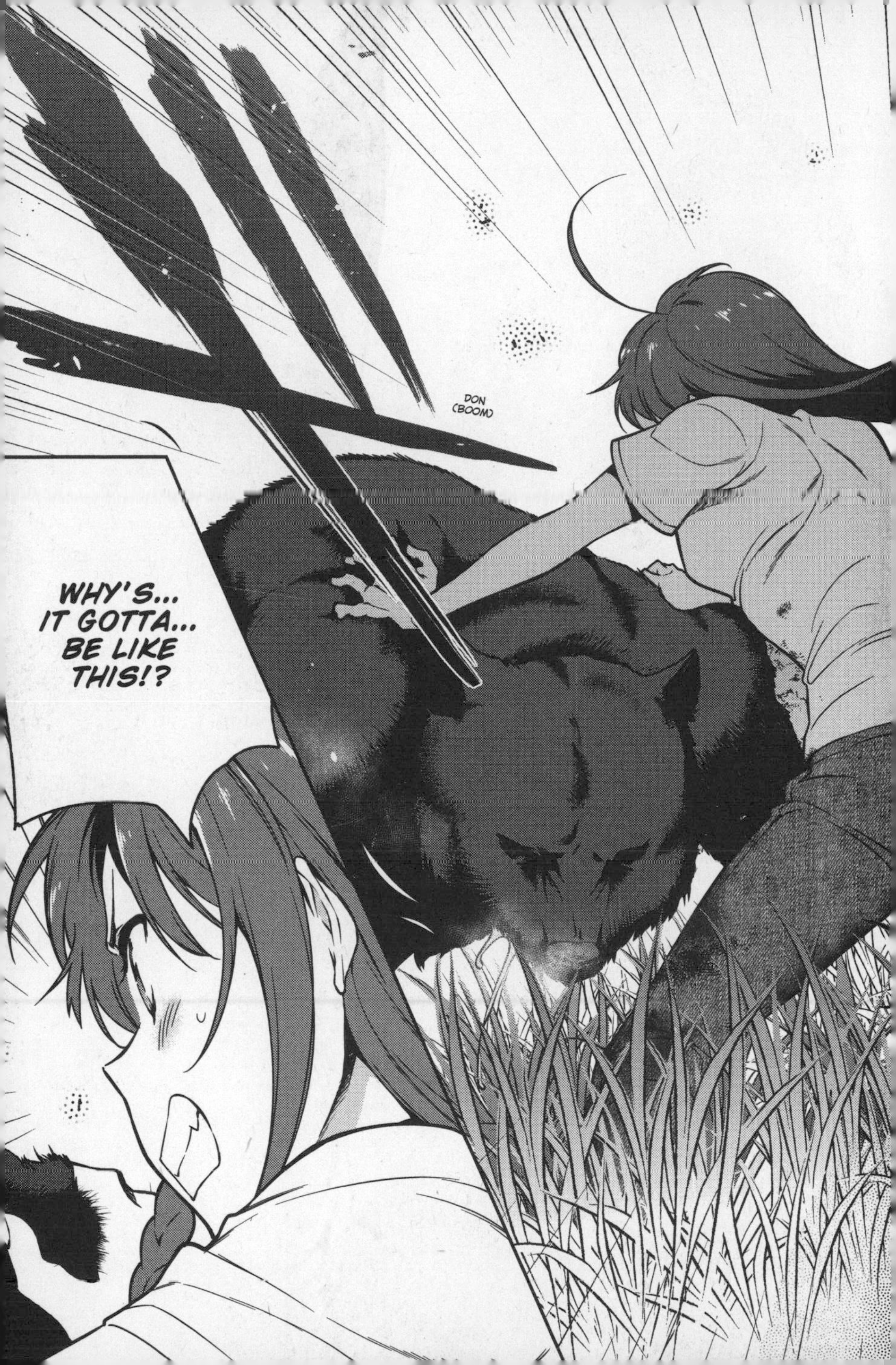
DON (BOOM)
WHY'S... IT GOTTA... BE LIKE THIS!?

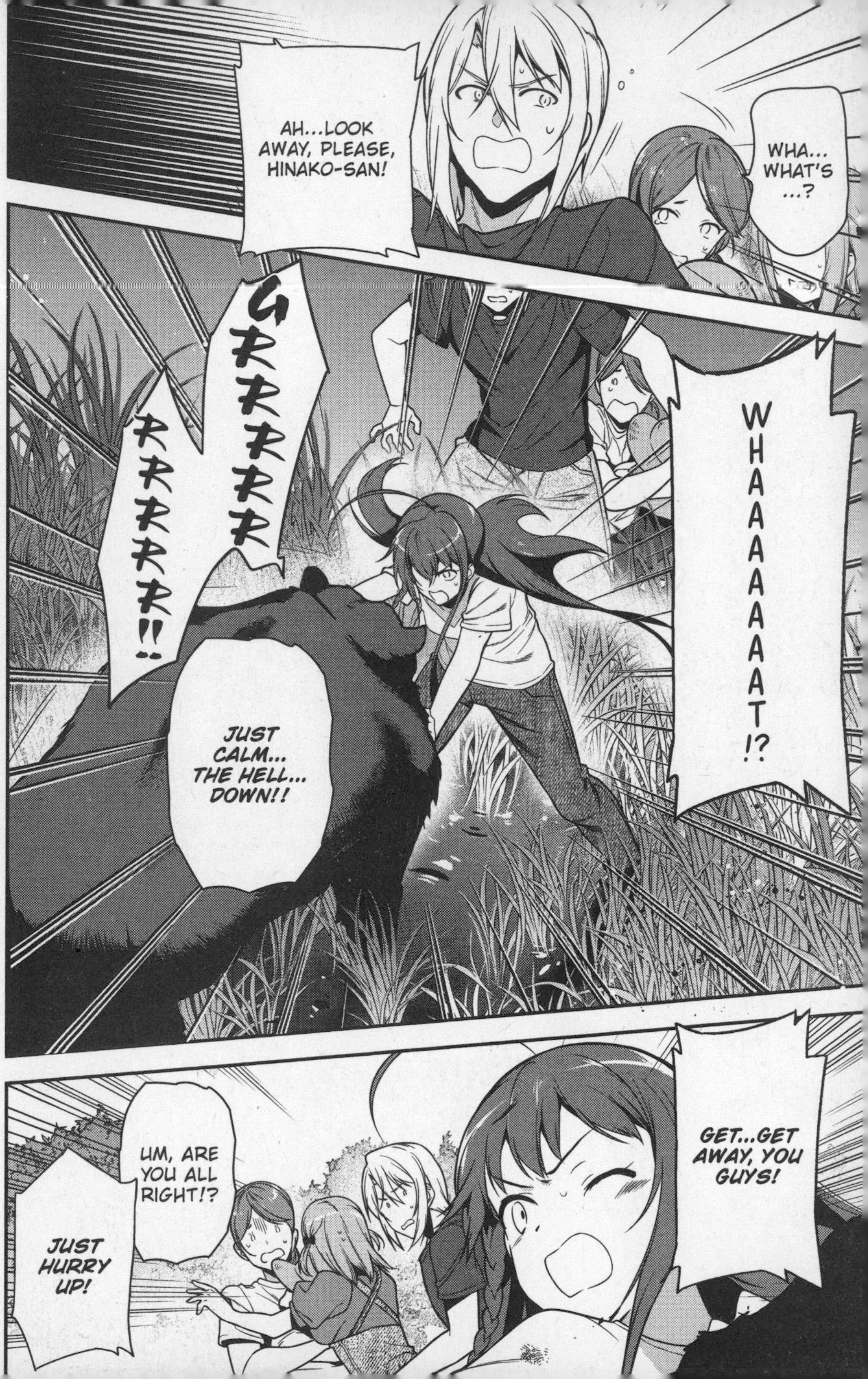
WHA... WHAT'S ...?
AH...LOOK AWAY, PLEASE, HINAKO-SAN!
WHAAAAAAAAAT!?
GRRRRRR RRRRRR!!
JUST CALM... THE HELL... DOWN!!
GET...GET AWAY, YOU GUYS!
UM, ARE YOU ALL RIGHT!?
JUST HURRY UP!

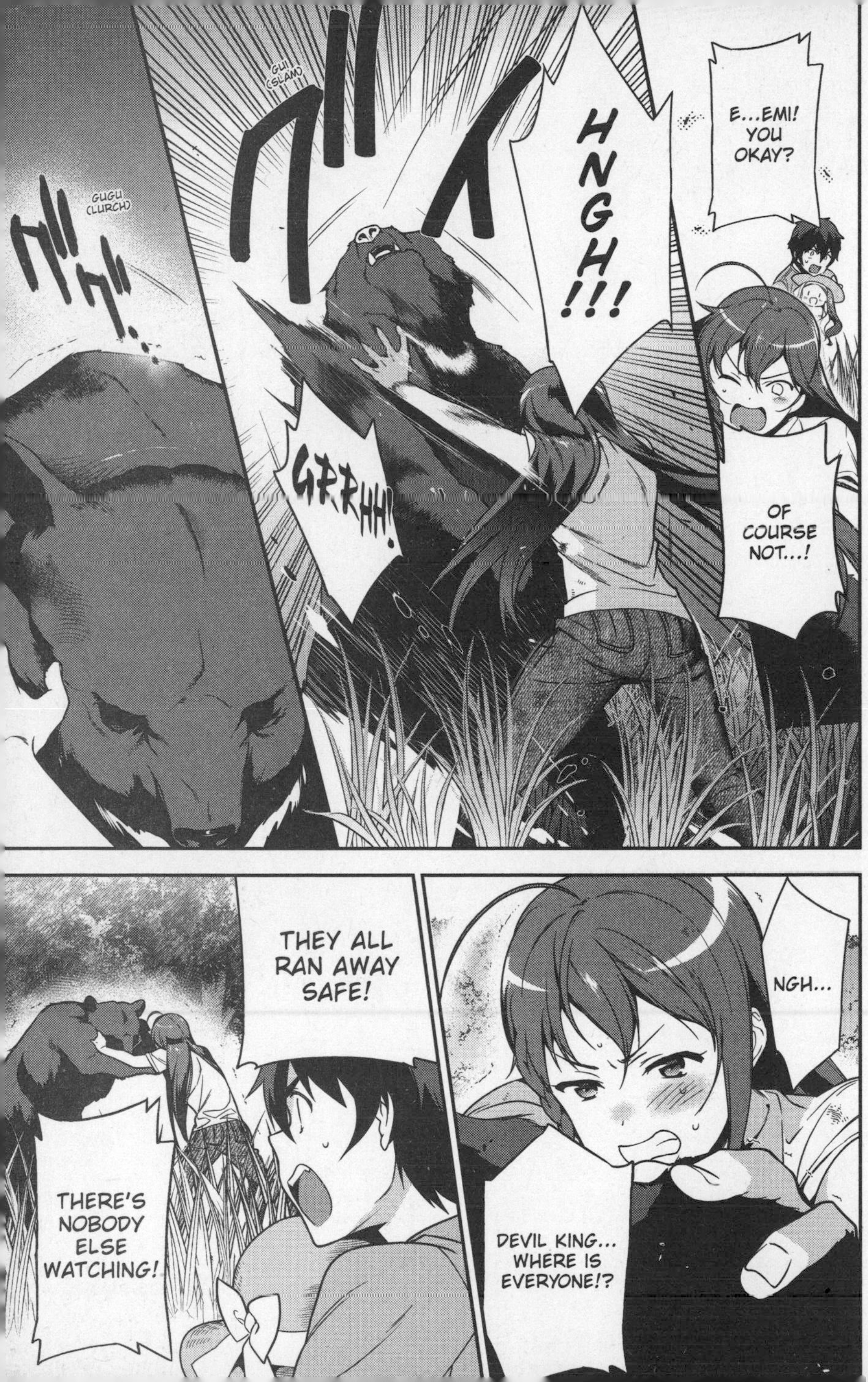
E...EMI! YOU OKAY?
HNGH!!!
GUI (SLAM)
OF COURSE NOT...!
GRRHH!
GUGU (LURCH)
NGH...
DEVIL KING... WHERE IS EVERYONE!?
THEY ALL RAN AWAY SAFE!
THERE'S NOBODY ELSE WATCHING!

IT'S THINNER THAN I EXPECTED.

I CAN FEEL ITS BONES UNDERNEATH ITS ARMS...

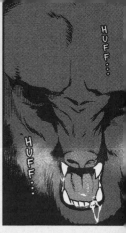

HUFF...

HUFF...

KIII (TWIIING)

...SORRY!

THIS BEAR MUST'VE TRAVELED HERE IN SEARCH OF FOOD.

BUT...

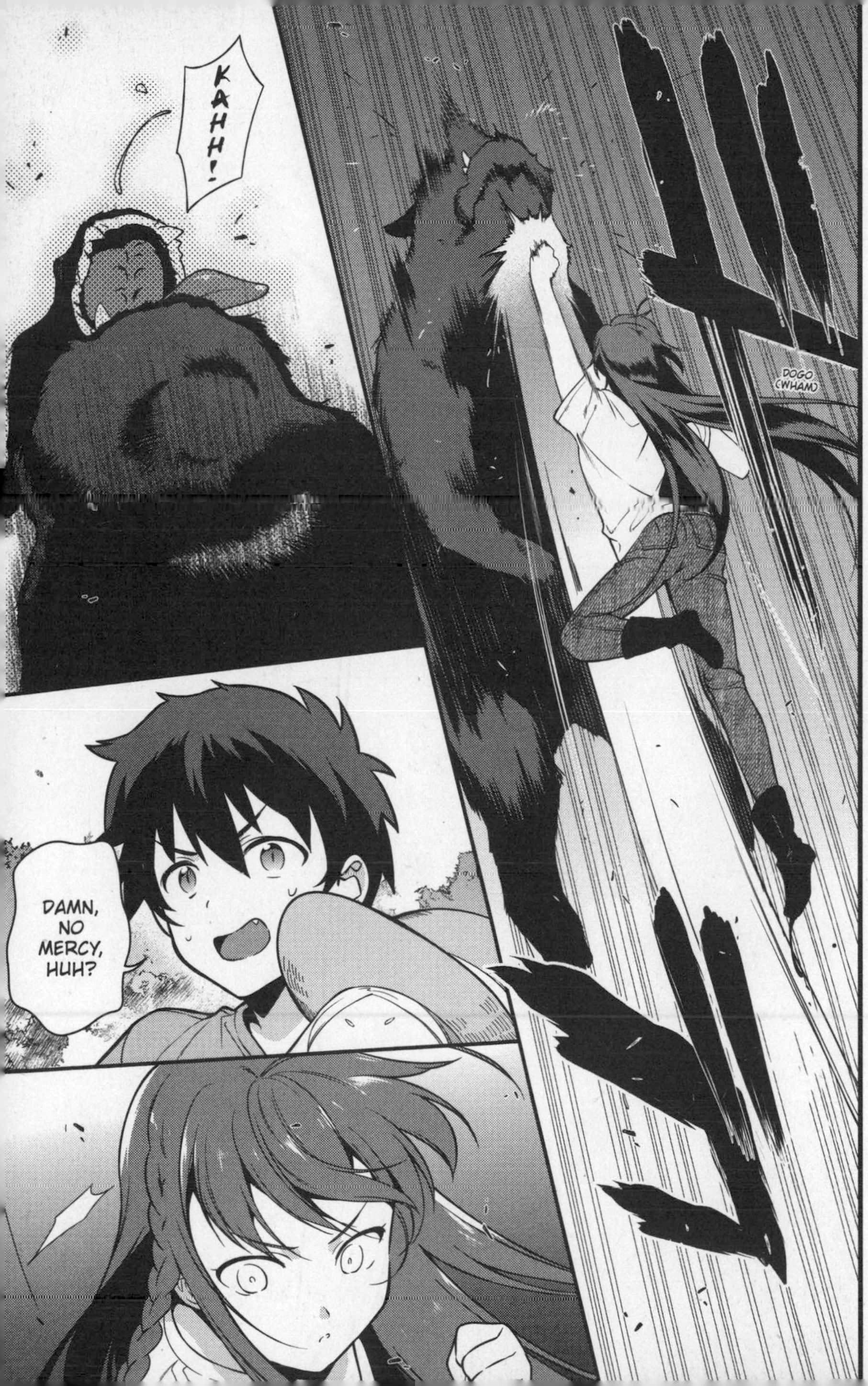
DOGO
(WHAM)
KAHH!
DAMN, NO MERCY, HUH?

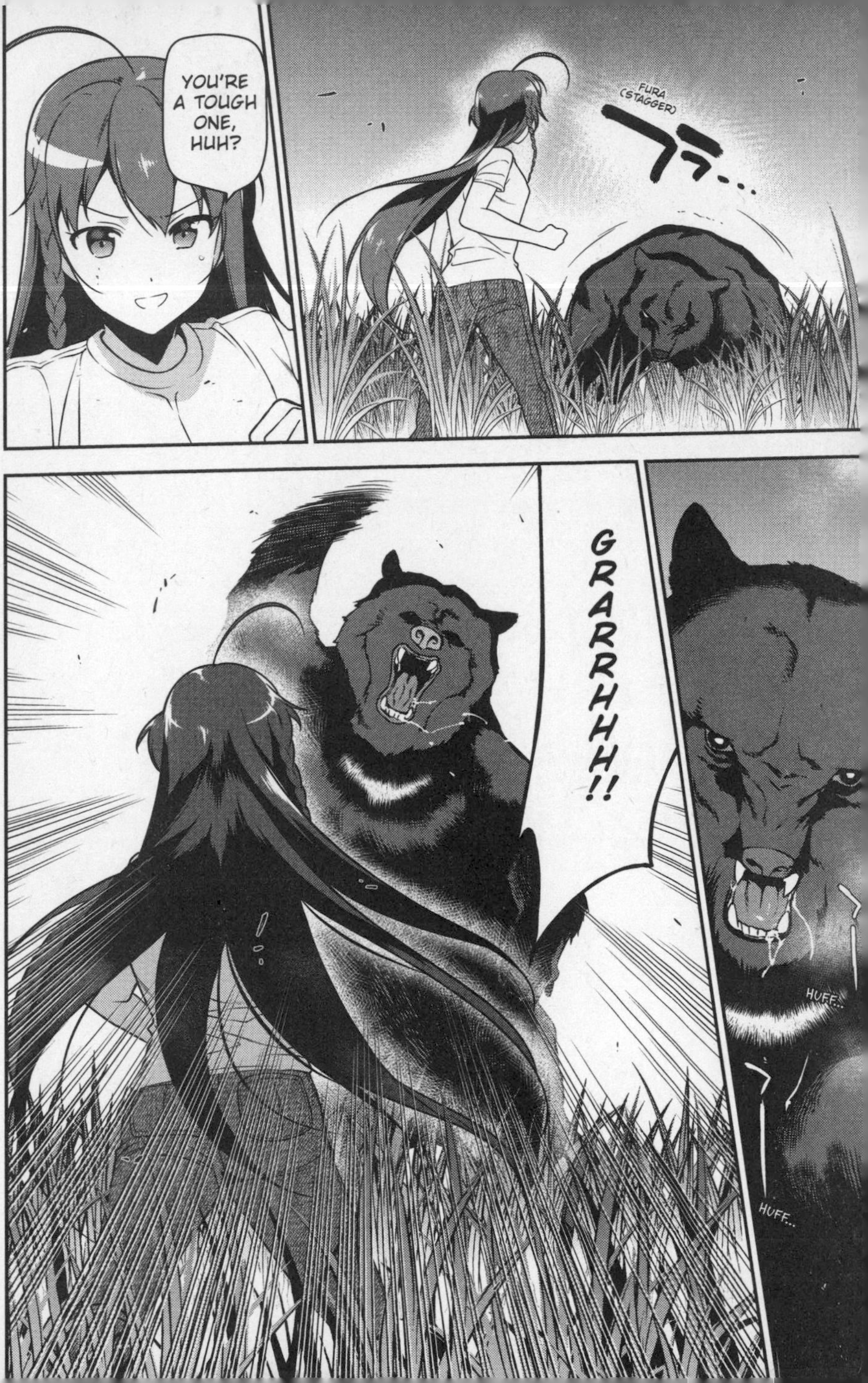
FURA (STAGGER)
YOU'RE A TOUGH ONE, HUH?
HUFF...
HUFF...
GRARRHHH!!

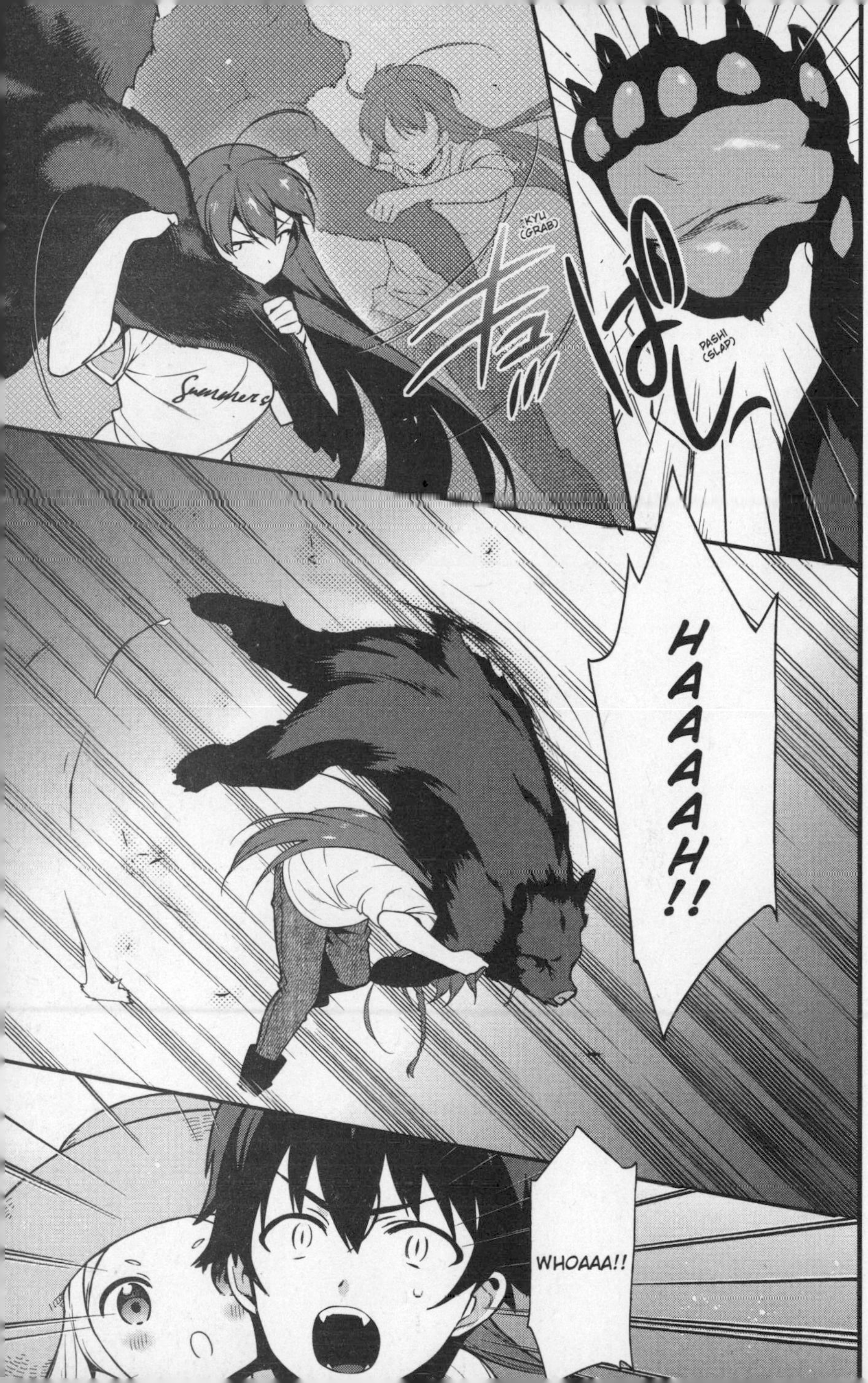
PASHI (SLAP)
KYU (GRAB)
Summers
HAAAAAH!!
WHOAAA!!

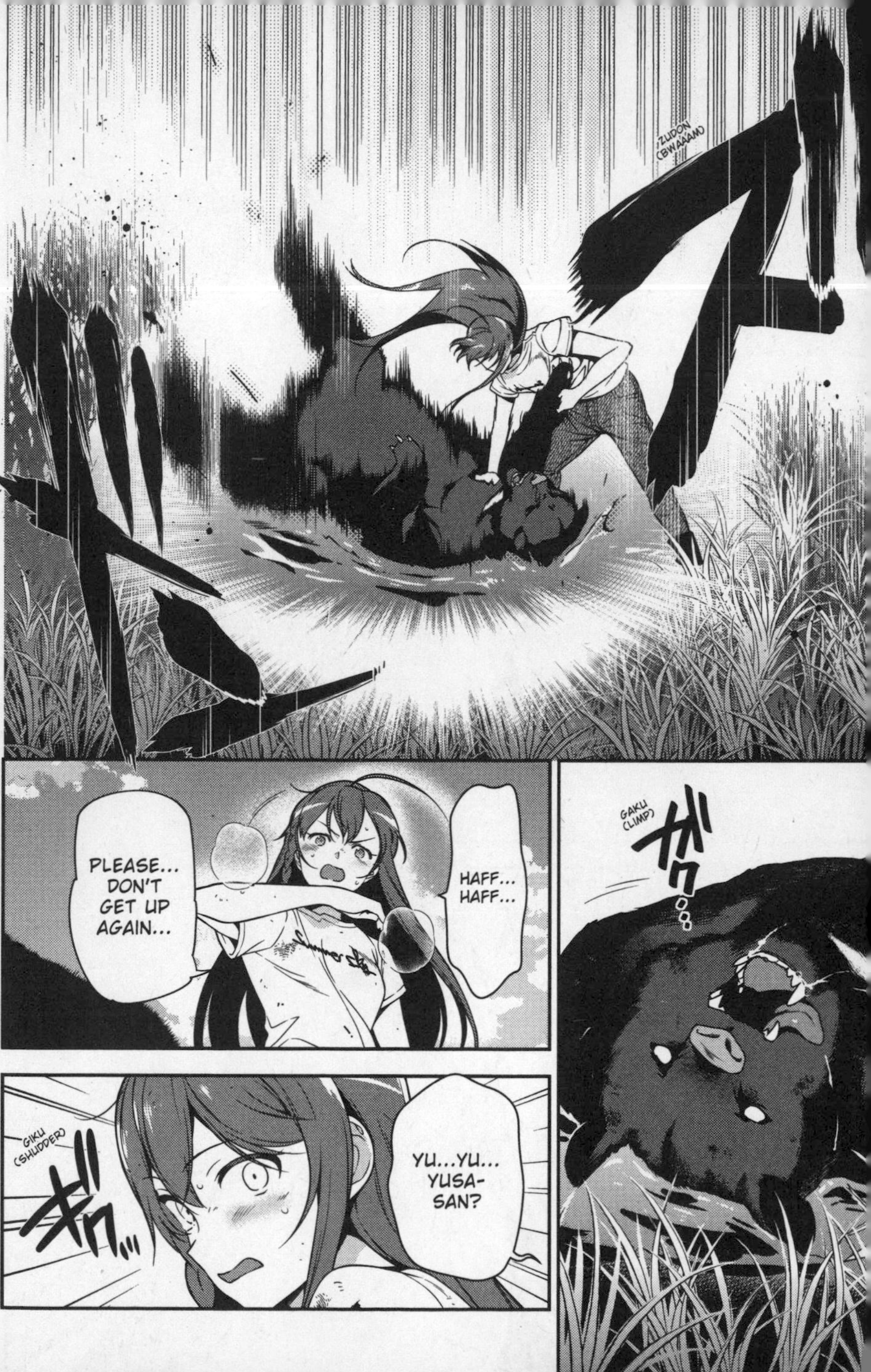
ZUDON (BWAAAM)
GAKU (LIMP)
HAFF... HAFF...
PLEASE... DON'T GET UP AGAIN...
YU...YU... YUSA-SAN?
GIKU (SHUDDER)

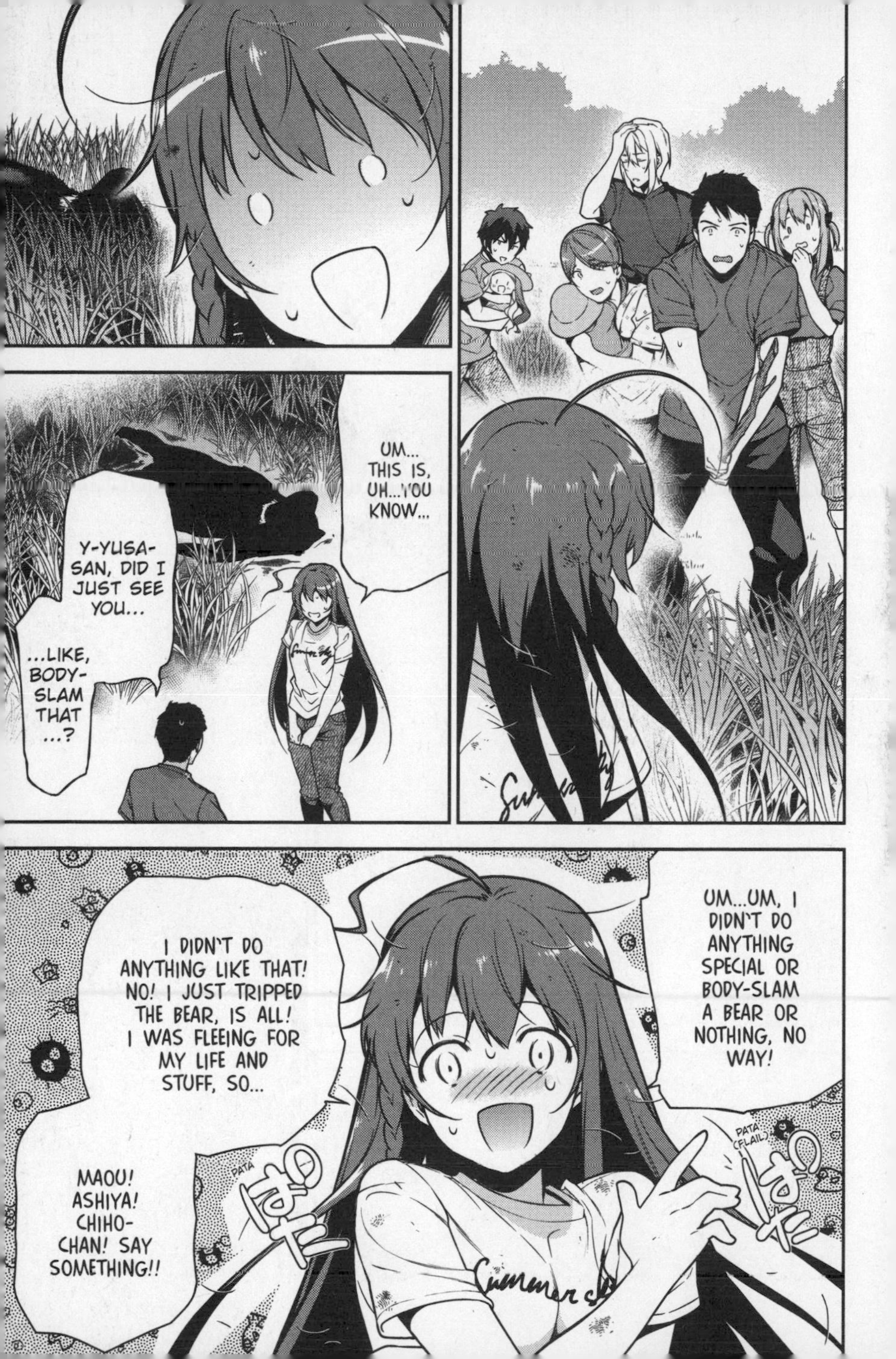
UM... THIS IS, UH...YOU KNOW...
Y-YUSA-SAN, DID I JUST SEE YOU...
...LIKE, BODY-SLAM THAT...?
UM...UM, I DIDN'T DO ANYTHING SPECIAL OR BODY-SLAM A BEAR OR NOTHING, NO WAY!
PATA (FLAIL)
I DIDN'T DO ANYTHING LIKE THAT! NO! I JUST TRIPPED THE BEAR, IS ALL! I WAS FLEEING FOR MY LIFE AND STUFF, SO...
PATA
MAOU! ASHIYA! CHIHO-CHAN! SAY SOMETHING!!

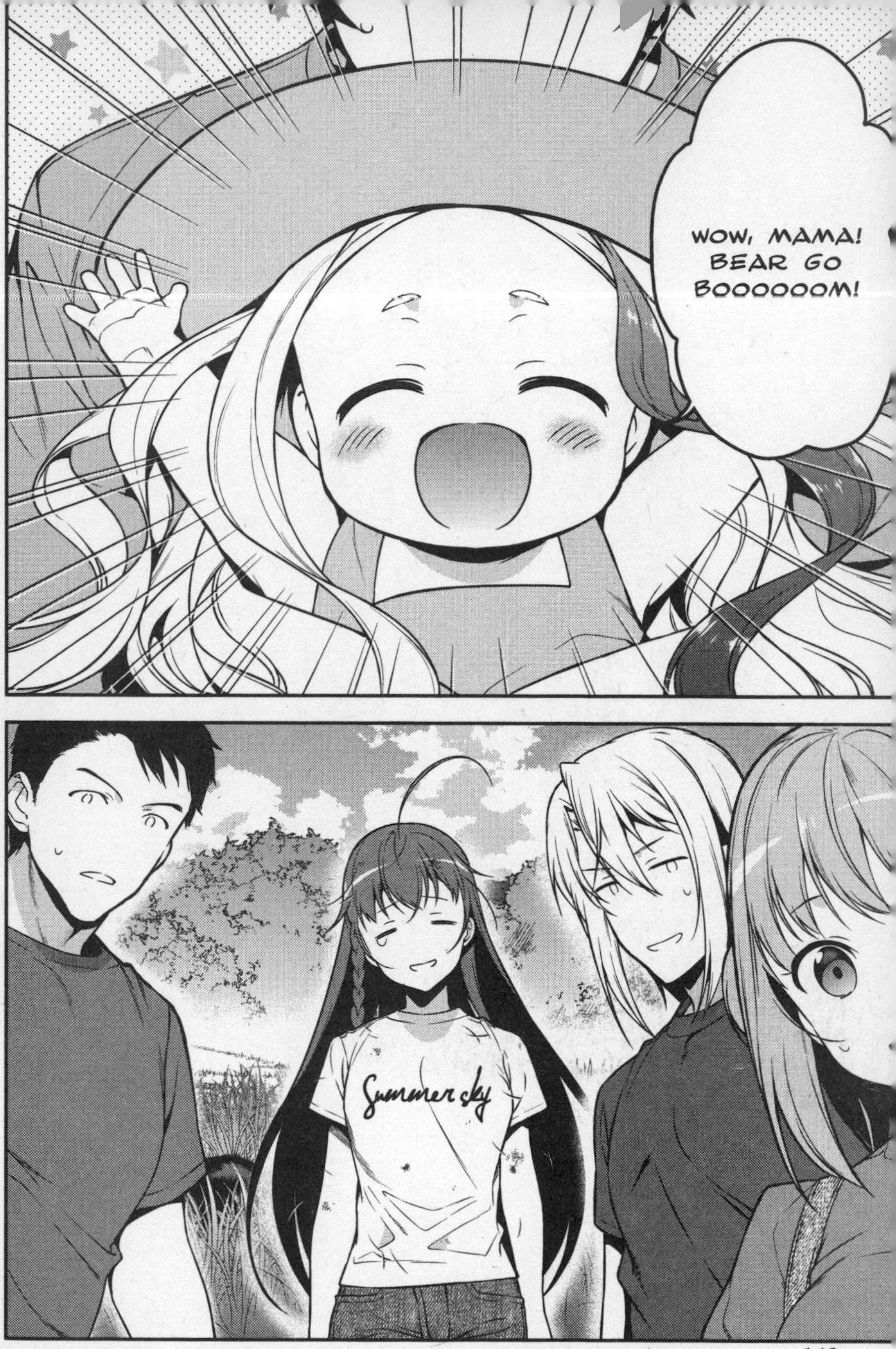
WOW, MAMA!
BEAR GO
BOOOOOOM!
Summer sky

Bear

THE DEVIL IS A PART-TIMER!

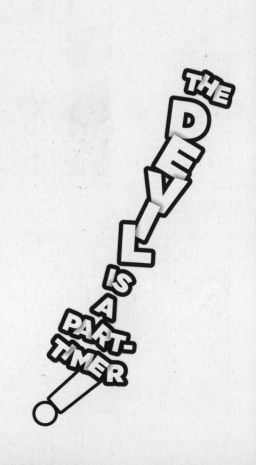

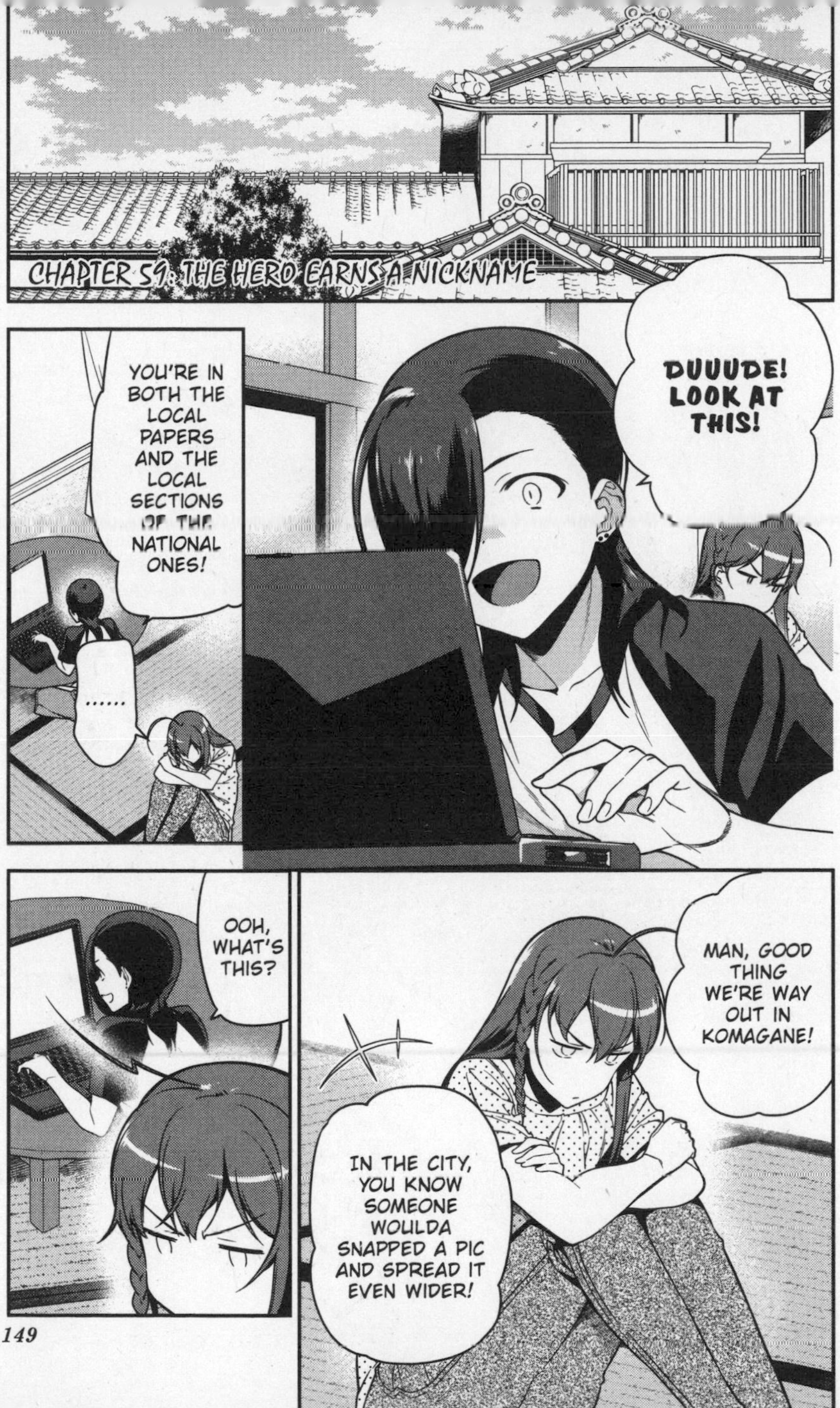
CHAPTER 59: THE HERO EARNS A NICKNAME
DUUUDE! LOOK AT THIS!
YOU'RE IN BOTH THE LOCAL PAPERS AND THE LOCAL SECTIONS OF THE NATIONAL ONES!
......
MAN, GOOD THING WE'RE WAY OUT IN KOMAGANE!
IN THE CITY, YOU KNOW SOMEONE WOULDA SNAPPED A PIC AND SPREAD IT EVEN WIDER!
OOH, WHAT'S THIS?

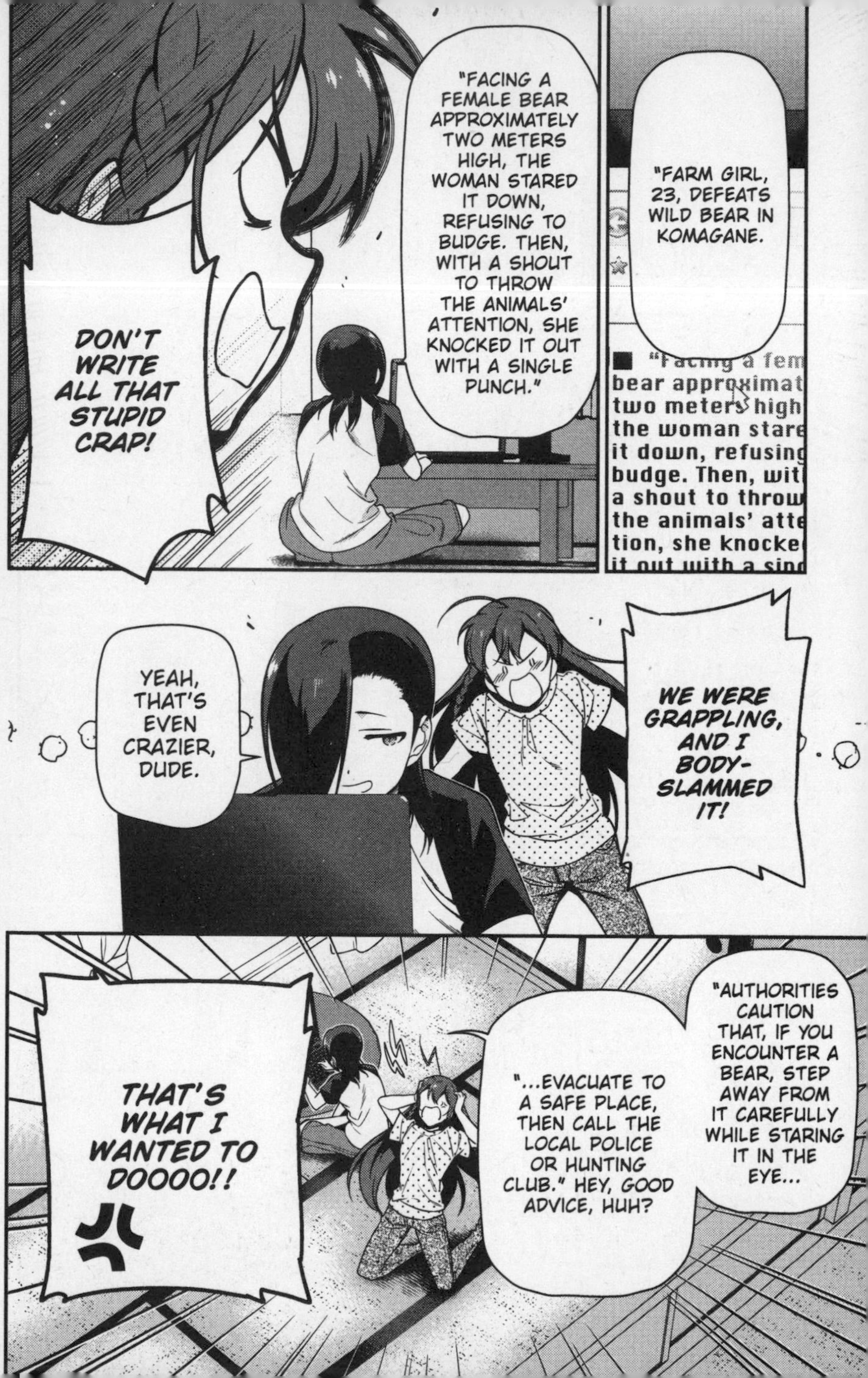
"FARM GIRL, 23, DEFEATS WILD BEAR IN KOMAGANE.
■ "Facing a fem bear approximat two meters high the woman stare it down, refusing budge. Then, wit a shout to throw the animals' atte tion, she knocke
"FACING A FEMALE BEAR APPROXIMATELY TWO METERS HIGH, THE WOMAN STARED IT DOWN, REFUSING TO BUDGE. THEN, WITH A SHOUT TO THROW THE ANIMALS' ATTENTION, SHE KNOCKED IT OUT WITH A SINGLE PUNCH."
DON'T WRITE ALL THAT STUPID CRAP!
WE WERE GRAPPLING, AND I BODY-SLAMMED IT!
YEAH, THAT'S EVEN CRAZIER, DUDE.
"AUTHORITIES CAUTION THAT, IF YOU ENCOUNTER A BEAR, STEP AWAY FROM IT CAREFULLY WHILE STARING IT IN THE EYE...
"...EVACUATE TO A SAFE PLACE, THEN CALL THE LOCAL POLICE OR HUNTING CLUB." HEY, GOOD ADVICE, HUH?
THAT'S WHAT I WANTED TO DOOOO!!

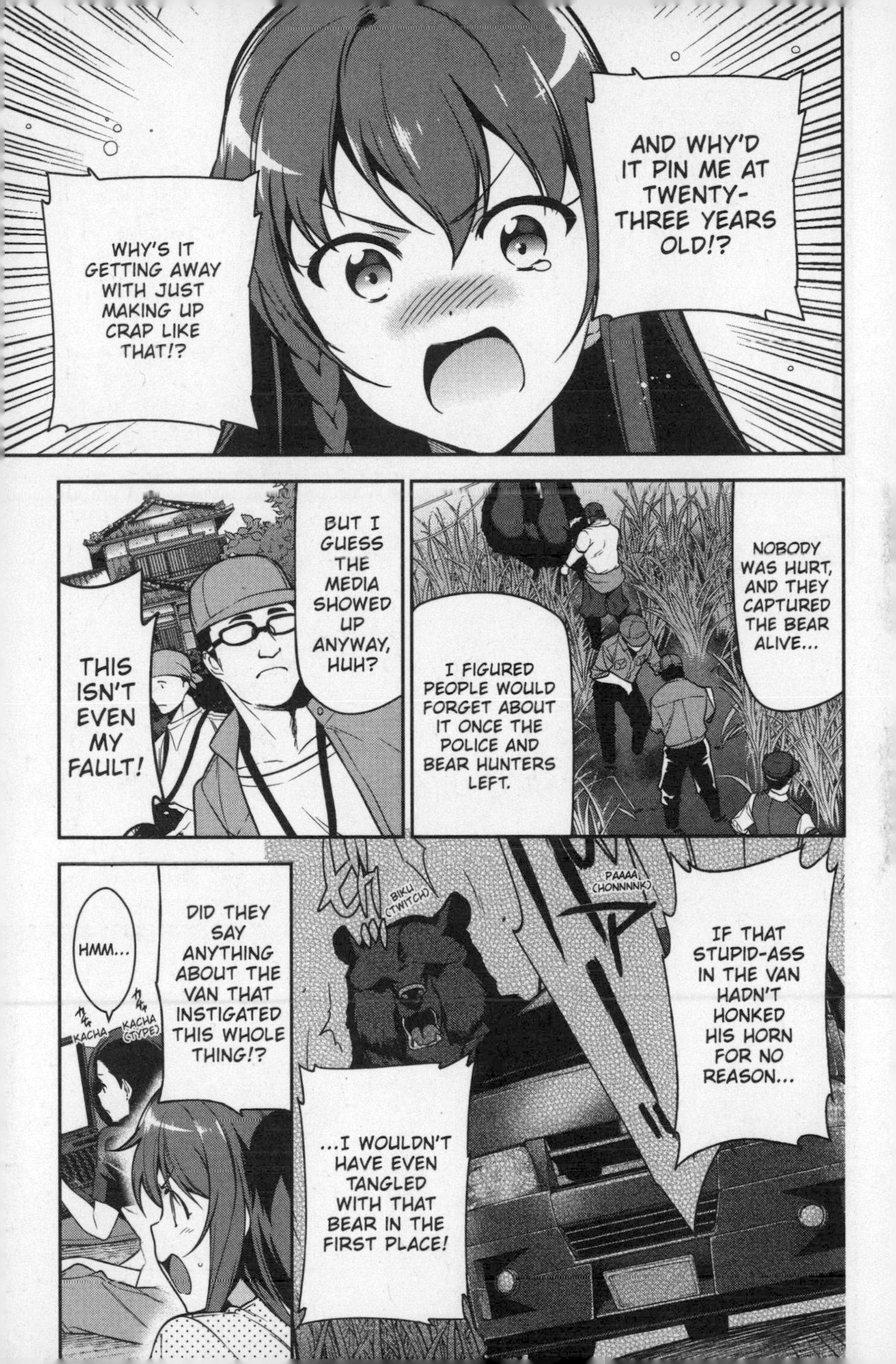
AND WHY'D IT PIN ME AT TWENTY-THREE YEARS OLD!?
WHY'S IT GETTING AWAY WITH JUST MAKING UP CRAP LIKE THAT!?
NOBODY WAS HURT, AND THEY CAPTURED THE BEAR ALIVE...
I FIGURED PEOPLE WOULD FORGET ABOUT IT ONCE THE POLICE AND BEAR HUNTERS LEFT.
BUT I GUESS THE MEDIA SHOWED UP ANYWAY, HUH?
THIS ISN'T EVEN MY FAULT!
PAAAA (HONNNNK)
BIKU (TWITCH)
IF THAT STUPID-ASS IN THE VAN HADN'T HONKED HIS HORN FOR NO REASON...
...I WOULDN'T HAVE EVEN TANGLED WITH THAT BEAR IN THE FIRST PLACE!
DID THEY SAY ANYTHING ABOUT THE VAN THAT INSTIGATED THIS WHOLE THING!?
HMM...
KACHA KACHA (TYPE)

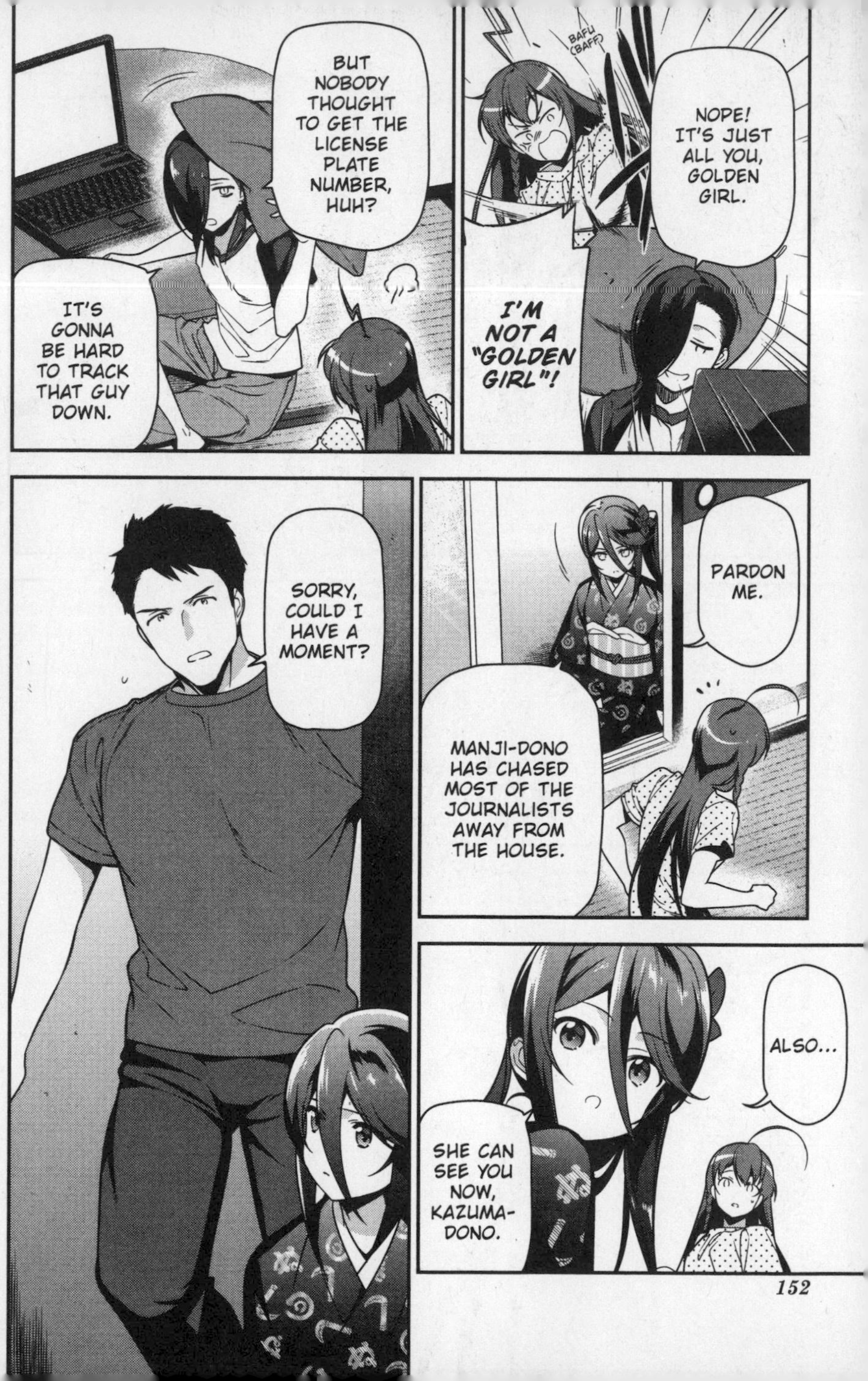
BAFU (BAFF)
NOPE! IT'S JUST ALL YOU, GOLDEN GIRL.
I'M NOT A "GOLDEN GIRL"!
BUT NOBODY THOUGHT TO GET THE LICENSE PLATE NUMBER, HUH?
IT'S GONNA BE HARD TO TRACK THAT GUY DOWN.
PARDON ME.
MANJI-DONO HAS CHASED MOST OF THE JOURNALISTS AWAY FROM THE HOUSE.
ALSO...
SHE CAN SEE YOU NOW, KAZUMA-DONO.
SORRY, COULD I HAVE A MOMENT?

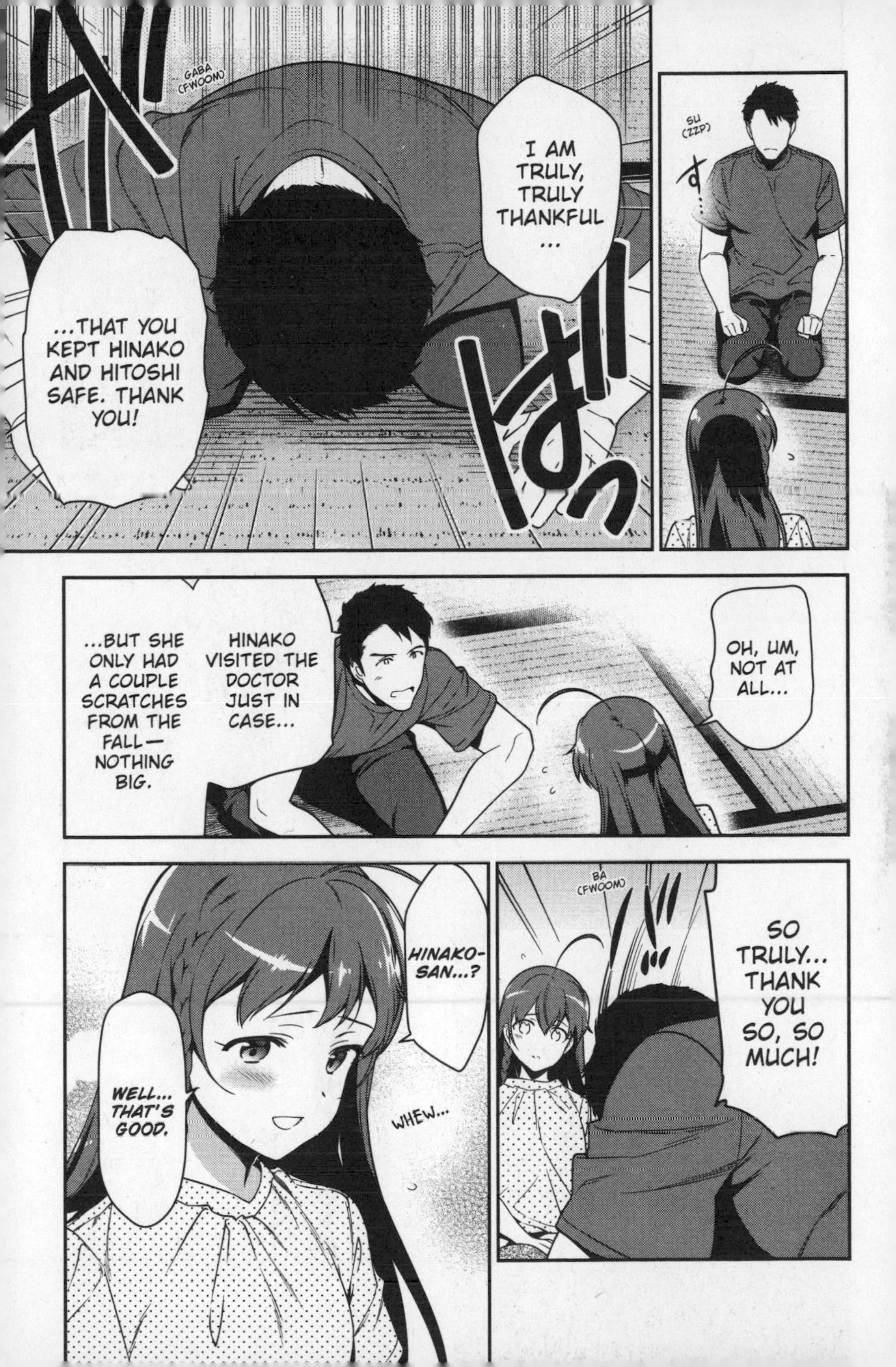
SU (ZZP)
す
GABA (FWOOM)
I AM TRULY, TRULY THANKFUL ...
...THAT YOU KEPT HINAKO AND HITOSHI SAFE. THANK YOU!
ばっ
OH, UM, NOT AT ALL...
HINAKO VISITED THE DOCTOR JUST IN CASE...
...BUT SHE ONLY HAD A COUPLE SCRATCHES FROM THE FALL—NOTHING BIG.
BA (FWOOM)
SO TRULY... THANK YOU SO, SO MUCH!
HINAKO-SAN...?
WHEW...
WELL... THAT'S GOOD.

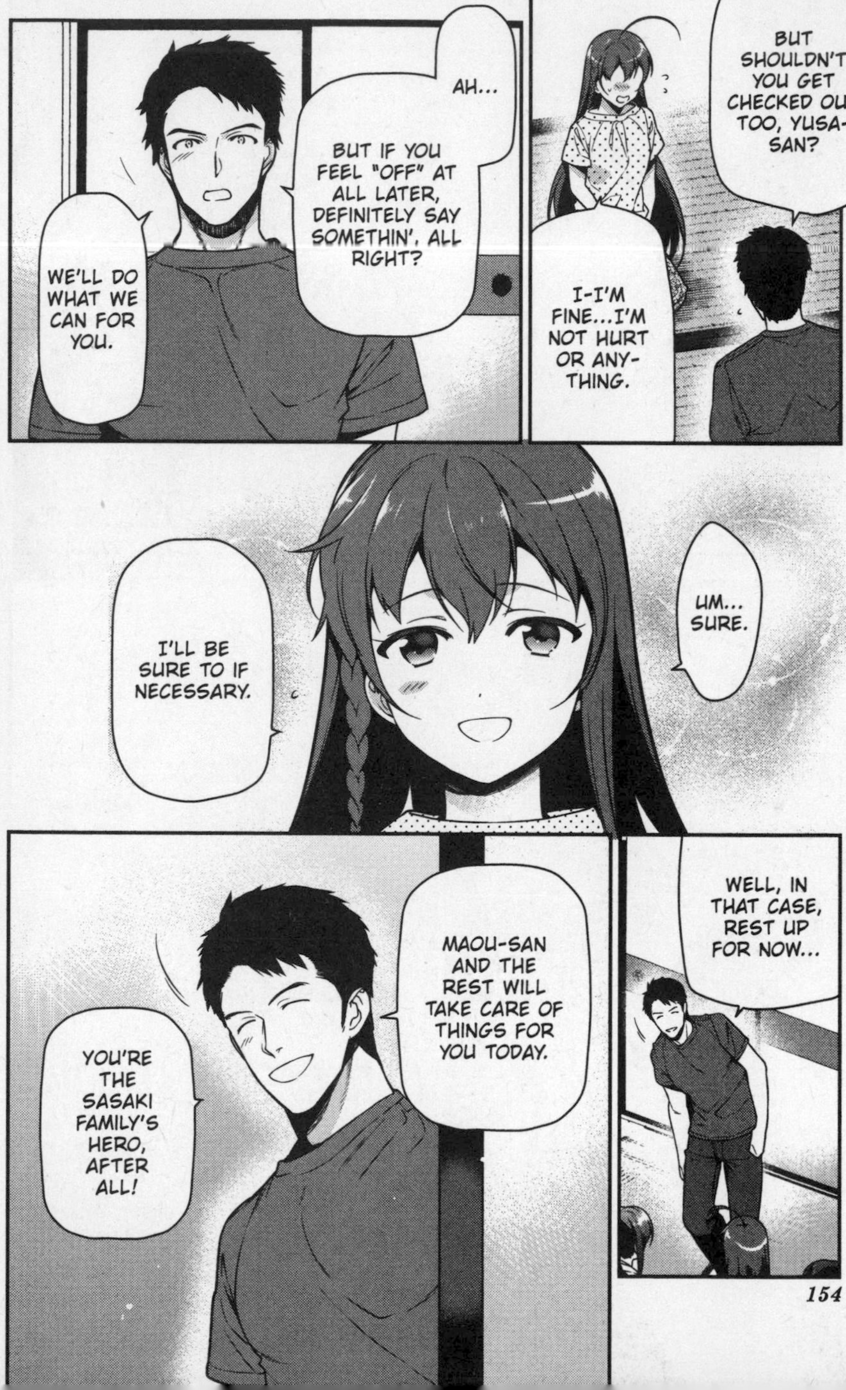
BUT SHOULDN'T YOU GET CHECKED OUT TOO, YUSA-SAN?
I-I'M FINE...I'M NOT HURT OR ANYTHING.
AH...
BUT IF YOU FEEL "OFF" AT ALL LATER, DEFINITELY SAY SOMETHIN', ALL RIGHT?
WE'LL DO WHAT WE CAN FOR YOU.
UM... SURE.
I'LL BE SURE TO IF NECESSARY.
WELL, IN THAT CASE, REST UP FOR NOW...
MAOU-SAN AND THE REST WILL TAKE CARE OF THINGS FOR YOU TODAY.
YOU'RE THE SASAKI FAMILY'S HERO, AFTER ALL!

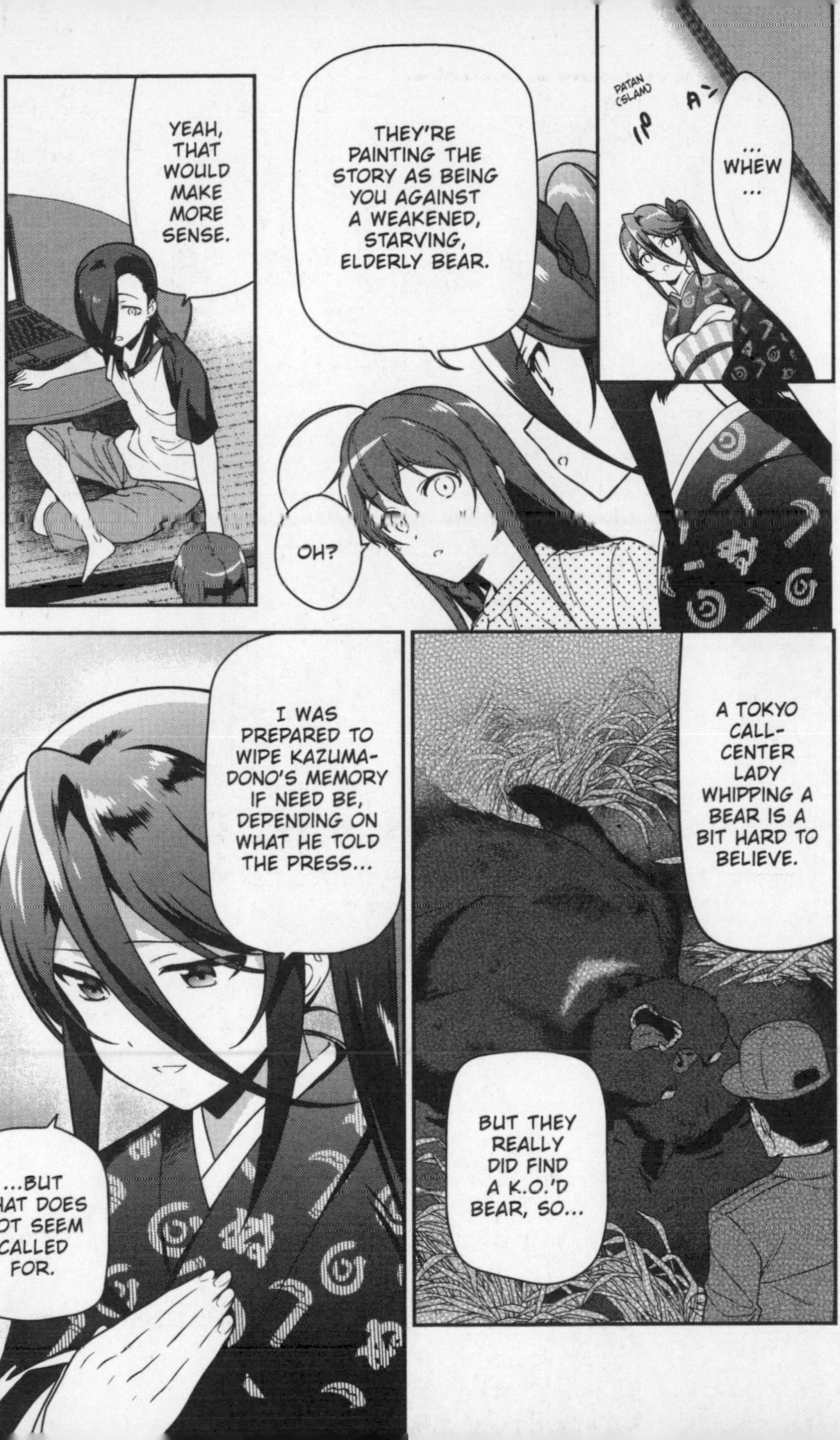
PATAN (SLAM)
...WHEW...
THEY'RE PAINTING THE STORY AS BEING YOU AGAINST A WEAKENED, STARVING, ELDERLY BEAR.
OH?
YEAH, THAT WOULD MAKE MORE SENSE.
A TOKYO CALL-CENTER LADY WHIPPING A BEAR IS A BIT HARD TO BELIEVE.
BUT THEY REALLY DID FIND A K.O.'D BEAR, SO...
I WAS PREPARED TO WIPE KAZUMA-DONO'S MEMORY IF NEED BE, DEPENDING ON WHAT HE TOLD THE PRESS...
...BUT THAT DOES NOT SEEM CALLED FOR.

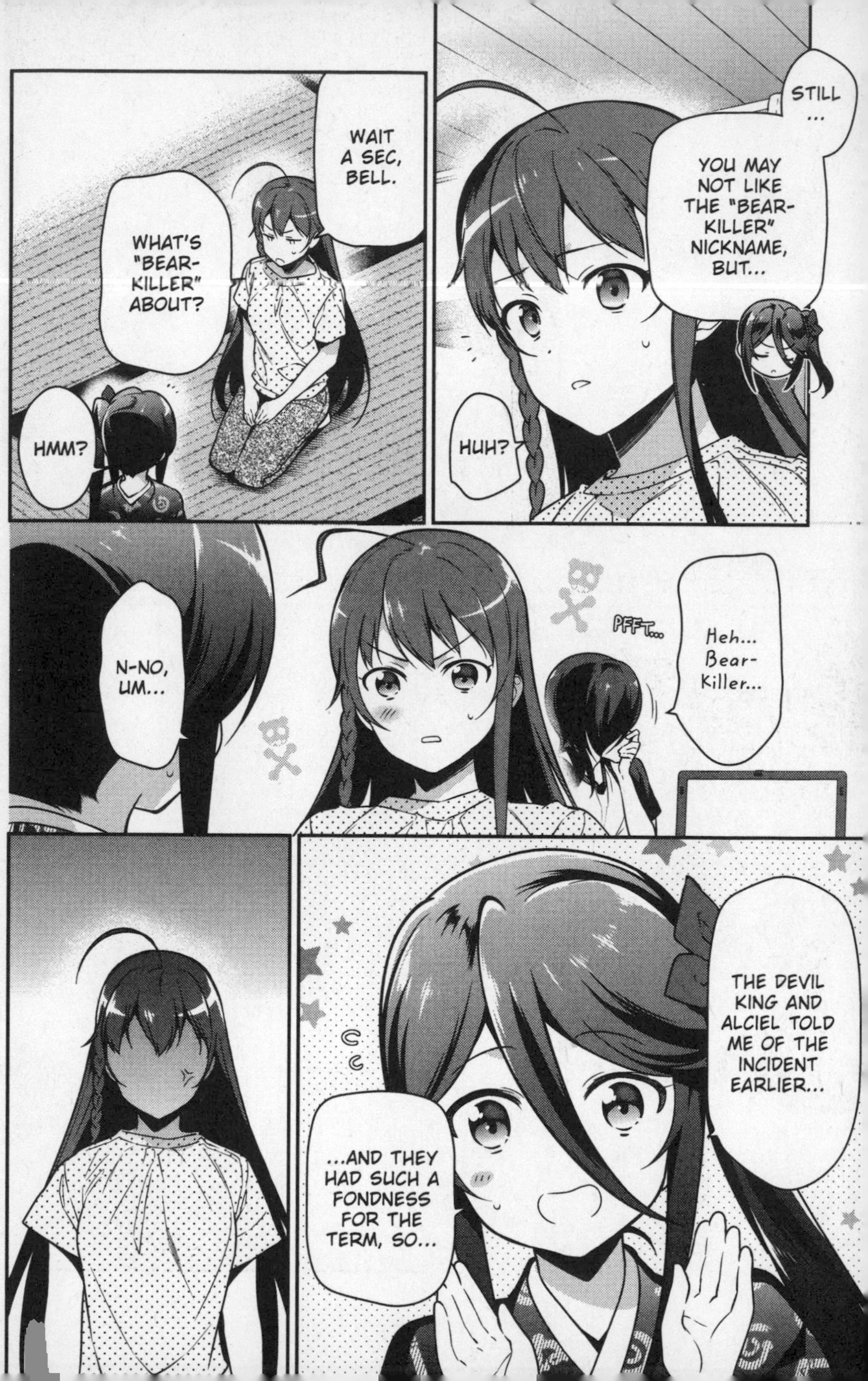
STILL...
YOU MAY NOT LIKE THE "BEAR-KILLER" NICKNAME, BUT...
HUH?
WAIT A SEC, BELL.
WHAT'S "BEAR-KILLER" ABOUT?
HMM?
Heh... Bear-Killer...
PFFT...
N-NO, UM...
THE DEVIL KING AND ALCIEL TOLD ME OF THE INCIDENT EARLIER...
...AND THEY HAD SUCH A FONDNESS FOR THE TERM, SO...

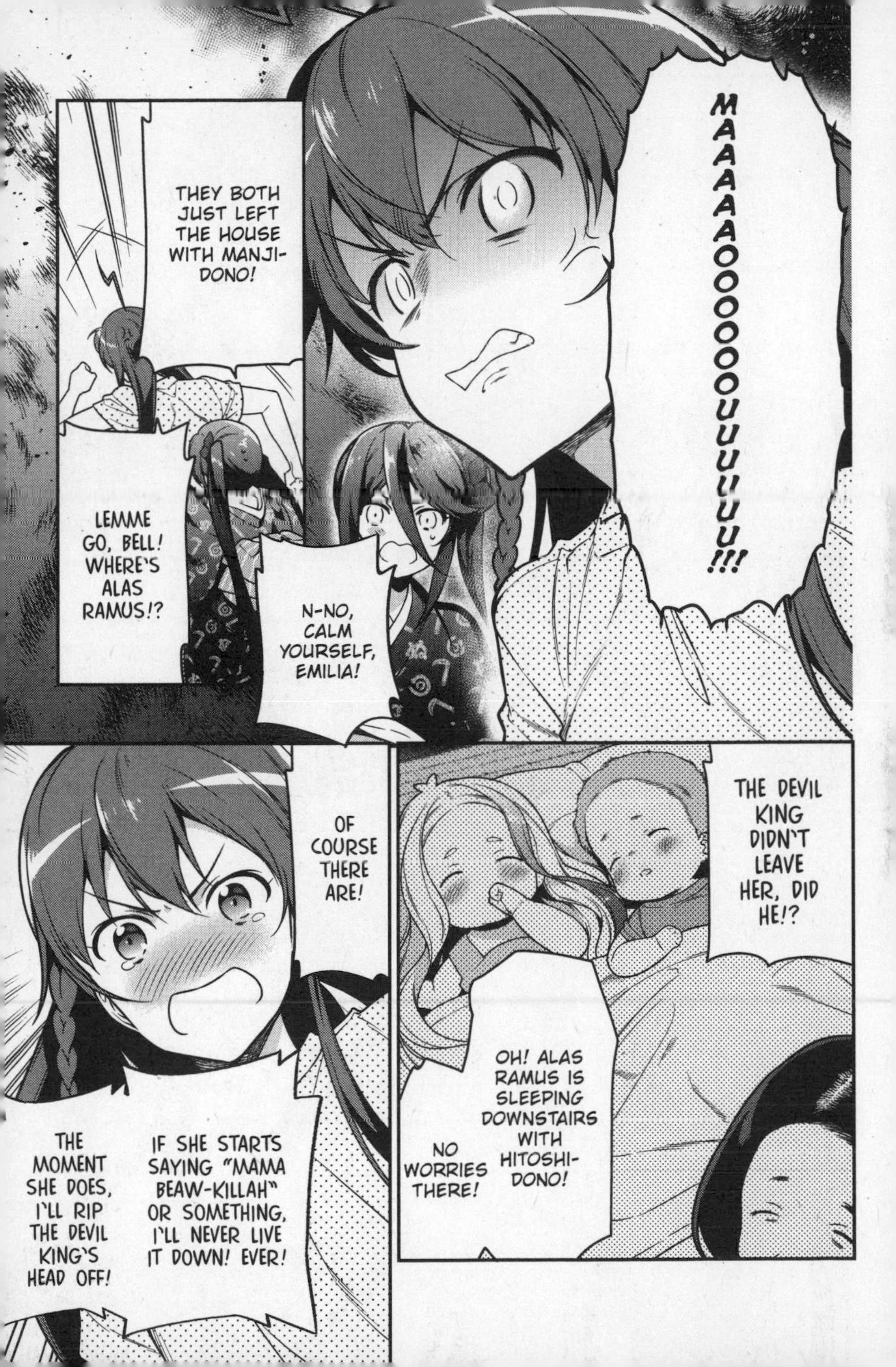
MAAAAAOOOOOOUUUUUU!!!
THEY BOTH JUST LEFT THE HOUSE WITH MANJI-DONO!
LEMME GO, BELL! WHERE'S ALAS RAMUS!?
N-NO, CALM YOURSELF, EMILIA!
THE DEVIL KING DIDN'T LEAVE HER, DID HE!?
OH! ALAS RAMUS IS SLEEPING DOWNSTAIRS WITH HITOSHI-DONO!
NO WORRIES THERE!
OF COURSE THERE ARE!
IF SHE STARTS SAYING "MAMA BEAW-KILLAH" OR SOMETHING, I'LL NEVER LIVE IT DOWN! EVER!
THE MOMENT SHE DOES, I'LL RIP THE DEVIL KING'S HEAD OFF!

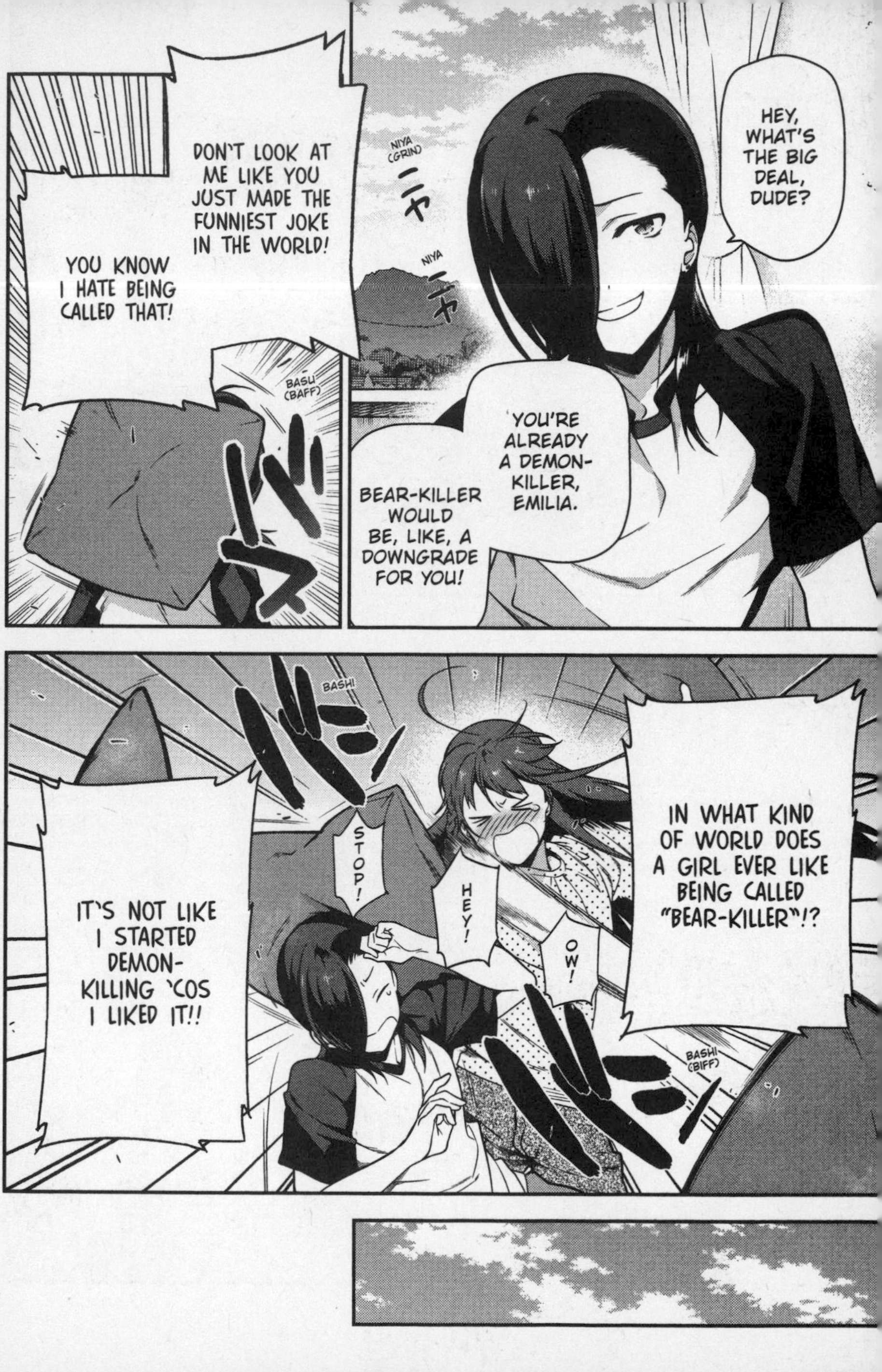
HEY, WHAT'S THE BIG DEAL, DUDE?
NIYA (GRIN)
NIYA
YOU'RE ALREADY A DEMON-KILLER, EMILIA.
BEAR-KILLER WOULD BE, LIKE, A DOWNGRADE FOR YOU!
DON'T LOOK AT ME LIKE YOU JUST MADE THE FUNNIEST JOKE IN THE WORLD!
YOU KNOW I HATE BEING CALLED THAT!
BASU (BAFF)
IN WHAT KIND OF WORLD DOES A GIRL EVER LIKE BEING CALLED "BEAR-KILLER"!?
BASHI
STOP!
HEY!
OW!
BASHI (BIFF)
IT'S NOT LIKE I STARTED DEMON-KILLING 'COS I LIKED IT!!

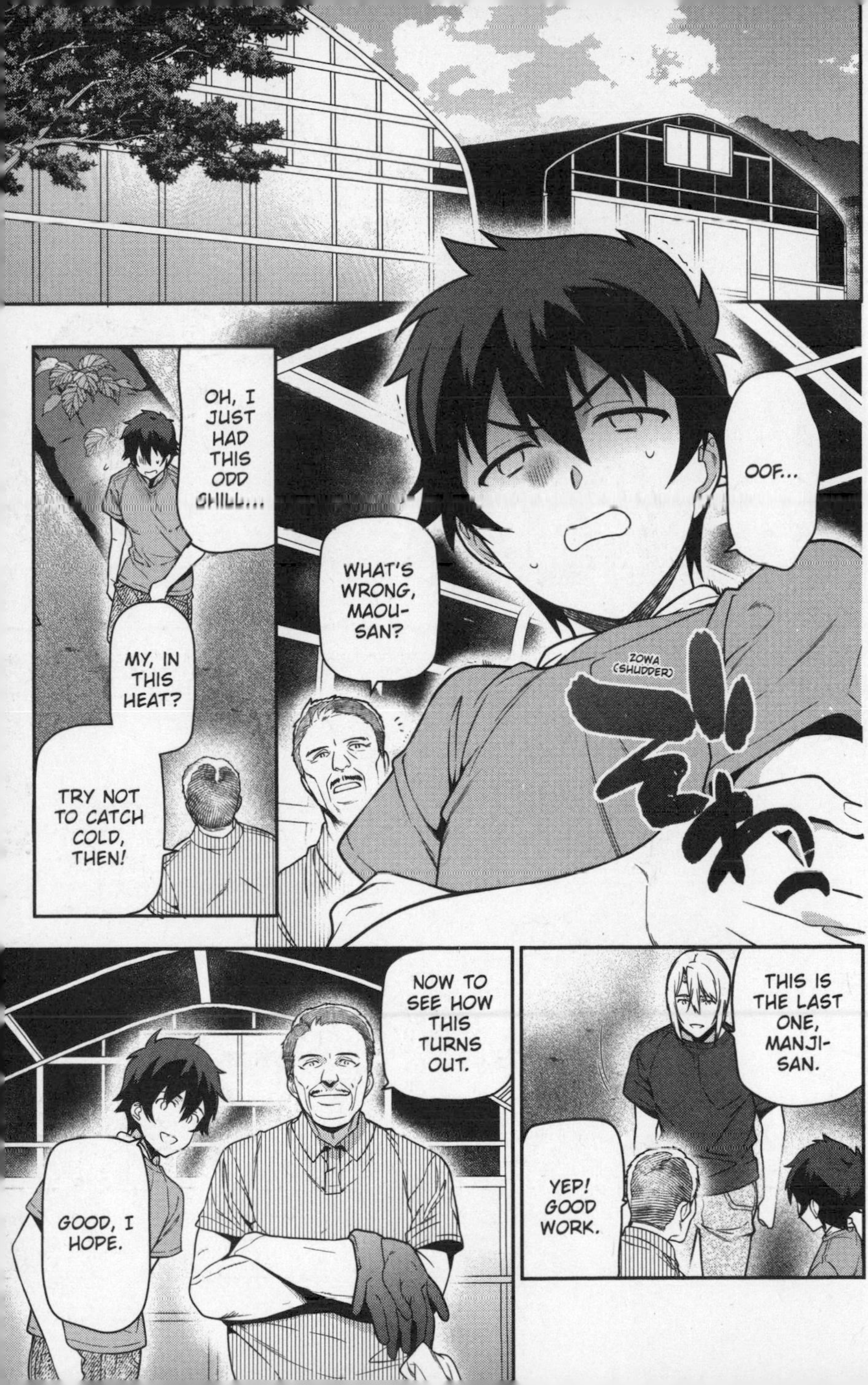
OOF...
ZOWA (SHUDDER)
ぞわっ
WHAT'S WRONG, MAOU-SAN?
OH, I JUST HAD THIS ODD CHILL...
MY, IN THIS HEAT?
TRY NOT TO CATCH COLD, THEN!
THIS IS THE LAST ONE, MANJI-SAN.
YEP! GOOD WORK.
NOW TO SEE HOW THIS TURNS OUT.
GOOD, I HOPE.

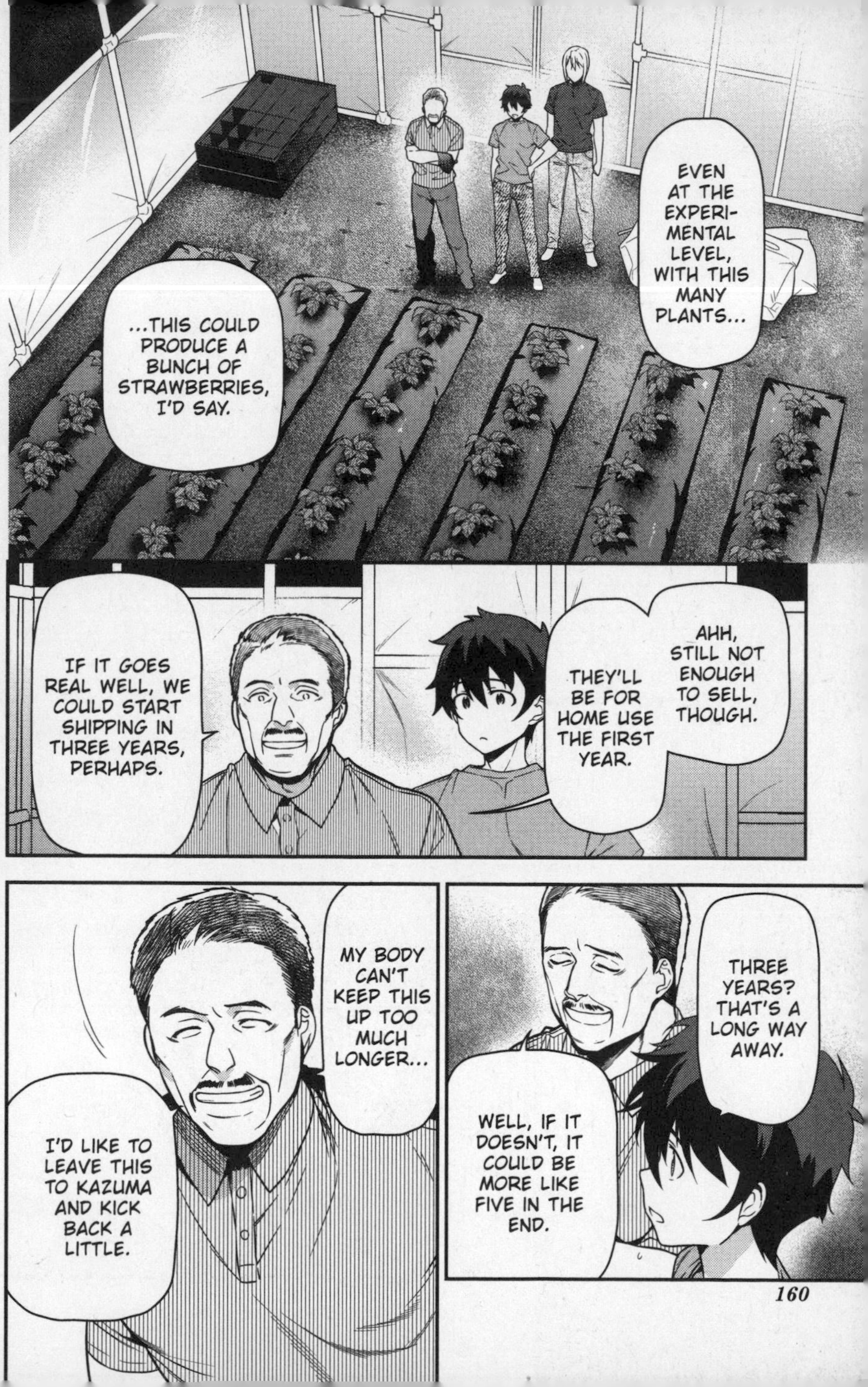

EVEN AT THE EXPERIMENTAL LEVEL, WITH THIS MANY PLANTS...
...THIS COULD PRODUCE A BUNCH OF STRAWBERRIES, I'D SAY.
AHH, STILL NOT ENOUGH TO SELL, THOUGH.
THEY'LL BE FOR HOME USE THE FIRST YEAR.
IF IT GOES REAL WELL, WE COULD START SHIPPING IN THREE YEARS, PERHAPS.
THREE YEARS? THAT'S A LONG WAY AWAY.
WELL, IF IT DOESN'T, IT COULD BE MORE LIKE FIVE IN THE END.
MY BODY CAN'T KEEP THIS UP TOO MUCH LONGER...
I'D LIKE TO LEAVE THIS TO KAZUMA AND KICK BACK A LITTLE.

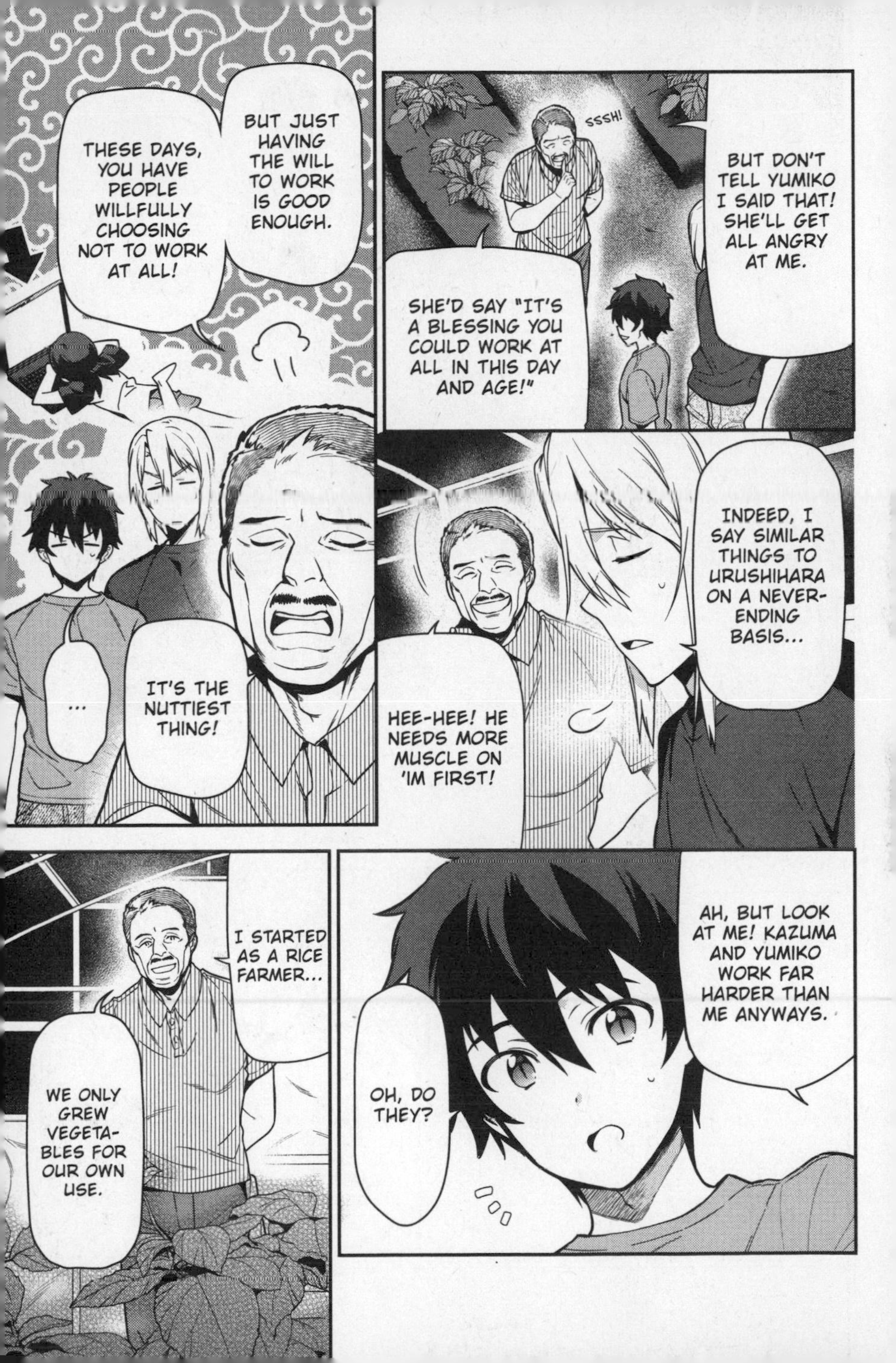
SSSH!
BUT DON'T TELL YUMIKO I SAID THAT! SHE'LL GET ALL ANGRY AT ME.
SHE'D SAY "IT'S A BLESSING YOU COULD WORK AT ALL IN THIS DAY AND AGE!"
INDEED, I SAY SIMILAR THINGS TO URUSHIHARA ON A NEVER-ENDING BASIS...
HEE-HEE! HE NEEDS MORE MUSCLE ON 'IM FIRST!
BUT JUST HAVING THE WILL TO WORK IS GOOD ENOUGH.
THESE DAYS, YOU HAVE PEOPLE WILLFULLY CHOOSING NOT TO WORK AT ALL!
IT'S THE NUTTIEST THING!
...
AH, BUT LOOK AT ME! KAZUMA AND YUMIKO WORK FAR HARDER THAN ME ANYWAYS.
OH, DO THEY?
I STARTED AS A RICE FARMER...
WE ONLY GREW VEGETA-BLES FOR OUR OWN USE.

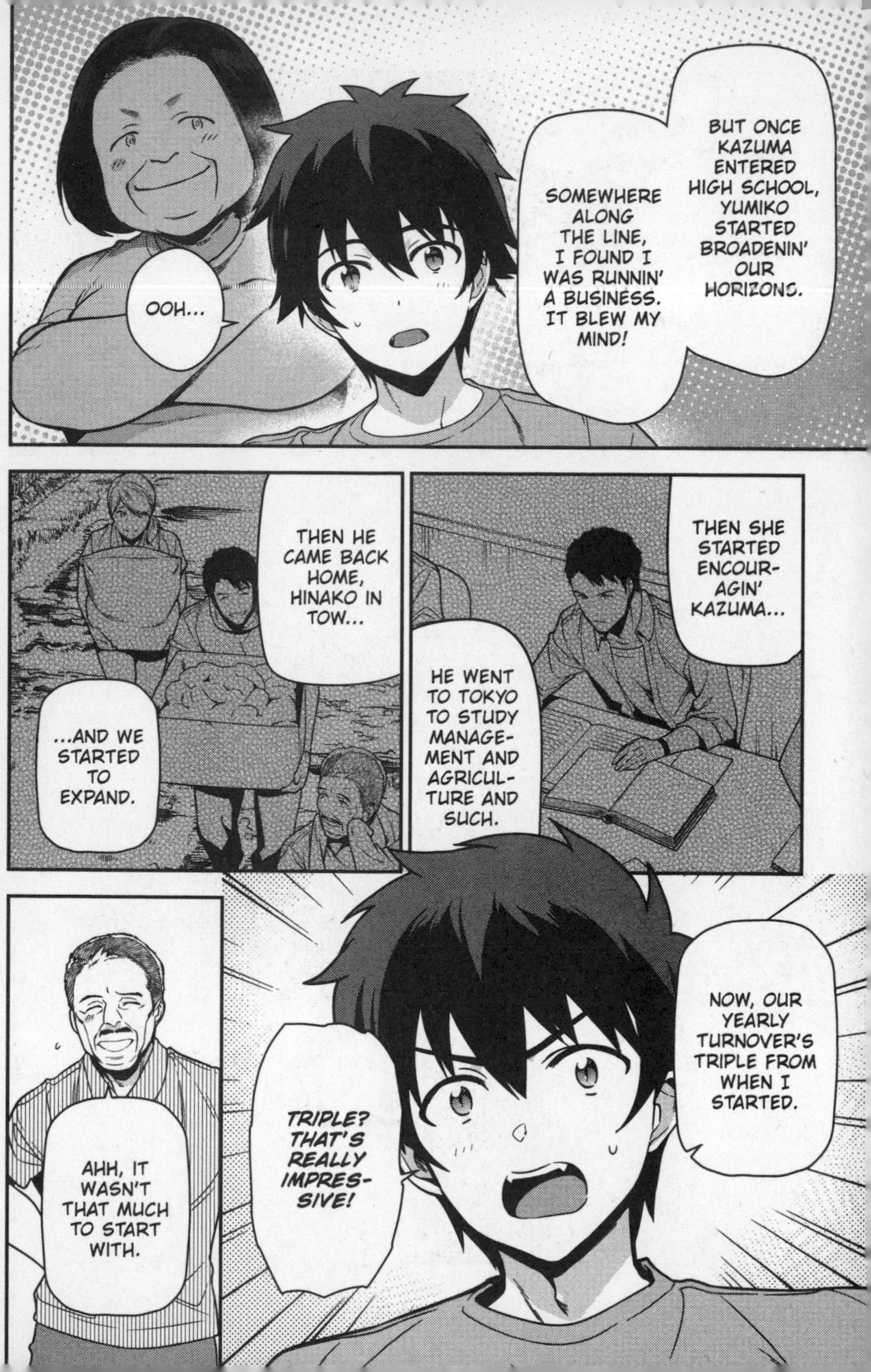
BUT ONCE KAZUMA ENTERED HIGH SCHOOL, YUMIKO STARTED BROADENIN' OUR HORIZONS.
SOMEWHERE ALONG THE LINE, I FOUND I WAS RUNNIN' A BUSINESS. IT BLEW MY MIND!
OOH...
THEN SHE STARTED ENCOURAGIN' KAZUMA...
HE WENT TO TOKYO TO STUDY MANAGEMENT AND AGRICULTURE AND SUCH.
THEN HE CAME BACK HOME, HINAKO IN TOW...
...AND WE STARTED TO EXPAND.
NOW, OUR YEARLY TURNOVER'S TRIPLE FROM WHEN I STARTED.
TRIPLE? THAT'S REALLY IMPRESSIVE!
AHH, IT WASN'T THAT MUCH TO START WITH.

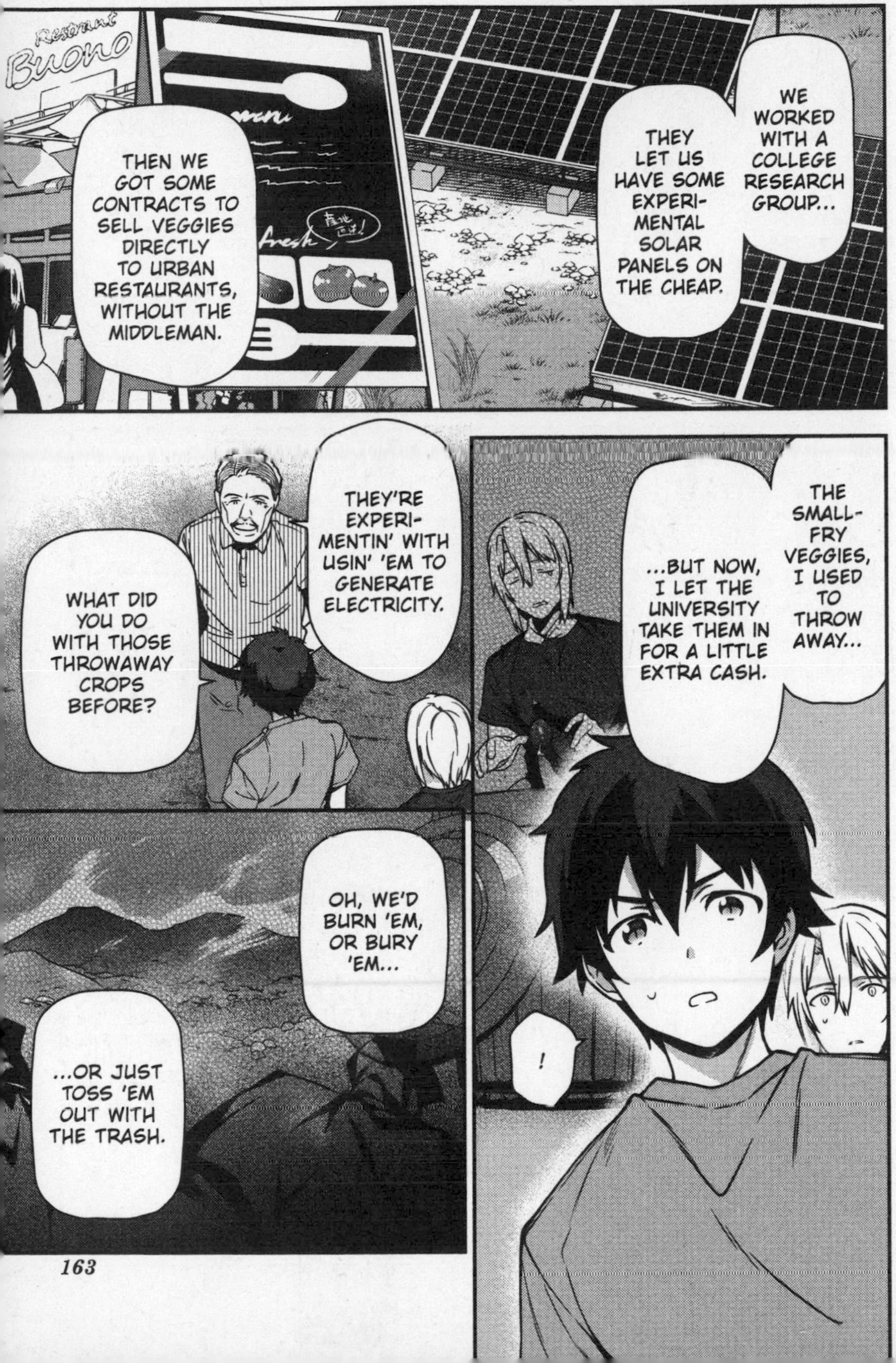
WE WORKED WITH A COLLEGE RESEARCH GROUP...
THEY LET US HAVE SOME EXPERIMENTAL SOLAR PANELS ON THE CHEAP.
Buono
Fresh
産地直送!
THEN WE GOT SOME CONTRACTS TO SELL VEGGIES DIRECTLY TO URBAN RESTAURANTS, WITHOUT THE MIDDLEMAN.
THE SMALL-FRY VEGGIES, I USED TO THROW AWAY...
...BUT NOW, I LET THE UNIVERSITY TAKE THEM IN FOR A LITTLE EXTRA CASH.
!
THEY'RE EXPERIMENTIN' WITH USIN' 'EM TO GENERATE ELECTRICITY.
WHAT DID YOU DO WITH THOSE THROWAWAY CROPS BEFORE?
OH, WE'D BURN 'EM, OR BURY 'EM...
...OR JUST TOSS 'EM OUT WITH THE TRASH.

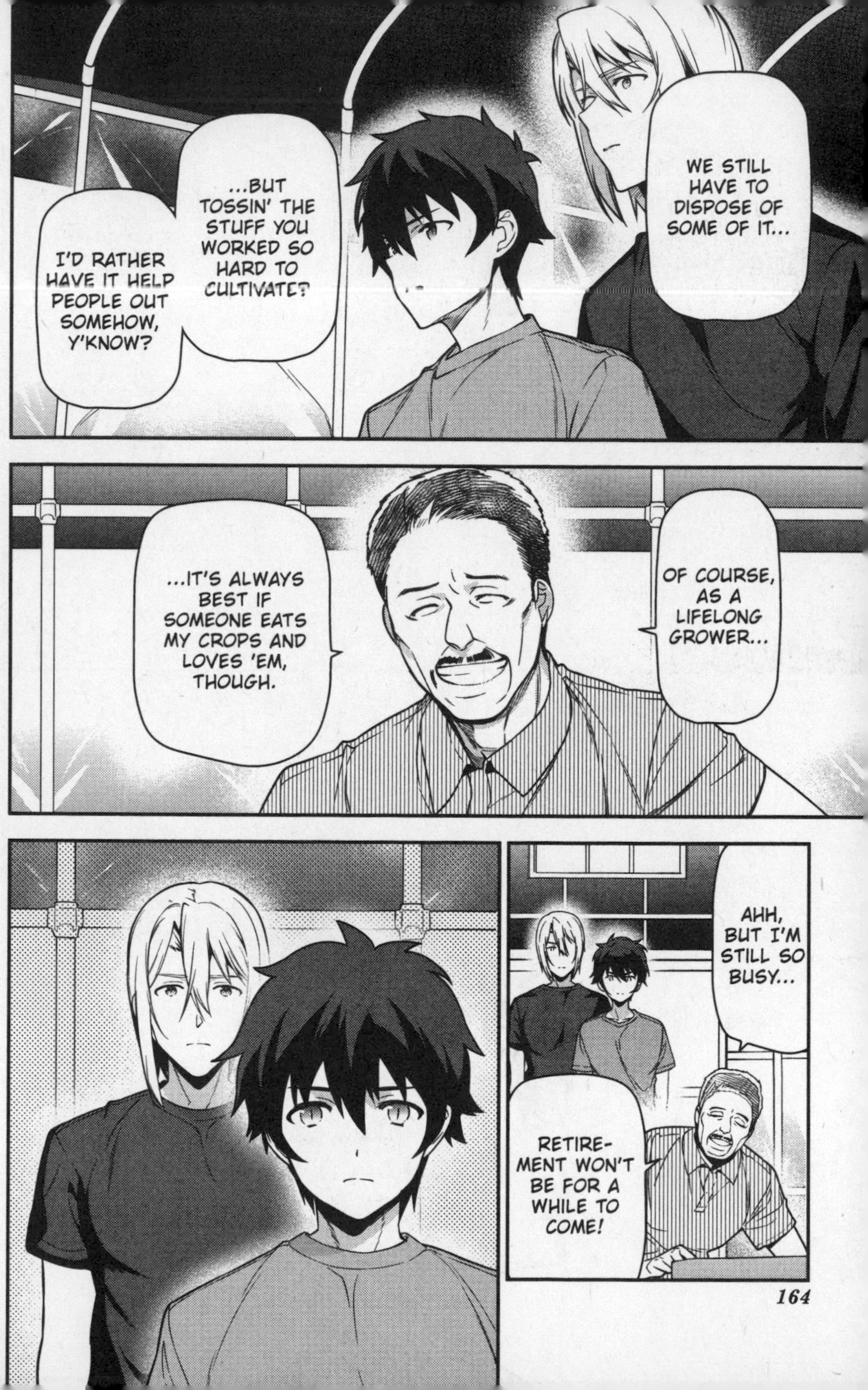
WE STILL HAVE TO DISPOSE OF SOME OF IT...
...BUT TOSSIN' THE STUFF YOU WORKED SO HARD TO CULTIVATE?
I'D RATHER HAVE IT HELP PEOPLE OUT SOMEHOW, Y'KNOW?
OF COURSE, AS A LIFELONG GROWER...
...IT'S ALWAYS BEST IF SOMEONE EATS MY CROPS AND LOVES 'EM, THOUGH.
AHH, BUT I'M STILL SO BUSY...
RETIRE-MENT WON'T BE FOR A WHILE TO COME!

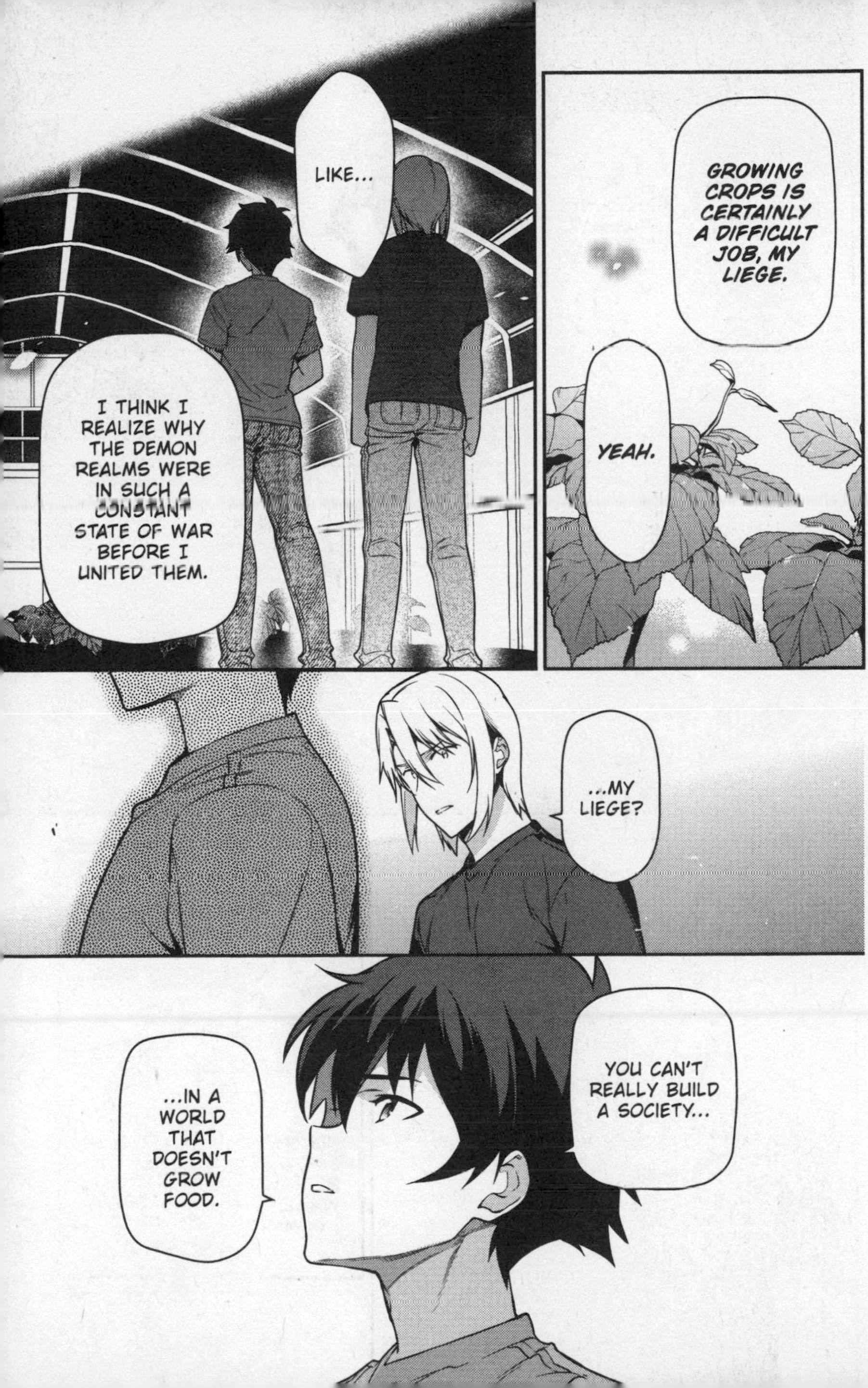
GROWING CROPS IS CERTAINLY A DIFFICULT JOB, MY LIEGE.
YEAH.
LIKE...
I THINK I REALIZE WHY THE DEMON REALMS WERE IN SUCH A CONSTANT STATE OF WAR BEFORE I UNITED THEM.
...MY LIEGE?
YOU CAN'T REALLY BUILD A SOCIETY...
...IN A WORLD THAT DOESN'T GROW FOOD.

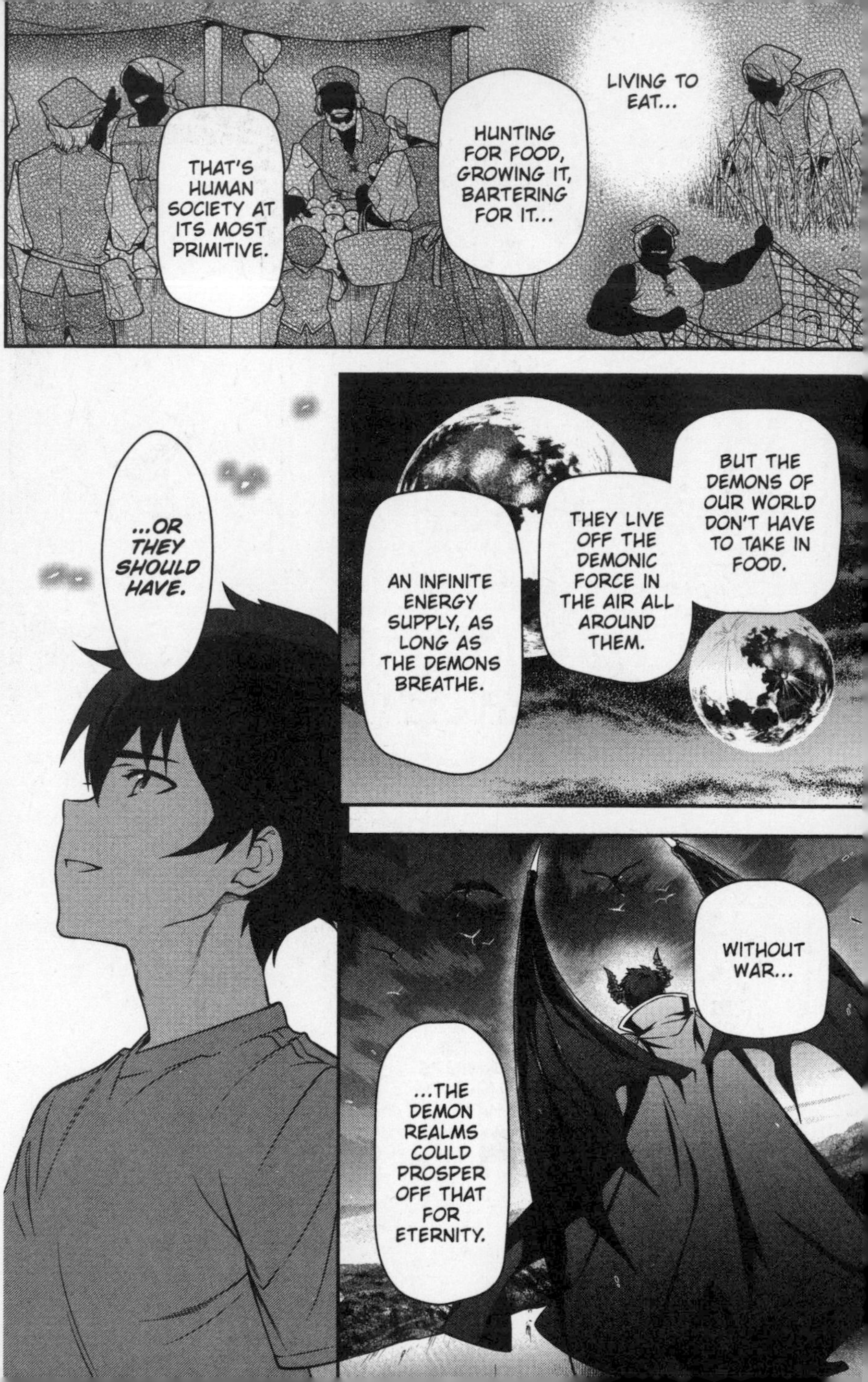
LIVING TO EAT...
HUNTING FOR FOOD, GROWING IT, BARTERING FOR IT...
THAT'S HUMAN SOCIETY AT ITS MOST PRIMITIVE.
BUT THE DEMONS OF OUR WORLD DON'T HAVE TO TAKE IN FOOD.
THEY LIVE OFF THE DEMONIC FORCE IN THE AIR ALL AROUND THEM.
AN INFINITE ENERGY SUPPLY, AS LONG AS THE DEMONS BREATHE.
WITHOUT WAR...
...THE DEMON REALMS COULD PROSPER OFF THAT FOR ETERNITY.
...OR THEY SHOULD HAVE.

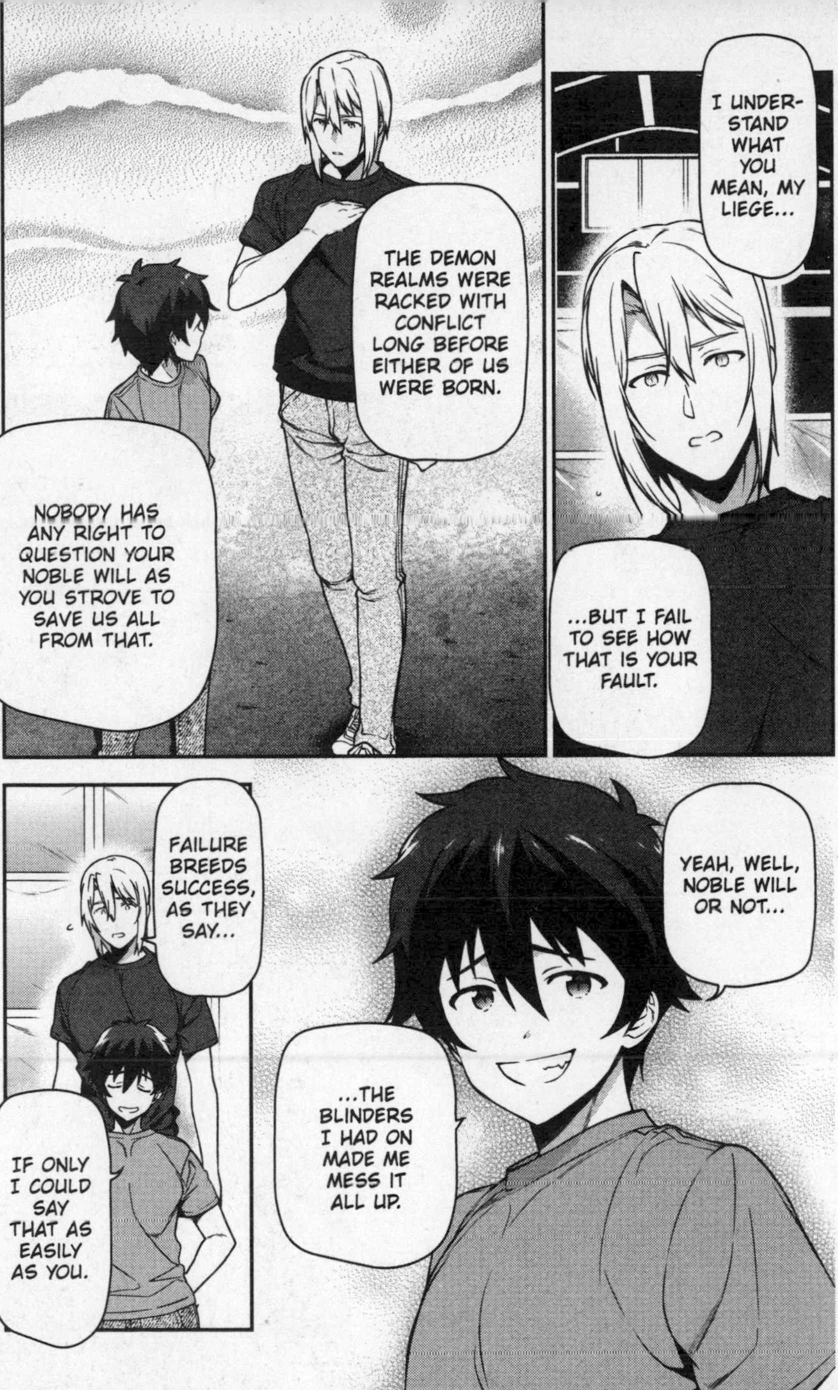
I UNDERSTAND WHAT YOU MEAN, MY LIEGE...
...BUT I FAIL TO SEE HOW THAT IS YOUR FAULT.
THE DEMON REALMS WERE RACKED WITH CONFLICT LONG BEFORE EITHER OF US WERE BORN.
NOBODY HAS ANY RIGHT TO QUESTION YOUR NOBLE WILL AS YOU STROVE TO SAVE US ALL FROM THAT.
YEAH, WELL, NOBLE WILL OR NOT...
...THE BLINDERS I HAD ON MADE ME MESS IT ALL UP.
FAILURE BREEDS SUCCESS, AS THEY SAY...
IF ONLY I COULD SAY THAT AS EASILY AS YOU.

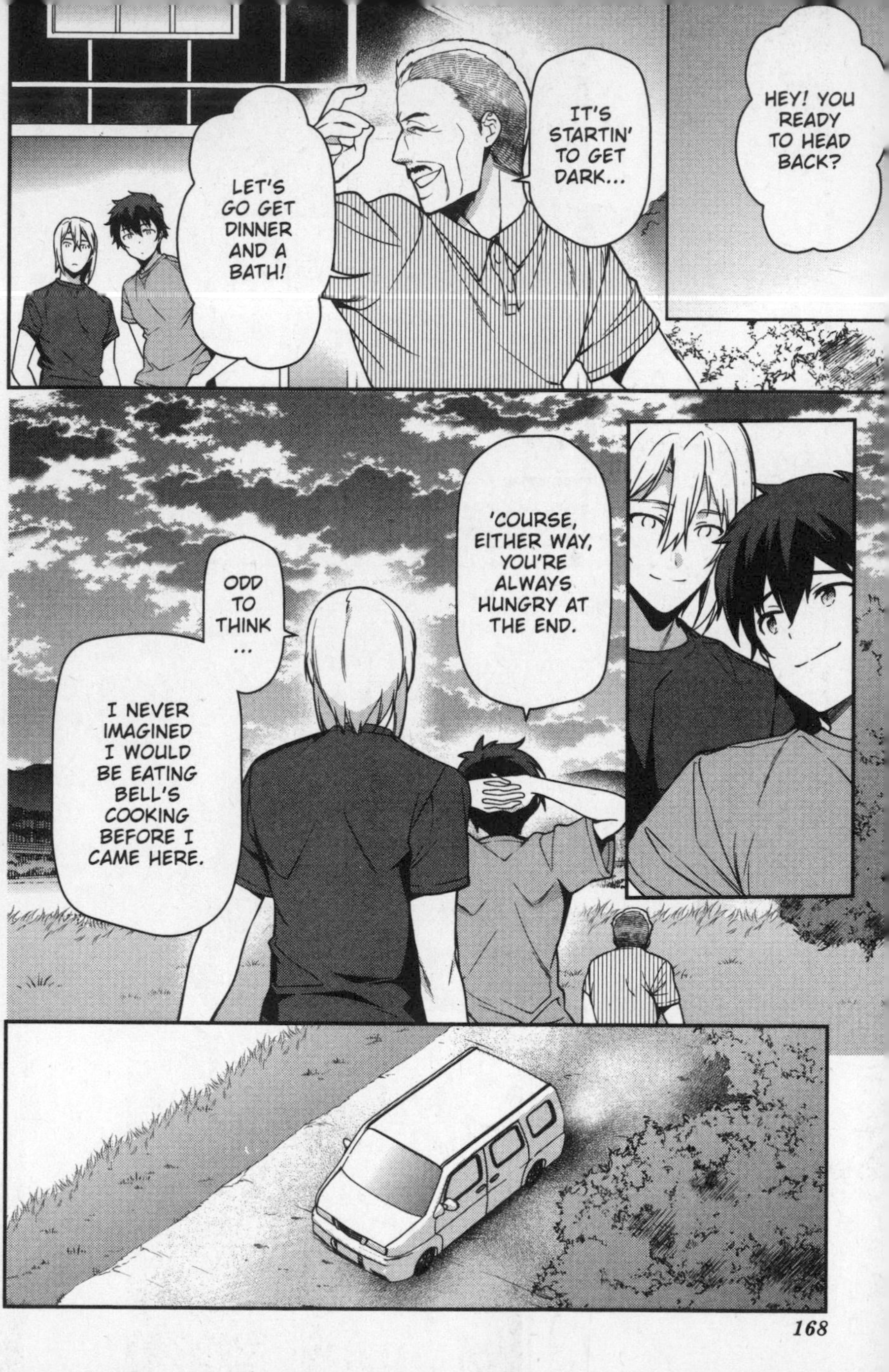
HEY! YOU READY TO HEAD BACK?
IT'S STARTIN' TO GET DARK...
LET'S GO GET DINNER AND A BATH!
'COURSE, EITHER WAY, YOU'RE ALWAYS HUNGRY AT THE END.
ODD TO THINK...
I NEVER IMAGINED I WOULD BE EATING BELL'S COOKING BEFORE I CAME HERE.

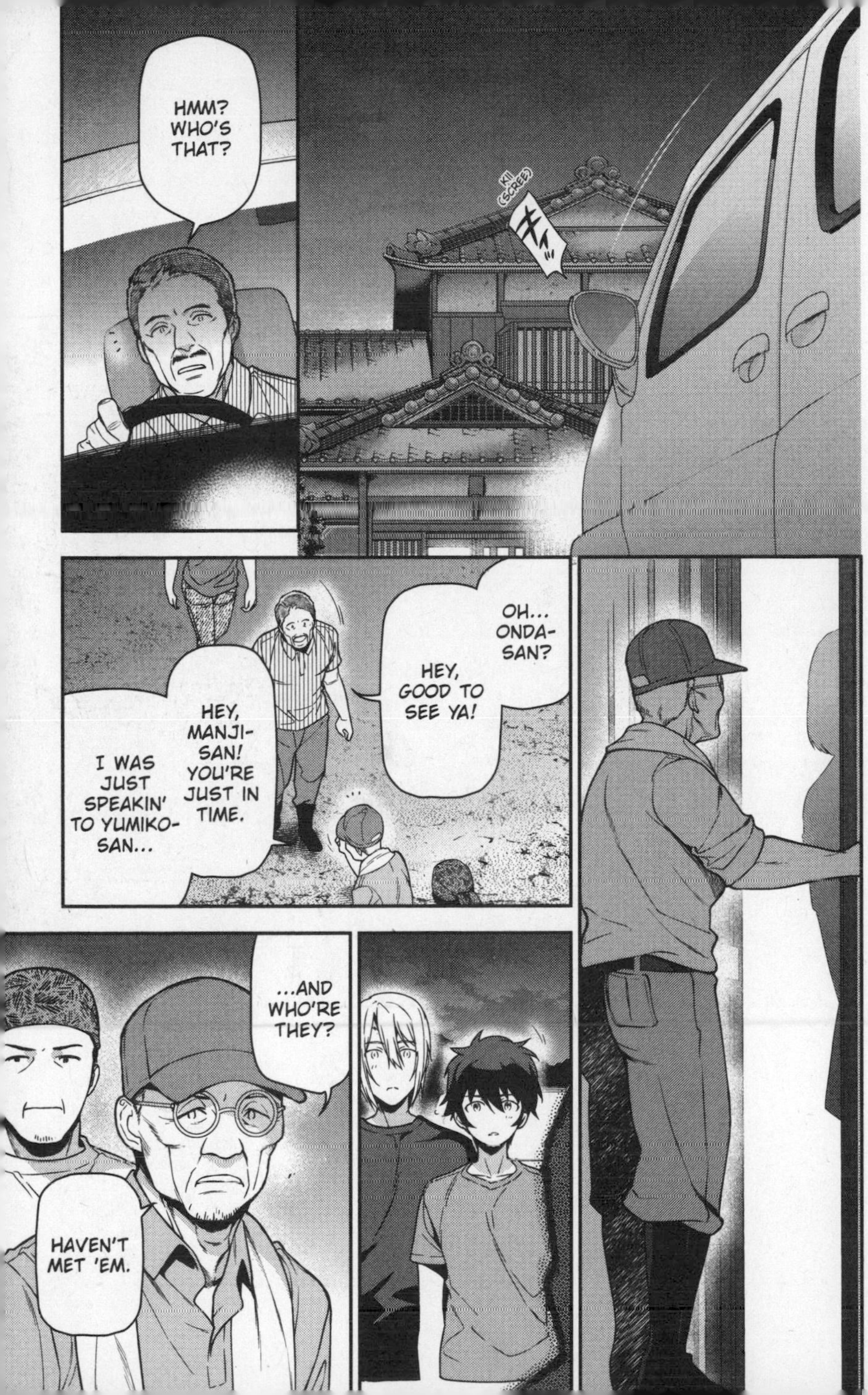
KII (SCREE)
キィ
HMM? WHO'S THAT?
OH... ONDA-SAN?
HEY, GOOD TO SEE YA!
HEY, MANJI-SAN! YOU'RE JUST IN TIME.
I WAS JUST SPEAKIN' TO YUMIKO-SAN...
...AND WHO'RE THEY?
HAVEN'T MET 'EM.

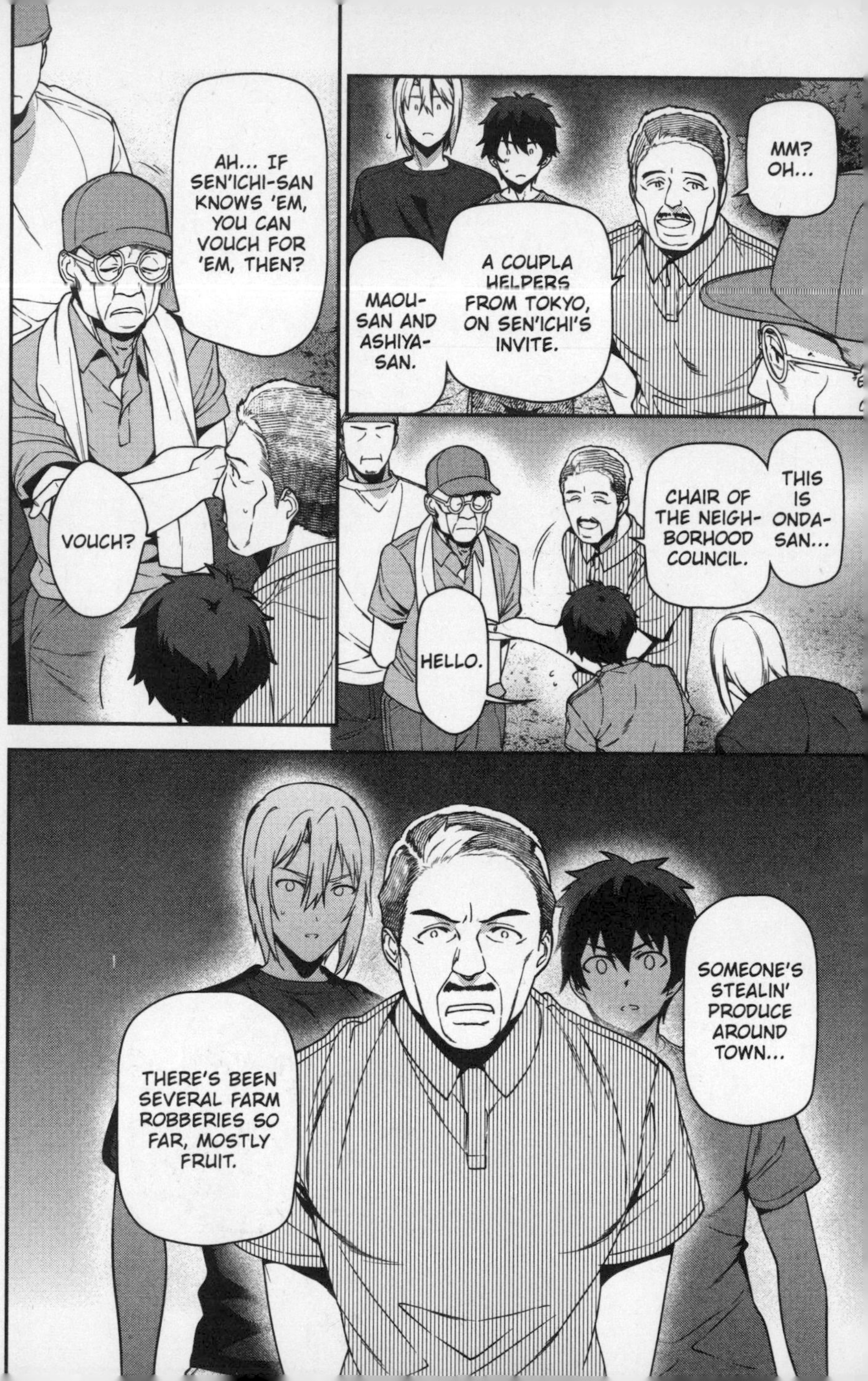
MM? OH...
A COUPLA HELPERS FROM TOKYO, ON SEN'ICHI'S INVITE.
MAOU-SAN AND ASHIYA-SAN.
THIS IS ONDA-SAN...
CHAIR OF THE NEIGHBORHOOD COUNCIL.
HELLO.
AH... IF SEN'ICHI-SAN KNOWS 'EM, YOU CAN VOUCH FOR 'EM, THEN?
VOUCH?
SOMEONE'S STEALIN' PRODUCE AROUND TOWN...
THERE'S BEEN SEVERAL FARM ROBBERIES SO FAR, MOSTLY FRUIT.

Suzuno
Kamazuki

THE KOMAGANE SASAKIS ROUGH SKETCHES

I HAD THE CHANCE TO DESIGN THE SASAKI FAMILY LIVING IN KOMAGANE. I DON'T ALWAYS DRAW THEM BASED ON THESE SKETCHES, BUT I THINK THE GENERAL LOOK HASN'T CHANGED MUCH. IT WAS HARD TO PIN DOWN GRANDMA EI'S LOOK.

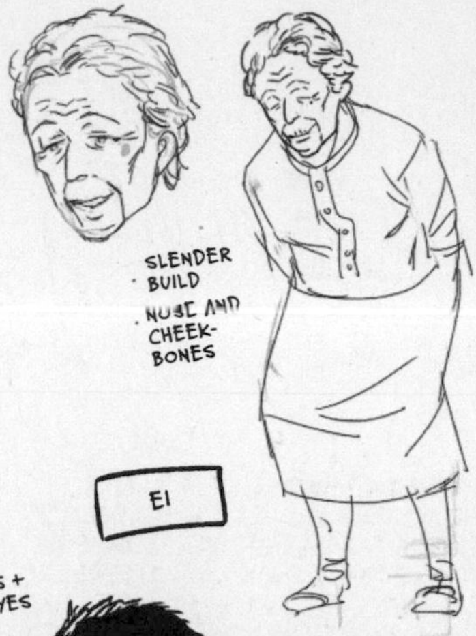

SLENDER BUILD
NOSE AND CHEEK-BONES
EI

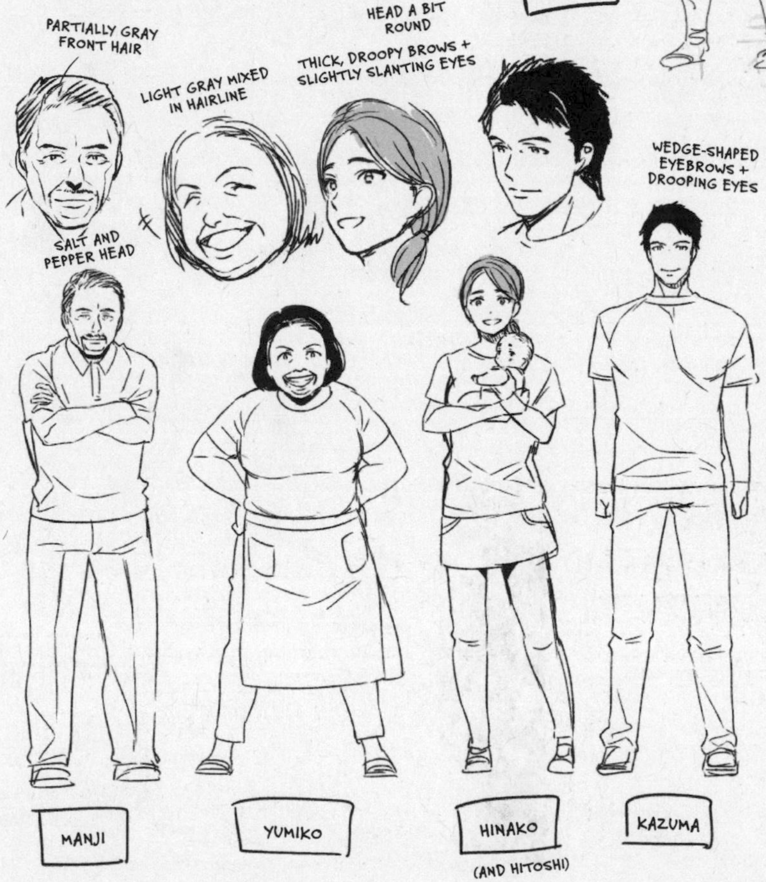

PARTIALLY GRAY FRONT HAIR
SALT AND PEPPER HEAD
LIGHT GRAY MIXED IN HAIRLINE
HEAD A BIT ROUND
THICK, DROOPY BROWS + SLIGHTLY SLANTING EYES
WEDGE-SHAPED EYEBROWS + DROOPING EYES
MANJI
YUMIKO
HINAKO
(AND HITOSHI)
KAZUMA

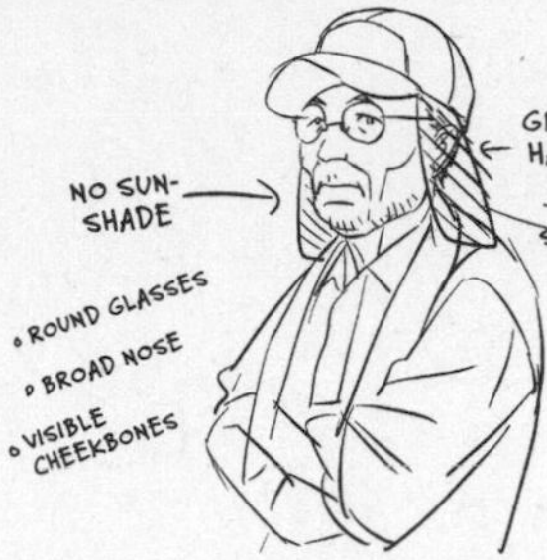
NO SUN-SHADE
GRAY HAIR
• ROUND GLASSES
• BROAD NOSE
• VISIBLE CHEEKBONES
SUNSHADE CAN BE BROUGHT DOWN

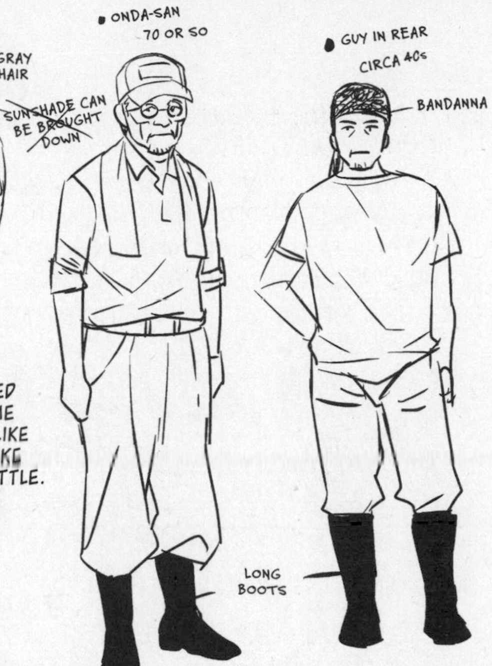
• ONDA-SAN
70 OR SO
• GUY IN REAR
CIRCA 40s
BANDANNA
LONG BOOTS

THESE TWO SHOW UP FOR ONLY A BIT, BUT WAGAHARA-SENSEI SEEMED TO LIKE THEM A LOT, WHICH MADE ME GLAD. I DON'T DRAW CHARACTERS LIKE ONDA-SAN VERY MUCH, SO I FEEL LIKE I'VE EXPANDED MY REPERTOIRE A LITTLE.

OLD MAN ONDA AND GUY BEHIND HIM ROUGH SKETCHES

KOMAGANE SASAKI FAMILY HOUSE — EXTERNAL

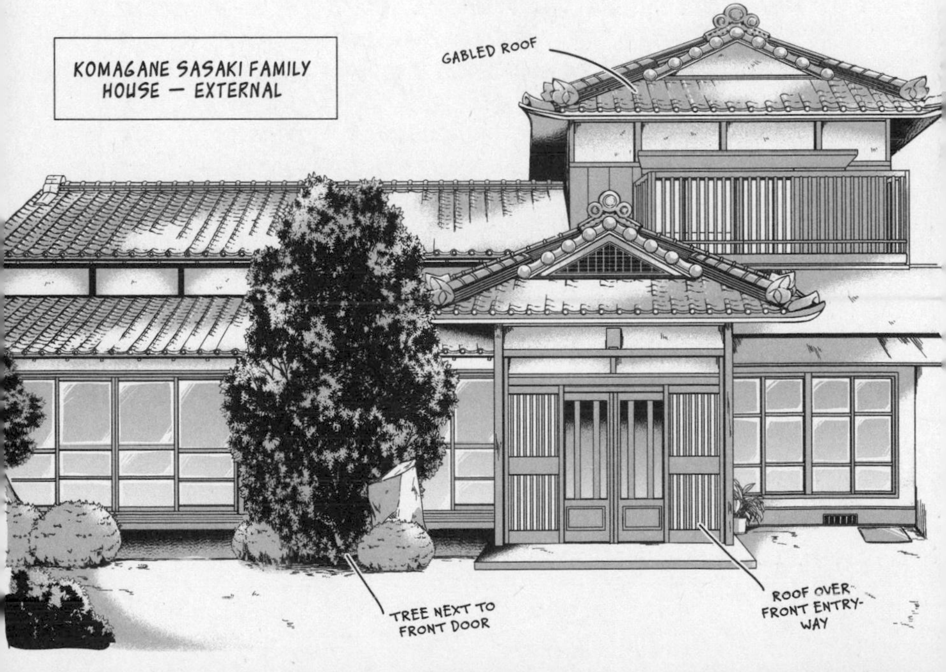
GABLED ROOF
TREE NEXT TO FRONT DOOR
ROOF OVER FRONT ENTRY-WAY

VOLUME 12 OF THE MANGA VERSION OF *THE DEVIL IS A PART-TIMER!* HAS SPECIAL MEANING TO ME, AND NOT JUST BECAUSE IT MEANS I CAN START COUNTING THIS SERIES'S VOLUMES BY THE DOZEN.

THE STORY IN THIS VOLUME IS BASED ON *THE DEVIL IS A PART-TIMER! 5.5*, A SPECIAL NOVEL THAT I WROTE AS A BONUS FREEBIE FOR THE BD/DVD RELEASE OF THE ANIME VERSION. ANIME DISCS ALWAYS COST A LOT MORE THAN PAPERBACK BOOKS, AND THIS STORY WAS A LIMITED-EDITION BONUS AS WELL, SO I FIGURED IT'D ONLY BE SEEN BY A SELECT FEW PEOPLE. WHEN THE EDITORS AT THE DENGEKI DAIOH SUGGESTED MOVING ON WITH 5.5 AFTER COVERING UP TO VOLUME 5 IN THE MANGA, THEN, IT WAS REALLY A BIG SURPRISE.

THANKS TO HIIRAGI-SAN'S HARD WORK, MAOU AND HIS FRIENDS ARE HAVING ANOTHER ONE OF THEIR "WORKPLACES" DEPICTED IN A BRAND-NEW WAY, RIGHT IN YOUR HANDS. IT'S A REALLY MOVING THING TO SEE. THE SCENE MAY HAVE SHIFTED FROM THE SASAZUKA NEIGHBORHOOD OF SHIBUYA WARD, TOKYO, TO THE CITY OF KOMAGANE IN NAGANO PREFECTURE, BUT I HOPE YOU'LL CONTINUE ENJOYING MAOU, ASHIYA, URUSHIHARA, EMI, CHIHO, AND SUZUNO AS THEY TOIL AWAY UNDER THE HOT SUN AND BRIGHT BLUE SKY!

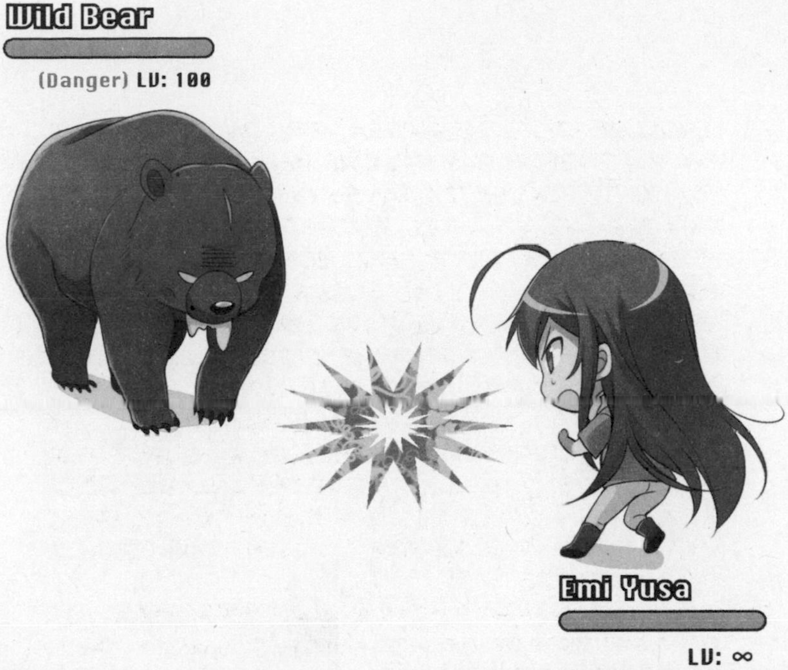
Wild Bear
(Danger) LV: 100
Emi Yusa
LV: ∞

THE COMIC VERSION'S REACHED VOLUME 12 IN WHAT SEEMS LIKE NO TIME FLAT...I NEVER THOUGHT IN A MILLION YEARS THAT WE'D START COVERING BONUS CONTENT IN THE MANGA, TOO, SO NOW ALL THESE TOP SCENES OF MINE—ASHIYA GETTING HIS HAIR PULLED BY THE KID, EMI DEFEATING A BEAR, CHI-CHAN AND MAOU GETTING CLOSE AGAIN—IN FULL VISUAL FORMAT FOR THE FIRST TIME MAKES ME HAPPIER THAN EVER!

I CAN'T WAIT TO SEE HIIRAGI-SAN'S VIVIDLY ILLUSTRATED DEMON KING GANG AS THEY KEEP HAVING THEIR ADVENTURES!

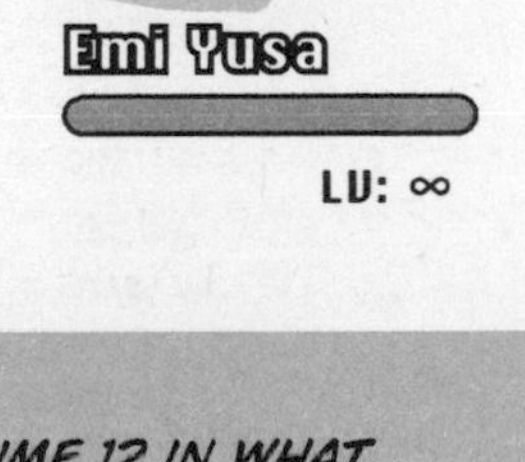

THIS VOLUME FEATURES THE COMIC RENDITION OF "THE DEVIL PICKS UP SOME FARMWORK," PART OF VOLUME 5.5 OF THE DEVIL IS A PART-TIMER! INCLUDED WITH THE FIRST PRESSING OF THE ANIME DVD/BLU-RAY VOLUME 1. I WAS HOPING I'D GET TO DRAW THIS EPISODE IN MANGA FORM SOMETIME, SO SEEING THAT WISH COME TRUE MAKES ME REALLY HAPPY.

MANY THANKS GO OUT TO WAGAHARA-SENSEI, 029-SENSEI, AND EVERYONE ELSE INVOLVED FOR SO GLADLY AGREEING TO THIS REQUEST. AND MANY THANKS, AS ALWAYS, FOR THE READERS WHO MAKE ALL OF THIS POSSIBLE.

THIS VOLUME FEATURES A LOT OF THINGS YOU WOULDN'T NORMALLY SEE IN DEVIL—COUNTRYSIDE NATURE, ELDERLY WOMEN, AND...WELL, BEARS, I SUPPOSE (HEH). IT WAS A LOT OF FUN TO DRAW.

THE STORY CONTINUES IN THE NEXT VOLUME! ONE THAT, I'M HAPPY TO ADD, FEATURES A REALLY COOL DEVIL KING CLIMAX SCENE I'LL GET TO BRING TO YOU. I HOPE YOU'LL CONTINUE TO PROVIDE YOUR SUPPORT!

SPECIAL THANKS:
AKIRA HISAKI / SHIBA
AND YOU!

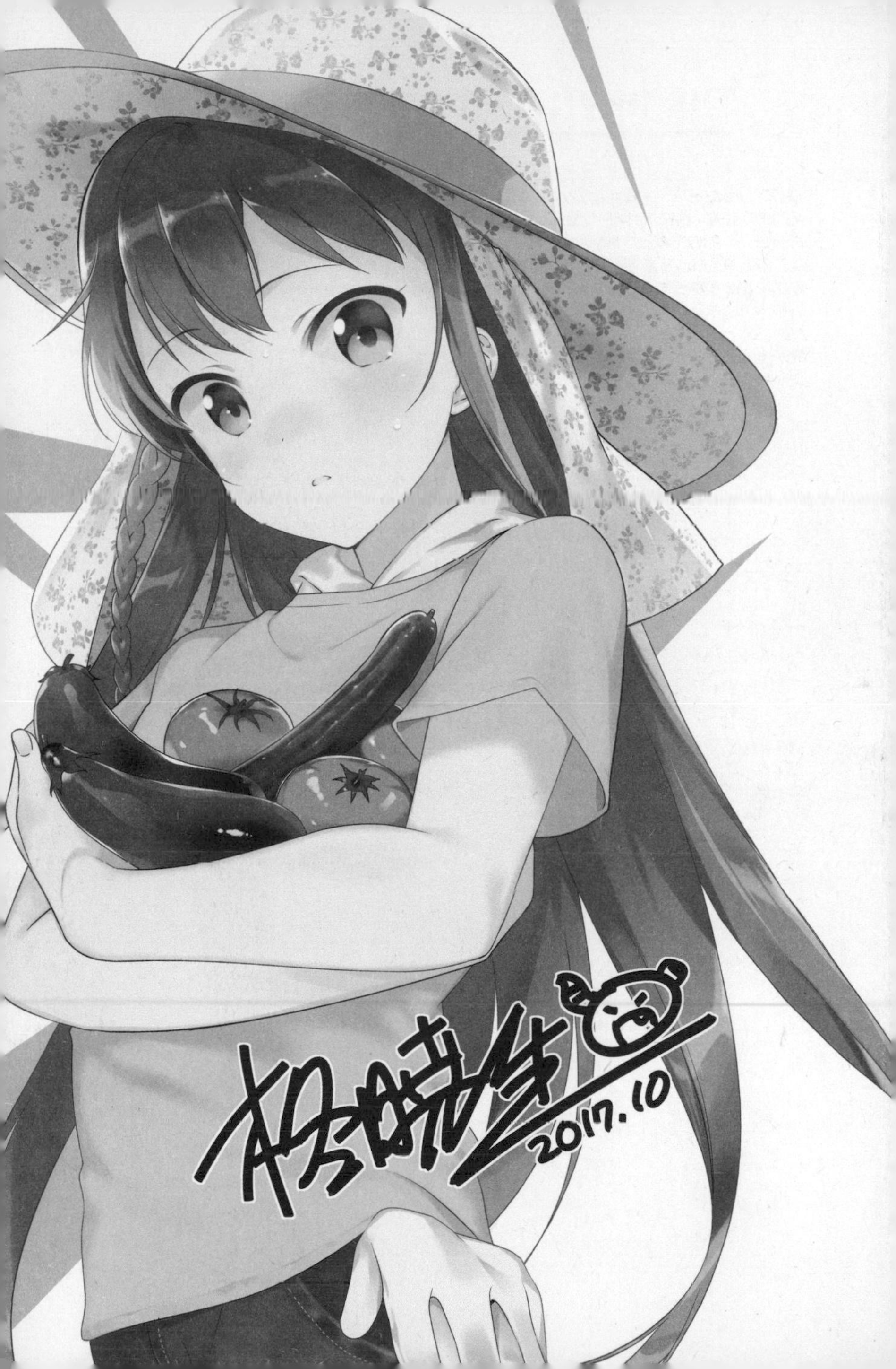
2017.10

THE DEVIL IS A PART-TIMER! ⑫

Art: Akio Hiiragi
Original Story: Satoshi Wagahara
Character Design: 029 (Oniku)

Translation: Kevin Gifford

Lettering: Brndn Blakeslee

HATARAKU MAOUSAMA! Vol. 12
© SATOSHI WAGAHARA / AKIO HIIRAGI 2017
First published in Japan in 2017 by KADOKAWA CORPORATION, Tokyo.
English translation rights arranged with KADOKAWA CORPORATION, Tokyo, through Tuttle-Mori Agency, Inc., Tokyo.

English translation © 2018 by Yen Press, LLC

Yen Press
1290 Avenue of the Americas
New York, NY 10104

Visit us at yenpress.com
facebook.com/yenpress
twitter.com/yenpress
yenpress.tumblr.com
instagram.com/yenpress

First Yen Press Edition: October 2018

Yen Press is an imprint of Yen Press, LLC.
The Yen Press name and logo are trademarks of Yen Press, LLC.

Library of Congress Control Number: 2014504637

ISBNs: 978-1-9753-0182-8 (paperback)
978-1-9753-0276-4 (ebook)

10 9 8 7 6 5 4 3 2 1

WOR

Printed in the United States of America